Migration and Society in Early Modern England

Edited by

Peter Clark and David Souden

Hutchinson

London   Melbourne   Auckland   Johannesburg

Hutchinson Education

An imprint of Century Hutchinson Ltd

62–65 Chandos Place, London WC2N 4NW

Century Hutchinson Australia Pty Ltd
P O Box 496, 16–22 Church Street, Hawthorn,
Victoria 3122, Australia

Century Hutchinson New Zealand Ltd
P O Box 40–086, Glenfield, Auckland 10,
New Zealand

Century Hutchinson South Africa (Pty) Ltd
P O Box 337, Berglvei 2012, South Africa

First published 1987

Set in Linotron Times
by Input Typesetting Ltd, London

Printed and bound in Great Britain by
Anchor Brendon Ltd, Tiptree, Essex

British Library Cataloguing in Publication Data

Migration and society in early modern England.
  1. Migration, Internal—England—
  History
  I. Clark, Peter, *1944*–   II. Souden, David
  304.8′0942   HB1952
  ISBN 0 09 173220 4

Contents

Figures and maps

Contributors

Jeremy Boulton is a Fellow of New Hall, Cambridge and a member of the ESRC Cambridge Group for the History of Population and Social Structure.

Peter Clark is Professor of Economic and Social History and Director of the Centre for Urban History at the University of Leicester.

James Horn is Lecturer in History at Brighton Polytechnic.

John Patten is a former lecturer in Geography at the University of Oxford, and is currently a British government minister.

Roger Schofield is a Fellow of Clare College, Cambridge, and Director of the ESRC Cambridge Group for the History of Population and Social Structure.

Paul Slack is a Fellow and Tutor at Exeter College, Oxford, and chairman of the editorial board of *Past and Present*.

David Souden is a former Research Fellow of Emmanuel College, Cambridge, and is currently a freelance producer and writer of television documentaries.

Acknowledgements

The editors and publisher are grateful to the authors and journals for permission to reprint these articles:

P. Clark, 'Migration in England', first appeared in *Past and Present*, **83** (1979), pp. 57–90.

J. Patten, 'Patterns of migration and movement of labour', first appeared in *Journal of Historical Geography*, **ii** (1976), pp. 111–29.

R. S. Schofield, 'Age-specific mobility', first appeared in *Annales de démographie historique 1970* (Paris, 1971), pp. 261–74.

P. A. Slack, 'Vagrants and vagrancy', first appeared in *Economic History Review*, 2nd series, **xxvii** (1974), pp. 360–79.

D. Souden, ' "Rogues, whores and vagabonds"? Indentured servant emigrants', first appeared in *Social History*, **iii** (1978), pp. 23–41.

Preface

In Britain the study of migration during the pre-industrial period has made important strides in recent times. There has been a stream of work on the geography of human movement, types of movers, the reasons why people took to the road, the impact of official controls, and the wider demographic and social implications of large-scale physical mobility. All the signs are that migration was a dynamic and powerful force in the changing face of the demographic landscape of early modern England. Most of the material published so far however has appeared in scattered articles, quite often in less accessible locations. There has been little attempt to produce a methodological framework or to present a coherent overview of the state of research.

This volume is concerned not only with the nature of migration but with its interaction with society as a whole. Collected here are a number of key articles from the published literature and a number of new essays covering major aspects of the subject. Two chapters are included on migration connections with colonial North America, seen as an extension of internal migration patterns. The introduction outlines the methodological problems of studying migration – problems too often swept under the carpet – as well as sketching the broad scenario of migration in the period, to set in context the detailed chapters which follow. The collection is by no means exhaustive, but we hope that it will stimulate further teaching and research of a complex phenomenon which is central to our understanding of social relationships and the economic transformation of English society between the sixteenth and eighteenth centuries.

We are grateful to Jenny Clark for checking the proofs and to Louise Clark for helping with the index.

P.A.C.   D.C.S.

1
Introduction

Peter Clark and David Souden

Migration is the movement of individuals or groups which involves a permanent or semi-permanent change of usual residence. The basic definition is easy.[1]* Everything else in the study of physical movement is harder, especially for the past where the capture of statistical information and of evidence on attitudes is particularly difficult. But, in the early modern period, the simple actions of moving from place to place underpinned most aspects of demographic, social, and economic activity. So finding out why and how people moved around is essential for our understanding of English society.

How and why an individual moved are probably the most difficult questions to determine, although if detailed autobiographical material survives we can gain an unrivalled insight into moves and motivation. The Birmingham self-made businessman William Hutton wrote such a life story in the eighteenth century, celebrating his own tale of success.[2] Born the son of a Derby woolcomber in 1723, Hutton was sent at the age of 4 to live with his relations in Mountsorrel, Leicestershire, for fifteen months, his 'family being distressed'. That was his first recorded residential move; but in 1738 (after a seven-year apprenticeship in a local silk mill) he was apprenticed again, to his uncle, a stocking-maker in Nottingham.

There he stayed until 1746, serving out his apprenticeship and remaining as a journeyman until his uncle's death. But during that time he had run away, and had one week of great mobility. His uncle had beaten him, and off he went, 'a lad of seventeen, not elegantly dressed, nearly five feet high, rather Dutch built', with

---

* Superior figures refer to the Notes and references which appear at the end of the chapters.

11

some food, a change of clothing, a sun-dial, and his best wig. 'I had only two shillings in my pocket, a spacious world before me, and no plan of operations.'[3] So he wandered – and was rejected everywhere as being a runaway – visiting Derby, Burton-on-Trent, Lichfield, Walsall, Birmingham, Coventry, Nuneaton, Hinckley, Ashby-de-la-Zouch, and finally, repentant, back to Derby and thence to his uncle.[4] By the mid 1740s Hutton was very interested in books and binding; so, finding himself excluded from the distressed Leicester hosiery trade, he set himself up in 1748–9 as a bookseller and binder, buying proper equipment in London (a nine-day round trip walk) and taking a shop in Southwell. Then in 1750 he moved to Birmingham, where by degrees he established himself as a bookseller, paper merchant, antiquarian, and leading citizen. He remained in the town, buying property nearby (and later in Hertfordshire), until ousted by the 'Jacobin' riots of 1791 during which his house was sacked. In 1806 he made his second visit to London, to secure more Hertfordshire property; and he died an aged and respected figure in 1815.[5]

William Hutton described what we shall see was a pretty standard pattern: relatively high mobility in early years, residence in households other than that of his immediate family, followed by a lengthy period of settled life (and marriage) until old age or death. What animates this story is the wealth of description and Hutton's account of his reasons for making a particular move.

This class of autobiographical information, which provides details about movements and about motivation and attitudes, is exceedingly rare and highly individualistic.[6] It can be argued that those who left posterity information of this kind were far too individualistic to be properly representative of the population as a whole.[7] Movement was such an ingrained feature of everyday life that comment, particularly informed comment, is hard to find except in extraordinary circumstances.

Fortunately, for early modern England there is abundance of other more mundane material for the detailed analysis of migration. As we shall see, the sources are not without serious difficulties, but deploying them with care and imagination it is possible to achieve an understanding of migration and mobility as a major phenomenon in English social and economic life from the sixteenth to the eighteenth centuries. In this collection our concern is with the varied aspects, both quantitative and qualitative, of mobility – as part of the demographic *cursus*, as an aspect of wealth and poverty, as an index of regionality, and as a vital feature of urbanization and colonization. We are concerned not only with who were movers, but why they took to the road and what happened to them on their travels. As well as reporting on the current state of the art, it is hoped that the book will point the way towards new questions and new approaches in the study of migration.

I

But to start we need to go back to first principles, and attendant methodological problems. If we begin with a fairly idealized version of the world, and then progressively build in historical reality, the task of definition and comprehension should be made easier. Imagine therefore a simple and unchanging rural world which conforms to the basic social rules of pre-industrial English household economies.[8] Marriage is late, households are new (not extensions of existing ones) and are simple, and service, either in the household or on the farm, and apprenticeship are the norm.[9]

In that world there are two villages, V_1 and V_2, of equal size. The action of the prevailing social rules ensures some exchange of people between them, exchange of roughly equal intensity. In *stable populations*, that is those with unchanging demographic parameters, some families will have surplus children, some too few to carry on the family work and line.[10] Therefore there would be some movement of offspring to fill vacancies, take up inheritances, or be adopted into new households. Children are swapped between households as servants.[11] Pressures towards exogamy are great, especially in small places, for not only does movement diminish the risks from inbreeding, but it also enlarges the pool of potential marriage partners.[12] In populations even of a few hundred, the number of people of the opposite sex of the right age and status to marry will be very small.[13] Short-term labour requirements may persuade families to move from one place to another; the elderly may move to a smaller, cheaper property or to be near other members of their family.[14] An active property market together with a tendency towards impartible inheritance would again promote movement.[15]

Even in small out-of-the-way places there may be considerable movement. This is migration of minor consequence, in that it does little or nothing to disturb the status quo.[16] But such basic levels of movement provide considerable insight into the way in which many ordinary people did in fact conduct their lives, and give us a benchmark for the stages which follow. We should not be surprised at the existence or the intensity of small-scale local movement in pre-industrial England – and should rather reserve our surprise for when mobility seems absent or less intense.

Now we must add village communities, V_3, V_4, . . . V_n to this semi-mythical world. Practical experience tells us that these villages will be of different sizes, and of different economic complexions. So the aggregate flows of people between all the places would tend, other things being equal, to vary with the relative population sizes of V_1–V_n.

Yet this does not begin to correspond to the real world. Different agricultural regimes have different labour requirements, with less stable year-round employment in pastoral farming, and generally more work for males in arable cultivation.[17] This too works against that simple one-to-one correspondence between V_1 and V_2. Moving a step nearer reality, while agriculture was the mainstay and the defining characteristic of the rural population, there was a whole range of other occupations, servicing the agricultural economy and processing and distributing its products, and a further array of industrial occupations, tied to a greater or lesser extent into the local rural economy.[18] Here the idea of a simple exchange of people weakens even further. Within an area, even one with a dual economy of farming and industry, two or more labour markets might be operating, for agricultural and for industrial skills.[19]

Now into this model world we introduce a town, T_1. It has an important function within an area, acting as a central market, as the place where a greater variety of skills and trades can operate, as a larger manufacturing base.[20] There will thus be a continuing and necessary interchange of people between town and country; and, given the greater size of a town and its possible inability to maintain its size through natural population increase, the balance of that flow will be towards town.[21] In addition to T_1 there are T_2 . . . T_n, towns each with their constellation of surrounding villages. So there will be overlapping migration 'fields': village to village, village to town, town to town. In general, the degree of movement should correspond with the size of town (and of village), larger places having more migratory activity than small.[22]

And finally we have a large centre, M. Here the great

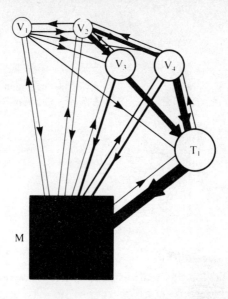

Figure 1 First migration model (for symbols see text)

administrative functions are concentrated, there is a super-urban
economy of specialization, production, and consumption, feeding
on and back into those constellations of towns and villages, drawing off a certain number of people, returning others to them.[23]

This is still not entirely real. But, as captured in the
accompanying diagram in Figure 1, it begins to approximate to a
world we can recognize as that of early modern, pre-industrial
England. What it suggests is a way of looking at the movement
of people from place to place as being entirely 'natural'. The idea
of exchange of people is built into the simplest groupings of places.
And even at levels above that of the small independent village
there is of necessity interchange of people, for demographic or
economic reasons. The width of the arrows suggests the relationship between population size and movement flow. In the aggregate
of all moves, small-effect and local moves would predominate;
but there is also a sense of growing purposiveness and increasing
distance higher up this hierarchy of places.

Other ways of building migration into a model can use individual motivation rather than the spatial and demographic
relationship between places. In Figure 2 the axes on the graph
are labelled 'distance' and 'definitiveness'.[24] 'Distance' in this

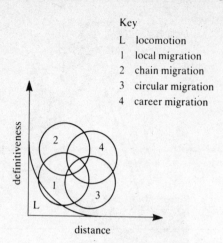

Key

L   locomotion
1   local migration
2   chain migration
3   circular migration
4   career migration

Figure 2   Second migration model

sense may be the physical distance moved (the most commonly measured characteristic of migration) or may be some form of mental distance, the difference between two cultures, the financial or opportunity costs of making a move. 'Definitiveness' expresses the degree of divorce from the place of origin. The first curve encloses an area marked 'circulation', the physical movement of people which is excluded from our present interests – a daily journey to work, a weekly trip to market, a monthly visit to the city. There are however four 'clouds' containing different but overlapping varieties of movement.

'Local' migration is, as we have just seen, the backbone of this system of migration, both in terms of volume and ubiquity, as individuals relocate themselves within a local area, moving within a labour, agricultural, or marriage market, or within geographical boundaries.[25] At the other end of the scale, 'career' migration lifts individuals out of their initial home environment and transports them elsewhere. Their new homes are the result of taking up the opportunities inherent within the career structure of their occupation, and may have little or no connection with their origin.[26] The classic example of this pattern has always been apprenticeship of boys into a trade or craft; and indeed many other professions, notably the Church and the law, had a similar redistributive function.[27]

The characteristic feature of 'circular' migration is of individuals moving away, and returning to their starting point after a sequence of moves. Circular migration can take a special form, seasonal migration, usually an aspect of employment patterns designed to eke out the family economy or to relieve short-term imbalances in the labour market. Thus there were Cornish farmers in James I's reign who travelled across the Atlantic annually to fish for and dry cod;[28] there were chapmen in western England in the seventeenth century who moved eastwards and back again, buying and selling small goods;[29] there were harvest gangs in the eighteenth and nineteenth centuries;[30] and into the twentieth century East End families from London journeyed into Kent for the hop-picking season.[31]

On the other side is the phenomenon of 'chain' migration, where individuals move, one after another, along a fairly determined path, taking advantage of established structures and contacts.[32] Peter Clark writes about this mechanism in chapter 9 in his discussion of clubs and personal ties.[33] Particular places might have long-term contacts with particular institutions – witness the recruitment to certain north-eastern coalfields from individual areas of eastern Scotland,[34] or indeed the large Italian population currently living in Luton and Bedford, continuing to come even after the great demand for their labour has passed, and showing the cultural as well as economic determinism of migration flows.

We may have begun to identify the mechanics of migration, using demographers' abstractions. But there is the question of what they really mean in an early modern context. The evidence available to the historian is not suited to analysing many of these features, and the categories we have described all tend to overlap. How, for instance, would we relate William Hutton to these schemes of migration? A clergyman returning to take up a benefice in his family's gift would be a career and a circular migrant. A domestic servant working in a wide variety of households before returning to her family's parish to marry would be a local and a circular migrant. A boy apprenticed to a town trade with which his home village had a special connection might be a local migrant, a career migrant, and a chain migrant. At different points in the life cycle individuals might be each type of migrant in turn. Hutton was. The second encapsulation of migration has some advantages over the first in being more closely based on the motivation of individuals. But neither model derives from direct measurement. Rather, they are an idealization of and an abstraction from the real world of early modern society.

II

In a less than ideal world the historian has to take pot luck in terms of documentary evidence. The sources for the study of English migration in the early modern period are numerous and illuminating, but as we have said they rarely provide a neat match with our theoretical abstractions, although they can help us towards understanding them. Several of the contributions below look at specific sets of records and their problems. Here we need to consider the general biases of the documentation as a whole.

The material for the historian of the early modern period can be divided into three main categories – with two main focuses, the individual and the group.

1 Sources which give origin and destination information for a general group, of whom all, or more usually a proportion, are migrants.
2 Sources from which the results of the migration process can be seen (or inferred), but which do not themselves provide point to point data on movement.
3 Sources which provide inferential evidence on migration through its overall effects.

In the first of these categories are those sources which have been extensively mined by historians who have studied migration: registrations of apprenticeship;[35] the depositions of witnesses appearing before church courts;[36] the papers thrown up in the workings of the poor laws and settlement legislation – settlement certificates, removal orders, and examinations;[37] residential information in marriage registers (especially after Hardwicke's Marriage Act of 1753);[38] the records of arrested vagrants;[39] and personal data collected on emigrants, notably indentured servants bound for North America and the West Indies.[40] Unlike Swedish practice for the last two centuries, British local and central authorities have not kept continuous population registers, tracking people and their movements.[41] So however wide their coverage none of these English sources encompasses an entire population; rather, each covers a select, and usually a different, group. Only with a chance and rare survival, such as the listing for the Bedfordshire village of Cardington on which Roger Schofield's paper, in chapter 8, is based, do we have pretty detailed information on migration across a population.[42]

The second category is dominated by listings of inhabitants

which, if they are available serially, indicate the extent of *'turn-over'* in a population – those who have gone, those who have arrived, those who have stayed, during the interval between two listings. This was the form of analysis undertaken by Peter Laslett in his pioneering study of two such pairs of local censuses for the midland villages of Clayworth and Cogenhoe in the seventeenth century;[43] and in chapter 6 James Horn similarly assesses evidence for population turnover patterns in the New World.[44]

Nineteenth- and twentieth-century analyses of migration more commonly feature in the third category. The advent of the published record of the decennial census and of civil registration have provided opportunities to investigate general pictures of inter-regional migration flows, while birthplace data in the manuscript census returns provide rich material for the local study of migration and its impact.[45] For the earlier period, the advent of large-scale demographic databases, especially aggregative series of births, marriages, and deaths, now permits some of these techniques and insights to be taken back into the seventeenth and eighteenth centuries.[46]

It was largely on the basis of nineteenth-century published census returns that E. G. Ravenstein propounded his 'laws of migration' in the 1880s.[47] This was essentially the first attempt to devise theories in social science based on sources in an historical context. Ravenstein's laws have guided (perhaps one is tempted to say straitjacketed) migration studies ever since. Ravenstein concluded:

1 The majority of migrants move only a short distance.
2 Migration proceeds step by step, in that the places of outmigrants are filled by inmigrants from more remote areas.
3 Each migration current produces a compensating counter-current.
4 Longer distance migrants tend to go to towns.
5 The urban-born are less prone to migrate than the rural-born.
6 Females are more migratory over shorter distances, males over longer.
7 Most migrants are adults.
8 Large towns grow by migration more than by natural increase.
9 Migration increases in volume with economic and transport improvements.
10 The major migration flow is from agricultural areas to large towns.
11 The major causes of migration are economic.[48]

These statements of tendency ('laws' is surely too strong and deterministic a word) have been tested many times, in a variety of cultures, and are usually found to hold up, although various refinements have been added. The size–distance rule has been reformulated mathematically into 'gravity models', and further refined by the concept of 'intervening opportunities' – that the number of migrants over a certain distance is proportional to the opportunities at that distance, and inversely related to the opportunities that may exist in between. In other words, you may be enticed by opportunities closer to home if they emerge.[49]

Much of Ravenstein's picture has a resemblance to the first model of early modern English economy and society outlined above, derived from basic principles. Some of the ideas stemming from his analysis have been used by historians of the early modern period: for example, the idea of intervening opportunities has helped explain the contraction of the volume of apprentice migration from northern England to London between the mid sixteenth century and the later seventeenth, as the attractiveness of growing northern towns increased.[50]

But Ravenstein's early success has tended to cast his conclusions as iron rules, whereas empirical research tries to square the contradictions which are found in reality. The laws, for instance, fail to recognize the human and historical reality of the different life-cycle components of migration, with mobility generated by the formation and dissolution of households, the timing and incidence of marriage, the location and variety of work, and local economic and demographic circumstances. Even more significant, detailed research using a wider variety of evidence suggests that there are often small but crucial variations in movement over space – between countries, regions, and localities, between town and countryside – and variation over time. The exceptions are infinitely more interesting and important than the rule.

III

The study of migration, then, is the study of the redistribution of people. It has not only an important demographic dimension, but also wide social ramifications. At the same time, as we have seen, there are many difficulties and frustrations when we try to examine the subject in depth in the context of early modern society. Abstract demographic concepts, mainly derived from work on contemporary societies, are difficult to match with the data and documentation accessible to the historian. Most sources provide descriptions of migration patterns, usually of point to point movement, but it is not easy to relate these moves to a population 'at risk', and so to compute migration rates.[51] In the same way we can find material on the changing spatial shape of mobility, but it is problematical how far this relates to the early modern population as a whole.[52]

Taking another approach, how far can contemporary perceptions and comments provide a guide to the social and demographic realities of migration in early modern England? Certainly a great head of official steam was provoked in the Tudor and Stuart era. Crown, county magistrates and town rulers were constantly exercised over the movement of the tramping poor and vagrants, and the pressure of incomers particularly upon urban economies. In the 1560s the Kentish town of Sandwich complained of the 'sundry vagrant and stout vagabonds [that] do now very much resort to this town', while in the reign of Charles I the Manchester court leet protested that the town was 'intolerably troubled and daily more and more charged with the relief of poor people . . . finding the receiving of many strangers and inmates . . . to be the chief cause of such multitudes of poor'.[53] In official eyes the distressed migrants not only created rising local poverty but posed a serious threat to public order. Their fears were fanned by an extensive pamphlet literature exaggerating the scale and organization of vagrancy. By contrast, official interest in better-off movement was only sporadic. Moreover, with advancing economic prosperity and political stability from the end of the seventeenth century both central and local government paid declining attention to population movement in general, except in places suffering economic decline or where the parish worthies sought to exclude newcomers or to enhance their local control.[54]

If the upper classes exhibited only partial (albeit well-documented) awareness of the processes of migration which affected the lives of the majority of English men and women, ordinary people themselves were even more reticent. The very ubiquity of movement made it a little-remarked phenomenon. Little direct evidence survives for the attitude of villagers and townspeople to the waves of internal movement which swept through their communities. Open expressions of hostility to outsiders as such are rare even in the combustible, inebriated atmosphere of the local alehouse (although the outbursts recorded in seventeenth-century defamation cases might include some reference to sexual dalliance with pedlars!).[55] Mobility was so pervasive that it was seen as much a natural part of the life cycle as being born or dying. Compared with official attitudes towards the itinerant poor, ordinary inhabitants had a more sympathetic approach. Perhaps their main hostility was reserved for foreign immigrants: there were attacks on Dutch and Walloon refugees in the sixteenth century, the Scots in the seventeenth, the Jews and above all the Irish in the eighteenth.[56] At the core of that hostility was economic disadvantage: foreign immigrants could take away jobs – although they were welcomed when and where skills and people were needed.[57]

Contemporaries were perhaps more likely to note the absence of mobility than its presence. Celia Fiennes was moved to crack one of her worst jokes when meeting a curiously immobile community in the Peak District, for they 'scarce ever go two or ten mile from thence, especially the women, so may be termed good housekeepers'; William Hutton remarked with surprise upon a village where he was made to feel unusually unwelcome as a stranger.[58]

All in all, contemporary opinion by itself is of limited value for the study of migration in the early modern period. There is usually the bias of other circumstances at work in producing comment, often economic disadvantage, potential or real. If we were to rely simply on contemporary comment we might well have a distorted picture of migration patterns over time. While economic difficulties in the later sixteenth century were accompanied by vociferous comment on migrants and their habits, there is, perversely, less public comment on (and documentation for) migration in the eighteenth century when the volume of movement increased with accelerating urban and industrial growth.[59]

IV

Clearly there are severe methodological problems confronting the student of migration in early modern England. At the same time, the importance of the subject cannot be doubted. Recent research on economic and social developments in the period has brought to the fore the wide-ranging role of mobility as both an important force for stability within the social system, maintaining the status quo, and as a dynamic and quite often disruptive force for change.

In the context of the national population it is evident from the preceding sections that the relationship between migration and the classic demographic triumvirate of birth, marriage, and death is close, and particularly close in the case of England. By comparison with continental Europe this country was, demographically, astonishingly homogeneous: English regions were close to each other in terms of the level and direction of change of basic demographic variables.[60] No less important, fertility and nuptiality (rather than, as has usually been supposed, mortality) played the overall decisive role in engineering structural population change in England.[61] Since the action of fertility is relatively slow and extra children take many unproductive years to mature, migration was of crucial importance, mediating between changing levels of economic demand and national population supply, and also compensating for the differential rates of population growth between regions, towns, and villages.[62]

Migration also affected demographic trends more directly. In the period before the Civil War it is arguable that urban immigration, in combination with heavy mortality rates in larger towns, served as a providential check on the accelerating pace of population increase in the kingdom as a whole.[63] Thereby widespread famine was perhaps avoided. After the Restoration migration to London and the major cities, along with emigration to the colonies, may well have choked off demographic growth and precipitated the marked decline of the national population between the 1650s and 1690s.[64] It was not only that migrants continued to stand a strong risk of dying in towns because of high levels of epidemic and endemic disease and insanitary conditions, but also the character of migratory activity in the later seventeenth century may have depressed overall marriage and fertility rates. Recent work has shown that the period saw high inflows of female migrants to towns, leading to unbalanced sex ratios in both rural and urban communities with inevitable effects on reproductive ability and performance.[65]

The movement of people was also positively engaged in the maintenance of an effective relationship between town and countryside in pre-industrial society. With most larger towns and many smaller ones (throughout western Europe) afflicted by large demographic deficits, with burials in many years greatly exceeding baptisms, immigration provided the life-blood of the urban community. Such a statement may hide significant local variation, and it is still a matter of debate whether the 'native' population of a major city was less affected by the depredations of disease and urban life. Some historians, like Allan Sharlin, have argued that the general supposition of a whole urban population being unable to reproduce itself is a statistical mirage, and that only the immigrant population was specifically so affected. The evidence is problematical, but contemporary as well as historical data point to the widespread operation of demographic deficits among urban populations.[66]

Be that as it may, labourers, artisans, traders, professional men, and gentry flocked to town, principally from the countryside. But in numerical terms the largest contingents comprised unskilled young people, boys and girls who served as the infantry of town life, trained (if they were lucky) as apprentices, working as tapsters in inns, servants in households and in shops, doing dirty jobs like sweeping chimneys and cleaning latrines. In the late seventeenth century the annual number of immigrants into Norwich was at least 400; in the case of London the figure may have exceeded 8000.[67] Without such an influx towns would not have been able to function effectively, or to grow in size. Massive immigration was crucial in enabling urban populations to recover rapidly from the catastrophic outbreaks of epidemic disease, most ferociously bubonic plague, which recurred in the sixteenth and seventeenth centuries.[68]

Although poorly documented and much less studied by historians, outmigration from the towns to the countryside was also important. Some urban families made good and moved into landowning, others fled from the harsh realities of urban life. The movements of skilled artisans may have contributed to the diffusion of craft skills in the hinterland of industrial towns, further promoting demographic and economic growth. Part of the process of 'proto-industrialization' often involves the setting up of industry in rural households, using previously urban-based skills and techniques.[69] Outmigration could also play an important part in urban decline, as in the case of Coventry in the early sixteenth century and some small market towns in the eighteenth century.[70]

Movement was also of social and economic significance in maintaining social and family relations between town and country, not least by sustaining kinship networks. As Peter Clark suggests in chapter 9, kinship networks were an important mechanism for the assimilation of newcomers to towns.[71] But no less important was the constant ebb and flow of migrants, teenagers apprenticed to urban relations or friends of relations, or townspeople returning to their home village to help bring in the harvest, which helped reinforce kinship links, especially outside the tight nuclear family. Less speculative migration was deeply implicated in the transfer of economic resources between town and country. By the later Stuart period landowners and other members of the rural elite were paying large premiums for their sons to be apprenticed to leading town traders. The aggregate sums represented a quite significant injection of capital into the urban economy.[72] In the reverse direction and on a more limited scale, country gentry collected handsome dowries for their sons' marriages to the daughters of city patricians eager to consecrate commercial fortune with the trappings of gentility. These same city worthies often acquired and (less commonly) retired to country houses and acres.[73]

The single most significant transfer of wealth occurred as the result of the growth of social migration to English towns in the seventeenth and eighteenth centuries. After the Restoration the attraction of the town as a place to politick, shop, frequent coffee houses, gamble at cock-fights and horse races, parade at assemblies, and otherwise display fashion and wealth became inescapable for many of the landed classes. Gentry families owned or rented property on a growing scale, not only in London, but in regional capitals and numerous country and resort towns.[74] Whole new fashionable quarters developed, with the West End leading the way. The cost was paid for by a massive transfusion of rental income.[75] Social, socialite migration was one of the pillars underpinning the golden age of urban prosperity in Georgian England.

In theory a prime function of migration is to shift surplus labour from relatively backward to economically developing areas. As far as early modern towns were concerned that process was by no means perfect. During the sixteenth and seventeenth centuries push factors led to large-scale movement from the poverty-stricken uplands of the north and west towards the more prosperous south.[76] But subsistence migration like this was not effectively targeted. Many urban communities in the lowlands receiving large numbers of poor migrants were themselves experiencing economic setbacks in the years before the Civil War and the influx threatened serious social problems.[77] Paradoxically, major urban-industrial growth in the midlands and the north in the eighteenth and early nineteenth centuries was not accompanied by a sizeable relocation of surplus labour from the increasingly over-populated rural counties of the south.[78] As we are about to see, the reason for this was the localized pattern of migration which predominated in England, notably after the late seventeenth century. Constraints on the mobility of labour may have been a stimulus to major technological advances.[79]

In the countryside migration was an essential lubricant for the working of the agrarian economy. Roger Schofield, in his analysis of the eighteenth-century census of Cardington, demonstrates that a high proportion of workers, servants and labourers in a village community comprised migrants from neighbouring villages. Circular mobility (the idea of exchange, which was a major feature of the first model we discussed) was common in England, from the fifteenth century and probably long before.[80] Servant migration within rural society was encouraged by the growing, and codified, importance of hiring fairs, particularly after the Restoration, and by the growing pressure of the settlement laws.[81] In the eighteenth century physical movement was further under-lined as a dynamic element in the economy of the countryside by the growing distinctiveness of 'open' and 'closed' parishes.[82] The latter were often small communities under the control of a single landowner or small group of farmers, in which poor law and settlement measures, including action against the building of cottages, were used to force young people and the 'undeserving' poor to leave the village.[83] By contrast, in open parishes controls were lax and agricultural occupations were increasingly supplemented by industrial trades which often depended on an inflow of migrant workers.[84]

As we shall see below, the latter half of our period also witnessed the increasing importance of seasonal, mainly harvest, migration which was closely associated with rising agricultural efficiency and specialization. Migrants not only provided an important part of the labour force for the rural economy, but may also have been a significant factor in the spread of new farming techniques and practices. Ann Kussmaul's research has revealed a ripple-type spread of agricultural innovation across the country from the mid seventeenth century, which is compatible with the idea of migrants as vectors of information.[85]

On the other hand, it is important to bear in mind that while migrants may have had their part to play in the advance of econ-omic integration, patterns of rural and largely localized migration may also have helped confirm sub-regional boundaries, giving demographic substance to village perceptions of a local 'country' or *pays*.[86]

So far we have been mainly concerned with the positive and dynamic aspects of migration's function in early modern society but, as the authorities complained before the Civil War, migration could also cause serious social problems. In chapter 2 Paul Slack confirms that vagrancy or subsistence movement was a widespread phenomenon in those years, with thousands of near-destitute and landless labourers tramping the trackways of the kingdom.[87] Mobility of this kind almost certainly contributed to the increase of unemployment and poverty in towns, just as the authorities complained. Most poor newcomers had limited skills and virtually no capital, and they joined an urban labour-market glutted with local workers through population increase and sluggish economic growth. In this way poor migration almost certainly contributed to the general slide of real wages and the surge of poverty.[88] Official complaints that migration led to a rise in crime and disorder are more contentious. A. L. Beier and others have shown that the scare stories of large and highly organized vagrant gangs, which figure prominently in the pamphlet literature of the time, were literary fabrications.[89] In rural society a relatively high proportion of indicted offenders were migrants, but this was in part because of other more informal sanctions against local people.[90]

Not enough work has been done on urban crime to come to positive conclusions about the role of migrants. In chapter 4 Jeremy Boulton makes a strong case against the conventional picture of metropolitan society being swamped by torrents of immigrants, destroying the social organization of local neighbourhoods and networks. In Boulton's view, established householders often stayed for quite long periods in a neighbourhood, usually only travelling short distances to adjoining streets when they did move. These people played a key role in maintaining a sense of social cohesion and solidarity, countering high levels of total mobility in the community.[91]

Nonetheless it is difficult to avoid the impression that high levels of immigration generated major difficulties of adjustment and integration for both movers and host communities. Peter Clark suggests in chapter 9 that traditional urban mechanisms of assimilation (apprenticeship, kinship, and regional solidarities) found it hard to cope with the tide of subsistence migrants in the sixteenth and early seventeenth century. But by the eighteenth century the process of integration may have been working more smoothly, with traditional arrangements being supplemented and supported by new bodies, voluntary societies, commercial agencies, and the like.[92] No less influential was growing local sophistication in the deployment of poor relief and settlement controls, together with the expansion of urban housing stock, which was advancing ahead of population growth in some towns by the end of the eighteenth century.[93] Hanoverian cities were further able to contain their social problems because of marked changes in the overall pattern of migration with the evolution of more specialist and targeted types of movement. Fundamental to all these developments was the emergence of a more sophisticated urban economy with a growing service sector.[94]

Everything then would suggest that migration had an ambivalent role in early modern England. It helped supply and regulate the populations of town and countryside. It was a reflection of general population trends of expansion and contraction, yet it could also work in opposition to those trends. It fuelled the operation of the economy and lubricated the machinery of the social system. However, it also might pose serious social and administrative problems for communities and their authorities. Above all, migration was a dynamic force, not only responding to demographic, economic, and social developments, but also creating and changing structures in later Stuart and Hanoverian society.

V

Earlier discussion made clear the problems of conceptualizing, documenting, and analysing physical mobility in the early modern period.[95] Nonetheless, migration has a central importance for understanding the changing face of English society in this period. Despite the difficulties it is essential to try to sketch the main contours of migratory activity between 1500 and 1800, drawing together material from a number of recent, often source-specific studies (several of which are reprinted in subsequent chapters). Given the problems of the sources discussed above, the resulting picture will be incomplete and perhaps puzzling. Not all the elements will add up, for those reasons we have already discussed.

But with some of the major landmarks visible we should be able to view the broad sweep of mobility in the period.

What seems fairly clear is that the pattern of physical movement in England shifted from one of muzzy, relatively undifferentiated migration activity before the Civil War to one increasingly overlaid by specialist, and in some measure institutionalized, flows in the later seventeenth and eighteenth centuries. This shift paralleled, and was almost certainly related to, structural change in the nature of national economy and society.

Beginning with the situation in Tudor and early Stuart England, all our evidence is that mobility rates were high throughout the country. In Buckinghamshire under Elizabeth over 80 per cent of witnesses appearing before the church courts had moved at least once in their lives. The comparable figure for countrymen in the Kent and Sussex Weald between 1580 and 1649 was 77 per cent; in early Stuart Suffolk and Norfolk 82 per cent.[96] Even so there were significant differences between the sexes, men moving further but not necessarily more often than women, and according to social and economic status. More respectable members of local society tended to be less mobile than small craftsmen, servants, and labourers.[97] No less important, the affluent tended to migrate shorter distances than lesser folk. In the Weald only 19 per cent of yeomen had journeyed over 20 miles when they moved, compared with over 64 per cent of labourers.[98] As we know, the poor were particularly prone to long-distance movement at this time, many travelling from the backward north to the southern lowlands. In Paul Slack's sample of vagrants half had migrated over 40 miles, and nearly a quarter over 100; Joan Kent's work on poor travellers in midland counties likewise indicates substantial numbers of long-distance movers in the early seventeenth century.[99]

It is possible to identify two main phases of lower-class longer distance movement in the Tudor and early Stuart period. There was migration to marginal, mostly woodland and pastoral, areas. The Forests of Whittlewood and Selsey in Northamptonshire and the Forest of Arden in Warwickshire all experienced high population growth from the sixteenth century, much of it stemming from immigration. Poorer folk were attracted to the woodlands by the relative freedom of open, unregulated settlements where they might engage in wood, leather, and other trades, keep livestock and smallholdings, and clear space to build their cottages among the trees. The account of Cambridge villages by Margaret Spufford, and the classic description of the Shropshire village of Myddle by Richard Gough, likewise suggest the appeal of pastoral areas with spare land.[100] By the last part of the sixteenth century however pauper movement was increasingly dominated by the drift to town. Wages were higher in London and other southern towns than in the countryside; jobs were available in the expanding marketing and dealing sectors of the economy. In the wake of the repeated epidemics which decimated the major urban centres, wiping out earlier generations of migrants, job and housing opportunities were good. In addition there was the lure of better-organized poor relief and, if all else failed, the chance to take up begging, petty crime, or prostitution.[101]

For many poor people the attractions of woodland, pasture, or town were less crucial in propelling them onto the road than the oppressive push factors at home. The sharp rise of the English population in the years between the mid sixteenth century and the mid seventeenth (from 2.98 million in 1561 to 5.09 million in 1641) created many pressures for an economy in which agricultural and industrial expansion was tardy and hard to achieve.[102] There is some debate about the trend in living standards over this period, but the balance of evidence would suggest that it was a time of mounting difficulty and distress for many smallholders, petty craftsmen, and labourers. High prices, declining real wages, under- and un-employment, together with rising rents and land shortages, all conspired to make poorer people leave home.[103] The situation was particularly acute in the upland regions. Andrew Appleby's work reveals how in Cumberland and Westmorland substantial demographic growth combined with the fragmentation of holdings and poor crop yields precipitated major subsistence crises in the 1590s and 1620s, with widespread famine, from which many escaped by taking the road south.[104] In times of severe hardship such as the 1620s and 1630s group migration became common, with whole families tramping in a random, erratic fashion across the provinces, from town to town. As we have seen, lower-class subsistence migration aggravated the social problems in many communities, particularly towns, and provoked a storm of upper-class condemnation.[105]

The tramping poor travelling long distances formed only one group of migrants in those years before the Civil War. A high proportion of movement was of a more conventional localized nature, on the pattern found in earlier centuries.[106] Ann Kussmaul has suggested that in the countryside servants in husbandry frequently moved in a limited circuit not too far from home, hired by the year at wage rates set by local justices.[107] Working on urban apprenticeship records, John Patten in chapter 3 confirms the suggestion that better-off migrants moved relatively short distances: the great majority of outsiders apprenticed in Norwich, Ipswich, and Yarmouth in this period had come from between 8 and 20 miles. At Southampton half of the migrant apprentices came from Hampshire, and even in the case of London with its enormous drawing power, nearly four out of ten boys apprenticed to city gilds had originated in the home counties and in the south midlands.[108] Evidence from civic freedom records likewise confirms that those respectable outsiders, mainly merchants and master craftsmen, who could afford to pay the freedom fines mostly came from the adjoining areas.[109] For these migrants the opportunities for advancement and betterment in town were more influential in determining their movement than were push factors. Respectable outsiders also faced fewer difficulties in establishing themselves in towns than did their poorer counterparts.

However while it is possible to distinguish broad streams of longer-distance subsistence migrants and more localized, respectable, betterment movers in the great tide of internal migration in sixteenth- and early seventeenth-century England, one should be careful of drawing too rigid or clear-cut a distinction. Apprenticeship was no guarantee of economic and social success, and for many teenagers and young men it ended in failure and disenchantment, especially in lesser trades. Many boys dropped out of service after only a few years, quite often drifting into vagrancy. Many of the vagrants arrested in London between 1597 and 1608 were former apprentices.[110] Other types of service were perhaps less formalized than they later became. It is uncertain quite how widespread hiring fairs were for domestic and farm servants, and many servants in town and country were retained on a casual basis or for a term shorter than the standard year. Some may have had to resort to longer-distance movement to find work; with a large surplus of younger workers, it was a buyer's market. According to Ann Kussmaul, the proportion of rural living-in servants was declining in the late sixteenth and early seventeenth centuries, and urban evidence points in the same direction. With rising food prices and falling wages it was cheaper to employ wage labourers than to house living-in servants.[111]

The overall picture for much of the period up to the middle of the seventeenth century is one of a relatively ill-defined and undifferentiated system of migration. More basic, localized movement shaded into longer-distance travelling. Crude subsistence or push factors were a vital part of the migration matrix. Pull factors were not matched to the precise needs of the economy.

By the later Stuart period however all the signs are that migration was developing in new directions, reflecting changes in society as a whole. Looking at the global dimensions of physical mobility various features are clear. Firstly, although aggregate mobility rates remained high (certainly by comparison with a number of European societies[112]), the period between 1650 and 1750 witnessed a small but significant increase in immobility, at least among the more settled, married portion of the population. The shift is a general phenomenon and can be measured for instance through family reconstitution-based studies of lifetime movements in local populations.[113] Diminished mobility is particularly notable in western England. For instance, among the witnesses appearing before the church courts in the diocese of Bath and Wells, the proportion of non-movers rose from something over a third before the Civil War to nearer a half in the late seventeenth century; by contrast, non-movers in the diocese of Norwich remained a small minority, only a sixth of witnesses after the Restoration. Quite why there was this regional difference and divergence remains unclear.[114]

Regional performance appears much more uniform in respect to the second major development of this period: the decline of long-distance migration. As Peter Clark makes plain in chapter 7, throughout the country migration was becoming increasingly localized. Subsistence migration out of the highlands had largely disappeared by 1700.[115] A fundamental reason was the decline in national population, from 5.28 million in 1656 to 5.05 million in 1701, and its laggardly recovery thereafter. In conjunction with rising and increasingly specialized agricultural output, this led to a decisive advance in real living standards and the virtual disappearance of subsistence crises.[116] One also needs to emphasize the proliferation of new industries with many of them in or near upland areas and, related to this, the growing economic diversity and sophistication of northern towns.[117]

Improvements in rural poor relief and the tightening up of settlement controls may also have moderated the old push forces in popular society, encouraging people to stay at home. The effects of the settlement laws have often been misunderstood. They were not a blanket restraint on migration, and indeed to some extent only *codified* existing patterns of movement (particularly that of young people in service and apprenticeship).[118] As Christopher Pond's researches have indicated, the settlement laws operated to regulate movement according to local economic need. Enforcement was often stricter where economic growth and demand for labour were limited; by contrast, in the fast-growth industrial cities little attention was paid to the laws except in time of trade crisis.[119]

A further development was a greater degree of convergence in the migration experience of different social groups. Not only were levels of mobility and distances moved often broadly similar across the social spectrum, but women were closer to men in their pattern of mobility.[120]

While at the aggregate level there are indications of increased homogeneity in English migration in a number of important respects, it is also clear that within this framework there was an emerging differentiation between more specialized types of migration behaviour. In the countryside the decades after the Restoration were the great age of the servant in husbandry, servants being kept in large numbers, moving usually every spring or autumn when changing masters. As living costs fell there was now an incentive for farmers to hire living-in servants rather than higher-cost, and possibly itinerant, labourers. Service of this kind was regulated by the settlement laws, especially from the 1690s, and lubricated by hiring fairs. Movement was not only increasingly institutionalized but also very localized; in Hertfordshire, for instance, farm servants moved on average only 3 or 4 miles.[121]

More formalized, regular mobility of farm servants in the post-Restoration period may have served to counterbalance the trend towards somewhat lower levels of mobility among farmers and their families.[122] Another dynamic element in the rural scene was the growth of seasonal migration. Before the Civil War seasonal migration seems to have been sporadic and ad hoc, but by the eighteenth century it had become widespread, helping farmers over the labour peaks and troughs of the agricultural year. People from the uplands journeyed into the south for harvesting;

Londoners travelled into the home counties for hop-picking; and Welsh girls came to the nurseries and market gardens around London.[123] Like old-style subsistence movement, harvest migration was often long distance, but it was also organized and directed. Other types of rural movement also deserve attention. With mounting prosperity among ordinary villagers, there were growing tribes of itinerant traders selling at alehouses and inns, to the increasing number of village shopkeepers or at market. Pedlars of earlier days, barely distinguishable from vagrants, were transmuted into respectable chapmen, warehousemen, ballad sellers, and bagmen; quite a few of these were Scottish. When the same people tried to sell in town, they provoked protests from established retailers.[124] The spread of rural industries may also have generated longer-distance movement by skilled workers, although this was probably never as important as in the case of urban artisans.[125]

In town society there is substantial evidence that old-style apprenticeship migration was on the wane by the start of the eighteenth century. At Norwich and Southampton the total numbers enrolled around 1700 were little more than a tenth of the figure a hundred years before. A rising proportion of apprentices came from the home town, and in many places outsiders were almost wholly recruited from the local hinterland. No less important, apprenticeship was geared increasingly to servicing the wealthier trades, such as distribution and victualling, and the professions.[126] The reasons for the eclipse of the old pattern of urban apprenticeship are touched on below in chapter 9. The decline of town gilds and the opening up of town economies made it easier to trade without having been apprenticed, while there was a multiplication of new trades in which apprenticeship failed to become established.[127]

With formal apprenticeship migration now focused more narrowly on serving the upper tier of urban occupations, the wider needs of the urban labour-market being more readily met by artisan and female migration. By the early Georgian period a distinct movement of skilled workers is evident, often inter-urban and involving travel over relatively long distances. In eastern England over a fifth of urban craftsmen in one large sample had migrated over 50 miles; those in high-status crafts had often moved furthest.[128] E. G. Thomas has identified flows of skilled workers in the textile crafts out of towns in Essex and also into Berkshire and Oxfordshire towns.[129] Emerging social institutions like 'houses of call' and trade clubs (usually based at alehouses) helped to structure artisan movement. In addition to aiding itinerant craftsmen when they arrived in a community, these bodies circulated news about jobs within the craft, encouraging skilled workers to migrate further afield into centres of expanding employment.[130] There were clear and positive links between migration and literacy: the more literate a person, the greater the access to information on occupational opportunities elsewhere, and perhaps the greater the distances moved.[131]

Female migrants were also well established as a distinctive force in urban migration by 1700. This led to a growing imbalance in urban communities compared with the countryside. At York, for example, sex ratios at death had shown a surplus of males over females in the years between 1600 and 1660, but this was reversed in the decades that followed. Similar situations were found elsewhere. By the 1690s the sex ratio (number of males per 100 females) at Leicester was 87.1, at Gloucester 81.0, and as low as 80.2 in Bristol.[132] After the Restoration women flocked to town to work as domestic servants in the houses of merchants, gentry and professional men, and to serve in the burgeoning numbers of inns and shops, while the new consumer industries also employed groups of female workers. Some women found work through the gilds – by the later seventeenth century girls were being apprenticed in various towns, Coventry and York among them – and other jobs were available through the register offices and newspaper advertisements.[133] At the same time, because many female migrants had moved only short distances, a considerable proportion probably relied on family connections to get a toehold in urban society.

Social migration, which we examined briefly above, was another type of movement characterizing towns of the late seventeenth and eighteenth centuries. By the early Hanoverian period lesser gentry as well as county magnates stayed in town for weeks or months of the year. Shrewsbury in the 1690s had over seventy resident gentry with their households; in the next century it had several hundred. Eighteenth-century Norwich, Lincoln, and Exeter all had major contingents of gentry visitors, many smaller towns likewise. Bury St Edmunds, with its annual fair, became a byword for gentility.[134] But London was the mecca. From the Restoration it attracted many thousands of landowners to the season, meeting together in a smart urban world of coffee houses, theatres, assemblies, clubs and societies.[135]

Vagrancy stood at the other end of the social spectrum. Unlike earlier, when it had embraced a wide variety of the tramping poor including unemployed labourers and craftsmen, vagrancy in the years after the Restoration was more restricted. Numbers probably diminished, and movement of this type was limited more to a rump of petty criminals, sharks, entertainers, tramps, ne'er-do-wells, and Scots and Irish, swollen during and after wars by hundreds of itinerant soldiers and sailors with their families. In the later eighteenth century, larger-scale vagrancy reappeared, mainly due to a great influx of Irish poor.[136]

So far our discussion of trends in physical mobility in England has concentrated on internal migration. Emigration and immigration also require our attention. During the sixteenth and seventeenth centuries, alien migrants formed specialist flows, complementing the less well-differentiated patterns of internal movement. Dutch and Walloon refugees brought skilled trades, particularly in the new draperies, to London and the other provincial centres.[137] Sephardic Jews after the Restoration became active in the financial sector, while at about the same time Huguenot refugees fleeing from Louis XIV developed the silk-weaving industry in east London, and became established in many luxury trades.[138] Welsh and Scottish immigrants were less cohesive, and less involved in specific trades, though by the end of the seventeenth century Scots were linked with itinerant retailing and in London with hairdressing and tailoring.[139] The new immigrant waves of the eighteenth century, Ashkenazi Jews from northern Europe, and the Irish, seem to have fitted in less well with the increasingly complex and specialist pattern of English migration. In part this was because of their lack of skills; it also reflected the rising level of skill within the native population. Ghettoization may have been more common among these aliens than their predecessors, given their growing difficulties of integration.[140]

Historically (and to the present day) it appears that for England net migration has always been outwards – that is to say, emigrants have consistently outnumbered immigrants. During the later sixteenth century and the early years of the seventeenth, the principal destination was almost certainly Ireland (although there was a small but steady movement to the Low Countries, especially from East Anglia).[141] But from the 1630s and 1640s the colonies in North America and the West Indies were to take most emigrants. One estimate has put the British trans-Atlantic contingent at some 380,000 in the course of the seventeenth century, while Wrigley and Schofield's calculation for net emigration from England over the same period is something approaching half a million people. These figures do not cover quite the same universe, but show just how substantial the movement overseas must have been. For in proportional terms this was a very considerable leakage of population, and at its height in the 1650s emigration probably approached the rates seen in the middle of the nineteenth century.[142]

Of those bound for the colonies, only a tiny fraction went to New England. The Pilgrim Fathers were not typical members of the flow of trans-Atlantic emigrants. Most who left England went to the West Indies, to Virginia and Maryland. A considerable proportion went as indentured servants, working for a fixed term on a plantation in return for their passage and board.[143] That system continued, albeit at a lower ebb, in the eighteenth century. There was also a not inconsiderable convict population transported across the Atlantic, at least until 1776.[144] The shift in migration patterns at home also affected movement to the colonies. In the great efflux of the mid seventeenth century a small proportion of the emigrants were highly skilled. Indeed, in chapter 5 David Souden argues for seeing emigration patterns as an extension of patterns of internal migration, with large numbers of long-distance subsistence migrants taking ship. But by the early eighteenth century a much higher proportion, of a much smaller flow of English settlers, was highly skilled.[145] Once they arrived in the plantations many settlers did not forget their English heritage of high mobility. As James Horn demonstrates in chapter 6, internal migration was an important element in the social world of the middle-American colonies.[146]

Thus from the later Stuart period the major demographic and economic changes affecting the country, which included the stagnation in population growth, the advance of innovation and specialization in agriculture, trade, and industry, were having a powerful effect on the pattern of English migration. Subsistence movement fell away; local migration seems to have predominated to a greater extent; immigration and emigration played variations on the main themes of development. Our picture is by no means perfect however. Most of our evidence is for the late seventeenth and early eighteenth centuries. One of the great mysteries still is what happened in the later eighteenth century as the industrial revolution took wing.

Documentation is a serious problem. David Souden suggests in chapter 10, with only sparse evidence available from conventional sources, what may be achieved by devising indirect, back-door techniques for exploiting parish register data. What he shows is evidence for considerable net differences between various English regions. By inference these are migration differences with distinct male and female migration patterns in the regions. Total volumes of mobility probably remained high (see the analysis of the Cardington census by Roger Schofield in chapter 8) and may well have increased towards the end of the century.[147] The quickening pace of urbanization (in contrast, it may be noted, with continental Europe) saw a swelling tide of urban migrants, given the continued inability of many urban populations to maintain natural increase. Who those migrants were remains a largely undetermined question. As for the distances migrants travelled, the evidence would appear to point, as ever, to the primacy of short-range movement.[148] The anomalies in regional sex-specific distributions of population highlighted by David Souden in the final chapter also signal the existence of some longer-distance flows, many centred upon London. The great attraction of London is clearly one constant in the equation, the magnet of the metropolis continuing to dominate all else, absorbing a good part of the natural increase in the southern and eastern counties.[149] So there is a real sense in which the old, 'natural' patterns persisted. There was also a trend towards greater local variability in migration: the first model outlined earlier in this introduction is less valid for the end of our period of study than for the beginning. For the variegation was probably associated with the development of increasingly differentiated if inter-connected regional economies; but it may also have been influenced by highly localized differences in the operation of administrative and social controls.

*

Thus there are still many pieces missing from our puzzle. More problems will be solved (and more will arise) in the course of fitting in those pieces. But as the following chapters confirm, the central place and broad configuration of migration in early modern England is already emerging.

Notes and references

1 For a comprehensive introduction to the definitions and varieties of explanation for migration, see R. P. Shaw, *Migration theory and fact* (Philadelphia, 1975); L. A. Kosinski and R. M. Prothero (eds), *People on the move: studies on internal migration* (1975).

2 W. Hutton, *The Life of William Hutton*, 2nd edn (1817).

3 *Life of Hutton*, pp. 70–106

4 *Life of Hutton*, pp. 106–20.

5 *Life of Hutton*, pp. 131ff.

6 See, for instance, M. Spufford, 'First steps in literacy: the reading and writing experiences of the humblest seventeenth-century spiritual autobiographers', *Social History*, iv (1979), pp. 407–35; D. Vincent, *Bread, knowledge, and freedom: a study of nineteenth-century working class autobiography* (1981), pp. 1–38; A. Macfarlane (ed.), *The diary of Ralph Josselin, 1616–83* (1976); E. P. Thompson, 'Anthropology and the discipline of historical context', *Midland History*, i (1971–2), pp. 41–55; A. Kussmaul (ed.), *The autobiography of Joseph Mayett of Quainton, 1783–1839*, Bucks Record Society, xxiii (1986); D. Souden and D. Starkey, *This land of England* (1985), pp. 124–30.

7 For example, Thompson, 'Anthropology and the discipline'.

8 P. Laslett, 'Characteristics of the western family considered over time' in P. Laslett, *Family life and illicit love in earlier generations* (Cambridge, 1977), pp. 12–49; R. M. Smith, 'Fertility, economy, and household formation in England over three centuries', *Population and Development Review*, vii (1981), pp. 595–622.

9 J. Hajnal, 'Two kinds of pre-industrial household-formation system' in R. Wall *et al.* (eds), *Family forms in historic Europe* (Cambridge, 1983), pp. 65–104; E. A. Wrigley and R. Schofield, *The population history of England 1541–1871: a reconstruction* (1981) pp. 466–80.

10 E. A. Wrigley, 'Fertility strategy for the individual and the group' in C. Tilly (ed.), *Historical studies of changing fertility* (Princeton, 1978), pp. 135–54, esp. pp. 137–48, 153–4; R. M. Smith, 'Some issues concerning families and their property in rural England 1250–1800' in R. M. Smith (ed.), *Land, kinship, and life-cycle* (Cambridge, 1984), pp. 1–86, esp. pp. 38–62.

11 Wrigley, 'Fertility strategy', p. 147.

12 See the comments in A. Kussmaul, *Servants in husbandry in early modern England* (Cambridge, 1981), pp. 24–7.

13 See the calculations in D. C. Souden, 'Pre-industrial English local migration fields', unpublished University of Cambridge PhD thesis, 1981, pp. 11–13.

14 For an extreme view on these possibilities, see K. Snell, 'Parish registration and the study of labour mobility', *Local Population Studies*, 33 (1984), pp. 33ff.

15 This question has been addressed rather more for the medieval world than the early modern: see Smith, 'Some issues concerning families and their

property'; A. Macfarlane, *The origins of English individualism* (Oxford, 1978), pp. 94–101, 139–40.

16 Various Scandinavian historians have drawn particular attention to this sort of low-level but ubiquitous movement. See, for example, S. Langholm, 'Short-distance migration, circles and flows: movements to and from Ullensaker according to the population census lists of 1865', *Scandinavian Economic History Review*, **xxiii** (1975), pp. 36–62. Jean-Pierre Poussou in his comprehensive survey of French studies refers to this as 'micro-poussière', J.-P. Poussou, 'Les mouvements migratoires en France et à partir de la France de la fin du XVᵉ siècle au début du XIXᵉ siècle: approches pour une synthèse', *Annales de démographie historique 1970* (Paris, 1971), pp. 11–78.

17 A. Kussmaul, 'Agrarian change in seventeenth-century England: the economic historian as paleontologist', *Journal of Economic History*, **xlv** (1985), pp. 1–30.

18 J. Thirsk, 'Industries in the countryside' in F. J. Fisher (ed.), *Essays in the economic and social history of Tudor and Stuart England in honour of R. H. Tawney* (Cambridge, 1961), pp. 70–88.

19 See the inter-relationships between agriculture and industry, and changes in them, shown in P. Large, 'Urban growth and agricultural change in the west midlands during the seventeenth and eighteenth centuries' in P. Clark (ed.), *The transformation of English provincial towns 1600–1800* (1984), pp. 169–89.

20 J. Patten, *English towns, 1500–1700* (Folkestone, 1978), pp. 146–96.

21 E. A. Wrigley, 'Parasite or stimulus. The town in a pre-industrial economy' in P. Abrams and E. A. Wrigley (eds), *Towns in societies* (Cambridge, 1978), pp. 295–309.

22 T. Hägerstrand, 'Migration and area. Survey of a sample of Swedish migration fields and hypothetical considerations on their genesis', *Lund Studies in Geography*, Series B, **xiii** (1957), pp. 27–158.

23 See E. A. Wrigley, 'A simple model of London's importance in changing English society and economy 1650–1750', *Past and Present*, **37** (1967), pp. 44–70; A. L. Beier and R. A. P. Finlay (eds), *London 1500–1700: the making of the metropolis* (1986), pp. 17ff; D. Ringrose, 'The impact of a new capital city: Madrid, Toledo, and New Castile 1560–1660', *Journal of Economic History*, **xxxiii** (1973), pp. 761–91.

24 The diagram and part of the discussion which follows draws upon C. Tilly, 'Migration in modern European history' in J. Sundin and E. Söderlund (eds), *Time, space and man: essays on microdemography* (Stockholm, 1979), pp. 175–97.

25 Above, p. 13–14; A. Constant, 'The geographical background of inter-village population movements in Northamptonshire and Huntingdonshire, 1754–1943', *Geography*, **xxiii** (1948), pp. 78–88; D. Souden and G. Lasker, 'Biological inter-relationships between parishes in east Kent: an analysis of the Marriage Duty Act returns for 1705', *Local Population Studies*, **21** (1978), pp. 30–9; Schofield, below, pp. 256ff. For a Scandinavian comparison, see Langholm, 'Short-distance migration'.

26 C. Jansen, 'Some sociological aspects of migration', in J. A. Jackson (ed.), *Migration* (Cambridge, 1969), pp. 69–71.

27 J. H. Pruett, *The parish clergy under the later Stuarts: the Leicestershire*

experience (Urbana, 1978); P. Clark, *English provincial society from the Reformation to the Revolution* (Hassocks, 1977), p. 277.

28 J. Scantlebury, 'John Rashleigh of Fowey and the Newfoundland cod fishery 1608–20', *Journal of the Royal Institution of Cornwall*, new series, **viii** (1978–81), pp. 61–71.

29 M. Spufford, *The great reclothing of rural England: petty chapmen and their wares in the seventeenth century* (1984), pp. 23–8.

30 E. J. T. Collins, 'Migrant labour in English agriculture in the nineteenth century', *Economic History Review*, 2nd series, **xxix** (1976), pp. 38–59.

31 J. Kitteringham, 'Country work girls in nineteenth century England' in R. Samuel (ed.), *Village life and labour* (1975), pp. 75–138, esp. pp. 108–10.

32 V. Brodsky Elliott, 'Mobility and marriage in pre-industrial England', unpublished University of Cambridge PhD thesis, 1978, pp. 152–244; curious trans-Atlantic migrant chains are examined in H. Charbonneau, *Tourouvre-au-Perche aux XVIIᵉ et XVIIIᵉ siècles* (Paris, 1970).

33 Below, pp. 271–3, 281–2.

34 See the forthcoming work of Keith Wrightson and David Levine on Tyneside mining communities.

35 See bibliography, section B. v, pp. 337–8.

38 See bibliography, section B. iv, pp. 336–7.

37 See bibliography, section B. ii, pp. 334–5.

38 See bibliography, section B. i, pp. 333–4.

39 See bibliography, section C. i, p. 338.

40 See bibliography, section C. ii, pp. 338–40.

41 See A.-S. Kälvemark, 'The country that kept track of its population' in Sundin and Söderlund (eds), *Time, space and man*, pp. 221–38.

42 Below, pp. 253–66. An original copy of the census which Schofield used has come to light, with updated information on the families for the following few years, between 1782 and 1791: Bedfordshire RO, P38/28/1/2.

43 P. Laslett, 'Clayworth and Cogenhoe' in Laslett, *Family life and illicit love*, pp. 50–101.

44 Below, pp. 172–203.

45 Particular illumination has been and will be thrown on the topic by the work of Michael Anderson: see, for example, 'Urban migration in nineteenth century Lancashire: some insights into two competing hypotheses', *Annales de démographie historique 1971* (Paris, 1972), pp. 13–26. Many of the items included in section F of the bibliography, pp. 342–3, are based on the census schedules and returns.

46 P. Deane and W. A. Cole, *British economic growth 1688–1959*, 2nd edn. (Cambridge, 1967), pp. 106–22; Souden, below, pp. 292–328.

47 E. G. Ravenstein. 'The laws of migration', *Journal of the [Royal] Statistical Society,* **xlviii** (1885), pp. 167–227, and **lii** (1889), pp. 214–301. See also D. B. Grigg, 'E. G. Ravenstein and the "laws of migration" ', *Journal of Historical Geography,* **iii** (1977), pp. 41–54.

48 Grigg, 'Ravenstein and the "laws of migration" '; E. S. Lee, 'A theory of migration' in Jackson (ed.), *Migration*, pp. 282ff.

49 S. A. Stouffer, 'Intervening opportunities: a theory relating mobility and distance', *American Sociological Review,* **v** (1940), pp. 845–67.

50 M. Kitch, 'Capital and kingdom: migration to later Stuart London' in Beier and Finlay (eds), *London 1500–1700*, pp. 224–51.

51 W. Haenszel, 'Concept, measurement and data in migration analysis', *Demography*, iv (1967), pp. 253–61; D. Courgeau, *Migrants and migrations* (Paris, 1979: reprinted translation from *Population*); Kosinski and Prothero (eds), *People on the move*, pp. 1–19.

52 This problem is discussed in Souden, 'Migrants and the population structure'.

53 Kent Archives Office, Sa/AC5, fo. 6; J. P. Earwaker (ed.), *The court leet records of the manor of Manchester*, iii (Manchester, 1886), p. 122; see also Clark, below, pp. 277–9.

54 See Slack, below, pp. 49–50, 52; also A. L. Beier, *Masterless men: the vagrancy problem in England 1560–1640* (1985), p. 7 and *passim*; Clark, below, pp. 279–80; K. Wrightson and D. Levine, *Poverty and piety in an English village: Terling 1525–1700* (1979), pp. 69, 72.

55 P. Clark, *The English alehouse: a social history 1200–1830* (1983), pp. 130–1.

56 A Pettegree, *Foreign Protestant communities in sixteenth-century London* (Oxford, 1986), pp. 284 ff; P. Clark (ed.), *The European crisis of the 1590s* (1985), pp. 52–3; D. H. Willson, *King James VI and I* (1956), pp. 176, 255; M. D. George, *London life in the eighteenth century* (1965), p. 137; Clark, below, pp. 274–6.

57 J. Thirsk and J. P. Cooper (eds), *Seventeenth-century economic documents* (Oxford, 1975), pp. 713–50.

58 C. Morris (ed.), *The journeys of Celia Fiennes* (1947), p. 94; W. Hutton, *An history of Birmingham* (Birmingham, 1806), p. 91.

59 For the methodological problems of studying eighteenth-century migration, see Souden, below, pp. 292ff.

60 E. A. Wrigley and R. S. Schofield, 'English population history from family reconstitution: summary results 1600–1799', *Population Studies*, xxxvii (1983), pp. 157–84; A. J. Coale and S. C. Watkins (eds), *The decline of fertility in Europe* (Princeton, 1986), pp. 61–76.

61 E. A. Wrigley, 'The growth of population in eighteenth-century England: a conundrum resolved', *Past and Present*, 98 (1983), pp. 121–50.

62 Wrigley and Schofield, *Population history*, pp. 464, 469–78; for an interesting illustration of the different interactions between migration and other demographic variables, see D. Gaunt, 'Pre-industrial economy and population structure: the elements of variance in early modern Sweden', *Scandinavian Journal of History*, ii (1977), pp. 183–210.

63 P. Clark (ed.), *The early modern town* (1976), p. 207.

64 Wrigley and Schofield, *Population history*, pp. 469–72; Wrigley, 'Simple model of London's importance', pp. 47–8. For the European pattern, see J. de Vries, *European urbanization 1500–1800* (1984), p. 206.

65 Souden, 'Migrants and population structure', pp. 152–61. For a discussion of other feedback mechanisms at work, see Smith, 'Household formation and fertility'.

66 A. Sharlin, 'Natural decrease in early modern cities: a reconsideration', *Past and Present*, 79 (1978), pp. 126–38. For a general critique of Sharlin, see de Vries, *European urbanization*, pp. 180–95; for a discussion of the problem in modern urban demography, N. Keyfitz, 'Do cities grow by natural increase

or by migration?', *Geographical Analysis,* **xii** (1980), pp. 142–56, **xiii** (1981), pp. 287–99.

67 P. J. Corfield, 'The social and economic history of Norwich, 1650–1850', unpublished London University PhD thesis, 1976, pp. 172–4; Wrigley, 'Simple model of London's importance', pp. 46–7.

68 P. Slack, *The impact of plague in Tudor and Stuart England* (1985), p. 184.

69 For a brief discussion, D. Palliser, *Tudor York* (Oxford, 1979), p. 99; W. T. MacCaffrey, *Exeter 1540–1640* (Cambridge, Mass, 1975), pp. 260–1; S. R. H. Jones, 'The development of needle manufacturing in the west midlands before 1750', *Economic History Review*, 2nd series **xxxi** (1978), pp. 354–68; D. Levine, *Family formation in an age of nascent capitalism* (1977); R. B. St George, 'The decentralization of skill in New England society 1620–1820', paper read at Anglo-American social history conference, Williamsburg, Va., 1985.

70 C. Phythian-Adams, *Desolation of a city* (Cambridge, 1979), pp. 64–6, 235–7, 281; S. J. Wright, 'Small towns and urban networks: a study of the home counties and south midlands', paper read at colloquium on small towns, Leicester, 1986; also see for an analysis of famous examples of decline, S. A. Hipkin, 'The economy and social structure of Rye 1600–1660', unpublished Oxford University, DPhil thesis, 1985, pp. 45ff.; D. Dymond and A. Betterton, *Lavenham: 700 years of textile making* (Woodbridge, 1982).

71 Below, pp. 271–3.

72 P. Clark, 'The migrant in Kentish towns 1580–1640' in P. Clark and P. Slack (eds), *Crisis and order in English towns 1500–1700* (1972), pp. 135–7; R. Grassby, 'Social mobility and business enterprise in seventeenth century England' in D. Pennington and K. Thomas (eds), *Puritans and revolutionaries* (Oxford, 1978), pp. 364–5; K. J. Smith (ed.), *Warwickshire apprentices and their masters, 1710–60*, Dugdale Society, **xxix** (1975); for eighteenth-century premiums, see R. Campbell, *The London tradesman (1747)* (Newton Abbot, 1969), pp. 331–40.

73 R. G. Lang, 'Social origins and social aspirations of Jacobean London merchants', *Economic History Review*, 2nd series, **xxvii** (1974), pp. 41ff; Grassby, 'Social mobility', pp. 358–9.

74 P. Borsay, 'The English urban renaissance: the development of provincial urban culture c. 1680–c. 1760', *Social History*, **ii** (1977), pp. 582–97; P. Corfield, *The impact of English towns, 1700–1800* (Oxford, 1982), pp. 51ff; Souden and Starkey, *This land of England*, pp. 150–4.

75 M. G. Davies, 'Country gentry and payments to London, 1650–1714', *Economic History Review*, 2nd series, **xxiv** (1971), pp. 15–36.

76 Clark, 'The migrant in Kentish towns', pp. 126–8, 138–45; see below, pp. 62ff.

77 P. Slack, 'Social problems and social policies', in C. Phythian-Adams *et al., The traditional community under stress* (Milton Keynes, 1977), pp. 81ff.; P. Slack (ed.), *Poverty in early-Stuart Salisbury*, Wiltshire Record Society, **xxxi** (Devizes, 1975), pp. 1–7; A. L. Beier, 'The social problems of an Elizabethan country town: Warwick, 1580–90', in P. Clark (ed.), *Country towns in pre-industrial England* (Leicester, 1981), pp. 48ff.

78 A. Redford, *Labour migration in England, 1800–1850*, 3rd edn (Manchester,

1976), esp. pp. 182–7. This is elegantly demonstrated for Preston in the first half of the nineteenth century in Anderson, 'Urban migration'.

79 Kussmaul, 'Agrarian change in seventeenth century England'.

80 Schofield, below, pp. 256ff; P. J. P. Goldberg, 'Marriage, migration, servant-hood and life-cycle in Yorkshire towns of the later Middle Ages', *Continuity and Change*, i (1986), pp. 147–9: J. A. Raftis, *Tenure and mobility: studies in the social history of the medieval English village* (Toronto, 1964), pp. 173–5; P. McClure, 'Patterns of migration in the late Middle Ages: the evidence of English place-name surnames', *Economic History Review*, 2nd series, xxxii (1979), pp. 167–82.

81 Kussmaul, *Servants in husbandry*, pp. 49–69.

82 B. A. Holderness, ' "Open" and "close" parishes in England in the eighteenth and nineteenth centuries', *Agricultural History Review*, xx (1972), pp. 126–39.

83 Wrightson and Levine, *Poverty and piety*, pp. 69, 72, 133, 182–3.

84 W. G. Hoskins, *The midland peasant* (1965), pp. 211–12; Levine, *Family formation in an age of nascent capitalism*, p. 58; M. Spufford, *Contrasting communities: English villagers in the sixteenth and seventeenth centuries* (Cambridge, 1974), pp. 121–64; V. Skipp, *Crisis and development: an ecological case study of the Forest of Arden, 1570–1674* (Cambridge, 1978).

85 See below, pp. 33–4; Kussmaul, 'Agrarian change in seventeenth-century England', pp. 1–28; E. J. T. Collins, 'Migrant labour', pp. 38–59.

86 C. Phythian-Adams, 'Little images of the great country', paper presented at Anglo-American social history conference, Williamsburg, Va., 1985; P. Styles, 'A census of a Warwickshire village in 1678' in P. Styles, *Studies in seventeenth century west midlands history* (Kineton, 1978), pp. 103–6; A. Everitt, 'Country, county, and town: patterns of regional evolution in England', *Transactions of the Royal Historical Society*, 5th series, xxix (1979), 79–107.

87 See below, pp. 50ff; also Beier, *Masterless men*, pp. 14–48.

88 Clark, 'The migrant in Kentish towns', pp. 138–45.

89 Beier, *Masterless men*, p. 123; also below, pp. 68–9. The older view is preserved in J. F. Pound, *Poverty and vagrancy in Tudor England* (1971).

90 M. J. Ingram, 'Communities and courts: law and disorder in early-seventeenth-century Wiltshire' in J. S. Cockburn (ed), *Crime in England 1550–1800* (1977), pp. 127–8, 132; K. Wrightson, *English society 1580–1680* (1982), pp. 155–9.

91 See below, pp. 107–38.

92 See below, pp. 269ff.

93 P. Styles, 'The evolution of the law of settlement', in Styles, *Studies in seventeenth century west midlands history*, pp. 187–207; K. D. M. Snell, *Annals of the labouring poor: social change and agrarian England 1660–1900* (Cambridge, 1985), esp. ch. 3; J. S. Taylor, 'The impact of pauper settlement, 1691–1834', *Past & Present*, 73 (1976), pp. 42–74; D. Marshall, *The English poor in the eighteenth century* (1926); C. W. Chalklin, *The provincial towns of Georgian England* (1974), pp. 305–8

94 Borsay, 'Urban renaissance'; Corfield, *Impact of English towns*, p. 97; Souden, 'Migrants and the population structure'; E. A. Wrigley, 'Men on the land and men in the countryside: employment in agriculture in early nineteenth century England' in L. Bonfield, R. M. Smith, and K. Wrightson (eds),

The world we have gained: histories of population and social structure (Oxford, 1986), pp. 295–336.

95 Above, pp. 13–20.

96 H. Hanley, 'Population mobility in Buckinghamshire 1573–83', *Local Population Studies*, **15** (1975), pp. 33–9, esp. p. 34; the Wealden data were generously provided by Brian Phillips of the University of Kent; Souden, thesis, p. 77.

97 Souden, thesis, pp. 77–8, 80–1; Clark, 'The migrant in Kentish towns', pp. 122–3.

98 *Ex inform.* B. Phillips; Clark, 'The migrant in Kentish towns', p. 129.

99 Below, p. 59; J. R. Kent, 'Population mobility and alms: poor migrants in the midlands during the early seventeenth century', *Local Population Studies*, **27** (1981), p. 43.

100 P. A. J. Pettit, *The Royal Forests of Northamptonshire*, Northants Record Society, **xxiii** (1968), pp. 142 ff; Skipp, *Crisis and development*, p. 18; Spufford, *Contrasting communities*, pp. 151–60; D. G. Hey, *An English rural community: Myddle under the Tudors and Stuarts* (Leicester, 1974), pp. 9–10; R. Gough, *The history of Myddle* (ed. D. Hey, Harmondsworth, 1981).

101 P. Clark and P. Slack, *English towns in transition, 1500–1700* (1976), pp. 86ff., 121ff.; Beier and Finlay (eds), *London 1500–1700*, pp. 17–19.

102 Wrigley and Schofield, *Population history*, p. 528.

103 For the orthodox view, see D. C. Coleman, *The economy of England 1450–1750* (1977), pp. 18ff.; for a more optimistic viewpoint, D. Palliser, *The age of Elizabeth* (1983), esp. ch. 13.

104 A. B. Appleby, *Famine in Tudor and Stuart England* (Liverpool, 1978).

105 Kent, 'Population mobility', pp. 42–3; Clark, 'The migrant in Kentish towns', pp. 143–4.

106 Souden, thesis, pp. 120–40.

107 Kussmaul, *Servants in husbandry*, ch. 4.

108 Patten, below, pp. 86–7; A. J. Willis and A. L. Merson (eds), *Calendar of the Southampton apprenticeship registers, 1609–40*, Southampton Record Society, **xii** (1968), p. xxix; R. Finlay, *Population and metropolis* (Cambridge, 1981), p. 64; Brodsky Elliott, thesis, pp. 57–82, 197–220. There are further references to studies employing apprenticeship registers in the Bibliography, section B. v, pp. 337–8.

109 For example, at York: Palliser, *Tudor York*, p. 128; D. Palliser, 'A regional capital as magnet: immigrants to York, 1477–1566', *Yorkshire Archaeological Journal*, **lvii** (1985), pp. 111–23.

110 Beier, *Masterless men*, p. 44; see also Clark, below, pp. 269–70.

111 M. K. McIntosh, 'Servants and the household unit in an Elizabethan English community', *Journal of Family History*, **ix** (1984), p. 16; Kussmaul, *Servants in husbandry*, pp. 97–8, 101–3.

112 For various European comparisons, see P. Goubert, *The ancien regime* (transl. S. Cox, 1973), pp. 42ff.; Poussou, 'Les mouvements migratoires en France'; E. Todd, 'Mobilité géographique et cycle de vie en Artois et en Toscane au XVIIIᵉ siècle', *Annales, E. S. C.*, **xxx** (1975), pp. 726–44; Tilly, 'Migration in modern European history'. Other references will be found in the bibliography, section E, pp. 341–2.

113 D. Souden, 'Movers and stayers in family reconstitution populations', *Local Population Studies*, **33** (1984), pp. 11–28.

114 Souden, thesis, pp. 72–97; see also Clark, below, pp. 220–2; Souden, below, p. 315.

115 Clark, below, pp. 228–9, 236–8; also Souden, thesis, p. 144.

116 Wrigley and Schofield, *Population history*, pp. 528–9; Coleman, *Economy of England*, ch. 6; A. B. Appleby, 'Grain prices and subsistence crises in England and France 1590–1740', *Journal of Economic History*, **xxxix** (1979), pp. 865–87.

117 J. Thirsk, *Economic policy and projects* (Oxford, 1978), pp. 167–9; J. D. Marshall, 'The rise and transformation of the Cumbrian market town, 1660–1900', *Northern History*, **xix** (1983), pp. 128–209, esp. pp. 153–69.

118 Styles, 'Evolution of the law of settlement'; Taylor, 'Impact of the law of settlement'; Snell, *Annals of the labouring poor*, pp. 61, 105–37.

119 C. C. Pond, 'Internal population migration and mobility in eastern England in the eighteenth century', unpublished University of Cambridge PhD thesis, 1980, pp. 25–37, 253–4; E. G. Thomas, 'The treatment of poverty in Berkshire, Essex, and Oxfordshire 1723–1834', unpublished PhD thesis, University of London, 1971, pp. 217ff. Recent economic analyses of the effect of the Old Poor Law have tended to play down the effects of the supposed curb on labour mobility that it represented: see G. R. Boyer, 'The Poor Law, migration, and economic growth', *Journal of Economic History*, **xlvi** (1986), pp. 419–30; J. P. Huzel, 'The demographic impact of the Old Poor Law: more reflexions on Malthus', *Economic History Review*, 2nd series, **xxxiii** (1980), pp. 367–81. Some of the fine detail of individual cases concerning settlement and poor relief is shown in D. Vaisey (ed.), *The diary of Thomas Turner 1756–1765* (Oxford, 1984), pp. 120 and *passim*.

120 See below, pp. 220ff; Souden, thesis, pp. 80ff., 128.

121 Kussmaul, *Servants in husbandry*, pp. 56–8, 100–1; A. Kussmaul, 'The ambiguous mobility of farm servants', *Economic History Review*, 2nd series, **xxxiii** (1981), pp. 222–35; Laslett, 'Clayworth and Cogenhoe', pp. 72–4.

122 Souden, thesis, pp. 80–2, 127, 247ff. The highly directed movement of farmers in the rather better-off later eighteenth century is discussed in J. R. Walton, 'The residential mobility of farmers and its relationship to the parliamentary enclosure movement in Oxfordshire' in A. D. M. Phillips and B. J. Turton (eds), *Environment, man and economic change: essays presented to S. H. Beaver* (1975), pp. 238–52. The migration effects of agricultural change and especially enclosure have long been a subject of inquiry. Various recent direct and indirect methods for assessing the impact of such change are to be found in Snell, *Annals of the labouring poor*, and N. F. R. Crafts, 'Income elasticities of demand, and the release of labor by agriculture during the British industrial revolution: a further appraisal' in J. Mokyr (ed.), *The economics of the industrial revolution* (1985), pp. 151–63.

123 Beier, *Masterless men*, pp. 88–9; Collins, 'Migrant labour'; Kent Archives Office, Q/SB 2, fo. 48, Q/SB 32, fos 25, 210; E. Jones, 'The Welsh in London in the seventeenth and eighteenth centuries', *Welsh History Review*, **x** (1980–81), p. 473.

124 Spufford, *The great reclothing*; D. Hey, *Packmen, carriers, and packhorse*

roads: *trade and communications in north Derbyshire and south Yorkshire* (Leicester, 1980), pp. 195–204.

125 Pond, thesis, pp. 63–8; Thomas, thesis, pp. 233ff.

126 See Patten, below, pp. 89–90; Willis and Merson (eds), *Southampton apprenticeship registers*, pp. xxvi-ix, xli; *ex inform.* Prof. Ralph Davis.

127 Below, p. 270: For the wider context of pauper apprenticeship in the eighteenth century, see Snell, *Annals of the labouring poor*, pp. 228–319.

128 Pond, thesis, pp. 68–70; Souden, thesis, pp. 124–5.

129 Thomas, thesis, pp. 233–43.

130 C. R. Dobson, *Masters and journeymen: a pre-history of industrial relations 1717–1800* (1980), pp. 38–46; E. Hobsbawm, 'The tramping artisan' in E. Hobsbawm, *Labouring men* (1964), ch. 4; H. R. Southall, 'The tramping artisan revisits: the spatial structure of early trade union organization', paper presented to Economic History Society conference, Cheltenham, 1986.

131 Souden, 'Migrants and population structure', pp. 143–4.

132 D. J. Hibberd, 'Urban inequalities: social geography and demography in seventeenth century York', unpublished PhD thesis, University of Liverpool, 1981, p. 313; Souden, 'Migrants and population structure', p. 150.

133 M. J. Walker, 'The extent of the guild control of trades in England c. 1660–1820', unpublished University of Cambridge PhD thesis, 1986, pp. 189ff.; see Clark, below, pp. 285–6.

134 Borsay, 'English urban renaissance'; A. McInnes, *The English town 1660–1760* (1980), p. 25-n; Everitt, 'Country, county, and town', p. 95; P. Corfield, 'A provincial capital in the late seventeenth century: the case of Norwich', in Clark and Slack (eds). *Crisis and order*, pp. 290–3; F. Hill, *Georgian Lincoln* (Cambridge, 1966), pp. 5–16; R. Newton, *Eighteenth century Exeter* (Exeter, 1984), pp. 18 and *passim*; D. Defoe, *A tour through the whole island of Great Britain* (1962 ed.), i, pp. 51–2; Souden and Starkey, *This land of England*, pp. 136–54.

135 L. Stone, 'The residential development of the West End of London in the seventeenth century' in B. Malament (ed.), *After the Reformation* (Manchester, 1980), pp. 174ff.; J. Summerson, *Georgian London* (1978), pp. 98–112.

136 Below, pp. 239–40; L. D. Schwarz, 'Conditions of life and work in London c. 1770–1820, with special reference to east London', unpublished University of Oxford DPhil thesis, 1976, pp. 40–1; Snell, *Annals of the labouring poor*, pp. 124–8.

137 R. D. Gwynn, *Huguenot heritage* (1983), ch. 4.

138 Cf T. Mendelman, *The Jews of Georgian London* (Philadelphia, 1979), p. 19 and *passim*; Gwynn, *Huguenot heritage*, pp. 67–70. There is a useful review of literature on immigrants and their communities in M. Greengrass, 'Protestant exiles and their assimilation in early modern England', *Immigrants and minorities*, iv (1985), pp. 68–81.

139 Jones, 'The Welsh in London'.

140 Below, pp. 274–6; for hostility to Palatine Germans in the reign of Anne, Kent Archives Office, PS/Se 1, pp. 116 ff.

141 N. Canny, 'Migration and opportunity: Britain, Ireland, and the New World', *Irish Economic and Social History*, xii (1985), pp. 7–32.

142 H. A. Gemery, 'Emigration from the British Isles to the New World,

1630–1700: inferences from colonial populations', *Research in Economic History*, v (1980), pp. 179–231; D. Souden, 'English indentured servants and the trans-Atlantic colonial economy' in S. Marks and P. Richardson (eds), *International labour migration: historical perspectives* (1984), pp. 19–33.

143 Souden, below, pp. 156, 162; Horn, below, p. 175; Souden, 'English indentured servants and the trans-Atlantic colonial economy'.

144 M. Campbell, 'English emigration on the eve of the American Revolution', *American Historical Review*, lxi (1955–6), pp. 1–20; also B. Bailyn, *Voyagers to the West* (New York, 1986), esp. ch. 5; A. R. Ekirch, 'Bound for America: a profile of British convicts transported to the colonies, 1718–75', *William and Mary Quarterly*, xlii (1985), pp. 184–200.

145 Souden, below, pp. 156ff; Horn, below, pp. 174ff; D. W. Galenson, *White servitude in colonial America* (Cambridge, 1981). Bailyn points to the greater incidence of unskilled workers in Scottish emigration in the eighteenth century (*Voyagers*, pp. 91ff.).

146 Horn, below, pp. 182ff.

147 Souden, below, pp. 292ff; Deane and Cole, *British economic growth*, pp. 106–22; R. Lawton, 'Regional population trends in England and Wales 1750–1971', in J. Hobcraft and P. Rees (eds), *Regional demographic development* (1979), pp. 31ff.

148 Redford, *Labour migration*, p. 183; E. A. Wrigley, 'Urban growth and agricultural change: England and the continent in the early modern period', *Journal of Interdisciplinary History*, xv (1984–5), pp. 683–728.

149 Wrigley, 'Simple model'; Souden, below, p. 313; Corfield, *Impact of English towns*, pp. 66–81.

2
Vagrants and vagrancy in England 1598–1664

Paul A. Slack

Paul Slack uses mainly official lists of vagrants to chart the social and geographical background of the migrant poor before the Civil War. His main conclusions are that a high proportion of vagrants were young single people, predominantly males, who moved long distances. There were significant regional variations with strong flows from the disadvantaged upland areas towards the wood pasture and urban areas of the south. A limitation of this approach is the insufficient attention paid to how the policies of the authorities may have determined the configuration of detected vagrancy. The evidence used for occupations and movements may not be wholly reliable and the sample is skewed regionally. But this general picture of vagrant movement has been substantiated by more recent studies.

I

'The greatest part' of rogues, wrote Richard Younge, in 1654, 'are an uncircumcised generation, unbaptized, out of the Church, and so consequently without God in the world.'[1] He was echoing a condemnation which had risen in volume and violence over the previous century. Social commentators of all kinds were unanimous, from the royal physicians concerned about the danger to public health and Bacon appalled at this 'seed of peril and tumult in a state' to magistrates and ministers like Lambarde and Perkins who agreed that the laws against vagrants were 'grounded upon the laws of God and nature itself'.[2] Vagabonds became the scapegoats for all social problems. They were carriers of rumour, sedition, and disease, and they infected others with their 'licentious liberty'.[3] The threat posed by their needless idleness and reckless mobility seemed immediate and overwhelming. In spite of the continuing interest in poverty and the growing amount

49

of work on migration in this period, however, historians have seldom been able to penetrate the haze of rhetorical abuse to see the vagabond as he was, to define his status, or assess the significance of his mobility.

A recent survey of migrants in one English county has suggested that mobility among the lower strata of society was both long distance and frequent,[4] and the literary reactions to vagrancy would support this hypothesis.[5] But sources which throw light on vagabonds themselves are difficult to find. There are, for example, no hospital records of the kind so helpful to French historians. Yet according to the vagrancy statute of 1597 each parish should have kept its own register of vagrants whipped and returned to their place of birth or residence.[6] It is clear that these were compiled and referred to in the early seventeenth century, but few of them remain.[7] Information would be most valuable for large urban communities where vagrants were common. Here vagrants' passports were sometimes entered haphazardly in order books or council minutes along with other business.[8] But in two towns at least, separate lists of passports were kept for long periods in the seventeenth century and these still survive.

The first and most thorough register was compiled in Salisbury between 1598 and 1638. The record lists 557 passports containing the names of 651 vagrants. All were described as wandering and – unless pregnant, disabled, or under the statutory age of seven – were whipped; and all were ordered to be passed from constable to constable back to their birthplace or parish of residence. The second register which survives for the town of Colchester records the similar treatment of 237 vagrants in a list of all strangers expelled from the town between 1630 and 1664.[9] The evidence from these two towns of eastern and southern England may be compared with information from other parts of the country in the returns made by justices of the peace to the Privy Council in the 1630s. These certificates provide information about 132 vagrants found in Hertfordshire,[10] 614 in the counties of Kent, Sussex, and Surrey,[11] 296 in Devon and Cornwall,[12] and 916 vagrants discovered in Lancashire and Westmorland.[13] Finally, the printed minutes of the Norwich Court of Mayoralty record the punishment of 161 vagrants expelled from the town between 1630 and 1635.[14] These samples permit some comparison with the more detailed continuous registers of Salisbury and Colchester, and, together recording some 3000 individuals, they suggest general conclusions about the problem of vagrancy and the characteristics of vagrants in the early seventeenth century.

The limitations inherent in the records are, however, evident. The amount of information they provide is uneven, only names and places of origins being regularly recorded. Even the Colchester and Salisbury series are difficult to interpret, since it is never clear how far variations in the numbers of vagabonds punished from year to year reflect changing levels of enforcement or a change in the actual volume of vagrancy. Certainly those apprehended were only the tip of the iceberg and can tell us little about the quantitative as distinct from the qualitative features of the vagrant phenomenon. The most serious difficulty, however, concerns the reliability and significance of the evidence of vagrant origins provided by these records. The parish to which a vagrant was returned might be either his birthplace or the parish where he last resided for at least a year. But in either case the record does not tell us how long or where the vagrant had been wandering since he left the parish to which he was returned. This is a vital qualification to be made in any calculation of the distances which vagrants moved. Again, the authorities were dependent on the vagrant's own testimony for evidence of his place of origin. If he wished to visit London he need only say that he was born there. A Salisbury vagabond, for example, who alleged that he lived in Colchester, later confessed 'that he dwelleth not in Colchester but hath friends there dwelling and abiding and desireth to travel thither'.[15] Nevertheless, the variety of places given, many of them tiny obscure hamlets, and the detail of parishes or even streets which were often added in the case of large towns, suggest some truthfulness on the part of many vagrants; and where it has proved possible to check the vagrant's allegations with parish registers, birth- or dwelling-places have been confirmed for a striking proportion of cases, granted that we are looking for individuals in the social category most likely to escape parochial registration.[16]

Like other evidence bearing on those who were on the very margins of society, or, as contemporaries thought, completely outside it, the information provided by vagrancy passports can never be taken entirely at its face value. But in the absence of other sources it cannot be ignored, and it may be used to provide significant, if tentative, conclusions. In particular it suggests that vagrants were a recognizable and limited social group, and it illuminates the patterns of their mobility and possibly those of lower-class migrants in general.

II

The first problem for the historian, as for contemporaries, is to know who the vagrant actually was, to define his status. For vagrant and vagabond were emotive, elastic terms. Were vagrants, as statutory definitions often suggest, the useful or picturesque wandering pedlars and minstrels whom MPs on occasion wished to protect,[17] or those able-bodied professional beggars of the criminal underworld painted so definitively by Harman and his successors? Or were they simply unskilled migrant labourers and paupers, distinguishable on the one hand from the non-migrant poor and on the other from migrants of higher social status moving in search of work? The statute of 1597 tried to protect the two latter groups by insisting on wandering or 'loitering' and the absence of any visible 'living . . . to maintain themselves' in vagrants.[18] But it seems from the resolutions of the assize judges in 1629 and 1633 that they were not in practice always immune: it was necessary to insist that justices were not to 'meddle either with the removing or settling of any poor, but only of rogues', and to condemn 'illegal unsettling . . . for none must be enforced to turn vagrant'.[19] Consequently it has sometimes been implied that the vagrancy laws, like the ideological preconceptions and social prejudices which lay behind them, were employed against lower-class mobility of all kinds or against the able-bodied poor as a whole.[20]

It is certainly true that the categories of potential vagrant enumerated above were by no means distinct. Fortune-telling and theft were alternative sources of income for any poor migrant whose hope of finding regular employment in the economic conditions of the early seventeenth century was slim. The native poor of a parish once pushed out by parish authorities or pulled by a husband or parent would find return virtually impossible. Similarly, the hitherto respectable tradesman, seeking better opportunities in another town, might be expelled without punishment as a stranger or inmate under the strict (if usually informal and local) settlement regulations of the period, and at his next port-of-call find himself treated as a vagrant. Servants at the end of their term or those dismissed by their masters ran similar risks.[21]

On occasion the records allow us to glimpse this descent of the social scale, to follow the process which ended in vagrancy. Thomas Coxe, his wife, and two children had an apprentice with them when they were whipped and sent from Salisbury to Gaddesden, Hertfordshire, in March 1624. Eleven months later the family was taken in Salisbury again, but the apprentice and one of the children had disappeared.[22] This complete family was being fragmented. The death or flight of a parent or husband left a woman liable to 'become a vagrant' because she was 'harbour-less'. In the six months after her father left Essex, Susan Tomalin 'begged about the Marshes', while Agnes Symons 'wandered up and down in several shires begging' for two years after the death of her father in Somerset.[23] Pretexts might be found to force the native poor of a town on to the road. Stephen Poole of Salisbury deserted his sick wife and went to Romsey 'because the parish would not give more for his wife's maintenance'; she was sent after him with a passport. After the inhabitants of a Norfolk village put Denys Amys in a Norwich hospital he was treated as a vagrant by the city authorities.[24] When parishes were quicker to expel the poor than to welcome their return, the chances of the drummer boy from Devizes found with a passport saying he was 'minded to travel until he be settled' were minimal.[25] Once the first step had been taken, whether voluntarily or not, the road to vagrancy was an easy and precipitous one.

Most of the vagrants found in these records, however, seem to have been far from any past reality or present hope of respectability. Humphrey Reade and his wife, taken in Salisbury in 1610, had no 'certain place of dwelling and have wandered many years'. Anne Standley had been wandering for a year and 'hath received punishment three times before this time'. Others had been following the progress of the court or moving from fair to fair for months.[26] It is not surprising, therefore, that a few had turned to the traditional occupations of the wayfaring life as popular entertainers. Among the Salisbury vagrants were a fortune-teller, a minstrel, a morris-dancer, and two conjurors.[27] Others fit closely the categories of professional beggar described by Harman. There were 'counterfeit Bedlams' and a counterfeit cripple in Hertfordshire.[28] One of the Salisbury vagrants was a 'Dummerer', pretending 'he hath no tongue'. Some used the role of a guide for cripples as a pretext for begging and migration, like the married couple who had walked with the husband's lame brother all the way from Northumberland. One Amazon manipulated sickness as a threat rather than an object of pity, terrifying Salisbury citizens by running into their houses 'affirming herself to have the plague'. The settlement regulations of the period presented opportunities of a more sophisticated kind. There was a wholesale trade in counterfeit passports of the sort prescribed by the Statute of Artificers for those travelling in search of work.[29] One Salisbury vagrant had a certificate made 'by a stranger under a hedge'; another paid 3s. for one in London, while the price in Dorset was 2s. Forged certificates claiming losses by fire[30] or allowing travel as maimed soldiers were even more useful. Two rogues claiming to have been wounded in Ostend were given money by a string of county treasurers for maimed soldiers in 1602, before they admitted that their passports were forged by a man in Shoreditch.[31]

Yet this sort of information is provided in only a small proportion of cases. The picturesque or professional rogue appears to have been the exception not the rule. Men and women with stated occupations were rather less rare, though again in a small minority. Of the 651 Salisbury vagrants, seventy were accredited with trades. There was a joiner, a shoemaker, a wire-drawer, and two weavers. But a third of these were petty chapmen or pedlars, reflecting at this social level the contemporary expansion in the society of wayfaring traders.[32] One sold ballads, another rapiers and daggers, and a third was found 'selling of small books seeming to be distracted'. Other pedlars doubled as receivers of stolen goods, like Margaret Legg alias Jackson alias Smith, found in possession of a stolen cloak, who claimed that a beating from her husband had prevented her practising her trade.[33] Apart from professional rogues and wandering pedlars, there were two other noticeable sub-groups among the vagrants listed. The first were allegedly runaway apprentices and servants, some of them maltreated by their masters, others suspiciously pregnant.[34] They numbered eighteen of the Salisbury vagrants and four of those taken in Colchester. The second distinct group were the Irish. Nineteen of them were punished as vagrants in Salisbury, twelve between 1629 and 1633 when Irish famine pushed hundreds of emigrants into the western counties.[35] They were more conspicuous than their numbers suggest, since they often moved in bands of a dozen or more. In Colchester in October 1631 one Irishman, five women, and four children were apprehended together; in the Colyton division of Devon a few years later fifteen Irish adults and fourteen children were taken in a band.[36] Odd travelling Irishmen might sometimes be supported from parish doles,[37] but these gangs were an immediate problem for local constables and the probable foundation of Irish scares in the next decade.[38]

The Irish bands, like the other groups already mentioned, were, however, exceptional. English vagrants travelled in ones and twos. They might have their familiar haunts in a local alehouse, an isolated barn, or a lodging-house like that of John Matthew, a Salisbury hosier,[39] but whether they relied on petty crime or persuasive begging for their livelihood, or were genuinely seeking work, their chances of success depended on their relative solitude.[40] They also often depended on a certain anonymity, hence the frequency of aliases in these records. As a result the vagrant's physical appearance was often his most notable characteristic, as with Elizabeth Taylor, a Lancashire woman 'having black hair, a green waist-coat, a red petticoat and tall of stature, being great with child'.[41] But vagrants are usually described in the record merely by a name and a place of origin, and the majority of them appear as isolated individuals about whom only the simplest and broadest generalizations are possible.

Like migrants in other societies, English vagrants appear to have been normally young adults, although ages are commonly given only in three records.[42]

Table 1 The age of vagrants

Found in	7–9	10–14	15–19	20–9	30–9	40–9	50–9	60+	Total known	Total unknown
Colchester	3	13	12	8	14	8	5	10	73	164
Crondall 1598–1622	2	3	2	7	7	3	2	0	26	29
Westmorland	1	2	14	27	17	13	13	5	92	19
Total	6	18	28	42	38	24	20	13	191	212

The concentration of vagrants between adolescence and middle age is clearer in the Westmorland than in the Colchester evidence, partly because in the latter exceptional ages such as 90, 75, and 70 seem to have been particularly noted. In Westmorland, on the other hand, those old people who were found wandering the roads were thought not to 'deserve to be whipped or stocked' and were given alms rather than punished.[43] Local policies may have varied somewhat. A handful of old, lame, and blind men or women and some young children, one of them a boy of nine 'like to perish and die in the streets with cold', are to be found among the Salisbury vagrants. But those apprehended and punished were commonly young able-bodied adults.

They were also single and largely male.

Table 2   The status of vagrants
All figures in brackets expressed as percentages.

Found in	Single men	Single women*	Husbands and wives†	Children‡	Total
Salisbury 1598–1638	343	171	86	51	651
Colchester 1630–64	103	48	32	54	237
Norwich 1630–5	97	31	20	13	161
Kent, Sussex, Surrey 1632–9	208	147	132	127	614
Hertfordshire 1636–9	68	41	12	11	132
Lancashire and Westmorland 1634–8	561	254	80	21	916
Devon and Cornwall 1634–8	166	56	26	48	296
Total	1,546	748	388	325	3,007
	(51.4)	(24.9)	(12.9)	(10.8)	(100.0)

* Includes wives deserted by or running away from their husbands. †Includes alleged marriages.
‡ Those described as 'children' and those under the age of 15 where ages given.

It is clear from Table 2 that at the time of apprehension half the vagrants were single men and a further quarter were single women. Only the figures for the south-east, with high proportions of married couples and children, are exceptional.[44] But even here over half the vagrants were adults who were either unmarried or travelling without their spouse. This evidence on family structure may slightly distort the facts, since a few apparently single vagrants may have had families wandering with them who escaped detection, and children under the statutory age of 7 may sometimes not have been recorded although wandering with a parent. An Irishman whipped in Salisbury was later found in Warminster with a wife and children, for example.[45] But the predominance of men among vagrants is evident.[46]

It is also unlikely that the paucity of complete families grossly misrepresents reality. For vagrant liaisons, whether legal or not, were unstable and temporary. There were seventeen couples among the Salisbury vagrants described as 'living lewdly together, being unmarried'; ten single women were spared punishment because they were pregnant; another seventeen were sent back to their husbands, while one man alleged that he 'travelleth from place to place to seek his wife who is departed from him, and here he persuaded one Felton's daughter that he would marry her'. Their children felt the consequences. The Salisbury justices twice had to send for the mothers of young boys deserted in the town and a Hertfordshire rogue 'had left a child of his in a barn and foresaken it'.[47] The attitude of authority to alliances of this kind was predictably ambivalent. On the one hand, justices concerned with the growing number of poor tried to discourage their marrying; but as upholders of the institutions of 'civil society' they could also find ample excuse for the punishment of vagrants who did not 'range themselves into families, but consorted together as beasts'.[48]

Yet, however misinterpreted or exaggerated by contemporaries, the characteristics which lay behind this reaction served the important function of distinguishing vagrants from other social groups who might otherwise have been included among them. The vagabond class was in practice a limited one even if its boundaries were roughly defined and based on ready social prejudices. The recognized domestic poor of a town usually comprised the old and young and contained a large proportion of women.[49] If able-bodied unemployed men might be 'forced to turn vagrant' by local authorities, it was more difficult to treat these groups in a similar way. Equally there were categories of migrant who did not conform to the characteristics of the vagrant described above, and who might gain some imperfect protection from this fact. For local authorities distinguished between the migrants who could be punished as vagrants and those against whom other settlement regulations must be invoked. In Colchester and Norwich the many 'strangers' who were simply ordered to leave the town, sometimes 'on pain of punishment as a vagrant' if they returned, or who had to find sureties to 'save the town, harmless', were included in the same record as vagrants; in Salisbury they were entered in the parish poor accounts. In many cases these strangers were legally distinguishable from vagrants, because they had obtained employment, or recently rented accommodation in the town, or had certificates to travel in search of work.[50] But they were also socially distinct. Of the 100 strangers presented by the parochial authorities in Salisbury between 1629 and 1635, for example, thirty-eight were travelling with a spouse and twenty-eight were children;

there were only twenty-four single men and ten single women among them.

Contemporary definitions of and attitudes towards vagrancy were sufficiently clear-cut, therefore, to restrict the penalties for the offence to only one section of the migrant population. Indeed, those whipped as vagrants did not even include all the most destitute wanderers. Lists of 321 'poor distressed travellers' who were provided with lodging or alms by the constables of Coventry in the 1640s contained no less than 106 children and sixty husbands and wives. Many were cripples, maimed soldiers, or other victims of civil war. But others were poor wanderers of the kind who were given charity rather than a whipping at other periods and in other towns.[51] Only twelve people were described as vagrants in these lists. Those punished as vagabonds were a roughly identifiable sub-group among migrants, shading into other categories of wanderers and paupers, but marked out at the extreme by an absence of complete families and a predominance of single men among them.

III

The most important characteristic of the vagrant was, however, his long-term and often long-distance mobility. Many vagrants knew the roads of England like the backs of their hands. Sometimes they had a regular itinerary. Edward Yovell, for example, a Londoner by birth, began wandering after ending his apprenticeship in Worcester. Twice in two years he took up casual work in London where he had friends, then helped with the harvest at his uncle's in Surrey, next worked at various inns in Chichester, and finally returned to Worcester via Salisbury, Bristol, and Gloucester, presumably for the winter. Other vagrants had a single destination in view. Yovell's companion suggested they might break their circuit through the rich southern counties and go to 'Andover and from Andover to Newbury and from Newbury to Oxon and from Oxford directly to York', to pastures new.[52] But in the case of most vagrants we can determine only two points in their journey: their place of punishment and the birth- or dwelling-place to which they were returned. The distance between these two points, measured in a straight line and including any sea or estuary crossings, is clearly only the crudest indicator of distance actually moved. But such a measurement does suggest the geographical horizons of the vagrant class, and since similar information has been used for other sections of the population it can be manipulated for comparative purposes.

Studies of other groups of migrants have suggested that although mobility was common it normally took place within a relatively confined area. Of the witnesses appearing before archdeaconry courts in east Sussex between 1580 and 1640, most had moved from their place of birth, but less than 5 per cent had gone more than 40 miles. Less than 7 per cent of those moving into Sheffield to be apprenticed between 1625 and 1649 and less than 15 per cent of a group of apprentices moving into Salisbury between 1598 and 1640 came more than that distance. Apprentices moving into Southampton in this period and to Birmingham rather later had similarly come from a restricted area. There were local differences. In particular, inhabitants of the East End of London had often travelled more than 50 miles.[53] But with the exception of London's extensive pull on the whole of lowland and much of highland England, it is probable that the existence of competing urban centres of attraction made most mobility essentially local.

Vagrants, however, had often come much greater distances and moved deliberately from one urban centre to another. Table 3 shows that of 2651 vagrants whose place of origin can be determined, 50 per cent had travelled more than 40 miles and 22 per cent had gone more than 100 miles.[54] Although the majority had moved less than 50 miles and the median distance was rather

Table 3 Distances between places of origin and punishment of vagrants
(Number of vagrants expressed as percentage of total)

Vagrants found in	Distances to place of origin in miles								Total	
	0–20	21–40	41–60	61–80	81–100	101–50	151–200	200+	Per cent	(No.)
Salisbury	16·5	26·2	14·2	15·6	7·7	11·4	3·9	4·5	100·0	648
Colchester	15·7	14·0	36·0	3·4	2·5	11·9	2·5	14·0	100·0	236
Norwich	52·5	18·1	3·8	4·4	8·8	6·3	3·1	3·1	100·0	160
Kent, Sussex, and Surrey	19·2	20·3	12·6	8·8	5·1	20·3	5·6	8·1	100·0	605
Hertfordshire	10·6	41·2	4·7	22·4	3·5	17·6	0·0	0·0	100·0	85
Lancashire and Westmorland	43·5	30·5	12·3	4·7	3·7	2·6	2·1	0·6	100·0	653
Devon and Cornwall	21·6	10·6	8·3	5·7	5·7	9·5	34·8	3·8	100·0	264
Total (per cent)	26·2	23·3	13·8	8·8	5·4	11·0	6·6	4·9	100·0	—
(no.)	694	617	365	234	143	292	176	130	—	2,651

less than 45 miles, substantial numbers of vagrants had wider geographical horizons than other mobile groups in the population.

There were significant chronological and regional variations, however. It is clear that periods of bad harvest led to an increase in the number of vagrants punished in both Salisbury and Colchester. In each town the annual figure was highest at the beginning of the register, ninety-six vagrants being whipped in Salisbury in 1598 and fifty-nine in Colchester in 1631, no doubt in part as a consequence of initiative from the central government.[55] But the number of vagrants punished again rose significantly, to more than twice the annual average, in Salisbury in 1630 and in Colchester in 1648.[56] Dearth also had a disproportionate effect on particular groups of wanderers. In 1630 and 1631 an influx of Irish vagrants raised the proportion coming more than 200 miles to each town. But there is also some evidence that a run of bad harvests produced an increase in local vagrancy. This was particularly evident in 1598 when 40 per cent of Salisbury vagrants had come less than 20 miles; and in this year only, women outnumbered men among them. Although it is impossible to separate the administrative efficiency of authorities at the beginning of the record, or the readiness of local communities to co-operate in attacking vagabonds when food was short, from the distinctive effects of high grain prices on vagrancy itself, the two were related phenomena.[57]

The number of vagrants apprehended also varied from month to month, the peaks coming generally in March and October.

Table 4   Months in which vagrants were punished

Place	J	F	M	A	M	J	J	A	S	O	N	D	Total
Salisbury:													
1598	—	—	—	36	41	0	1	1	0	5	8	4	96
1599–1638	45	44	77	59	59	32	40	50	26	36	33	54	555
Colchester	18	20	45	19	12	18	14	8	7	42	20	14	237
Norwich	9	23	22	14	9	4	30	6	2	19	10	13	161
Total	72	87	144	128	121	54	85	65	35	102	71	85	1,049

Again local factors and enforcement influenced the figures. In Norwich, for example, the streets were regularly cleared of beggars in February and July before the visit of the assize judges.[58] Fairs like those in Salisbury in January and October, in Norwich in February, and in Colchester in March no doubt attracted additional migrants. The fall in numbers in September may be explained either by the availability of harvest work outside the towns or by official reluctance to enforce the laws at a time when extra migrant labour was needed and tolerated.[59] But the figures support the observation of contemporaries that vagrants began to move in the spring, as grain prices rose towards their peak and the condition of the roads improved.[60]

If the problem of vagrancy varied over time, it also differed from place to place, and it is the geography of English vagrancy which the records illuminate most clearly. Although there are important exceptions, Table 3 suggests that vagrants punished in highland England had moved much shorter distances than most of those found in the lowlands. Three-quarters of the vagabonds taken in Lancashire and Westmorland were recruited within 40 miles of their place of punishment, compared with 40 per cent of those in the south-eastern counties and 30 per cent of those in Colchester. While Irish vagrants account for the high proportion coming more than 150 miles into Devon and Cornwall, it would appear that Scotland did not provide a similar reservoir of poor migrants for at least the western side of the Pennines.

Even more striking, however, is the exceptionally high proportion of Norwich vagrants coming less than 20 miles, more than in any other region. Two-thirds of the total indeed were returned to places in Norfolk itself.[61] This was not due to any obvious lack of attraction of a rich and charitably well-endowed provincial capital for the vagrant class, but to its remoteness from the main lines of vagrant mobility. For the evidence suggests that, excluding movement within a short radius of major centres, the dominant stream of vagrant migration was towards the south-east, and specifically towards London. Given its situation, Norwich could not attract vagrants from long distances moving towards the Home Counties.

The Appendix shows the counties to which our sample of vagrants was returned and from it we can analyse in general terms the movement of vagrants in various parts of the country. Salisbury's contingent had the widest geographical experience, scarcely a county of England being unrepresented among them. This was partly the product of Salisbury's situation, at the junction of the main highways from London to Exeter and from Bristol to Southampton. As Map 1A suggests, the majority of vagrants were moving along these axes or on that route through the southern counties on which Harman commented.[62] Many had come from settlements clustered along the three main roads to Exeter via Taunton, Sherborne, and Dorchester, and ease of communication by river and road largely determined the local distribution of vagrant origins. Looking at the overall pattern, however, it appears that rather more of the long-distance migrants were moving from west to east than vice versa, although Salisbury was in a rich enough area also to attract vagrants from the Home Counties. Taking the counties south of a line from Bristol to London, 199 vagrants came from counties to the west of Wiltshire, 146 from those to the east. The position at Colchester was similar (Map 1B). Here the main routes were southwards through East Anglia and in both directions along the east coast from Newcastle to London and Kent. In lowland England, therefore, there was both general movement towards London and the Home Counties and a contrary stream away from the south-east.

When we look at vagrants caught in highland regions the picture is at once unambiguous and dramatic (Map 1C). Movement was towards the lowlands. The origins of 212 of the vagrants found in Devon can be traced. Of these twenty-six were from Cornwall, as many as seventy-seven from Ireland, and thirty-four from Devon itself. Only seventy-five, or 35 per cent, came from counties to the east. The pattern in the north-west is even clearer. Of 557 vagrants found in Lancashire whose origins may be discovered, 278 came from within the same county, many of them from parishes north of those in which they were found, or from 'beyond the Ribble'. Another 146 were from Westmorland, Cumberland, Northumberland, Durham, and Yorkshire, and thirty-seven from Scotland, 'the Borders' or 'the North'. Only ninety-six, or 17 per cent, were from counties further south or from Ireland. It is unfortunate that no similarly large sample can be used to examine vagrants caught in the midlands in order to follow these currents further and to see whether, as in 1571–2, there was similar movement from the Welsh highlands into England.[63] But the majority of the few vagrants whose origins were noted by the justices of Nottinghamshire had come from Yorkshire and the north-eastern counties; while only seventeen out of 112 vagrants taken in Monmouthshire in the 1630s were sent back to English parishes.[64]

This is not to say that most vagrants were intending to move to

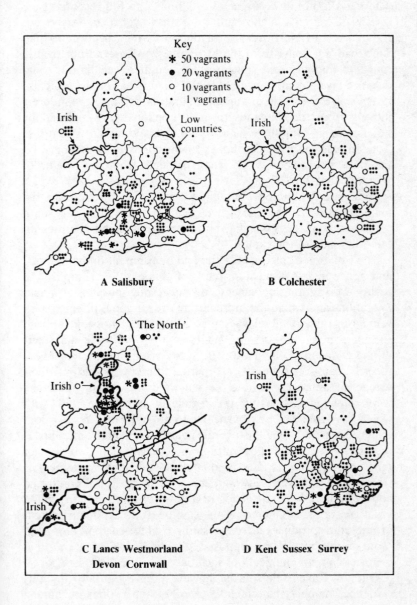

Map 1   The origins of vagrants by county

London. Many had no such single destination in mind and those who had did not always reach it. Although no full records of the origins of vagrants in the capital itself have yet been discovered, those taken in Hertfordshire in the 1630s may be comparable. They had not come from the extremities of England but from a range of midland and south-eastern counties, the largest long-distance group coming from Shropshire. One has in fact a picture in Ravenstein's terms of vagrant migration by stages, wanderers moving from the midlands towards London being replaced by others moving into the midlands from highland regions.[65] But that London was the magnet whose growth imposed its influence on the pattern of mobility elsewhere appears from the origins of vagrants found in Kent, Sussex, and Surrey (Map 1D). Apart from a good deal of local mobility towards and from London, the main streams of long-distance movement were along the south coast and from East Anglia, not from the midland counties on the other side of the capital.

The isolation of places of origin and punishment in the records, and hence in this discussion, tends of course to oversimplify the reality of vagrant movement, by suggesting purposeful linear migration rather than the more untidy irregular and often circular wandering of individual vagrants. Usually it is possible only to speculate about intervening stages in their journeys and their ultimate destinations. However, it seems probable that these records capture vagrants at many different points in their wandering and can illustrate the general directions in which they were moving, though not the regularity and deliberation with which they followed any particular route. With this reservation, it may be noted that the overall pattern of vagrant mobility is consistent with the generalizations suggested by studies of migration elsewhere. The predominant stream of movement is from highland towards lowland areas.[66] This pattern is confirmed and extended by the attraction of a 'town of rapid growth' and 'a great centre of commerce' in the south-east. 'Each main current of migration produces a compensating counter-current' along the same route but in the opposite direction, following personal contacts and communications facilities.[67]

One of Ravenstein's laws, however, only partially fits this evidence, namely that 'females appear to predominate among short-journey migrants'.[68] Of the adult vagrants travelling less than 40 miles to Salisbury and Colchester, 43 per cent were women, compared with 31 per cent of those coming more than that distance. But the difference is not great and in each case the proportion of women among those coming more than 200 miles was high, 50 per cent in the case of Colchester, nearly 30 per cent in the case of Salisbury, due largely to the numbers of women found among Irish immigrants. Regional differences may be more important than any associated with length of journey. Table 2 would suggest that there were more women to be found among vagrants in the south-east (and to some extent in Hertfordshire) than in south-western or north-western England. But whether this was a result of local authorities discriminating against unemployable women in the south-east or conversely of the attraction of parts of the home counties for female labour,[69] or whether it reflected an important highland/lowland distinction in migratory habits or sex ratios, the present evidence will not allow us to say.

In fact the precise push and pull factors at work in these patterns of migration are elusive. The attraction of towns may be readily appreciated. While their inns and alehouses provided lodging and rich travellers who might be mulcted, their poor law and charitable institutions, 'invited a swarm and surcharge of poor', as Bacon observed.[70] At the same time their suburbs and neighbouring villages were relatively or entirely free from municipal jurisdiction. Crowds of vagrants were found in villages round Hertford and St Albans and in Southwark, St Giles in the Fields, Blackheath, and Stepney around London.[71] But the forces which pushed men on to the roads in the first place are not easy to discern. Personal tragedies, the death of a parent or eviction from a house, or local disasters such as fires were no doubt often responsible though rarely referred to. Epidemics of plague might provoke flight from centres of infection but equally draw an influx of strangers to fill empty houses when the crisis was over.[72] Industrial depression and unemployment may have been a common cause of vagrancy, as the justices of Hertfordshire thought in 1637,[73] but again the sources used here give little direct information. Depression in the textile industries of East Anglia or the west country was at once too widespread and too sporadic for it to be easily associated with any single group of vagrants. Few vagrants are to be found in Colchester from other Essex towns in the 1630s, for example, presumably because it was apparent that employment conditions were no better there, while the movement of men from the clothing towns of the western counties into Salisbury is no more striking in the 1620s than before or after.

A comparison of 'woodland' and 'champion' country is rather more fruitful. The work of Dr Thirsk and Prof. Everitt has drawn attention to the expanding squatter populations of forest and pastoral areas in this period.[74] One cause of this growth, migration into these regions from more settled arable areas, can sometimes be traced in vagrancy records. In the 1630s, for example, a third of the vagrants found in the Bolton division of Lancashire, on the edge of pastoral moorland, had come up from the mixed farming lowlands around Wigan.[75] But much more conspicuous are the consequences of the growing populations only precariously supported by rural industry in pastoral areas. Vagrants from the Pennine uplands moved on in large numbers into other parts of the same region or into the lowland plain of Lancashire.[76] There was no doubt more mobility, much of it tolerated or ignored, from arable to pastoral areas than vagrancy records suggest, but it was movement in the opposite direction which was more threatening, out of those woodlands and pastures which were 'breeders and nurseries' of 'thieves, rogues and beggars'.[77]

The importance of wood-pasture regions is also evident in the case of vagrants found in towns. Since Colchester lay in the middle of a belt of wood-pasture farming stretching from London to Norwich, a predominance of vagrants from such origins is not surprising. Conversely, Norwich, on the boundary between two farming areas, drew rather more vagrants from the sheep–corn area to the north than the wood–pasture region to the south, as one might expect from the general direction of vagrant movement. In the case of the Salisbury vagrants, however, where local geography might seem to dictate no obvious pattern and where the number of vagrants is large enough to reveal local concentration, it is clear that the wood–pasture areas were major sources of recruits. Excluding those coming from within five miles of the town, fifty-five vagrants were sent back to the chalk country to the west, north, and east of the town. But forty-two vagrants had come up the Avon from places in or close to the New Forest; and thirty-seven vagrants came from the more distant wood–pasture region in the square formed by Devizes, Bath, Shepton Mallet, and Warminster, most of them from around Frome Selwood, an area well known for its poverty and vulnerability to harvest failure.[78] In both these areas rural industry and the growth of new settlements combined to produce sporadic unemployment, mobility, and perhaps a habit of vagrancy. It is no accident that woodlanders were attacked in language often reserved for vagrants, as 'mean people [who] live lawless, nobody to govern them, they care for nobody, having no dependence on anybody'.[79]

Still more decisive in the making of a vagrant than an environment of rural industry or woods and pastures, however, was the experience of urban life. The further a vagabond had moved, the more likely he was to have come from an urban setting. If we take as a town any place listed as such by Adams in his *Index Villaris* we can compare the importance of urban communities in the origin of vagrants coming from within the county where they were apprehended and from outside it.[80]

Table 5   Percentage of vagrants from urban origins

Found in	Vagrants from within the county	From outside the county	All vagrants
Salisbury (Wilts)	30·5	50·1	46·9
Colchester (Essex)	30·3	51·7	48·7
Norwich (Norfolk)	24·3	52·8	33·8

Unfortunately similar comparison cannot be made in the case of those rogues named in the justices' certificates of the 1630s.[81] But from this partial evidence from lowland England, it seems that experience of a town was an important factor in turning a man into a long-distance vagrant.[82] In particular the suburbs of towns, where immigration was an everyday phenomenon, provided the formative background for some vagabonds. The majority of those whipped back from Salisbury to London were from parishes outside the city walls, while three others came from 'St. Sidwell's without Eastgate in the suburbs of Exeter'.

Whether these vagrants of urban origin were the sons of immigrants or had themselves already made the initial move from country to town it is usually impossible to say. Only in the case of the Salisbury vagabonds can we compare those who gave their place of birth and those who cited their place of dwelling as their settlement.[83] Here at any rate the vagrant whipped back to a town was likely to have merely lived there for some time, while the vagrant who gave a rural parish as his place of origin had usually been born there.

Table 6   Percentage of Salisbury vagrants born in place of origin

	Within Wilts.	Outside Wilts.	All counties
Urban origin	54·8	42·3	43·7
Rural origin	75·4	58·4	62·4
Urban and rural	69·0	50·0	53·3

It is possible, therefore, that the making of a semi-permanent vagrant may be dimly discerned in the records which survive. A short first move to a local town or an area of rural industry could, after an interval of temporary employment in which settlement rights might be acquired, lead to further movement along the roads of England and to other towns, often in the direction of London. And those who had acquired this habit of vagrancy and the social characteristics associated with it brought odium and savage punishment on the heads of some less advanced in the downward vagrancy spiral as well as on themselves.

IV

The records of English vagrancy thus suggest general conclusions about lower-class migration in early modern England, its direction, and its potential consequences. But they refer only to a minority of migrants. Vagrants were not confused with wanderers of all kinds. More informal settlement regulations were utilized to deal with some of these and in urban societies a certain amount of in-mobility was necessarily tolerated to counterbalance the effects of relatively high mortality rates. For every migrant whipped as a vagrant, there must have been several who were accepted into the expanding populations of towns and areas of rural industry. Those who were punished were either unfortunate in being caught or exceptional because sought out by more efficient authorities as particularly unwelcome; and their exceptional characteristics helped to shape and to warrant contemporary definitions of the vagrant.

Nevertheless we must resist the temptation to go to the opposite extreme from the broad interpretation of the vagrant class and describe it in terms of a 'sub-' or 'counter-culture'. The vagrant bands of beggars or gipsies, with a canting language and a structured hierarchy, may sometimes have existed behind our evidence of individual vagabonds. But they were by no means as common as Harman and particularly his later plagiarists suggested. Their descriptions were the result of contemporary desires to define and perhaps to romanticize the vagrant phenomenon, to provide stereotypes in order to make the reality more explicable and more palatable. If not representative of a whole counter-culture, however, many vagrants were clearly exceptions to accepted social norms quite apart from their persistent mobility. Their inability to conform to any stereotype made them all the greater a threat to the prevailing ideology of early Stuart society. They were individuals with few household or kinship ties, and they had often fled from masters, husbands, or wives. These traits were determined or confirmed by experience of a rootless insecure existence in forests or towns or armies, and consolidated by the exigencies of an economy marked by seasonal and chronic underemployment.[84] When we see the special class of migrants who were punished as vagrants we can comprehend contemporary reactions to them as representatives of disorder.[85]

This is not to say that such reactions were justified. The harsh punishments for vagabonds and the increasingly narrow interpretation of settlement regulations helped to make men permanently vagrant. Some of them could still benefit from indiscriminate charity. Two Wiltshire women who had 'long wandered the county' were supported 'by the alms of good people as they did travel'. A deserted child, being transported from Essex to Kent wth a passport in 1594, was taken in by John Brewer who 'made it his adopted son, calling him by the name of John Brewer'.[86] But many more were whipped and ordered back home, to be disciplined in the local workhouse if they ever arrived. Others spent their lives and died on the road, like a 'stripling taken vagrant' found in Essex on his way back from London to Norwich, or were pressed into service as buriers of plague victims or, if in London, as reluctant emigrants to the colonies.[87] In such conditions the family and associated features of respectable society could scarcely survive. The stigma of whip and workhouse was as much a determinant of the special quality of vagrant life as conditions of overpopulation and underemployment. Harman's 'Walking Mort' spoke for many of her kind: 'God help, how should I live? None will take me into service. But I labour in harvest-time honestly.'[88]

Appendix   *Origins of vagrants*

Returned to	Salisbury 1598–1638	Colchester 1630–64	Norwich 1630–5	Kent, Sussex, Surrey 1632–9	Lancs. Westm. 1634–8	Devon Cornw. 1634–8	Herts. 1636–9	Total
Cornwall	15					71		86
Devon	59			4		34		97
Somerset	74			7		10	1	92
Bristol and Gloucestershire	29			13	2	4	1	49
Wiltshire	105	1		8				114
Dorset	51			7		14		72
Hampshire	80	4		70	1	6	1	162
Berkshire	16		1	6		2	1	26
Sussex	15	1		67		6		89
Surrey	9	1		15		2		27
Kent	26	18	2	169	2	13	11	241
London and Middlesex	35	42	10	41		3	1	132
Essex	11	33		30		7	18	99
Suffolk	4	29	7	9		1	4	54
Norfolk	2	26	107	25		1	1	162
Cambridgeshire	1	7	4	5		1	2	20
Hertfordshire	7	3	3	5			1	19
Huntingdonshire	2							2
Bedfordshire	4			1			6	11
Buckinghamshire	3			14			9	26
Oxfordshire	6			8		1	4	19
Northamptonshire	1	4	7	9	1		3	25
Leicestershire and Rutland	1	1		1	5			8
Warwickshire	7	2		11			6	26
Worcestershire	5	4		18	1		1	29
Herefordshire	8			6		2		16
Shropshire	3			4	4		12	23
Staffordshire	2	2		2	7			14
Cheshire	4	2	1	2	36	3		48
Derbyshire		5			5			10
Nottinghamshire	1	2		1	1			5
Lincolnshire	5	7	3	3	7	1		26
Lancashire	4	1		8	296			309
Yorkshire	10	6	6	17	96	2		137
Westmorland		2			56			58
Cumberland	2	1			74			77
Durham					5			5
Northumberland	3	5			7			15
'The North'					33			33
Scotland	1	3	3	1	7			15
Wales	17	4		6	11	9	2	49
Ireland	19	20	2	17	11	77		146
Low Countries	1		3					4
Not given	3	1	1	4	248	26	47	330
Total	651	237	161	614	916	296	132	3,007

Notes and references

1 Richard Younge, *The Poores Advocate* (1654), ch. xiv, p. 10.
2 PRO SP 16/533/17, fo. 39r; J. Spedding (ed.), *Letters and Life of Francis Bacon* (1861–74), IV, 252; C. Read (ed.) *William Lambarde and Local Government* (Ithaca, 1962), p. 173; C. Hill, *Society and Puritanism in Pre-Revolutionary England* (1964), p. 259.

3 *Orders and Directions* (1630), sig. G4*v*. Cf. *Historical Manuscripts Commission, Salisbury (Cecil) MSS,* xxii, 297; PRO SP 16/293/44; B. H. Cunnington (ed.), *Records of the County of Wilts.* (Devizes, 1932), pp. 10–11.

4 P. Clark, 'The Migrant in Kentish Towns, 1580–1640', in P. Clark and P. Slack (eds), *Crisis and Order in English Towns, 1500–1700* (1972), pp. 117–63. A suggestive summary of recent work is J. Patten, *Rural-Urban Migration in Pre-Industrial England* (Oxford University School of Geography, Research Papers, 6, 1973).

5 Summarized in F. Aydelotte, *Elizabethan Rogues and Vagabonds* (Oxford, 1913) and F. W. Chandler, *The Literature of Roguery* (Boston, 1907).

6 *Statutes of the Realm,* 39 Eliz. c. 4, clause iii.

7 There are references to parochial lists in PRO SP 16/210/44, 250/47, 239/129, 130, 349/73, 288/7 (xxxviii). Short surviving lists are described in E. Melling (ed.), *Kentish Sources: The Poor* (Maidstone, 1964), pp. 18–19; C. D. Stocks, *A History of Crondall and Yateley, Hants* (Winchester, 1905), pp. 29–30.

8 For example, Southampton Borough Records, Book of Instruments, 1597–1689, fo. 115 and *passim*; J. M. Guilding (ed.), *Reading Records: Diary of the Corporation* (1892–6), II, 262–3.

9 Salisbury Corporation Archives (hereafter SCA), Poor Accounts Z225, fos. 12–45; Colchester Borough Records (hereafter CBR), Shelf 1, Sessions of the Peace Book II, 1630–64. I am indebted to the Town Clerks of Salisbury and Colchester for permission to quote from the documents in their care.

10 PRO SP 16/319/85, 344/30, 347/67, 418/21.

11 PRO SP 16/220/33, 314/77, 319/64, 328/7, 61, 68, 347/68, 70, 363/100, 115, 122, 364/119, 393/76, 85, 99, 417/25, 424/112, 425/85, 426/87.

12 PRO SP 16/265/34, 93, 275/15, 289/58, 364/28, 395/21, 397/99.

13 PRO SP 16/273/23, 351/31, 364/122, 123, 366/90, 382/9, 81, 383/56, 388/7, 395/105, 106, 112, 397/36.

14 W. L. Sachse (ed.) *Minutes of the Norwich Court of Mayoralty, 1630–1* (Norfolk Rec. Soc., **xv**, 1942); idem, ed. *Minutes of the Norwich Court of Mayoralty, 1632–5* (Norfolk Rec. Soc., **xxxvi**, 1967). Only those strangers specifically described as vagrants or punished before being expelled from the town are included in this sample.

15 SCA, Z225, 6 August 1628. He was nevertheless sent to Colchester.—Cf. J. W. Horrocks (ed.), *Assembly Books of Southampton* (Southampton Rec. Soc., 1917–25), **II**, 55; Wiltshire Record Office (hereafter WRO), Quarter Sessions Minute Book 1610–16, pp. 25–6.

16 It has been possible to check the alleged place of origin of sixteen Salisbury vagrants; four have been confirmed and a further five are probable if mistakes in Christian names are assumed: for example, William Gill returned to Leeds in 1634 was baptized in Leeds in 1613.—G. D. Lumb (ed.), *The Registers of the Parish Church of Leeds, 1612–29* (Thoresby Soc., **III**, (1895), p. 11; Edmund Vye returned to Colyton in 1598 may be the Edward Vye baptized there in 1549.—A. J. P. Skinner (ed.), *The Register of Colyton, 1538–1837* (Devon and Cornwall Rec. Soc., 1928), p. 11.

17 S. D'Ewes, *The Journals of all the Parliaments of Elizabeth* (1682), p. 220; *Historical Manuscripts Commission, House of Lords MSS,* new series, **xi**, 8.

18 39 Eliz. c. 4, clause ii. The Vagrancy Act of 1657 weakened the strength of this latter qualification but it seems not to have affected the sort of vagrants

apprehended in Colchester.—C. H. Firth and R. S. Rait, *Acts and Ordinances of the Interregnum* (1911), II, 1098–9.

19 M. Dalton, *The Countrey Justice* (1682 edn). pp. 158, 166. For examples of doubts on this point see PRO Asz 24/20, fos. 29*v*, 72*v*; J. Lister (ed.), *West Riding Sessions Rolls* (Yorks. Arch. Soc. Rec. Series, **III**, 1888), pp. 85–6; R. H. Tawney and E. Power (eds), *Tudor Economic Documents* (1924), II, 363.

20 M. G. Davies, *The Enforcement of English Apprenticeship, 1563–1642* (Cambridge, Mass., 1956), p. 7; M. James, *Social Problems and Policy during the Puritan Revolution* (1930), p. 286. Cf. S. and B. Webb, *The Old Poor Law* (1927), pp. 319–20.

21 Cf. P. Styles, 'The Evolution of the Law of Settlement', *University of Birmingham Historical Journal,* **ix** (1963), pp. 38–9, 44–5; T. G. Barnes (ed.), *Somerset Assize Orders* (Somerset Rec. Soc., **LXV**, 1959), pp. 6–7, 29 and n.

22 For other cases of vagrants with servants see CBR. Sessions Book II, March 1648; PRO SP 16/314/77; and for examples of vagrants claiming to be gentlemen, PRO SP 12/81/22; CBR Sessions Book II, August 1642; SCA Z225, 27 August 1599; *Historical Manuscripts Commission, Various,* 1, 92.

23 PRO Asz 24/20, fo. 137*r*; CBR Sessions Book II, 7 March 1635; SCA Z225, 17 March 1617.

24 SCA Poor Accounts S162, fos. 191*v*, 194*r*; Sachse (ed.) *Minutes, 1632–5,* pp. 32, 59–60. Cf. E. Lipson, *Economic History of England* (1934), III, 460; J. Lister (ed.), *West Riding Sessions Records II* (Yorks, Arch. Soc. Rec. Series, **LIV**, 1915), p. 175.

25 WRO Sessions File, Mich. 1604, docs 147, 152.

26 SCA Z225, 15 August 1609, 8 August 1618, 12 September 1601; WRO Sessions Roll, Mich. 1604, doc. 151.

27 Vagrants practising these occupations were occasionally called 'gypsies' but very few genuine gypsies have been discovered. – PRO SP 16/281/83; *Historical Manuscripts Commission Various* 1, 129; Cunnington, ed. *Records of the County of Wilts,* p. 26.

28 PRO SP 16/385/43, 329/56. Cf. A. V. Judges, *The Elizabethan Underworld* (1930), pp. 86, 91.

29 Tawney and Power (eds), *Tudor Economic Documents* 1, 341. One forger carefully kept a list of the names of JPs in various counties.—Cunnington, ed. *Records of the County of Wilts,* p. 52.

30 Cf. WRO Sessions Roll, Hilary 1610, doc. 125; B. H. Cunnington, *Some Annals of the Borough of Devizes, 1555–1791* (Devizes, 1925), pt II, p. 41; SCA Z225, 31 March 1618.

31 SCA Q136b, deposition of 44 Eliz.

32 Cf. A. Everitt, *Changes in the Provinces: The Seventeenth Century* (Leicester University, Department of English Local History, Occasional Papers, 2nd series **1**, 1969), pp. 38–43.

33 SCA Q136b, exam. of 11 January 1610.

34 Cf. SCA Z225, 2 July 1608; Norfolk and Norwich Record Office, Norfolk Sessions Roll, 1627–8, petition of Nicholas Smith; *Historical Manuscripts Commission, Various* 1, 101.

35 C. J. Ribton-Turner, *A History of Vagrants and Vagrancy* (1887), p. 148; A. H. A. Hamilton, *Quarter Sessions from Queen Elizabeth to Queen Anne* (1878), p. 105; T. G. Barnes, *Somerset, 1625–40* (1961), p. 182; PRO SP 16/181/123.

36 PRO SP 16/265/34. Cf. SP 16/176/55, 234/57, 289/43; WRO Sessions File, Trinity 1629, doc. 112.

37 For example, Exeter City Muniments, St Kerrian's Churchwardens' Accounts, 1602–1700, 1643–4 account; Essex Record Office (hereafter ERO), D/P 128/5/1, fo. 64r; H. J. F. Swayne, *Churchwardens' Accounts of S. Edmund and S. Thomas Sarum* (Salisbury, 1896), pp. 176, 312.

38 Cf. PRO SP 16/141/75; R. Clifton, 'The Popular Fear of Catholics during the English Revolution', *Past and Present*, **52** (1971), 49–52.

39 SCA Q136b, 14 December 1601; Cunnington (ed.), *Records of Wilts*, pp. 38–9; PRO Asz 24/20, fo. 76r.

40 Only two large bands of English vagrants, largely children, have been found.— PRO SP 16/314/77, 363/100; WRO Sessions File, Easter 1632, doc. 170. Cf. Hext's comments in Tawney and Power (eds), *Tudor Economic Documents*, II, 345.

41 PRO SP 16/388/7(iii).

42 Cf. J. P. Poussu, 'Les Mouvements Migratoires en France et à partir de la France de la fin du XVe siècle au debut du XIXe siècle', *Annales de Démographie Historique* (1970), 15; J. A. Jackson (ed.), *Migration* (Cambridge, 1969), p. 63; T. H. Hollingsworth, *Migration* (Edinburgh, 1970), p. 97. I am grateful to Dr A. L. Beier for information from the list of the Hampshire village of Crondall, which is still in the parish church.

43 PRO SP 16/388/7 (xxiv, xxxvii).

44 The reasons for this difference, which may include regional variations in age at marriage, are unclear. – Cf. below, p. 374.

45 SCA Z225, 19 May 1630; W.R.O. Sessions Roll, Trinity 1630, doc. 135. Sixty-four of the single women and twenty-one of the single men in Table 2 had children wandering with them.

46 The predominance was even greater in eighteenth-century France.—O. Hufton, 'Begging, Vagrancy, Vagabondage and the Law', *European Studies Review,* **II**, (1972), 110.

47 PRO SP 16/329/56.

48 WRO Sessions Minute Book 1631–6, Mich. 1633; PRO SP 16/193/79; R. Younge, *The Poores Advocate*, ch. xiv, p. 11.

49 Cf. J. F. Pound (ed.), *The Norwich Census of the Poor, 1570* (Norfolk Rec. Soc. **XL**, 1971), pp. 95–6, Clark and Slack (eds), *Crisis and Order*, p. 166.

50 CBR Sessions Book II, April, July 1631, November 1632; Sachse (ed.), *Minutes, 1632–5*, pp. 70, 71, 73, 77, 102; SCA S162, fos. 1–2 and *passim*.

51 Coventry City Record Office, W1026/7–10. Mr C. V. Phythian-Adams kindly drew my attention to these documents. Similar poor travellers were given lodging in Ipswich.—J. Webb (ed.), *Poor Relief in Elizabethan Ipswich* (Suffolk Rec. Soc., **IX**, 1966), pp. 80–90.

52 SCA Q136b, 14 December 1601.

53 J. Cornwall, 'Evidence of Population Mobility in the Seventeenth Century', *Bulletin of the Institute of Historical Research,* **XL** (1967), 150; E. J. Buckatzsch, 'Places of Origin of a Group of Immigrants into Sheffield, 1624–1799', *Economic History Review*, second series **II** (1950), 305; SCA Tailors' Book EI/245 and Add. 3 apprenticeship indentures, 1612–14; A. J. Willis and A. L. Merson, *A Calendar of Southampton Apprenticeship Registers, 1609–1740* (Southampton Records Series, **XII**, 1968), p. xxix; R. A. Pelham, 'The Immigrant Population

of Birmingham, 1686–1726', *Transactions of the Birmingham Archaeological Society,* **LXI**, (1937) 45–64; D. Cressey, 'Occupations, Migration and Literacy in East London, 1580–1640', *Local Population Studies,* **5** (1970), 57.

54 In some cases it has proved impossible to trace the village to which a vagrant was whipped. Hence the totals in Table 3 do not entirely correspond with those in the Appendix. Except in the case of counties close to the place of punishment, however, the county town has been taken in doubtful instances. Where there are two possible places of origin with the same name, that nearer to the place of punishment has been used. Where the vagrant is simply described as 'Irish', distances have been measured to the nearest point on the Irish coast. Lancashire vagrants described merely as coming from Yorkshire or 'the North' have been taken as travelling 21–40 and 41–60 miles respectively, these being the usual distances of movement in similar cases where precise places of origin are also given.

55 The Salisbury record begins on 20 April 1598, shortly after the Privy Council's order enforcing the Vagrancy Act (*Acts of the Privy Council, 1597–8,* pp. 388–9); the Colchester register starts on 18 October 1630, but there were few entries before January 1631 when the Book of Orders was issued.

56 1596–7, 1629–30 and 1647–8 were years of high grain prices.—J. Thirsk (ed.), *The Agrarian History of England and Wales: IV, 1500–1640* (Cambridge, 1967), pp. 820–1.

57 Cf. A. Vexliard, *Introduction à la Sociologie du Vagabondage* (Paris, 1956), pp. 204–5; J. Meuvret, 'Demographic Crisis in France from the Sixteenth to the Eighteenth Century', in D. V. Glass and D. E. C. Eversley (eds), *Population in History* (1965), p. 512.

58 Sachse (ed.), *Minutes, 1632–5*, pp. 57, 159.

59 Cf. R. Steele, *Tudor and Stuart Proclamations* (Oxford, 1910), 1, 191 (1630); PRO SP 12/81/25.

60 Read (ed.), *William Lambarde*, p. 174; W. J. Paylor (ed.), *The Overburian Characters* (Percy Reprints, **XIII**, 1936), p. 73; PRO SP 16/234/57.

61 J. F. Pound informs me that there was a similar local recruitment of Norwich vagrants in the later sixteenth century.

62 Judges, *The Elizabethan Underworld*, p. 84. The Salisbury-London Road was a major haunt of vagrants.—Cf. Guilding (ed.), *Reading Records*, II, 143–4.

63 Welsh vagrants in Oxfordshire and Northamptonshire in 1571–2 are recorded in PRO SP 12/80/51, 57, 60, 81/14, 44, 46, 83/1, 86/16, 22.

64 PRO SP 16/329/63, 349/86 (Notts); SP 16/270/18, 271/92, 293/82, 310/107, 329/26 (Mon.). Cf. Lister (ed.), *West Riding Sessions Records*, 11, 17; A. D. Dyer, *The City of Worcester in the Sixteenth Century* (Leicester, 1973), p. 183.

65 E. G. Ravenstein, 'The Laws of Migration', *Journal of the Royal Statistical Society,* **XLVIII** (1885), 199.

66 Cf. E. Le Roy Ladurie, *Les Paysans de Languedoc* (Paris, 1966), 1, 96–101; J. Nadal and E. Giralt, *La Population Catalane de 1533 à 1717* (Paris, 1960), pp. 181–4.

67 Ravenstein, 'The Laws of Migration', 198, 199; E. S. Lee, 'A Theory of Migration', in Jackson, ed., *Migration*, pp. 292–3.

68 E. G. Ravenstein, 'The Laws of Migration', *Journal of the Royal Statistical Society,* **LII** (1889), 288.

69 Women may have been extensively employed in hop-picking in Kent.—Cf. C. W. Chalklin, *Seventeenth Century Kent* (1965), p. 94.

70 Spedding (ed.), *Letters and Life of Francis Bacon*, IV, 250–1.

71 PRO SP 16/354/184, 251/12, 259/28, 268/60, 347/29, 363/33, 382/52, 395/117, 415/95. Cf. A. H. French *et al.*, 'The Population of Stepney in the Early Seventeenth Century', *Local Population Studies,* **3** (1969), 47.

72 For complaints of the multitude of vagrants in plague years see WRO Sessions Rolls, Mich., 1603, doc. 209, Hilary 1627, doc. 111.

73 PRO SP 16/385/43.

74 Thirsk (ed.), *Agrarian History*, pp. 80, 111, 409–12. The following discussion is based on Dr Thirsk's analysis of farming regions.

75 PRO SP 16/364/122, 123. The growing textile industries of upland Lancashire are described in N. Lowe, *The Lancashire Textile Industry in the Sixteenth Century* (Chetham Soc., 3rd series, **xx**, 1972), especially pp. 82–3.

76 Into parts of Amounderness, for example.—PRO SP 16/383/56, 395/105. Cf. W. G. Howson, 'Plague, Poverty and Population in Parts of North-West England, 1580–1720', *Transactions of the Lancashire and Cheshire Historical Society,* **CXII** (1960), 55.

77 E. R. Foster (ed.), *Proceedings in Parliament, 1610* (New Haven, 1966), 11, 281.

78 PRO SP 16/185/40, 204/112. Cf. J. E. Jackson (ed.), *The Topographical Collections of John Aubrey* (Devizes, 1862), p. 11; WRO Sessions File, Mich. 1610, doc. 111; G. D. Ramsay, *The Wiltshire Woollen Industry in the Sixteenth and Seventeenth Centuries* (Oxford, 1943), p. 72.

79 Quoted in Thirsk (ed.), *Agrarian History*, p. 111.

80 J. Adams, *Index Villaris* (1680). This work distinguishes cities and market-towns from villages and parishes.

81 Too many vagrants were described there as coming merely from a county or country (usually Ireland) to permit valid comparisons. In the case of the three towns in Table 5, those few vagrants whose origins were given imprecisely have been taken as being of rural origin.

82 Cf. M. Garden, 'L'Attraction de Lyon à la fin de l'Ancien Régime', in *Annales de Démographie Historique* (1970), 215.

83 The other sources used here do not regularly differentiate between the two. Even the Salisbury record does not say whether fifty-six vagrants were born or lived in their place of origin, and these have been excluded from the calculations for Table 6. According to the statute of 1597 vagrants should be sent to their place of birth and only if this was not known to their place of last residence. The statute of 1 James I, c. 7, reversed this for incorrigible rogues, but the later resolutions of the judges imply that the 1597 procedure should be followed.—Barnes (ed.), *Somerset Assize Orders*, p. 68. An example of local disputes on this point is: WRO Sessions Roll, Hilary 1636, exam. of the inhabitants of Wootton Bassett.

84 Cf. D. C. Coleman, 'Labour in the English Economy of the Seventeenth Century', *Economic History Review,* 2nd series, **VIII** (1955–6), 280–95.

85 For the obverse view of beggars as 'the only freemen of a commonwealth', see C. Hill, *The World Turned Upside Down* (1972), p. 39.

86 Cunnington (ed.), *Records of Wilts.*, pp. 21–2; ERO D/P 91/1/1, West Tilbury parish register, fo. 1v.

87 ERO D/P 136/1/1, Little Chishall register, 11 November 1604; ERO Q/SBa 2/46, Easter 1642; PRO SP 16/224/65; R. C. Johnson, 'The Transportation of Vagrant Children from London to Virginia, 1618–22', in H. S. Reinmuth (ed.), *Early Stuart Studies in Honor of D. G. Willson* (Minneapolis, 1970), pp. 137–51.
88 Judges, *The Elizabethan Underworld*, p. 100.

3
Patterns of migration and movement of labour to three pre-industrial East Anglian towns

John Patten

This chapter exploits a single source, apprenticeship registers, to analyse and map the movements of indentured migrants to the East Anglian towns of Norwich, Great Yarmouth and Ipswich during the sixteenth and seventeenth centuries. The author emphasizes the high levels of physical mobility and reveals the significant variations in local migration fields, related to the differing economies of individual towns and their hinterlands. At the same time, the paper also demonstrates the heavily localized character of most apprenticeship mobility with this becoming accentuated in the later Stuart period. The paper probably underplays the difficulties of employing apprenticeship records for migration studies and may well overstate the typicality of this kind of movement for general migration.

Immigration undoubtedly contributed a great deal to both the demographic and economic health of towns in pre-industrial England. Actual rates of immigration will always remain hard to quantify exactly. The fact, however, that most towns of any standing could not really have grown in size, or have prospered, without such influxes of newcomers must now be regarded as established.[1] Little as yet is known, compared for example with the nineteenth century,[2] of patterns of movement then from country to town. Yet a variety of sources – from deposition books to settlement papers – exist to allow migration in pre-industrial times to be examined. In East Anglia, for example, a series of apprentice indentures survive for Norwich and Great Yarmouth in Norfolk, and Ipswich in Suffolk, for the sixteenth and seventeenth centuries: the evidence they contain permits an examination of the overall picture of movement of this sort of migrant to towns of different sizes, and different economic activities, purely at a macro-scale. More detailed explanatory discussion of why apparently apprentices chose to move, and what their migratory careers were, requires the amassing of a large sample of individual biographies, as much as that can be done; in the light of this, the study presented here pretends to provide no more than a descriptive framework.

Norwich, great provincial city and capital of its region, had perhaps 12,000 people at the middle of the sixteenth century, reaching a population of nearly 30,000[3] by the end of the seventeenth century; centre of the Norfolk worsted manufacture,[4] which for much of the period acted as a barometer of the city's changing economic fortunes, in its variety of shops and services offered[5] it aped the capital's style, if not its scale. Great Yarmouth and Ipswich by comparison were both smaller, regionally less important, and had their fortunes tied quite closely to the sea. Great Yarmouth, around 5000 in size at the middle of the sixteenth century had reached only 10,000 or more by the end of the next; Ipswich perhaps 4000 and around 8000 at the same dates. The former town had few noted manufactures, though it acted as an outlet for the export overseas of Norwich's textiles, and those of the villages around Worstead in north-east Norfolk. Important concerns were, on the other hand, with the North Sea herring fisheries; with trade across it, and to the Baltic and Iceland; and with associated activities like shipbuilding, and its allied trades. It was also an important stopping-off point on the coastal trade in sea coal, as was Ipswich. This Suffolk port, and capital of the eastern division of its county, had a rich agricultural and textile manufacturing hinterland;[6] it supplied dairy produce for the capital, though the export of broadcloth from the declining manufacture of the Stour valley[7] became less important after the end of the sixteenth century. Its position as an important coasting port, deeply involved in the eastern carrying trade to and from Newcastle and London, was similarly in decline in the seventeenth century,[8] 'eaten up' by London, though its fortunes remained relatively wedded to the sea throughout.

Sources

Altogether, as might be expected, these three towns proved to be 'magnets' of various strengths for young migrant labour from different directions. As far as is known, no further full series of indentures exists for any other town in this region. Nearly 6000 apprenticeship indentures exist for Norwich, largely in the middle and later sixteenth, and seventeenth centuries.[9] The number is very much smaller for Great Yarmouth and Ipswich, and they survive for a shorter period in each case. In Great Yarmouth nearly 500 were taken between the 1560s and 1660s;[10] the series is apparently deficient for a number of years during Elizabeth's reign. Only some 370 exist for Ipswich, taken between 1596 and 1651.[11] Small proportions of the total populations of the last two towns it is true, although enough to demonstrate overall patterns, in a similar fashion to those given by the 1200 depositions used by Clark for a study of migration to three Kentish towns over the sixty-year period, 1580–1640.[12] The disparities in the numbers of apprentices enrolled, as well as the different lengths of time over which the series for the three towns extend, affect their direct comparability. This is the case even though immigration could be expected to have been much less marked anyway to the two smaller ports; they did not have any noted manufacturing interests to provide employment opportunities on the scale of Norwich's textiles, for instance.

In their best, and most useful form, apprentice indentures give the name, occupation and place of residence of the apprentice's father; the name of the apprentice himself or more rarely herself; and the name and occupation of his prospective master. Not every indenture necessarily contains all, or even a large part, of this information. The regulation of labour was of national,[13] as well as of local concern. Of the three East Anglian towns considered here, only the regulations governing entry to the trades of Norwich have been subjected to any kind of detailed examination.[14] Such control, it must always be remembered, was not solely a matter of the prevention of what was thought of as 'unfair' competition between those engaged in the same craft within the same town, but was also intended to control what was thought of as equally unfair competition from the surrounding countryside from which so many eventual urban apprentices came. Such rural dwellers might have all the advantages of land holding and its revenues during times of slump in demand for craft manufactures, yet had none of the burdens of urban fees and dues, or civic responsibility, often so costly. The Statute of 1563 seems to have been specifically aimed against, amongst other activities thought of as abuses, countrymen taking craft apprentices; this was taking 'divers men's living into one man's hands'.[15] The Statute also limited apprenticeship in most skilled crafts, including weaving, to the sons of freeholders of land worth above £2 a year. This was increased to £3 a year for those going into apprenticeship in a corporate town – such as were Norwich, Great Yarmouth and Ipswich. It is not clear how far it was enforced in this context, and therefore what effect it may have had on apprenticeship generally.

The information contained in apprenticeship indentures does in some cases allow the place of origin of individuals coming from outside the town of eventual indenture to be stated, and thus general geographical patterns of migration to be constructed. Equally, when both father's and prospective master's occupations are given something can be found out about the occupational mobility of the boys, going perhaps from the house of a yeoman to that of a merchant. A great mass of criss-crossing spatial and occupational movements is apparent. It is difficult to estimate the exact proportion of apprentices in any of the towns at any one time. But within the overall body of indentured apprentices migrants played an important role. They made up about a third of all those indentured in Norwich and over a half of those in both Great Yarmouth and Ipswich. Any use of the evidence of these indentures must always be tempered by the realization that the already small numerical sample is representative only of apprentice migration, which was however fairly permanent; it is certainly not representative of characteristically more temporary movements as may be recorded in depositions[16] or in settlements. On the other hand, apprentices being young, and presumably both economically and socially motivated, were likely to be part of one notably mobile sector of the population, or at least the 'non-vagrant' sector. The most mobile section of the population today is undoubtedly comprised of the young adult; the same was probably true of pre-industrial England. Spufford suggests that the most mobile age group in the seventeenth century was that between fifteen years of age and marriage, particularly for living-in servants.[17] The one fact about migration which seems definitely established is that it is age-selective.[18] Reservations felt about drawing any general conclusions from such information may thus be tempered by the knowledge that apprentices were likely to be representative of at least those economically active migrants staying for any length of time in their new place of residence.

Patterns of migration

Patterns of short- and long-range migration must be carefully separated in the case of each town, the one being an important component of the overall and interrelated everyday economic system, the other largely comprising a few highly defined streams, representing contact between the three towns and certain parts of the rest of England, predominantly to the north. As such it is the *description* of patterns of migration within East Anglia which presents the biggest problem if the great mass of information is to be reduced to a semblance of order. The description of patterns of migration into East Anglia is, of course, a much more straightforward matter. In order to define and examine patterns of migration using the evidence available in apprentice indentures, maps illustrating the relative density of migrants within Norfolk and Suffolk going to each of the three towns were constructed. Information on the place of residence of immigrant apprentices is always available in a point form, viz. '. . . of Wymondham', '. . . of Beccles', etc. The home town or village is usually specified but nothing more; the actual place of residence of the migrant within what could be a quite large parish is almost never stated.[19] Such locational information is thus approximate. Given this, simple plotting of the places of origin of migrants to whichever town is under consideration, by the use of dots on a map, would tell something, but not enough, of the patterns of migration. For it would omit consideration of the actual numbers of migrants coming from each place, and equally omit any consideration of how important a fraction of population migrants might be. The relative density of migration needs to be examined to provide a more realistic framework. Density is thus defined as the number of migrants divided by the estimated approximate population of the home village or town, so providing a more meaningful description of patterns of migration than simple place of origin data. This ratio of density of migrants for each place – in practice the main settlement of each parish – forms the basic information subsequently mapped. Approximate information on population was derived for each period from sources such as lay subsidies, different communicant 'censuses' and hearth-taxes; this is described elsewhere.[20] Regular distribution of population within each parish's total area had to be assumed, as no more detailed information survives.

The labour of converting these to a density distribution map by conventional cartographic methods would be lengthy. In fact so lengthy as to make the whole exercise seem not worthwhile – as a consideration of the great volume of work required in plotting

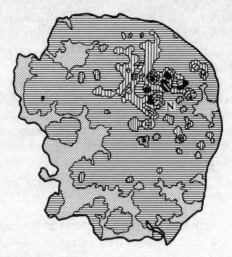

NORWICH 1510–1599

Absolute value range applying to each level
('Maximum' included in highest level only)

Maximum	0.0	0.00	10.71	21.43	32.14	42.86	53.57	64.29
Minimum	0.00	10.71	21.43	32.14	42.86	53.57	64.29	75.00

Percentage of total absolute value range applying to each level

	0.00	14.29	14.29	14.29	14.29	14.29	14.29	14.29

Frequency distribution of data point values in each level

Level	1	2	3	4	5	6	7	8
Symbols								
Frequency	514	181	82	26	5	4	4	2

0   10
miles

Figure 3   Migrant apprentices to Norwich, 1510–99

the location, and calculating the density, for the over 450 villages and towns which sent migrant apprentices to Norwich at one time or another, readily shows. The recent development of computer graphics, by which the speedy machine drawing of such maps is facilitated, allows these practical problems to be overcome; in addition, they are more accurate than the most experienced cartographer could attempt. A SYMAP V computer mapping

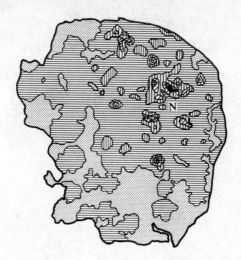

NORWICH 1600–1649

Absolute value range applying to each level
('Maximum' included in highest level only)

Maximum	0.0	0.00	6.72	13.45	20.17	26.89	33.61	40.34
Minimum	0.00	6.72	13.45	20.17	26.89	33.61	40.34	47.06

Percentage of total absolute value range applying to each level

	0.00	14.29	14.29	14.29	14.29	14.29	14.29	14.29

Frequency distribution of data point values in each level

Level	1	2	3	4	5	6	7	8
Symbols								
Frequency	581	123	64	20	9	6	0	1

```
|_____|
0    miles   10
```

Figure 4 Migrant apprentices to Norwich, 1600–49

programme[21] was used in this case, one which requires no more information than, variously, an exact location of each place as specified by mapping coordinates, the numbers of migrants in any period and the estimated population in any period. It makes no statistical demands on the data. The ratio of migrants to total population was therefore used in each case to present the average condition for each parish for which it was being calculated; the

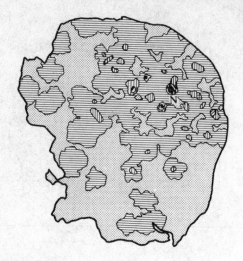

NORWICH 1650–1699

Absolute value range applying to each level
('Maximum' included in highest level only)

Maximum	0.0	0.00	5.29	10.58	15.87	21.16	26.46	31.75
Minimum	0.00	5.29	10.58	15.87	21.16	26.46	31.75	37.04

Percentage of total absolute value range applying to each level

	0.00	14.29	14.29	14.29	14.29	14.29	14.29	14.29

Frequency distribution of data point values in each level

Level	1	2	3	4	5	6	7	8
Symbols								
Frequency	715	62	46	7	0	2	0	1

0 ⊢——————⊣ 10
miles

Figure 5   Migrant apprentices to Norwich, 1650–99

point for which information was available, in practice the most
important settlement of each parish, was taken to be the *centroid*,
or average point in each parish for the computation of conventional isopleth maps. This in effect simply represents in a spatial
sense the same sort of reasoning whereby an average value is
acceptable in statistical computations. Every place in the two
counties not sending any recorded apprentices had also to be

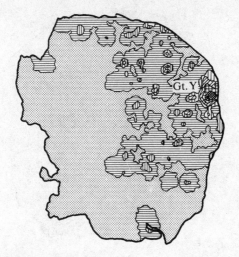

GREAT YARMOUTH 1563–1655

Absolute value range applying to each level
('Maximum' included in highest level only)

Minimum	0.0	0.00	3.86	7.72	11.58	15.44	19.31	23.17
Maximum	0.00	3.86	7.72	11.58	15.44	19.31	23.17	27.03

Percentage of total absolute value range applying to each level

	0.00	14.29	14.29	14.29	14.29	14.29	14.29	14.29

Frequency distribution of data point values in each level

Level	1	2	3	4	5	6	7	8
Symbols								
Frequency	741	28	36	11	10	2	1	1

0   10
miles

Figure 6   Migrant apprentices to Great Yarmouth, 1563–1655

taken into account in the program, being assigned a nil-value, so that the correct interpolations in constructing the density isopleth maps could be made. From the patterns mapped, which are in effect like three-dimensional surfaces with the 'peaks' of highest density standing up like icing on a cake, differences in migration fields can be examined (Figures 3 to 7).

In addition to these maps, information on the distances travelled

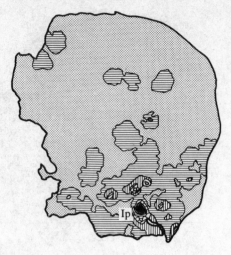

IPSWICH 1596–1651

Absolute value range applying to each level
('Maximum' included in highest level only)

Minimum	0.0	0.00	6.12	12.24	18.37	24.49	30.61	36.73
Maximum	0.00	6.12	12.24	18.37	24.49	30.61	36.73	42.86

Percentage of total absolute value range applying to each level

	0.00	14.29	14.29	14.29	14.29	14.29	14.29	14.29

Frequency distribution of data point values in each level

Level	1	2	3	4	5	6	7	8
Symbols								
Frequency	765	54	24	6	3	2	0	1

```
 L_____I
 0        10
    miles
```

Figure 7   Migrant apprentices to Ipswich, 1596–1651

to the three towns can be represented more conventionally on histograms. In this case (Figures 8 to 10), the numbers of migrants at increasing distances from each of the centres are shown. Of course, the 4-mile bands themselves increase in area with increasing distance from the towns and so have a greater chance of including progressively more and more migrants. Taking this into account, although for all three towns the greater part of the immigrant apprentices seem to come from between about 8 and about 20 miles, it is made clear by the maps that this was not necessarily the case in every direction; far more, or far less, than might be expected came in some cases from certain directions. Some of this irregularity could have been caused, variously, because of nearby areas being very highly, or very thinly, populated; by especial numbers coming because of a marked link between some of them and a town; or because of what might be called 'competition' for labour between nearby towns. Simple distance, therefore, is not enough to explain these variations. Distance, population distribution, special trading links, all need to be considered to explain migration patterns on a regional scale.

Norwich

Migration to the great provincial capital of Norwich was marked in the sixteenth and seventeenth centuries. A striking aspect appeared to be the relatively low number of migrant apprentices coming from within 7 or 8 miles of the centre (Figure 8), though these are interpolated across to a great extent in the small-scale maps. This might in part of course have been due to villages close by being recorded as part of Norwich, but this seems unlikely, considering the regulation of town freedom; indentures seem carefully to specify nearby places at a mile or two's distance, thus 'Eaton-next-Norwich'.[22] The relatively low numbers of apprentices moving in permanently from nearby might be explained by the attractions of staying as established outworkers for uban manufacture or of supplying specialized dairy and garden produce to the city, or even perhaps going into work on a daily basis. Many people would deliberately have chosen to practise manufacture or trade outside a town's walls in order to escape restrictive urban regulations on quality of manufacture or size of enterprise, and to avoid the burdens of contribution to poor relief, and other urban dues, while on the other hand benefiting from nearness to markets and other outlets. Certainly this kind of suburban expansion caused concern to many town governments. On more than one occasion Norwich corporation, or those weavers of influence in it, complained about manufacturing outside the town and asked that it should be brought at least under the same rigorous quality controls their workforce laboured under.[23] This was seen as a problem around London to a much greater extent of course.[24] A

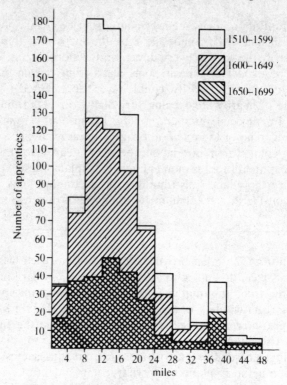

Figure 8 Migrant apprentices to Norwich

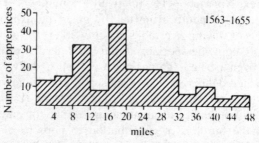

Figure 9 Migrant apprentices to Great Yarmouth

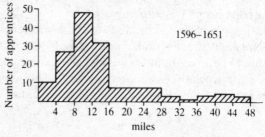

Figure 10 Migrant apprentices to Ipswich

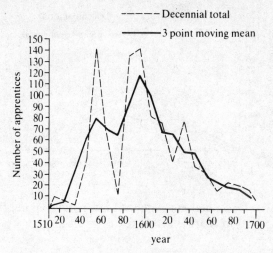

Figure 11   Decennial enrolment of migrant apprentices
to Norwich, non-textile trades

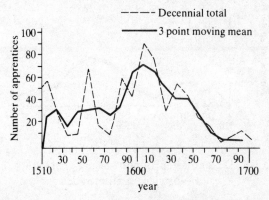

Figure 12   Decennial enrolment of migrant apprentices
to Norwich, textile trades

further major characteristic of the pattern of migration was that,
whilst the density of migrants declined with distance fairly evenly
from Norwich in most directions, this was not the case towards
Great Yarmouth, just over 20 miles to the east. Far fewer places
from the Great Yarmouth direction sent apprentices relative to
other areas at an approximately equal distance from Norwich, a
fact which cannot be explained away by reference to the low
population undoubtedly obtaining in some (only) of the poorly

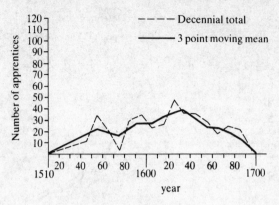

Figure 13   Decennial enrolment of indigenous apprentices to Norwich, non-textile trades

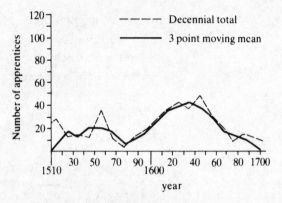

Figure 14   Decennial enrolment of indigenous apprentices to Norwich, textile trades

drained parishes in this region. Presumably this reflected the very marked local migration field of Great Yarmouth itself (see, for example, Figures 3 to 6); a pattern that was particularly apparent in the sixteenth century. Yarmouth seems, in this context, to have had its own restricted but definite field of influence, from which few apprentices went to Norwich; it never sent apprentices to Norwich in any number relative to its size, nor indeed received many from that city. Further away, the sandy and thinly populated Breckland to the west and south-west sent a small number of apprentices as might be expected, relative to other areas at similar distance. Villages of the extreme west of Norfolk sent almost none at all; otherwise the migration field of Norwich extended over most of the two counties with few exceptions. Yet only about ten apprentices can definitely be identified as coming from Essex to Norwich in the course of the sixteenth and seventeenth centuries.[25]

In contrast, larger numbers of migrants than might otherwise have been expected came from the north-east of the city, the textile villages around Worstead in particular. This can be much more easily explained, as connections of the two were close through their interrelated spinning and textile manufactures. Particularly high densities were to be found also in the rich arable area to the south and west of Norwich around large market towns like Wymondham and Attleborough. Sir Thomas Wilson, writing of England around 1600, noted that this area was very rich, exclaiming over the number of gentry there with money to spend. Such were the conditions about 'Windhame' (Wymondham).[26] Of course, migration was marked from most other towns, as might be expected on the grounds of their greater size alone, which increased the simple statistical chance of migrants being sent. In addition, it must also have been due to their greater connectivity with Norwich via markets, fairs and other trading links. Chance meetings between employer and prospective employee, or perhaps his father, must always have played a large role in setting up such actual contacts; knowledge about opportunities, or what the opportunities were thought to be, must always have played an important part in migration. We are only very rarely likely to get much information on exactly why people chose to move; indeed studies of contemporary societies in developing countries demonstrate that many migrants cannot, surprisingly, exactly identify why they chose to move, other than because of vague aspirations of betterment, often based on inadequate knowlege.[27] This may often have been the case in pre-industrial England.[28] But most other East Anglian towns sent numbers of apprentices to Norwich; for example, twenty-seven out of thirty places with market rights in Norfolk in fact did, and about two-thirds of those in Suffolk, twenty-two out of thirty-two.

Few notable changes took place in this general pattern in the sixteenth and seventeenth centuries, as comparison of Figures 3, 4 and 5 show; the first period which takes into account the relatively small number of apprentices enrolled in the first years of the sixteenth century is thus some thirty years longer than in the case of the second two fifty-year periods. The 'negative area' towards Great Yarmouth became less marked in the early seventeenth century, while on the other hand more apprentices seemed then to come from the agricultural areas of north-central Norfolk – the 'poor sands' of the day. It is difficult to advance any definite suggestions as to why this should be in these two cases. The apparent increase during the seventeenth century from the crowded, wood-pasture region of central high Suffolk is perhaps more easily attributed to population pressure there[29] at a time when employment opportunities in spinning for the declining Suffolk broad-cloth industry must have been lessening.[30] Even the Norwich weavers were turning more and more away from such sources of spun yarn towards those of areas like Westmorland.[31] Overall then the strictly geographical pattern of migration to Norwich from within the confines of East Anglia was marked by general stability over two centuries. Those concerned with rural/urban migration in other countries and other periods have found tremendous continuity in migration patterns also. Hägerstrand, studying migration patterns over a hundred years in Sweden, stressed that there was a striking lack of variation in both distances and directions involved,[32] emphasizing '. . . the stability of the rural migration field and the element of continuity in its changes'[33] and that,

if our opinion is correct, that the migration field is to be considered as a feedback process of historical continuity, the conclusion must be that it would be in vain to look for a deterministic theory connecting migration and distance, be it measured by km, cost or 'intervening opportunities'. The best we can hope for is a roughly adequate description of particular empirical materials.[34]

Certainly this was the case with the movement of apprentices to towns within East Anglia: the tendency for relatively fewer migrants than might be expected to come from within 8 miles of Norwich to that city was noted also for the later eighteenth century from evidence contained in the more numerous settlement papers. Between 1754 and 1788 for example the largest proportion of that class of migrants came from between 10 and 29 miles, strikingly similar to the pattern of apprentice migration in the sixteenth and seventeenth centuries.[35]

A small number of apprentices came from further afield (see Table 7). Many English counties sent at least one or two: some apprentices even came from London to Norwich, in addition to

the great number of Norwich folk who must have gone in the
opposite direction. This indeed points to Norwich's stature at the
time; the number of people who went from London to get their
training elsewhere must have been much less than those who
streamed to the capital in ever-increasing numbers. The only case
of any special long-range link seeming to develop was with Yorkshire, especially the West Riding, and other north-western counties apparently experiencing population pressure, like Lancashire
(mostly from north of the Ribble), Westmorland and Cumberland.
Indeed a part of the migration to Norwich from these counties
seems to have developed due to special links with the textile trade.
On the other hand, some of the movement into other trades and
occupations from Yorkshire may just have been a reflection of
that county's size, greater than other English counties; equally
neither that county[36] nor Cumberland, Westmorland and Lancashire were particularly prosperous agricultural regions.[37]

Table 7 Counties sending apprentices to Norwich

County	No.	County	No.
Yorkshire	157	Warwickshire	3
Lincolnshire	49	Nottinghamshire	3
Lancashire	31	Middlesex	2
Leicestershire	22	Cornwall	2
Westmorland	20	Worcestershire	2
Cambridgeshire	19	Shropshire	2
(London	15)	Northamptonshire	2
Cumberland	8	Isle of Ely	2
Durham	7	Berkshire	1
Essex	7	Denbigh	1
Cheshire	7	Gloucestershire	1
Kent	6	Oxfordshire	1
Huntingdonshire	5	Buckinghamshire	1
Northumberland	4	Hampshire	1
Derbyshire	4	(Berwick-on-Tweed	1)
Staffordshire	4	(Rotterdam	1)
Hertfordshire	4	(Amsterdam	1)
Bedfordshire	4		

The effects on the city of all three sorts of apprentices, those
born in Norwich, those coming from within its region or those

from other parts of the country, must have varied from year to year.[38] Certainly the enrolments for that city fluctuated quite widely from year to year in some cases (see Figures 11 to 14). Quite a large sector of Norwich's recorded apprentices came from elsewhere, for about a third (1932:5835) of all those indentured were immigrants and many must have continued to be mobile after they had served their apprenticeship. Indeed, of all apprentices – indigenous and migrant – as yet only about 17 per cent (995:5835) can definitely be said to have remained in the city at the end of their term, these being the ones who later took up their freedom.[39] Others of course may have stayed on as unrecorded journeymen, but it is certain that many must have moved on in a fashion very rarely recorded then,[40] and only recently much discussed now.[41] And they were equally occupationally mobile. Occupational information is given for about 95 per cent (5550:5835) of all apprentices in Norwich; in the case of migrants about 90 per cent of those for whom the necessary information is recorded (1238:1932) went to different jobs from those that their fathers were employed in.

Certainly the course of temporal trends of enrolment may at least indicate, though without much precision, something of the impact of apprenticeship on the city, as well as of the city on apprenticeship. Throughout the sixteenth and seventeenth centuries a lot of the economic activity of Norwich was concerned with, and therefore its prosperity dependent on, the manufacture of textiles.[42] At first largely the traditional worsteds, and then the new draperies. The draw of the textile and allied trades was marked then. Forty-eight per cent of apprentices who came to Norwich during this period, and who cannot be definitely traced as staying in the city, entered the worsted weaving and allied trades (2252:4605), and 15 per cent (762:4605) tailoring; the proportions of those entering these two trades who stayed more permanently, at least long enough to take up their freedom, was 28 per cent (271:945) and 18 per cent (172:945). This dominance of textiles is most marked. However, the decennial entry of apprentices in the worsted weaving trades fluctuated widely (see Figures 12 and 14). The peaks and troughs of enrolment represented there, present even when the more marked changes have been smoothed out by the use of a three-point moving mean, seem to echo to a large extent various changes in the prosperity of the textile trades themselves, though they must also have been much influenced by general population trends and the effects of plagues. This even without taking the impact of the Flemish into account. The textile trades, as Allison demonstrated, certainly were not in very good heart at the beginning of the sixteenth century. On the other hand, the fairly high numbers recorded as entering apprenticeship agreements between 1510 and 1520 probably indicates no more than the effects of reaction to legislation on crafts, and the registration of apprentices, introduced in 1511 after previous laxity in this respect.[43] Enrolments fell off once more in the 1530s and again in the 1560s and 1570s and the 1620s and 1630s. These trends in enrolment seem to follow the cyclical depressions of English manufacture brought about variously by the changing terms of foreign trade and the interruption of war. The slump in the 1550s and 1560s probably followed the crisis in Antwerp in 1551; a slump well known to older commentators on the economic affairs of the day.[44] Manufacturers concerned with the new draperies suffered badly again, particularly at the end of the first quarter of the seventeenth century.[45] And the trends of apprenticeship enrolments thus seemed broadly to reflect trends in the prosperity of the textile manufactures of the city. This is followed whether indigenous, East Anglian or longer-distance immigrant apprentices are considered. Numbers fell off towards the end of the seventeenth century, but this may well have simply followed some decline in administrative control over enrolment rather than any decline in the trade itself, not yet setting in.[46]

Enrolment of apprentices to all other trades followed roughly parallel to these movements (see Figures 11 and 13); it is of course impossible to do anything more than to suggest that the general decline in the economy of the whole city, consequent on poor conditions obtaining in the textile trade from time to time, may help to explain this. These apprentices certainly entered a broad spectrum of trades and services, about 105 in all.[47] It would be naive to propose that these graphs are finely adjusted to a number of economic, demographic, or even simple administrative factors – they instead broadly reflected their influence. Periodic inaccuracies in recording, fluctuations in prosperity, times of population pressure or replacement after plagues, all must be taken into account. It would, for example, be dangerous in the extreme to expect to be able to reflect accurately the demographic history of Norwich or any other town from figures of entry of apprentices or freemen.[48]

Great Yarmouth

Being smaller, Great Yarmouth had a much more restricted migration field than Norwich, but it was a thriving seaport, exporting, *inter alia*, some Norwich cloth as well as being a base for the herring fleet and scene of the great Herring Fairs.[49] It thus particularly attracted immigrants entering into maritime and mercantile trades. One hundred and twenty-one villages and towns in Norfolk and Suffolk sent migrants to Great Yarmouth at some time or another. As might be expected, a majority of these apprentices came from nearby. The most marked characteristic of its East Anglian migration field was that (see Figure 6) there was a notable density of migrant apprentices coming from 10 or 12 miles around the town, which then fell off sharply westwards as Norwich's influence presumably became stronger; this was what might be called the seaport's own local 'apprentice-shed', the area of local movement to the nearest town centre which was nothing out of the ordinary in pre-industrial England, which most English towns must have experienced, for which everyday 'mobility' is perhaps a better term than migration.[50] Almost all of the rest came from within central and eastern Norfolk and Suffolk; the town's pull or attractiveness to migrants extended only about halfway across East Anglia compared to Norwich which attracted people from all over the region. In contrast to Norwich migration was much more marked from coastal parishes and towns, and relatively much less from inland market and other towns. Only eight out of thirty market towns in Norfolk and seven out of thirty-two from Suffolk sent apprentices to Great Yarmouth, and these were all to the east of the region, near the port itself. Thus although even Norwich itself, together with some other smaller towns like North Walsham and Holt to the north-west and Beccles, Bungay, and Diss to the south-west, of Great Yarmouth, sent a number of apprentices, the burden from inland came from nearby rural parishes particularly to the north-west. Some of these were in the marshy areas of the broads, parishes like Bastwick and Martham; others were in a belt around Worstead and Colt-ishall which were engaged in textile manufacture, and also notably sent apprentices to Norwich. These areas were quite densely popu-lated and in times of slump such areas of rural textile and spinning outwork may have been hard-hit. Very few apprentices came from the thinly peopled area of the Suffolk Sandlings, to the south of the town.

It is the coastal pattern of migration which is most marked, however. Apprentices travelled to Yarmouth from many of the coastal areas of Norfolk and Suffolk, from as far as King's Lynn around the coast to Ipswich. That this should be so is not surprising considering the coasting trade in this busy and prosperous region, and much movement is thus accounted for. Most notable are high densities from the north and north-eastern fishing and coastal trading ports of Cley, Sheringham and particularly Cromer, as well as Lowestoft to the south. Some movement may have been due to the extreme poverty of coastal parishes, encouraging migration. Reports in the course of the sixteenth and seventeenth centuries repeatedly emphasized their poverty. The area was one of by-employment in slack periods of the farming and fishing year, for the knitting of stockings in particular.[51] In 1568, for example, the 'poor inhabitants' of the coasts of Norfolk in parishes like Sidestrand, Overstrand, Trimingham and Repps, which sent a number of apprentices to Great Yarmouth, petitioned the Queen for renewal of the concession which allowed them to export fish free of duty.[52] Nearly seventy years later there were complaints to the farmers of Customs against the merchant adventurers for refusing to trade in the stockings of the area because of their low quality.[53] And it was certainly the sea connection which also led to the one marked longer-distance stream of migrant apprentices going to Great Yarmouth (see Table 8) as in the case of Norwich. These again came from the north, but in this case from the coastal parts of Yorkshire, Durham and Northumberland. The evident connection between Yarmouth and these areas via the coastal coal and associated carrying trades would presumably have led to the setting up of this link. Others came from as far around the coast in the opposite direction as Dorset. These last represent movements the reasons for which cannot even be hinted at in a macro-scale study such as this, without detailed examination of the histories of individual migrants, the evidence for which may be often missing.

The number of apprentices enrolled at Great Yarmouth in the years 1563–1669, some 487 in all, was low at the beginning and end of the period, about twenty a decade or so, but reached a peak in the 1610s, 1620s and 1630s. It is difficult to suggest any particular reason for this other than administrative. Occupational

Table 8   Counties sending apprentices to Great Yarmouth

County	No.	County	No.
Yorkshire	21	Cheshire	2
Northumberland	15	Essex	1
Durham	11	Middlesex	1
Lincolnshire	6	Nottinghamshire	1
Dorset	6	Northamptonshire	1
Kent	4	Herefordshire	1
Sussex	3	Scotland	1
Westmorland	2	(London	2)

mobility was high, of immigrants some 90 per cent (194:207) entered jobs different from their fathers. Although they entered a wide range of trades, fifty-three in all, the dominance of the sea trades is apparent. The occupations entered by most, 464, are known. Thirty per cent (143:464) became mariners, 17 per cent apprenticed to merchants (81:464) and 11 per cent (54:464) to shipbuilders and services, ranging from shipwrights to anchor-smiths and compass makers. Twenty-five were also apprenticed to the cooper's trade. The dominance of these sea trades in the overall occupational structure of the town was marked, around 60 per cent. The allied activities of seafaring, trading and shipbuilding played a part in Yarmouth's economy as marked as that played by the worsted and textile trades in Norwich, which accounted for some 55 per cent of all trades entered there. By comparison with Norwich, however, over the whole period only two apprentices in Great Yarmouth were indentured to weavers, further confirmation of the stranglehold Norwich had on the urban manufacture of worsteds, for textiles produced in Great Yarmouth or King's Lynn had to be sent to that city for finishing.[54]

The influence of the sea seems to have been all penetrating, and many of the work people of Great Yarmouth ostensibly engaged in other trades, in fact may have spent some of their time involved in activities associated with it.[55] For example, one apprentice put to a cooper in Great Yarmouth was to be sent on one sea voyage a year; another was apprenticed to a tailor, but if he proved 'unfit or unwilling' he was to be put to sea.[56] The trading activities of the port were highly organized, an apprentice from Mundham in Suffolk, for example, being indentured to a merchant of Great

Yarmouth in 1612 'to keep books and accounts, after the manner of merchandise called debtor and creditor';[57] the links with Holland and the Low Countries in the 'North Sea community', were also marked. Apprentices were to 'learn the Dutch and French language' by being sent to reside in Holland for a year,[58] and (presumably) to conduct business for their masters abroad. Apparently much business in the Low Countries was conducted on behalf of the English merchants by factors or apprentices.[59] This certainly appears to have been the case, for example, with the young man apprenticed to a hosier in 1627, who was to be 'maintained half the year in Holland'.[60]

Ipswich

The Suffolk port of Ipswich, 'capital' also of the eastern division of that county, had on this evidence at least a restricted migration field compared even to Great Yarmouth, which was not much larger than it (Figures 6 and 7). Seventy-two of the ninety places in East Anglia which sent migrant apprentices to Ipswich were in Suffolk, and these mostly in the eastern part of that county. A notable density occurred around the port itself, falling off in intensity in most directions to the eastern and coastal parts of the county, while numbers came from the market towns to the north, like Stowmarket and Needham Market. Any migration from beyond the Norfolk/Suffolk border seems also to have come from market towns like Wymondham or East Dereham in the central and southern parts of Norfolk. Twelve out of thirty-one market towns in Suffolk sent apprentices to Ipswich but only seven out of thirty from Norfolk. The area of notable population density in the cloth-weaving regions of the Stour Valley to the north-west of Ipswich also sent a number, although few came from Bury St Edmunds and its immediate area. That town, for which few sources on migration survive as far as is known, presumably had its own equally marked local migration field. Ipswich's migration field was very local[61] and presumably it was similar in this respect to other east coast ports nearer London; Colchester[62] in the eighteenth century seemed to get most of the migrants from under 15 miles, for example, as settlement papers reveal and the picture is very similar for Maldon.[63] In comparison to Great Yarmouth the number from, for example, East Anglian coastal parishes was also much lower being restricted to the King's Lynn area and the Suffolk coast between Aldeburgh and Lowestoft. None came from

Great Yarmouth, or the Norfolk coast in between, and surprisingly few came from nearby Essex, most of these being from Colchester and Maldon.

Once more some apprentices came from a long distance, a number from the north-east coast, particularly Northumberland (see Table 9). The enrolment of apprentices reached peaks in the 1600s and 1630s, during the short period of 1596–1651 for which indentures survive, but as is the case with the similar fluctuations for Great Yarmouth, no particular weight can be given to these. But, like Great Yarmouth, the sea dominated those occupations entered, about twenty-five types in all. Of the 319 apprentices for whom occupational information is recorded 62 per cent (199) became mariners and 12 per cent (forty) entered the shipbuilding trades, yet only a bare 1 per cent (four) were apprenticed to those called 'merchants'. Whether this is a reflection of the town's trading position in the earlier seventeenth century, already 'eaten-up' by London, or simply a reflection of local usage, 'mariner' being interchangeable with 'merchant', it is difficult to discern. Certainly the port of Ipswich appears to have been in general depression during the seventeenth century.[64] Many people called 'mariners' may have been those concerned largely with the simple carrying of small broken lots of different sizes to different ports and creeks in the coastal trade. How much of the coal trade was in Ipswich's hands by the seventeenth century is not known. Both cloth and dairy products were exported through the port.[65] Otherwise new apprentices entered a variety of urban trades and services,[66] and occupational mobility was high, over 90 per cent (154:164) of migrants going into new jobs. It would be interesting to compare Ipswich, as well as Norwich and Great Yarmouth,

Table 9   Counties sending apprentices to Ipswich

County	No.	County	No.
Essex	17	Sussex	2
Northumberland	11	Wiltshire	2
Yorkshire	5	Bedfordshire	1
Cambridgeshire	3	Devon	1
Durham	2	Rutland	1
Kent	2	Shropshire	1
Leicestershire	2	Westmorland	1

with other smaller towns in East Anglia with respect to migration. As many questions are posed by an examination of apprentice indentures as are answered, particularly the fascinating problem of the actual mechanism by which a migratory movement set off. Presumably it was personal contact brought about by trade which induced the son of one Yorkshire badger to be apprenticed to an Ipswich oatmeal maker in 1601.

Conclusion

The discussion of the migration patterns to these three East Anglian towns has been essentially descriptive. The very brief description of the enrolment and trades of apprentices is based on traditional and simple methods of counting and cross-tabulating, which reveal equally simple facts about urban trade structures most briefly summarized here, although evidence of extreme occupational mobility is revealing. The description of migration patterns, however, is based on the less traditional but in fact equally simple method of computer mapping. As such, both approaches obviously suggest more questions than are answered, and leave much open to speculation. For example, there were many immigrants to Norwich from the cloth-weaving villages to its north-east. Many of these went into textile trades. But there is no more evidence than this to suggest there was therefore a *definite* link between the two, brought about by the textile manufacture. The nut of migration is not so easily cracked. It is also difficult to compare local patterns in other regions in this way as yet. But it is certainly the case that the East Anglian picture is likely to be repeated in other regions. On a regional scale the larger Norwich, as might be expected, attracted more apprentices over a wider area, both within the region and in the rest of England, than the smaller Great Yarmouth and Ipswich, even though these had their long-range contacts. On a national scale, in comparison, London would have attracted the greatest number of migrants of course, but it would be wrong to discount such movement to very much smaller places.[67] Certainly movement to places the size of all three East Anglian towns was far from rare. It was common enough to Bristol, the great provincial centre of the west at the time, to which marked numbers of long-range migrants came, many from the north-west of England, especially Westmorland.[68] It was common enough to a smaller port like Southampton[69] which apparently had a much more restricted migration field similar to Ipswich's with some marked local coastal connections. Inland towns of a similar size to Great Yarmouth and Ipswich such as York[70] or the smaller Worcester and Leicester[71] experienced similar local migration patterns, and some longer-range links; a whole interrelated network existed to some tiny towns in Kent.[72] London's pull covered the whole country; below it, provincial cities, county towns and market towns probably had their own hierarchy of migration fields decreasing in size as the size of the towns and their economic importance also decreased, although there were exceptions. Oxford, for example, with its nationally famous university, seemed to attract immigrants from a distance disproportionately further than its size would suggest in the sixteenth century, numbers of them from the northern and western parts of England.[73] Migration to them was not necessarily direct and could have involved intermediate stages between, for example, a remote north-western Norfolk marshland parish and the city of Norwich, taking in smaller towns en route. No direct evidence exists for this in apprentice indentures, it would have probably involved journeymen and adults rather more than apprentices bound for their first job; deposition books give evidence of this in plenty.[74] But, besides the aimless and hopeless movements of the destitute and vagrant, migration of a more permanent kind, as evinced by the evidence of apprentice registers, seems generally to have been densest from the immediate area of a town, from other smaller towns in the region and from areas with which they had a special link, such as similar manufacturing interests; it could also be marked from areas of high population and low agricultural or manufacturing opportunities, or those with which there was a link in landownership. Apprentices were of course only one group, a fluctuating one at that, amongst overall labour migration but an examination of their migration to these three East Anglian towns suggests much of the pattern and dynamics of migration of pre-industrial England.

Acknowledgements

I am most grateful to Dr J. Thirsk and Dr P. Slack for their kindness in reading early drafts of this paper. Any deficiencies of fact or interpretation remain the responsibility of the author of course.

Notes and references

1 See, for example, E. A. Wrigley, 'A simple model of London's rôle in changing English society and economy, 1650–1750', *Past and Present*, **37** (1967), pp. 44–70; P. Clark, 'The migrant in Kentish towns 1580–1640', in P. Clark and P. Slack (eds), *Crisis and order in English towns 1500–1700* (1972) pp. 117–63; J. Patten, *Rural-urban migration in pre-industrial England*, University of Oxford School of Geography, Research Paper 6 (1973); P. Spufford, 'Population mobility in pre-industrial England: I, The pattern of migration', *Genealogists' Magazine*, **XVII** (1973); S. N. Smith, 'The London apprentices as seventeenth century adolescents', *Past and Present*, **61** (1973), pp. 149–61; S. N. Smith, 'The social and geographical origins of the London apprentices 1630–60', *Guildhall Miscellany*, **IV** (1973), pp. 195–206; A. F. Butcher, 'The origins of Romney freemen, 1433–1523', *Economic History Review*, 2nd series, **XXVII** (1974), pp. 16–27; P. A. Slack, 'Vagrants and vagrancy in England, 1598–1664', *Economic History Review*, 2nd series, **XXVII** (1974), pp. 360–79.

2 For example, D. Friedlander and R. J. Roshier, 'A study of internal migration in England and Wales, 1851–1951: geographical patterns of internal migration', *Population Studies*, **XIX** (1966), pp. 239–79.

3 Population figures used for Norwich, Great Yarmouth and Ipswich are from J. H. C. Patten, 'The urban structure of East Anglia in the sixteenth and seventeenth centuries' (unpublished PhD thesis, University of Cambridge, 1972).

4 K. J. Allison, 'The Norfolk worsted industry in the sixteenth and seventeenth centuries', *Yorkshire Bulletin of Economic and Social Research*, **12** (1960), pp. 77–83, and **13** (1961), pp. 61–77.

5 For example, J. F. Pound, 'The social and trade structure of Norwich, 1525–1575', *Past and Present*, **34** (1966), pp. 49–69.

6 J. Thirsk (ed.), *The agrarian history of England and Wales, IV, 1500–1640* (Cambridge, 1967), pp. 40–9.

7 For example, J. B. Mitchell, *Historical geography* (1954), pp. 249–50.

8 For example, D. Defoe, *A tour through the whole island of Great Britain, I* (London, 1927), pp. 40–5; W. B. Stephens, 'The cloth exports of the provincial ports, 1600–1640', *Economic History Review*, 2nd series, **XXII** (1969), pp. 228–48.

9 W. M. Rising and P. Millican, *Apprentices indentured at Norwich 1510–1752*, Norfolk Record Society, **XXIX** (1959); P. Millican (ed.), *The Register of the Freemen of Norwich 1548–1713* (Norwich, 1934), Appendix.

10 Norfolk and Norwich Record Office (hereafter NNRO), C.4/258-C.4/357; NNRO, Great Yarmouth Corporation Assembly Books 1614–1637.

11 Ipswich and East Suffolk Record Office, A.IX.4. These indentures are calendared in Ms J. Glyde, Ipswich Reference Library, 942/64 (Ip.929–4).

12 Clark, 'The migrant in Kentish towns', pp. 120–2.

13 F. Unwin, *Industrial organisation in the sixteenth and seventeenth centuries* (1st published Oxford 1904; reprinted 1957), pp. 117–20; O. J. Dunlop, *English apprenticeship and child labour* (1912); M. G. Davies, *The enforcement of English apprenticeship 1563–1642* (Harvard 1956).

14 Millican, *The Register*, **XVI–XX**; Rising and Millican, *Apprentices indentured*

at Norwich, pp. xi–xiv; W. Hudson and J. Tingay, *The records of the City of Norwich*, II (1910), *passim*.

15 Unwin, *Industrial organisation*, p. 138; R. H. Tawney and E. Power (eds), *Tudor economic documents, I* (1935), p. 339.

16 Clark, 'The migrant in Kentish towns'.

17 P. Spufford, 'Population movement in seventeenth century England', *Local Population Studies*, 4 (1970), pp. 41–50.

18 Friedlander and Roshier, 'A study of internal migration', p. 246.

19 J. H. F. Brabney, *The comprehensive gazetteer of England and Wales* (Edinburgh and Dublin, 1911) gives, **V**, p. 37, some 690 ecclesiastical parishes for Norfolk (678 places are recorded in the Lay Subsidies of 1524–5) and for Suffolk, **VI**, p. 125, some 510 ecclesiastical parishes (505 places are recorded in the Lay Subsidies of 1524–5).

20 Patten, 'Urban structure of East Anglia', pp. 12–71.

21 See, for example, K. E. Rosing, 'Computer graphics' (unpublished PhD thesis, University of London, 1970), pp. 39–58; see also K. E. Rosing and P. A. Wood, *Character of a conurbation. A computer atlas of Birmingham and the Black Country* (1971).

22 Rising and Millican, 'Apprentices indentured at Norwich', *passim*.

23 For example, Calendar of State Papers Domestic (hereafter CSPD), Jas I, CLVII (1623), p. 34; M. Campbell, *The English yeoman under Elizabeth and the early Stuarts* (New Haven, 1942), p. 159.

24 J. R. Kellet, 'The breakdown of Gild and Corporation control over the handicraft and retail trades in London', *Economic History Review*, 2nd series, **X** (1958), pp. 381–94.

25 Patten, 'Urban structure of East Anglia', pp. 274–5.

26 Sir T. Wilson, 'The State of England Anno. Dom. 1600', *Camden Society*, **LII** (1936), p. 12.

27 A. K. Speare, 'A cost-benefit model of rural to urban migration in Taiwan', *Population Studies*, **XXV** (1971), pp. 117–30.

28 Clark, 'The migrant in Kentish towns'.

29 Thirsk, *The agrarian history*; *idem*, 'Industries in the countryside', in F. J. Fisher (ed.), *The economic and social history of Tudor and Stuart England* (1961).

30 N. C. P. Tyack, 'Migration from East Anglia to the New World before 1660' (unpublished PhD thesis, University of London, 1951).

31 A. E. Bland, P. A. Brown and R. H. Tawney (eds), *English economic documents* (1914), pp. 484–5; C. Wilson, *England's apprenticeship* (1965), pp. 77–191.

32 T. Hägerstrand, *Innovation and diffusion* (Chicago, 1967), p. 167.

33 T. Hägerstrand, 'Migration and area: A survey of Swedish migration fields', *Lund Studies in Geography*, Series B, **13** (1957), p. 77.

34 Ibid., 150.

35 I am indebted to Mr C. Pond of Queen's College, Cambridge, for this and other information on eighteenth-century settlements, *personal communication*.

36 Thirsk, *Agrarian history*.

37 Some apprentices from these parts certainly seemed to have returned to their home dales with newfound skills: see a letter, *Agricultural History Review*, **XVI** (1968), p. 84, and Patten, 'Urban structure of East Anglia', pp. 338–41.

38 Other important long-range flows both into and out of the region – such as the Fleming and French immigrations or the East Anglian emigration to the New World – cannot be examined here.

39 Calendared in Millican, *The Register*.

40 For example, R. Gough, *Antiquities and memoirs of the Parish of Myddle* . . . (Shrewsbury, 1875).

41 Clark, 'The migrant in Kentish towns'.

42 Allison, 'The Norfolk worsted industry'; D. C. Coleman, 'An innovation and its diffusion. The new draperies', *Economic History Review*, 2nd series, **XXII** (1969), pp. 417–29.

43 Allison, 'The Norfolk worsted industry'.

44 Blomefield, III, p. 382.

45 For example, Wilson, 'The State of England', pp. 69–79; B. E. Supple, *Commercial crisis and change in England 1600–1642* (Cambridge, 1959), *passim*.

46 For example, M. F. Lloyd–Pritchard, 'The decline of Norwich', *Economic History Review*, 2nd series, **III** (1950–1), pp. 371–7; P. Corfield, 'A provincial capital in the late seventeenth century: the case of Norwich', in P. Clark and P. Slack (eds), *Crisis and order in English towns 1500–1700* (1972).

47 Patten, 'Urban structure of East Anglia', pp. 334–6, 342–5.

48 As Bartlett seems to suggest for York, see J. N. Bartlett, 'The expansion and decline of York in the later Middle Ages', *Economic History Review*, 2nd series, **XII** (1959), pp. 17–33; but see also R. B. Dobson, 'Admissions to the Freedom of the city of York in the later Middle Ages', *Economic History Review*, 2nd series, **XXVI** (1973), pp. 1–22.

49 See, for example, D. Defoe, *A tour through the whole island of Great Britain*, *I* (1927), pp. 66–7; N. J. Williams, 'The maritime trade of the East Anglian ports, 1550–90 (unpublished DPhil thesis, University of Oxford, 1952), p. 72 *et seq*.

50 Patten, 'Rural-urban migration', pp. 23–5.

51 Thirsk, *Agrarian History*, p. 46.

52 CSPD, **XLVIII** (1568), p. 83.

53 CSPD, **CCLXXXVI** (1635), p. 37.

54 Allison, 'The Norfolk worsted industry', p. 74.

55 J. Patten, 'Freemen and apprentices', *Local Historian*, **9** (1971), p. 232.

56 NNRO C19/6, f.35.

57 NNRO C4/305, m.25.

58 NNRO C19/5, f.226.

59 G. D. Ramsay, *English Overseas Trade* (1957), pp. 18–19.

60 NNRO C19/6, f.53.

61 Dr Reed suggests a radius of about fifteen miles in the seventeenth century, see M. Reed, 'Ipswich in the seventeenth century' (unpublished PhD thesis, University of Leicester, 1973), p. 96.

62 *ex*. Mr C. Pond.

63 W. J. Petchey, 'The Borough of Maldon, Essex, 1500–1688' (unpublished PhD thesis, University of Leicester, 1972), pp. 77–114.

64 A. S. E. Jones, 'The port of Ipswich', *Suffolk Review*, **3** (1968), pp. 247–9.

65 Stephens 'The cloth exports'; Tyack, 'Migration from East Anglia'; Thirsk, *Agrarian History*.

66 Patten, 'Urban structure of East Anglia', pp. 357–8.
67 As Mr Spufford seems to do, 'Population movement', pp. 44 and 48.
68 D. Hollis (ed.), *Calendar of the Bristol apprentice book, 1532–1565 (Pt 1, 1535–42)*, Bristol Record Society, **XIV** (1948).
69 A. L. Merson (ed.), *A calendar of Southampton apprenticeship registers, 1609–1740*, Southampton Record Series, **12** (1968).
70 D. M. Palliser, 'Some aspects of the social and economic history of York in the sixteenth century' (unpublished DPhil thesis, University of Oxford, 1968), pp. 66–76, and map in end pocket.
71 A. D. Dyer, 'The city of Worcester in the sixteenth century' (unpublished PhD thesis, University of Birmingham, 1966), pp. 304–10, 490; *idem. The city of Worcester in the sixteenth century* (Leicester, 1973), pp. 169, 180–96; R. A. Jenkins and C. T. Smith, 'Social and administrative history, 1660–1835', *Victoria County History of Leicester*, **IV**, esp. pp. 193–4.
72 Clark, 'The migrant in Kentish towns'.
73 C. I. Hammer, 'The mobility of skilled labour to Oxford', *personal communication to author*.
74 For example, J. Cornwall, 'Evidence of population mobility in the seventeenth century', *Bulletin Institute Historical Research*, **XL** (1967), pp. 143–52; Clark, 'The migrant in Kentish towns'.

4
Neighbourhood migration in early modern London

Jeremy Boulton

Jeremy Boulton's study uses annual parish listings of household heads (the so-called Easter Books), together with parish registers, poor rates and so on, to illuminate intra-urban movement in the Southwark area of London in the early seventeenth century. The author takes issue with conventional arguments for the almost perpetual fluidity of London's population in this period and demonstrates the considerable level of residential persistence among householders; when they moved they often remained within the district. Promoting this degree of stability were kin-networks and neighbourhood structures. The sources do not cover the whole spectrum of intra-urban movements and concentrate on heads of household who by definition were older and more respectable than the majority of inhabitants, particularly servants and journeymen, who were almost certainly more mobile.

London: migration and mobility in the metropolis

London began to grow rapidly from the middle of the sixteenth century. With a population of 70,000 in 1550 the capital numbered 200,000 in 1600, 400,000 in 1650 and had reached 575,000 by 1700.[1] In the context of English urban society this growth was particularly striking in the century or so before 1670. It was largely thanks to London's uniquely rapid and large-scale growth that the proportion of the English population living in urban centres of 5000 or more increased significantly from the early sixteenth century to the later seventeenth century, from 5.31 per cent in 1520 to 13.5 per cent in 1670. In particular London's rapid sixteenth-century expansion offset the relative urban stagnation in other areas of the country in this period, a time when real wages (and hence demand for urban-based goods and services) were falling. Apart from London and Newcastle, a city whose

107

economic fortunes were linked closely to the capital, few large towns grew faster than the national population in this period.[2] After 1670 London's growth rate was equalled and then, in the eighteenth century, outstripped by the burgeoning manufacturing towns in the north and the midlands and by some provincial ports.[3]

The capital's remarkable growth was fuelled by immigration from the rest of England. Throughout the early modern period London's demographic regime was marked by 'natural decrease', that is a surplus of deaths over births. The capital's high population density and poor sanitation produced conditions facilitating the spread of diseases, notably bubonic plague, which produced devastating epidemics there in 1563, 1593, 1603, 1625 and 1665. Outside plague years other infectious diseases such as tuberculosis and smallpox took a heavy toll of London inhabitants.[4] In fact, despite the disappearance of plague from London after 1670, a compensatory increase in mortality from other diseases, notably smallpox, meant that the number of deaths in the capital continued to exceed births regularly. Mortality rates may have been most severe in London in the first half of the eighteenth century.[5] London's growth therefore required substantial numbers of immigrants from the rest of England if the city was to maintain and increase her population.

In many respects the patterns of immigration to London resemble those of other large towns and cities in pre-industrial England but quantitatively the flow of people to the capital took place on a unique scale.[6] The high mortality rates prevailing in London, the rapidity of the capital's growth and the scale of immigration meant that only a minority of the inhabitants had been born there. Of church court deponents from east London in the early seventeenth century only between 14 per cent and 22 per cent had been born in the metropolis.[7] London recruited its population from all parts of England in the sixteenth and seventeenth centuries. In line with what is known about the profile of English migration patterns, it was in the century or so before 1640 that the capital attracted the greatest proportion of long-distance migrants, thereafter the relative number of such immigrants declined. Thus of freemen enrolled in the mid sixteenth century some 36.9 per cent had come originally from the north-eastern and north-western counties of England. By 1690 only 11.1 per cent did so.[8] In addition to experiencing the contraction of migration fields in seventeenth-century England, London's immigrants seem to have possessed a similar age profile. As was common in other provincial towns and cities a large proportion of migrants were in their late teens and early twenties. In the early seventeenth century male apprentices formed a significant percentage, perhaps between one-third and one-half of the total annual inflow into the capital. At this time their age at arrival seems to have been about 19.5 years. Single women migrants also seem to have arrived in the capital in their late teens.[9] Sex- and age-specific immigration affected metropolitan society in the same way as it did that of provincial towns. In the early seventeenth century the sex ratio of the capital's population showed a surplus of men. This was caused by the exceptional numbers of apprentices in the population. One authority has calculated that, at this time, apprentices made up between 11.4 per cent and 17.8 per cent of the total population.[10] However, as the institution of apprenticeship declined as a means of recruiting London's population, as may have happened in other towns and cities in the later seventeenth century, so the number of apprentices in the capital's population diminished and the sex ratio came to favour women.[11]

The enormous size of London, the rapidity of its growth and its insatiable demand for immigrants acted as a significant brake on population increase in the rest of the country. This dampening effect was not particularly marked in the late sixteenth and early seventeenth century or indeed in the late eighteenth century, periods when the rate of natural increase, the surplus of births over deaths, in the rest of the country was relatively high. When the national birth and death rates moved closer together, however, in the period 1650–1750, the capital's annual deficit retarded national population growth. In the second half of the seventeenth century continual immigration to London, coupled with a considerable volume of emigration overseas, turned a small surplus of births in the rest of England into a deficit, causing a temporary fall in the national population.[12]

London's enormous size meant that direct experience of metropolitan society was widespread in Stuart England. This fact alone makes the study of the capital's social and economic institutions particularly important for historians interested in the relationship between migration and society. Something like 5 per cent, one person in twenty, of all English men and women lived in the capital in 1600. By 1650 this proportion had risen to 7 per cent and by 1700 had reached 11 per cent.[13] Moreover, experience of metropolitan life was greater than even these figures suggest. Since London's migrants consisted principally of individuals in their late teens each migrant represented the survivor from a larger number of births. Using this premise it has been calculated that in the period 1580–1650 something like one person in eight of all those surviving to adulthood in provincial England would have become Londoners at some point in their lives. A similar figure for the period 1650–1750 finds the proportion as high as one in six.[14]

In addition to the effects of heavy immigration on the age and sex structure of the capital's population, the society produced is thought by some historians to have been uniquely mobile. Some authorities have asserted that the sheer size of the capital and the population turnover which existed therein produced an anonymous, impersonal environment of the sort described in sociological studies of nineteenth- and twentieth-century cities. Cities containing 100,000 persons or more, it is thought, engender privacy and anonymity.[15] One writer has described the population turnover in seventeenth-century London as resembling that found in Los Angeles in the middle of the twentieth century.[16] Turnover of this sort is thought to have prevented the formation of self-conscious neighbourhoods by greatly restricting personal acquaintance. Such a conclusion is supported by the comments of at least one contemporary. Gregory King, an early writer on English population history, stated that one reason for defective returns deriving from the 1694 Marriage Duty Act (which required local officials to compile detailed listings of all households in their jurisdiction) was that,

For the parishes in England, there is scarce an assessor but knows every man, woman, and child in the parish but it is much otherwise in London, where the parishes have one with another 800 houses and 4000 souls and where an assessor shall scarce know 5 families on each side of him.[17]

However, some recent historians have taken a different view of the mobility of London's population. Roger Finlay has concluded that the stability of the capital's population has been underestimated and 'it is difficult to argue that [in many city parishes] people were less likely to know each other than in rural parishes, except of course in the case of some individuals in the population who were very mobile, for example the apprentices and servants'.[18] Finlay was writing, however, of those city parishes within the walls which were often extremely small. How stable was society in larger administrative units and are there sources which can measure accurately population turnover and residential mobility?

Case study: the Boroughside district of St Saviour's, Southwark

A valuable source for studying local population turnover and residential mobility exists for the Boroughside district of St Saviour's, Southwark. The parish of St Saviour's was located on the south bank of the Thames between London Bridge and Lambeth and formed, together with St Olave's, Southwark, part of the ring of poor suburban parishes which surrounded the city within the walls in the seventeenth century (see Map 2).[19] By the early seventeenth century this parish had become a populous administrative unit. Our best estimates of the population of the parish suggest that it shared in London's rapid population growth. It grew from about 3000 in 1547 to 7100 in 1603 and reached about 9300 in 1631.[20] At the opening of the seventeenth century St Saviour's was a bigger population centre than some provincial towns and cities such as Salisbury, Gloucester and Hull.[21] Comparing the figures for population growth in the parish with the natural decrease recorded in the parish register reveals that the parish's growth required sustained immigration from outside. *Net* annual immigration into the parish must have been running at around 200 persons per year throughout the later sixteenth and early seventeenth centuries.[22] The figure for *gross* immigration must have been much higher since newcomers would have been required not only to replace those who died and to promote growth but also to replace those individuals who left the parish every year. Moreover the volume of immigration must have fluctuated considerably over time and have been particularly heavy following the epidemics of bubonic plague which ravaged the parish regularly, as they did the rest of London.[23]

The parish of St Saviour's was divided into three administrative units, namely the Clink liberty, Parish Garden liberty and the Boroughside, the area chosen for this case study. A comparison of the number of subsidy payers in the parish in 1601 demonstrates that the Boroughside was a relatively wealthy part of the mother parish, containing twice as many persons contributing to that tax per capita.[24] The Boroughside had about 44 per cent of the total population of the parish so that it contained around 1320 persons

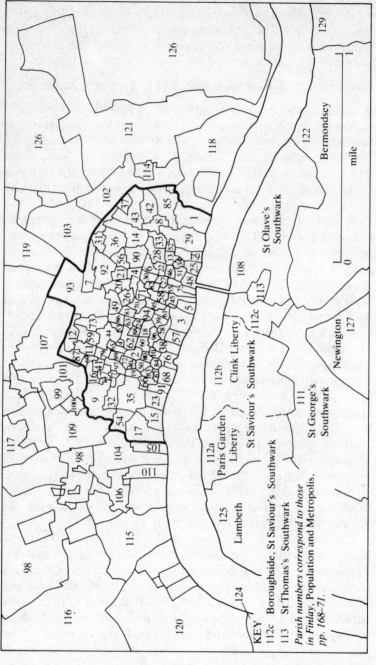

Map 2 London parishes

KEY
112c   Boroughside, St Saviour's Southwark
113   St Thomas's Southwark

Parish numbers correspond to those in Finlay, Population and Metropolis. pp. 168–71.

in 1547, 3100 in 1603 and about 4100 in 1631.[25] In addition to evidence for population expansion from the parish register of the mother parish other evidence also suggests the pressure of increasing immigration. From the late sixteenth century the churchwardens of St Saviour's made routine complaints about the daily increase in the numbers of poor and made regular appointments of officials to search out and eject poor immigrants.[26]

The Boroughside district therefore, in terms of size, resembles closely that hypothetical parish described by Gregory King. Moreover, one might well have expected to find a transient society here since the area acted as an important communications centre for the whole of London south of the river. The Boroughside was well known for the number and quality of its inns which lined the eastside of the High Street catering for visitors and tradesmen. It may have served merely as a staging post for many immigrants.[27] Some studies of migration, too, suggest that there may have been a considerable *outflow* of people from London, the capital acting as a 'revolving door' for England's migrant population.[28] Newcomers to the Boroughside may have intended to stay for only a short time in the area before returning home.

In order to understand fully the social background of the Boroughside we need to know something about its occupational structure because it has been suggested that social stability and cohesion might have been maintained in parts of towns occupied by individuals following similar occupations.[29]

The occupations of about three-quarters of the male householders resident in the Boroughside in 1622 are presented in Table 10. They have been recovered from individual entries in the St Saviour's parish register, manorial court records and from a wide variety of miscellaneous sources, notably wills and recognizances. The individuals whose occupations are tabulated are all listed by name in the sacramental token book for the district in 1622, the latter being the chief source for the study of population turnover and mobility.[30] In order to place the Boroughside's occupational structure in the context of Southwark's economic geography the trades and crafts of adult males living in the other two liberties of St Saviour's, Southwark, and its eastern neighbour St Olave's have also been analysed.[31] As the table makes clear the Boroughside possessed an exceptionally large number of occupations devoted to the production and retail of food and drink, employing 29.7 per cent of male householders compared to between 12.9 per cent and 14.7 per cent in other parts of Southwark. The size of this sector in the Boroughside reflected the commercial importance of the Borough High Street, the main artery linking London and the southern counties of England, and the effect of the market held in that street four days in every week.[32] However, unlike other Southwark districts which *were* dominated by particular occupations (watermen alone formed 39.8 per cent of *all* occupations in the Clink and Parish Garden liberties and feltmaking occupied about a quarter of all adult males buried in St Olave's) the local economy of the Boroughside was essentially heterogeneous. In addition to the numbers employed in building trades and crafts (4.6 per cent), the retailing of household goods and the provision of professional services (12.3 per cent in all), the manufacturing occupational groups were spread over a number of different categories, notably the leather industry (12.2 per cent), textiles (9.0 per cent) and clothing (8.1 per cent). Within these manufacturing sectors (despite evidence of large-scale breweries, dyehouses and soapmaking which probably had greater economic impact than their numbers alone would suggest) most householders worked in small-scale industries like shoemaking, miscellaneous weaving and tailoring. In addition to these callings about 10.7 per cent of male householders followed unskilled manual occupations such as porter, day labourer or carman. Such an occupational structure, by itself, would tell against the possibility of community solidarity and cohesion based on the congregation of large numbers of persons following similar occupations of the sort identified in early modern Oxford and eighteenth-century Newcastle.[33]

Population turnover and residential mobility

For the Boroughside district there is an important source, the sacramental token books, which enables us to place every household in a particular residential location and to trace his or her movements over time. Using this material it is possible to penetrate more deeply than ever before into the fabric of this urban society and to examine the forces which lay behind population turnover and residential mobility in the neighbourhood.

The sacramental token books of St Saviour's, Southwark, are annually compiled lists of householders. The books were compiled to record the delivery of, and payment received for, Easter communion tokens to every household in the parish. For this reason each book, in addition to the name of the household head,

Table 10 The occupational structure of the parishes of St Saviour's and St Olave's Southwark, 1604–25

Occupational category	Boroughside 1622 (Per cent)	Clink and Paris Garden 1619–25 (Per cent)	St Olave's Southwark 1604–23 (Per cent)
Agriculture	1.8	1.5	1.0
Building trades	4.6	2.8	8.5
Production and retail of food and drink	29.7	12.9	14.7
Retail of clothing and household goods	6.7	2.8	3.3
Transport and unskilled labour	10.7	46.7	19.4
Professions	5.6	3.5	3.5
Industry: Textiles	9.0	7.5	25.6
: Clothing	8.1	4.8	5.8
: Leather	12.2	6.8	6.8
: Rope	0.5	0.1	0.1
: Soap	1.1	0.8	0.3
: Wood	3.4	3.0	7.2
: Metal/glass	5.9	4.3	2.9
: Other	0.9	2.6	0.9
Number	657	1,056	1,616

Source: see text.

records the number of people of communicable age (about 16 or over) living in each household. Given supplemental information, the books can be made to shed light on popular religious practice in early seventeenth-century London.[34] In addition to their comprehensive coverage these listings identify the residence of each household. Households are listed street by street, the order in which they are named representing the path followed by the parochial officials who delivered the tokens. Since these officials almost invariably took the same route in the early seventeenth century, the names in the book represent the relative position of each household to the others in any particular year. In this way households can be 'fixed' on the listings relative to each other and to the street names given in the token book.[35] Topographical information contained in an exceptionally detailed parish clerk's notebook also helps to identify street names and the relative location of households. Using this source and this method it is possible to map the relative position of households in the Boroughside on a contemporary ground plan. Map 3 represents the ground plan of the Boroughside as depicted in John Roque's map of 1746.[36]

In order to trace persistence in the same dwelling all streets and alleys must be clearly identifiable on a ground plan and the exact position of one street to another discernible. Since tracing the persistence of every householder in the Boroughside at a number of different points in time over a ten-year period was not a practical proposition, samples of householders were taken. The sampling procedure adopted was to measure the persistence of every householder resident on the eastside of the Boroughside. The eastside has the advantage of being particularly well defined on the Roque map and of experiencing little major building since the first decade of the seventeenth century (see Map 3). The exact relative location of all households can therefore be ascertained.[37] On the map this area begins at Chequer Alley and ends at Axe Yard. It includes all the residential area to the left of the parish boundary (represented by the dotted line) as far as the High Street. This area also forms a particularly useful sample because both the rich on the High Street and the poorer sort in the back alleys receive reasonable coverage.[38] Despite the care taken the results will tend to overestimate the persistence of householders resident in back alleys because small residential movements in such districts cannot always be identified with certainty.

The sacramental token books list *all* the households in the parish. They are known to have recorded the delivery of tokens and listed the presence of paupers (who received free tokens), and even listed Catholic households and others who did not actually participate in the Anglican communion service. Members of foreign churches known from other sources to have been resident in the parish such as those attached to the Dutch or French churches in London were also listed.[39]

It is important to remember that it is only the turnover of household *heads* that can be measured from these books. Although each communicant received a token, only the household head was normally named. Consequently elements of London's

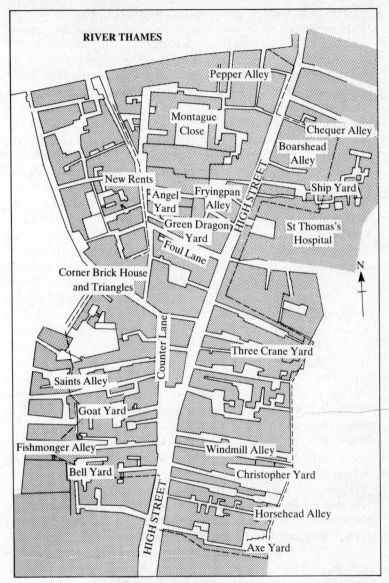

RIVER THAMES

Pepper Alley

Montague Close

Chequer Alley

Boarshead Alley

New Rents

Ship Yard

Angel Yard

Fryingpan Alley

Green Dragon Yard

HIGH STREET

St Thomas's Hospital

Foul Lane

Corner Brick House and Triangles

N

Counter Lane

Three Crane Yard

Saints Alley

Goat Yard

Fishmonger Alley

Windmill Alley

Bell Yard

Christopher Yard

HIGH STREET

Horsehead Alley

Axe Yard

Map 3 Boroughside, Southwark,
redrawn from J. Roque's *Plan of the City of London . . .*, 1746

population thought to have been more mobile, such as lodgers, apprentices and servants, are excluded. It might be argued, however, that the residential behaviour of the householder is of greater social significance than those other members of the population known to be in a transitory stage in the life cycle.[40] Only householders contributed to local taxation, qualified for poor relief or participated in local government and administration.[41] Household heads were responsible for the provisioning and disciplining of their immediate family, including servants and apprentices, and also provided the lion's share of the household income.[42] Furthermore, in many pre-industrial towns and cities where, particularly in poor districts, mean household size was often relatively small, householders formed a sizeable proportion of the total population. In 1631 out of a Boroughside population of 3708, 966 or 26.1 per cent were household heads.[43] It should be remembered that the movements of household heads would have determined (up to a point) the movements of all household members, including domestic servants and apprentices.

We need to know more, however, about the mobility experience of apprentices and servants within the capital's environs before we can appreciate fully the typicality of the residential experience of householders. There is some anecdotal evidence to suggest that some London servants led highly mobile and relatively isolated lives. One female servant in early seventeenth-century London testified in a church court that in her eight years of domestic service in the capital she had served three different masters in three different parishes.[44] Such cases may not have been typical. Other evidence suggests that servants and apprentices, after their initial move to the capital, may well have spent relatively long periods of time within one particular household and hence experienced similar mobility histories to their masters and mistresses. The average length of female domestic service in London households appears to have been over four years in early seventeenth-century London. Only about one in seven served their employers for less than one year.[45] Apprentices, in theory, were bound to their master for seven or eight years, although admittedly more than half never completed their training and their term of service could be interrupted by the death of their master and subsequent transfer to another.[46]

Four samples of householders were taken and their persistence in the same dwelling measured over time (see Table 11). The dates of each sample were determined by methodological considerations. The token books for the late sixteenth century did not survive in sufficiently large numbers for persistence over time to be measured in ten-year periods.[47] The disruption caused by the 1593 and 1603 plague epidemics was responsible for some of this patchy survival. The 1608 and 1609 books were the earliest which could be used to measure turnover for a relatively uninterrupted ten-year time span.[48] The 1618 and 1631 samples were chosen because taxation assessments survived for similar dates.

Table 11 Persistence of householders in the same dwelling 1608–1641

All figures in brackets are expressed as percentages

Number of years of persistence	1608 Number in sample	1609 Number in sample	1618 Number in sample	1631 Number in sample	Total
	257	258	313	330	1,158
1	197 (77)	214 (83)	245 (78)	254 (77)	910 (79)
2	167 (65)	—	—	218 (66)	
3	—	156 (61)	—	199 (60)	
4	134 (52)	—	153 (49)	170 (52)	
5	—	121 (47)	—	—	
6	102 (40)	—	125 (40)	129 (39)	
7	—	100 (39)	—	—	
8	88 (34)	—	76 (24)	—	
9	—	—	—	99 (30)	
10	63 (25)	74 (29)	57 (18)	87 (26)	281 (24)

Source: see text. Percentages expressed as a proportion of the original number of householders in each sample.

A householder was counted as persistent only if he or she remained resident in the same position relative to other householders in the original sample. In line with nineteenth-century studies, widows remaining in the same dwelling as their husbands or children continuing their parents' occupancy are not counted as persistent. The survival of families in the same dwelling will therefore be a few percentage points higher than that of household heads alone.[49]

After one year 79 per cent of the aggregated sample were living in the same dwelling and after ten years 24 per cent were still resident. If the 1618 sample, which included the 1625 plague crisis, is omitted persistence in the same dwelling was 27 per cent over a ten-year period.

A breakdown of two of the samples by wealth reveals that the richer householders were more likely to remain in the same dwelling than their poorer neighbours (see Table 12). In the 1618 sample 91 per cent of those householders paying the 1617 assessment for the Provost Marshall's wages were still resident in the same dwelling after one year, compared to only 74 per cent of those not assessed.[50] After ten years 29 per cent of those assessed were still resident, compared to only 14 per cent of the non-contributors. Similarly poor-rate payers were more likely to persist than non-rate payers. In the 1631 sample 86 per cent of all poor-rate payers were still resident after one year, compared to 72 per cent of non-rate payers, and after ten years 32 per cent persisted compared to 23 per cent.

Table 12 Persistence of householders in the same dwelling by wealth, 1618 and 1631

All figures in brackets are expressed as percentages

Number of years of persistence	1618 Number of householders not assessed in 1617	1618 Number of householders assessed in 1617	1631 Number of non poor-rate payers	1631 Number of poor-rate payers
	228	85	205	125
1	168 (74)	77 (91)	147 (72)	107 (86)
2	—	—	121 (59)	97 (78)
3	—	—	107 (52)	92 (74)
4	85 (37)	58 (68)	90 (44)	80 (64)
5	—	—	—	
6	78 (34)	47 (55)	64 (31)	65 (52)
7	—	—	—	
8	43 (19)	33 (39)	—	
9	—	—	48 (23)	51 (41)
10	32 (14)	25 (29)	47 (23)	40 (32)

Source: see text. Percentages expressed as a proportion of the original number of householders in each sample.

Mortality among household heads played a significant but not a predominant part in turnover. To examine the role of mortality the turnover in the 1609 sample caused by death of household heads was measured using information contained in the token books and the parish burial register (see Table 13).[51] Of the original sample 29 per cent were still resident in the same dwelling ten years later, whilst 25 per cent had died locally and the remaining 46 per cent had moved out of their dwelling. Of the total turnover (the number of householders no longer resident in the same dwelling) 35 per cent had been caused by mortality. The observed difference in persistence between rich and poor does not seem to have been caused by selective mortality. Reworking the 1618 sample backwards in time to eliminate the effect of mortality confirmed that the wealthier and poorer sort exhibited different levels of residential stability.[52]

Table 13 Role of mortality in turnover of householders 1609–19
All figures in brackets are expressed as percentages.

Number of years of persistence	Number of householders in 1609 sample	Total turnover of householders	Turnover caused by mortality	Mortality loss as a percentage of turnover
	258			
1	214 (83)	44	19	43
3	156 (61)	58	16	28
5	121 (47)	35	6	17
7	100 (39)	21	15	71
10	74 (29)	26	9	35
Total		184	65	35

Source: See text.

Measuring persistence in the same dwelling, however, has its limitations. There is, as yet, no comparable material available before the nineteenth century and more seriously it is overall persistence within a particular *area* that has important social consequences.[53] Studies of this latter sort might reveal something about the extent to which individuals identified with the Borough-side district and the importance they attached to neighbourhood ties.

It is clear from occasional memoranda on the token books that their compilers were conscious of movement from house to house and from alley to alley within the area. In the 1612 token book, for example, Thomas Berry, listed in Ship Yard, was reported to be 'in the Close', Simon Fowler, resident on the High Street, was reported to have moved to 'Foul Lane', and John Smith and Robert Clarke, both resident in Horsehead Alley, were noted to be 'in Bell Yard' and '3 Crane Yard' respectively. The compiler also noted intra-alley movement. Nicholas Rogerson in Horsehead Alley was reported to be resident on the 'south side' of the alley in 1612, a move confirmed by the token book itself.[54]

The baptism entries in the parish clerk's notebook supply a crude estimate of the amount of residential mobility within the Boroughside.[55] Since each entry supplied both the address and occupation of the father, the residential behaviour of all individuals baptizing two or more children in the period covered by the notebook can be measured. Between March 1619 and September 1625 243 householders baptized two or more children in the Boroughside area. Of these, 165 or 68 per cent consistently supplied the same address. Hence for example all the five children of William Stubbes, baker, were born in his dwelling on 'the High Street', and both those of Edward Tart, silkweaver, in his house in Saints Alley. However seventy-seven or 32 per cent clearly made one or more residential moves during the period. Thus Nicholas Wyburne, tailor, lived on the High Street at the baptism of his sons Nicholas and William in 1621 and 1623 but in Christopher Yard at the baptism of his daughter Elizabeth in 1625. In all cases the residential movement indicated by the baptism entries is confirmed by the addresses of the householders in the sacramental token books. In this way each source can confirm the reliability of the other. However, the token books indicate that the baptism entries overestimate the number of 'stayers' since they do not detect residential changes within an alley or between particular dwellings on the High Street or in Counter Lane and the Close. In addition it might be suspected that householders baptizing children are predominantly younger than other householders and therefore represent a sample biased towards the more mobile. Any detailed examination of residential mobility should be based on the token books, which are more sensitive to movement, and which represent both old and young householders. This internal movement is important since it raises the possibility that many of those inhabitants who vacated their dwellings may, nonetheless, have remained within the district.

Persistence within the Boroughside area as a whole was traced by indexing complete token books at different dates and tracing householders from one book to another. Care was taken to overcome the problems of nominal linkage that inevitably arose, such as individuals of similar surnames or sons succeeding fathers in the same dwelling.[56] There might well be a small number of wrong linkages but these will have been more than compensated for by the underestimation in persistence caused by the difficulty of linking individuals with common surnames, such as Smith, Jones or Brown. Wherever possible moves were checked against the entries in the parish clerk's notebook. The samples were selected to correspond to indexes compiled for other purposes. Hence because indexes had been compiled for the 1622 and 1624 token books the overall persistence of householders living on the eastside of the Boroughside in 1612 and 1614 was examined.[57] In order to look at the stability of the whole district the persistence of all householders was looked at for two four-year periods, 1618–22 and 1631–35 and one nine-year period, 1622–1631. The particular periods were determined by the amount of other information available. This methodology can only distinguish between those householders who made no moves in a given period and those who made one or more. Between 1619 and 1625, the parish clerk's notebook records that eight of the 111 individuals (7.2 per cent) baptizing three or more children made two or more residential moves within the Boroughside area. To recover the number of moves made by each householder in any given period, however, would have required the indexing of every token book in each period, a task which was not thought to justify the probable return.

Short-range residential mobility was a means by which the Boroughside achieved a measure of stability, much in the manner of some parts of nineteenth-century cities.[58] Thus after nine years 30 per cent of the original 1631 sample of householders were resident in the same dwelling (see Table 11) but 45 per cent were still living in the Boroughside district. Similarly of the 559 householders resident in the Boroughside in 1612 and 1614, 238 or 43 per cent were still to be found in the district ten years later. Between 1618 and 1622, 435 of the original 891 householders (49 per cent) remained in the same dwelling and a further 141 (16 per cent) made short residential moves within the Boroughside. In a similar fashion, between 1631 and 1635, 474 of the 966 house-holders resident in 1631 (49 per cent) remained in the same dwelling but overall 616 (64 per cent) remained within the district. The longer one spent in the Boroughside the greater the chance of moving house. Between 1622 and 1631, 169 of the 958 house-holders resident in 1622 (18 per cent) remained in the same dwelling and a further 160 (17 per cent) moved to a different residence within the area. The 1625 plague reduced the overall level of persistence of the 1622–31 generation.

The overall levels of persistence found in the Boroughside compare favourably with those found in some rural areas of pre-industrial England.[59] Some 52 per cent of household heads were still resident in Cogenhoe after a ten-year period and 50 per cent of householders in Clayworth after a twelve-year period, compared to the 43 per cent of householders persisting within the Boroughside between 1612–14 and 1622–4. This suggests that the relative stability of the district was considerable and adds weight to Finlay's conclusion that 'the stability of London's population has been underestimated'.[60] It should also be remembered that the individuals who crossed parish boundaries and moved out of observation may not have moved very far, staying within a restricted social area. Much movement from rural parishes took place within limited geographical areas.[61] There is some evidence that, in the Boroughside too, some of those who crossed adminis-trative boundaries settled in adjacent districts.[62]

Direct comparison with other areas of pre-industrial London suggests that overall persistence of household heads varied according to the size and social composition of the district in question (see Table 14). Overall persistence in the Boroughside, was considerably higher than in the three small city parishes analysed by Finlay. This difference is largely a product of size. Even short residential moves in the city parishes would have taken individuals across parish boundaries and out of observation. Goldsmith's Row (located in the parishes numbered 97, 72, 89 and 2 on the London parish map, see Map 2) probably owed its high stability to its position as the premier centre of the London goldsmiths' trade. This relatively high level of persistence also followed a substantial amount of residential mobility within the Row.[63] Recently, a wide-ranging and complex reconstruction of an adjacent area of Cheapside housing (covering the parishes numbered 4, 62, 88, 63 and 53 on the London map, Map 2) found similar short-range residential mobility within that district in the late fifteenth century:

moving house was . . . a common occurrence, and a large number of moves were over very short distances to other houses in the same street or parish.[64]

Table 14 Overall persistence within districts of sixteenth- and seventeenth-century London
Figures in brackets are expressed as percentages

District and dates of samples	Number of householders	Number of householders persistent after ten years
St Christopher le Stocks, 1576–80[a]	227	64 (28)
St Bartholomew by the Exchange, 1626–40[a]	1,004	337 (34)
St Margaret Lothbury, 1642–6	406	112 (28)
Boroughside, 1612 and 1614[b]	559	238 (43)
Goldsmith's Row, Cheapside 1558[c]	61	30 (49)

Source:
[a] Figures calculated from those given in Finlay, *Population and Metropolis*, pp. 46–7. Finlay's parishes are numbers 26, 20 and 49 represented in Fig 1.
[b] See text.
[c] Reddaway, 'Goldsmith's Row', pp. 192–206. After an eleven-year period.

The context of neighbourhood mobility

How are we to explain such levels of turnover and mobility in this London suburb? Clearly future studies of pre-industrial urban housing types and forms must take into account the fact that levels of attachment to particular dwellings are likely to have been low. One reason for this may have been that the type of tenure by which metropolitan housing was held facilitated mobility. By the early seventeenth century very few householders in Southwark owned the freehold of their dwelling house. Most housing in the Boroughside was held by lease or rented 'at will' from another person or an institution.[65] Perhaps as a result it was extremely unusual for such householders to display any sort of sentimental attachment to the physical fabric of their dwelling house. Phrases used by those making wills such as 'the house wherein I now dwell' suggest the temporary nature of much occupancy. In its most extreme form property not nowadays normally regarded as divisible from a dwelling might be bequeathed separately. Thus George Payne, citizen and grocer, left his son the 'wainscot about my hall and all shelves in the house'. A wealthy widow when bequeathing her property to a nephew felt constrained to include an explicit clause to the effect that 'the leaden cistern with the leaden sink and pump in the kitchen shall remain in the house together with all cupboards and other necessaries as are fixed to the said house'.[66] Joshuah Phinnies, citizen and leatherseller, was therefore an exception when he ordered that his dwelling house 'which my father estated me [i.e., settled on me]' should pass 'successively from one heir male to another heir male bearing the name Phinnies'.[67] Housing seems to have been regarded in a strictly functional way. Some testators concerned to order domestic arrangements after their death required the physical dismemberment of their dwellings. Thus Elizabeth Snelling, a widow living in the Clink liberty, ordered that after her death her dwelling-house should be divided equally between her son and daughter, her son to 'have the three fore rooms, the cellar and the yard'. Similarly a waterman, Thomas Elhorne, living in Paris Garden liberty, required that following the death of his wife his riverside dwelling was to be divided between his son and grandson 'the three fore rooms to the Thames ward [i.e., side] and half the wharf shall be for my son . . . And the 3 rooms towards the Garden [for his grandson] . . . and the other half of the wharf and the garden to be divided between them both'.[68] In fact division of housing by lessees or occupants rather than additions to the housing stock by new building was the most important means by which population increase in the Boroughside was accommodated in the early seventeenth century.[69] The ease with which pre-industrial housing could be adapted to the demands made upon it has been remarked upon by other scholars.[70] In fact, the house, particularly for those in the lower social orders, as Philip Ariès has suggested, was not the most important living place or 'home' that it is today, but was only a place to eat and shelter. A great deal of social activity took place outside the house, notably in local taverns and alehouses, in the street or in the market place.[71]

If the terms by which housing was occupied might go some way to explain the relatively low attachment to any particular dwelling, *differences* in forms of housing tenure, as well as differences in the way such structures were seen, might have caused the lower levels of persistence in the same dwelling displayed by the poorer householders. It was better quality housing, such as that on the High Street, which was normally held by lease but the poorer tenements in the back-street alleys and yards were held 'at will'.[72] The lengths of leases varied somewhat but evidence from the properties owned by the hospital of St Thomas, Southwark, suggests that for a dwelling house, twenty-one years was the normal period.[73] The advantage of leasehold tenure was greater tenurial security. Landlords needed to go to law to evict unsatis-factory leasehold tenants but 'tenants at will' could be more easily disposed of. In 1611 the parish vestry of St Saviour's, the ruling body of the parish, ordered that:

The churchwardens shall warn all those that are tenants to the parish (which are but tenants-at-will and have no leases) to come in at the next vestry to the end it may be known which are fit tenants and which are not and that the unfit tenants shall have warning to avoid.[74]

Donald Lupton, a contemporary pamphlet writer, also contrasted the greater security of the lease to the insecurity of the tenant-at-will, the latter being 'men that will take short warning a quarter of a year . . . they are not unlike courtiers for they often change places'.[75]

Another reason for the frequency of moving house in the locality may lie in the wide and heterogeneous range of dwellings available in the Boroughside district. In order to appreciate the importance of the urban environment at the micro level it is helpful to make some distinction between the various types of residential district contained in the Boroughside. The complex patterns and sheer variety of different environments that might be contained in even small districts of pre-industrial towns and cities is beginning to be appreciated by urban historians.[76] In particular, in an urban parish it was access to a thoroughfare which was of prime social and economic importance. Households located on thoroughfares would have been exposed to commercial traffic but in alleys and yards, usually possessing only one entry, non-residents might rarely have entered. In such places exposure to strangers was far more limited than life in a crowded and expanding city like London would at first have suggested. The classification of 'sub-districts' which is adopted here depends to a great extent on the volume of traffic entering them.[77] Using our evidence from the token books and our knowledge of the location of these streets on the ground plan it is possible to identify four distinct 'sub-districts'. The High Street (see Map 3) was the chief throughfare and the most superior residential district. Access to this street meant access both to the market site and to the considerable traffic passing in and out of London via London Bridge. John Strype praised the size and quality of much of this High Street housing and the wealth of its inhabitants.[78] Counter Lane and Foul Lane were both secondary thoroughfares that linked the 'New Rents' to the main street. Strype described Counter Lane in 1720 as 'a street of pretty good account, indifferent large and square with well built and inhabited houses having trees before the doors, which renders it pleasant'. The Close and Pepper Alley constituted a third district. The area was the only one in the Boroughside to possess riverside frontage and in addition its inhabitants claimed exemption from certain jurisdictions, a situation which attracted a small Catholic population. The area was physically distinctive enough to be numbered separately in the 1622 token book and as late as 1795 the Close gates were shut up every evening. Alleys and yards constituted a fourth type of environment. Running off the High Street Strype noted many yards and back alleys of 'little account' and 'meanly inhabited'. Physically, such alleys were narrow and hid from the passer-by the condition of the inmates. Thus Windmill Alley was described as a 'dark entrance and narrow within but poorly inhabited and very ordinary buildings'.[79]

By analysing the number of households in each of these sub-districts according to their locally perceived poverty or by their local poor-rate assessment it is possible to add a little statistical precision to this residential topography. Table 15 therefore analyses the residential location of those considered poor in a survey of 1618 and those able to contribute to the local poor-rate assessment in 1631; the latter assessment is recorded in an exceptionally detailed token book which supplied information about household size and population distribution.[80]

Table 15 Residential location of poverty in 1618 and poor-rate payers in 1631

All figures in brackets are expressed as percentages

Residential sub-district	Number of households 1618	Number of households described as poor 1618		Number of households 1631	Number of households paying poor-rate 1631	
High Street	198	2	(1.0)	196	167	(85.2)
Close and
Pepper Alley	94	18	(19.2)	102	39	(38.2)
Counter Lane	118	23	(19.5)	137	43	(31.4)
Alleys and
Yards	481	177	(36.8)	531	65	(12.2)
Total	891	220	(24.7)	966	314	(32.5)

Source: see text.

The High Street was dominated by the wealthier inhabitants. Of the 196 householders located on the High Street in 1631 over 85 per cent were assessed for the poor rate. The wealth of main street dwellers is an established topographical feature of pre-industrial London.[81] The wealth of the High Street was in sharp contrast to that of the other three sub-districts. Only 38.2 per cent of householders in the Close and 31.4 per cent of those in the Counter Lane area were assessed for some form of taxation. As one might expect alleys and yards were the poorest residential district with only 12.2 per cent of their inhabitants rated.

Poverty like wealth was distributed unevenly among the four residential sub-districts. The wealthiest area, the High Street, contained only two poor households in 1618 (1 per cent of the total) compared to eighteen (19.2 per cent) in the Close and twenty-three (19.5 per cent) in Counter Lane. Poverty was concentrated in the alleys and yards, 36.8 per cent of whose households were considered poor in 1618. The residential pattern of poverty, however, was more complex than Table 15 suggests, since it is apparent that the poor crowded together in particular alleys and yards. Those on the eastside of the High Street between Chequer Alley and Christopher Yard (see Map 3) were better off than others elsewhere. Hence only 12.5 per cent of the householders in Christopher Yard were poor and 17.8 per cent in Ship Yard compared to such desperate areas as Axe Yard (51.3 per cent poor), Green Dragon Yard (62.5 per cent poor), Angel Yard (52.6 per cent poor) and Saints Alley (48.3 per cent poor). Such differences suggest that there were finer gradations in back-street housing. A few of the smaller alleys were clearly superior 'social enclaves' of the sort identified elsewhere in London. In 1622 Chequer Alley included two subsidy men and also three poor-rate payers among its six householders and even one hundred years later was described by Strype as 'small, but pretty well built and inhabited'.[82]

It is apparent that the 'social intermingling' observed in early Stuart London and elsewhere also existed in the Boroughside.[83] There was no rigid social segregation. Although the majority of rate payers inhabited the High Street 147 out of 314 (46.8 per cent) lived in other sub-districts. Over 20 per cent were located in alleys or yards in 1631. Many of these, of course, paid at relatively lower rates of assessment than their High Street neighbours.

The impression of some social mixing and the existence of gradations within alleys and yards is reinforced by combining the information contained in two housing surveys taken in 1635 and 1637. A 1637 survey listed the number of 'poor tenements' in many of the alleys and yards in the Boroughside and these figures can be compared with the number of householders listed in the 1635 token book. It is clear that most householders lived in 'poor tenements' since in alleys and yards inhabited by 414 householders in 1635 some 363 (87.7 per cent) were reported. The 1635 survey gave brief general descriptions of this type of housing. The tenements in Ship Yard were 'all for the most part divided houses consisting of 1 and 2 rooms apiece'. The thirty-two tenements in Christopher Yard each contained two or three rooms. Rents for such tenements varied within the 40 to 60 shillings a year range. The average rent for seventy poor tenements in Horsehead Alley was 40 shillings per annum while most Ship Yard tenements were 'let at 50s or £3 a tenement' and those in Christopher Yard at between 40 and 60 shillings a year. Back-alleys and -yards also contained a small number of higher quality tenements. Christopher Yard contained 'other good tenements', Horsehead Alley also contained 'some good' tenements. Of the fifty-four householders resident in Goat Yard in 1635 forty-two inhabited 'poor tenements

. . . consisting of 1, 2 and 3 rooms apiece some dwelling in cellars underground . . . which pay in all about £130 per annum'. But the 1635 survey also revealed higher-quality dwellings. In Goat Yard, of twenty-two tenements whose rents were listed, fourteen were let at 50 shillings, one at 80 shillings, six at £5 and one at £8 per year. It should be remembered that, in the local economy of the poor, the distinction between a 40-shilling and 60-shilling tenement may have been as significant as that between High Street houses worth £20 and £30 per year.[84]

Surveys suggest that even on the High Street housing quality varied considerably. Three-storey dwellings were immediately adjacent to those of four stories, frontages ranged from as little as 8 feet to as large as 22. The houses, as was common in main streets in early modern towns and cities, were long and thin, with relatively narrow street frontages, designed to maximize the number of households who had access to the commercial traffic of the High Street. Thus the house of Francis Grove, grocer, had a street frontage of 15 feet but went back 56 feet. William Sledd, an ironmonger, possessed 10 feet of frontage, but his house stretched back 42 feet.[85] All these High Street houses included storage space in the form of either cellars, vaults or warehouses.[86] Many houses, wherever they were located, lacked basic social amenities. Only half of the fourteen properties surveyed by the hospital possessed a kitchen, reminding us of the important social functions still performed by local alehouses and cooks and the amount of social activity, eating and drinking and so on that was done outside one's dwelling place.[87] Apart from warehouses attached to the larger properties specialized rooms were only referred to twice. Henry Clift, butcher, possessed a small slaughterhouse adjoining (conveniently) his kitchen, and the house of his next-door neighbour George Idle, victualler, contained 'a shop or drinking house' abutting the High Street.[88]

The impression that High Street housing varied considerably in size and quality is reinforced by the evidence of rent. Thus relatively modest housing such as the three-storey single chamber house occupied by one Widow Seow was held on a twenty-one-year lease at £5 a year and a £35 entry fine; a similar but slightly smaller dwelling held by Christopher Fawcett, shoemaker, was held on a twenty-one-year lease at £4 per year and a £20 fine. A few yards down the street from this dwelling Francis Grove, grocer, held a much larger property on a twenty-five-year lease for £10 per year and a £100 entry fine. James Pollard, ironmonger, and a close neighbour of Grove, was also paying about £10 a year with a £120 fine.[89]

The topography of the Boroughside reflected rather than moderated its heterogeneous occupational structure. There was little sign that occupational groups congregated together in particular streets or alleys in the classic medieval fashion and as they still did in some parts of London.[90] Thus, by identifying the locations of householders with known occupations on the ground plan it can be shown that the High Street between Chequer Alley and the Hospital Gate (see Map 3) contained a baker, a cheese-monger, five grocers, a linendraper, a servingman, a tailor, a soapboiler, a pewterer, a smith, a goldsmith, a victualler, a wool-lendraper, a shoemaker and a haberdasher. Alleys and yards displayed similar occupational heterogeneity. Ship Yard contained a huckster, three tailors, two silkweavers, five shoemakers, a cooper, two porters, a sawyer, a sailor, a spectaclemaker, an ostler, a baker, two butchers, a labourer, a glover, a sheargrinder, a cutler, a victualler and a fruiterer.

Only two areas of the Boroughside were dominated by particular occupations. The wealthy butchers, who, as we have seen, might have required specialized housing that included an attached slaughterhouse, were grouped into a large shambles sited on the westside of the High Street from the Bridgefoot to Fryingpan Alley (see Map 3). This shambles was described by Strype.[91] However, even the shambles included a tailor, two cheesemongers and a shoemaker and was punctuated by the ubiquitous victualler. The riverside frontage of the Close and Pepper Alley gave it a unique occupational composition. All the Boroughside dyers were clustered in the sub-district, drawn to the water supply. Strype noted that the Bankside (of which Pepper Alley was technically a small part) contained many dyers 'seated for the conveniency of the water'. The riverside location also explains a concentration of watermen in Pepper Alley; Pepper Alley stairs were 'much frequented by watermen', reported Strype. The existence of loading and river transport facilities prob-ably explains a concentration of woodmongers in the Close.[92]

The heterogeneous housing stock within the Boroughside gave many of its inhabitants the opportunity to make residential adjust-ments to their life style *within* the very immediate locality. The actual motives which lay behind individual moves are, however, too variable to be quantified or even identified easily. Studies of local migration in eighteenth- and nineteenth-century cities suggest that personal whim, the births or deaths of children, life-cycle stage or the desire to alter business premises might each cause an individual to move house.[93] Evidence from seventeenth-century Chester suggests a relationship between the age of house-holders and the size of their dwellings.[94] Life-cycle changes are thought to have lain behind the exchange of houses by two Cheap-side grocers in 1531.[95] Because of the complexity of motives which lay behind residential moves no simple relationship between any variable other than wealth, such as occupational calling, could be established.[96]

A few individual careers can, however, be reconstructed to show how residential moves might be linked to changes in indi-vidual circumstances. Thus Roger Cotten, victualler, married his wife Edith in 1594 and set up house in the New Rents. By 1609 he had moved to a High Street dwelling and was assessed at one penny in the 1622 assessment, but in that year he moved from the High Street into Goat Yard. Cotten was not rated in 1631. He twice petitioned the vestry for relief in the early 1630s and eventu-ally died in a parish almshouse in 1636. Edith Cotten, twenty years his senior, died in 1634 and a year before her death had been a recipient of the charity of Henry Smith, when she was described as a 'poor aged woman [receiving] a petticoat and a waistcoat with a badge of HS on the breast of the waistcoat'.[97] Roger Cotten's petitions confirm his financial decline showing:

that your petitioner having been a parishioner these 50 years and upwards and a man of good demeanour in times past and one whose behaviour hath been lawful and honest in his demeans and carriage and one which hath paid scot and lot in the parish all the time of their abode here in the parish. But now so it is . . . that your poor petitioner with his aged wife is grown into years whereby their labours are both past that they cannot take pains whereby to relieve themselves by reason of their decrepit old age but are in election to come to great misery and want.[98]

Michael Mossendue was a £3 subsidy man in 1622 and assessed at 2*d* for the poor-rate. He had arrived in the parish by virtue of a second marriage to a Boroughside widow, Alice Greene, in 1614 and lived on the High Street. Mossendue's troubles may well have begun with the death of Alice in 1623. In 1626 the vestry authori-ties purchased the freehold of his house; 'the dagger', for £110 and at the end of December 1627 Mossendue was bound for £30 to pay £14 arrears of rent. In March 1628 the churchwardens decided to sue him for the rent and by May 1628 Mossendue had given up his main street dwelling and removed to poorer housing in Axe Yard. He was not rated in 1631. By 1635 he had moved into Goat Yard.[99]

Another subsidy payer who ended upon parish relief was one John Mee, described as a tallowchandler at his burial on 3 February 1655. Mee was born in 1583, the son of William Mee, a wealthy vestryman, citizen and tallowchandler. John continued his father's occupancy of a main-street house and in 1622 was rated at 3*d* in the poor-rate and at £4 in the subsidy books. By 1631 however John Mee was not rated for the poor-rate though still living on the High Street. Between 1631 and 1635 he moved into poorer accommodation in Goat Yard and in 1640 was dwelling in the New Rents. In 1638 he became a recipient of the charity of Henry Smith receiving a badged coat.[100]

It is clear, too, that *improvements* in financial position could lead to residential changes. For those householders involved in occupations that required a retailing outlet or a particular site moves may have been an integral part of financial advancement. Hence David Soane, butcher, arrived in the Boroughside in 1613 in Axe Yard. In 1617 he moved to Boarshead Alley and in 1622 moved from there to the High Street butchers' shambles. Between 1622 and 1631 his poor-rate assessment increased from one half penny to one and a half pence. In 1635 Soane was renting a stable in Goat Yard from a local innkeeper.[101]

If we can explain the volume and direction of residential mobility in this area by reference to the heterogeneous housing stock and the functional way in which it was treated by local residents adjusting to changes in their careers and fortunes, we need to say something more about the relatively high levels of persistence found within the area.

The sociological questions raised are too complex to be treated in full here but one that suggests itself is the implication that many householders had relatively restricted social horizons. There is certainly evidence which indicates that the geographical horizons of seventeenth-century Londoners may have been restricted considerably by poor intra-metropolitan communications. The capital's newsbooks did not carry advertisements regularly until the middle of the century and the first advertising sheet, too, dates from 1657. Despite the rapid expansion of advertising in the late seventeenth century information concerning travel within the metropolis remained poor and mostly centred on inns.[102] Access to printed advertisements and newsheets was of course denied to the illiterate. Although London had relatively low rates of illiteracy by 1640 compared to the rest of England, illiteracy rates amongst some of the poorer trades and crafts in the capital remained high. Furthermore no really useful street map of the capital was available before 1676.[103] As late as 1690 a Scottish visitor remarked on the sociological effects of poor intra-metropolitan communications.

The city is a great vast wilderness. Few in it know the fourth part of its streets, far less can they get intelligence of the hundredth part of the special affairs and remarkable passages in it, unless by public printed papers, which come not to every man's notice. The most attend their business, and an inquisitive stranger will know more of the varieties of the city than a hundred inhabitants.[104]

There are more positive reasons to suppose that the overall levels of persistence in the Boroughside demonstrate more positive social forces than what urban sociologists have described as merely 'the heterogeneous nature of the local housing stock and the inefficient flow of information about housing vacancies over long distances'.[105] Most individuals worked as well as lived in this same district. Moving out of a neighbourhood might therefore result in serious financial dislocation. A Southwark tailor complained in 1624 that, following a dispute with his employer, he had been,

enforced to . . . depart from his said house and liberty albeit to his utter undoing in driving your said subject from amongst all his acquaintance and custom of trade into a strange unknown place where he was and yet is lost of all acquaintance and friends, and hath thereby lost all his custom of work to his utter overthrow and decay of his trade and maintenance.[106]

Marriage horizons were relatively restricted; about 80 per cent of all partners chosen by St Saviour's inhabitants were drawn from within the parish boundary.[107] Moreover households were involved in complex locally-based networks of neighbourly and kin-relationships which must have given them significant emotional attachment to the Boroughside neighbourhood.[108] Indeed choice of residential location was affected directly by local kin networks. Of 172 households thought to have been related by blood or marriage to another in the locality thirty-five (20.4 per cent) lived within five dwellings of their relatives, often in fact next door.[109]

In addition to important informal social ties to the area many Boroughside householders were involved closely with the more formal institutions of local government. Something like one in nine adult male householders served in various executive and legislative organs of the local administration in 1622.[110] Membership of the vestry, the prestigious and most important organ of parochial government, required a minimum residence qualification of eight years as well as a wealth qualification.[111] For the poorer household the neighbourhood might prove an important source of poor relief, for which they only qualified if they were permanent residents of the parish. In 1621–2 109 out of 958 households received poor-relief payments from the local overseers of the poor for the Boroughside.[112] Qualification for entry into the local almshouse, the College of the Poor, also required long-term residence in the parish. Those poor who petitioned the ruling vestry for relief not unnaturally therefore tended to emphasize the length of time they had spent in the parish.[113] Involvement in that well-known centre of neighbourhood life, the church, was also far from negligible. The vast majority of householders and their families attended an annual communion service and observed those ecclesiastical ceremonies associated with childbirth and death in the early seventeenth century.[114]

The levels of persistence and volume of short residential moves made within the Boroughside district should be seen in the context of what urban sociologists would describe as an 'urban local social system': a society where social relationships and bonds are centred on a relatively restricted urban district.[115] This is not to claim that the local nature of much social activity meant that the Boroughside was a self-enclosed society. Membership of city companies, family or property ties to outlying rural areas and participation in national and even international trading networks must have made 'extra-local' claims on many inhabitants. It may well be the case, too, that the pattern of social activity and width of social horizons was particularly broad at the top of the social scale but narrowed progressively further down. The social world of the wealthy and literate merchant in contact by letter or in person with distant kin, trading partners and friends was likely to be far wider and more cosmopolitan than that of more humble tradesmen and artisans who lacked the financial resources, time and perhaps literacy, to maintain more distant social connections.[116] Overall, however, in seventeenth-century London as in some large Third World cities today, many people in practice knew and lived in only a limited part of their native city.[117]

Intra-district migration in early modern England

The usual sources available to historians of migration in our period do not normally reveal much about very short moves which individuals made between houses and streets. Apprenticeship bindings or the records of admission to the freedom of towns and cities normally supply only the birthplace of the individual listed. They do not record that individual's total mobility experience.[118] Witnesses in church court cases did not normally, in their depositions before the court, refer to very local moves but only to movements between parishes. Thus studies of the percentage of 'immobile' or 'stationary' deponents are talking usually of witnesses claiming never to have moved from their parish of birth, i.e., never to have moved outside that administrative unit. The larger the geographical size of, and number of local opportunities within, a parish the less the necessity for movement outside its boundaries and hence the greater the apparent immobility as revealed in certain types of historical source material. Since we know in fact that most moves made in the past were over short distances it seems probable that movement within parishes would have occurred.[119] Two exceptionally detailed listings indicate that in rural areas short moves between dwellings were common. In 1782 in the village of Cardington in Bedfordshire seven out of the twelve families who moved in that year remained within the parish boundary.[120] Again in the late eighteenth century a unique series of listings of the poorer householders in the village of Binfield, Berkshire, seems to reveal that over a twenty-year period moving house within the parish was as common as remaining in the same dwelling.[121] There are also scattered references to the existence of such mobility in early modern towns and cities.[122] Such moves are not revealed by the sources normally available to historians of migration in early modern England.

This study has demonstrated that there are good reasons why in studying early modern society one should take account of the extent of local mobility in towns and cities. The amount of such movement, its volume and direction, may be an important measure of the degree of the attachment to neighbourhoods within the towns and cities of early modern England. Such studies would also be valuable indicators of the fluctuations and movements within the life cycle of urban inhabitants. Urban historians have paid a considerable amount of attention to the urban housing stock, describing the functions and appearance of buildings, the amount of living space available to each occupant, and so on.[123] There has been little attention paid, however, to the *length* of time spent in any particular dwelling. Urban dwellers might have experienced a *range* of housing types and qualities.

It might be necessary, therefore, for those interested in housing and domestic interiors in towns and cities to relate house type to life-cycle stage. The individual biographies reconstructed above suggest at least one pattern of urban domestic experience. For the urban inhabitant early married life might have begun in a small one- or two-room tenement located in a back-street alley or on a secondary thoroughfare. For many of those in poorly paid or underemployed occupations this type of housing might be all that they could ever aspire to. Financial improvement, however, could result in residential moves to larger premises. The peak of the urban life cycle and business success might be represented by a move to a relatively large main-street house possessing specialized rooms such as shops and kitchens. Decline with old age or business failure could result in loss of physical living space and a return, perhaps, to the type of housing experienced in early married life. The degree to which such movement took place within urban neighbourhoods was related to the strength of local institutional and social ties, the nature of the local housing stock, available economic opportunities and the efficiency of intra-urban information flows. Obviously, it would be premature to claim a general application for such a model. Individual householders began independent life with very different social and financial advantages and pursued trades and crafts that might require specialized types of housing. Retirement and saving strategies, remarriages, and the high adult mortality rates commonly found in early modern cities would also produce a more complex reality. In neglecting the subject of residential mobility, however, historians miss an important dynamic element within early modern urban society.

Notes and references

1 For the growth of London's population see R. Finlay, *Population and Metropolis: The demography of London 1580–1650* (1981), p. 51; E. A. Wrigley, 'Urban Growth and Agricultural Change: England and the Continent in the Early Modern Period', *Journal of Interdisciplinary History*, **15** (1985), p. 688.

2 Wrigley, 'Urban Growth', pp. 683–95.

3 Wrigley, 'Urban Growth', pp. 689–95; P. J. Corfield, *The Impact of English Towns 1700–1800* (1982), pp. 1–16; P. Corfield, 'Urban development in England and Wales in the sixteenth and seventeenth centuries', in D. C. Coleman and A. H. John (eds), *Trade, Government and Economy in Pre-Industrial England* (1976), pp. 214–47.

4 For mortality in the metropolis see Finlay, *Population and Metropolis*, pp. 83–132; I. Sutherland, 'When was the Great Plague? Mortality in London, 1563 to 1665', in D. V. Glass and R. Revelle (eds), *Population and Social Change* (1972), pp. 287–320; A. Appleby, 'Nutrition and Disease: The case of London 1550–1750', *Journal of Interdisciplinary History*, **6** (1975), pp. 1–22; P. Slack, *The Impact of Plague in Tudor and Stuart England* (1985), pp. 144–72. For a contemporary view see J. Graunt, *Natural and Political Observations made upon the Bills of Mortality* (1662), reprinted in P. Laslett (ed.), *The earliest classics: John Graunt and Gregory King* (1973).

5 See J. M. Landers, 'Some problems in the historical demography of London 1675–1825', (Unpublished PhD thesis, University of Cambridge 1984), especially pp. 29–78, 124–32.

6 For the recent research on migration patterns in provincial England see P. Clark, 'Migration in England during the late seventeenth and early eighteenth centuries', below, pp. 213–52; D. Souden, 'Pre-industrial English local migration fields' (unpublished PhD thesis, University of Cambridge 1981); P. Clark, 'The migrant in Kentish towns 1580–1640', in P. Clark and P. Slack (eds), *Crisis and Order in English Towns 1500–1700* (1972), pp. 117–63; J. Patten, *Rural–Urban Migration in Pre-Industrial England* (University of Oxford School of Geography Research Paper 1973); J. Patten, 'Patterns of migration and movement of labour to three pre-industrial East Anglian towns', above, pp. 77–106; M. Siraut, 'Physical mobility in Elizabethan Cambridge', *Local Population Studies*, **27** (1981), pp. 65–7. For a particularly illuminating and novel source see J. R. Kent, 'Population mobility and alms: poor migrants in the Midlands during the early seventeenth century', *Local Population Studies*, **27** (1981), pp. 35–51.

7 See D. Cressy, 'Occupations, migration and literacy in East London 1580–1640', *Local Population Studies*, **5** (1970), pp. 57–8.

8 Finlay, *Population and Metropolis*, p. 64. For recent work on migration to London see, in particular, V. Brodsky Elliott, 'Mobility and marriage in pre-industrial England', (unpublished PhD thesis, University of Cambridge 1978); S. R. Smith, 'The social and geographical origins of the London apprentices, 1630–1660', *Guildhall Miscellany*, **4** (1973), pp. 195–207; J. Wareing, 'Changes in the geographical distribution of the recruitment of apprentices to the London companies 1486–1750', *Journal of Historical Geography*, **6** (1980), pp. 241–9; J. Wareing, 'Migration to London and transatlantic emigration of indentured servants, 1683–1775', *Journal of Historical Geography*, **7** (1981),

pp. 356–78; G. D. Ramsay, 'The recruitment and fortunes of some London freemen in the mid sixteenth century', *Economic History Review,* 2nd series, **31** (1978), pp. 526–40; D. V. Glass, 'Socio-economic status and occupations in the City of London at the end of the seventeenth century', in P. Clark (ed.), *The Early Modern Town* (1976), pp. 216–32; M. J. Kitch, 'Capital and kingdom: migration in later Stuart London', in A. L. Beier and R. Finlay (eds), *The Making of the Metropolis, London 1500–1700* (1986), pp. 224–51. One of the first authorities to draw attention to the late seventeenth-century contraction of migration fields was Lawrence Stone; see L. Stone, 'Social mobility in England, 1500–1700', *Past and Present,* **33** (1966), pp. 16–55, and especially pp. 31–3. For this contraction in provincial England see also Clark, 'Migration in England', pp. 227–36; Souden, 'Local migration fields', pp. 313–17.

 9 For the role of apprenticeship and age at arrival in early modern London see Elliott, 'Mobility and marriage', pp. 162–221. For the experience of migrant women see also V. Brodsky Elliott, 'Single Women in the London Marriage Market: Age, Status and Mobility, 1598–1619', in R. B. Outhwaite (ed.), *Marriage and Society. Studies in the Social History of Marriage* (1981), pp. 81–100. The median age at arrival of Cressy's church court deponents was 26.9 years, probably reflecting the inclusion of older immigrants. See Cressy, 'Occupations, migration and literacy', p. 57. For apprenticeship and migration to London in the mid sixteenth century see also S. Rappaport, 'Social Structure and Mobility in Sixteenth-Century London: Part I', *London Journal,* **9** (1983), pp. 107–35. For this enduring feature of migration to towns see also Clark, 'Migration in England', pp. 228–9; Souden, 'Local migration fields', p. 104. These latter two authors also suggest that, over the seventeenth century, the proportion of teenage migrants fell. There is, however, as yet little direct evidence for this in London.

10 Elliott, 'Mobility and marriage', pp. 214–15. For slightly lower estimates based on this same source see Finlay, *Population and Metropolis*, p. 67. These figures may well be too high because each of these authors assumed that 85 per cent of apprentices completed their service. In fact, it has been known for some time that rarely more than half of all apprentices bound completed their service. An unknown number of these simply returned home contributing to the outflow of persons from London. See Smith, 'Social and geographical origins', pp. 197–8; Rappaport, 'Social structure and mobility', pp. 116–17. For the sex ratio of London's population in the early seventeenth century, see Elliott, 'Mobility and marriage', pp. 216–20; Finlay, *Population and metropolis*, pp. 140–2. For provincial towns see D. Souden, 'Migrants and the population structure of later seventeenth century provincial cities and market towns', in P. Clark (ed.), *The Transformation of English Provincial Towns* (1984), pp. 158–9.

11 See Elliott, 'Mobility and marriage', pp. 214–16; Finlay, *Population and Metropolis*, pp. 66–7; Wareing, 'Changes in the geographical distribution of apprentices', pp. 247–8; J. R. Kellett, 'The breakdown of gild and corporation control over the handicraft and retail trades in London', *Economic History Review,* second series, **10** (1958), 381–94. For the decline of apprenticeship in provincial cities see Souden, 'Local migration fields', p. 164, n. 29; Clark, 'Migration in England', pp. 216–7, 226. The decline of apprenticeship in

London may have anticipated that of provincial towns and cities. This contro-
versial topic is discussed in K. Snell, *Annals of the Labouring Poor. Social
Change and Agrarian England 1660–1900* (1985), pp. 228–69. For evidence
for a surplus of females in London and elsewhere in the later seventeenth
century see D. V. Glass, 'Notes on the demography of London at the end of
the seventeenth century', in D. V. Glass and R. Revelle (eds), *Population
and Social Change* (1972), pp. 279–82; Finlay, *Population and metropolis*,
pp. 141–2; Souden, 'Migrants and the population structure', pp. 149–58.

12 See the classic exponent of this view, E. A. Wrigley, 'A simple model of
London's importance in changing English Society and Economy 1650–1750',
Past and Present, **37**, (1967), pp. 45–8. For empirical confirmation see E. A.
Wrigley and R. S. Schofield, *The Population History of England 1541–1871*
(1981), pp. 166–70, 219–24.

13 See Wrigley, 'Urban Growth', pp. 685–8.

14 The original method of calculating this figure was devised by Tony Wrigley.
See Wrigley, 'A simple model', pp. 48–50. See also Finlay, *Population and
Metropolis*, pp. 8–9.

15 P. Burke, 'Some reflections on the Pre-industrial City', *Urban History Yearbook* (1975), p. 19.

16 Stone, 'Social mobility in England', p. 31. For similar sentiments see P. Clark
and P. Slack, *English Towns in Transition 1500–1700* (1976), p. 142.

17 Quoted in Finlay, *Population and Metropolis*, p. 77.

18 Finlay, *Population and Metropolis*, p. 77. For a similar view of the stability
of the population of the parish of St Katherine Coleman Street in the late
seventeenth century, see S. M. Macfarlane, 'Studies in poverty and poor relief
in London at the end of the seventeenth century' (unpublished DPhil thesis,
University of Oxford 1982), p. 129. For a wide-ranging and challenging view
of the social stability of inner-city parishes see also V. Pearl, 'Change and
Stability in Seventeenth-Century London', *London Journal*, **5** (1979),
pp. 3–34.

19 For the relative poverty of St Saviour's, Southwark, see J. Boulton, 'The social
and economic structure of early seventeenth century Southwark' (unpublished
PhD thesis, University of Cambridge 1983), pp. 122–3. A revised and
expanded version of this thesis has been published as *Neighbourhood and
Society: a London suburb in the seventeenth century* (1987). For the social
geography of early modern London see Finlay, *Population and Metropolis*,
pp. 77–9; D. V. Glass (ed.), *London inhabitants within the Walls 1695*,
London Record Society, **2** (1966), pp. xxi–xxiv; R. W. Herlan, 'Social articu-
lation and the configuration of parochial poverty in London on the eve of the
Restoration', *Guildhall Studies in London History*, **2** (1976), pp. 43–53.

20 Boulton, 'Early Seventeenth Century Southwark', p. 21.

21 Wrigley, 'Urban Growth', p. 686.

22 Between 1546 and 1630 an aggregative count of the number of baptisms and
burials recorded in the St Saviour's parish register shows that burials exceeded
baptisms by 11,389. Given that the population increased by about 6300 in the
period this implies net immigration of 210 per year. The real discrepancy
between the number of births and deaths would have been smaller, however,
since proportionally more births were omitted from the parish register than
deaths. If baptisms under-registered births by 7 per cent, as they did in some

of the poorer parishes of London at this period, then the size of the natural decrease in St Saviour's would have been 10,008, implying net immigration of 194 per year. For the parish register of St Saviour's see Greater London Record Office (GLRO) P92/SAV/35a, 3001–3004. For the under-registration of births see, Finlay, *Population and Metropolis*, p. 31.

23 Boulton, 'Early Seventeenth-Century Southwark', pp. 36–7. See also note 4 above.

24 Ibid., pp. 58–9.

25 Ibid., p. 21. The population estimates used here incorporate an arbitary 10 per cent addition to allow for a 'floating population' of temporary residents such as lodgers, inmates and guests.

26 For the appointment of these officials see the entries in the St Saviour's vestry minute book, 15 January 1592, 11 August 1601, 17 August 1606, 6 July 1618, GLRO P92/SAV/450. For their reports see P92/SAV/1314, 1315, 1422, 1423. See also H. Raine, 'Christopher Fawcett against the inmates', *Surrey Archaeological Collections,* **61** (1969), pp. 79–85. For routine complaints see, for example, a petition sent to the Lord Mayor, GLRO P92/SAV/1471.

27 For the pre-industrial suburb as a staging post see Clark, 'Migrant in Kentish towns', pp. 141–2; I. Roy and S. Porter, 'The Social and Economic Structure of an Early Modern Suburb: the Tything at Worcester', *Bulletin of the Institute of Historical Research,* **53** (1980), p. 203. For the Boroughside's inns see Boulton, 'Early Seventeenth-Century Southwark', pp. 59–60, 84. Some descriptions and examples are given in J. A. Chartres, 'The Capital's Provincial Eyes: London's Inns in the Early Eighteenth Century', *London Journal,* **3** (1977), pp. 24–39; W. Rendle and P. Norman, *The Inns of Old Southwark* (1888).

28 See Souden, 'Local migration fields', p. 146; Clark, 'Migration in England', p. 232; Smith, 'Social and Geographical Origins', p. 198; Glass, 'Socio-Economic Status and Occupations', pp. 228–30 and note 10 above.

29 Clark and Slack, *English Towns*, p. 142.

30 For the construction of this table and a comprehensive list of the manuscript sources used see Boulton, 'Early Seventeenth-Century Southwark', pp. 60–70. The figures presented here have been revised slightly. For the 1622 token book see GLRO P92/SAV/211.

31 The principal source for constructing the occupational structure of the Clink and Paris Garden was an exceptionally detailed parish clerk's notebook: see GLRO P92/SAV/406. Information on occupations of all adult males buried in St Olave's comes from the parish register: see GLRO P71/OLA/9–11.

32 Boulton, 'Early Seventeenth-Century Southwark', pp. 66–7, 75–80.

33 See J. Ellis, 'A dynamic society: social relations in Newcastle-Upon-Tyne 1660–1760', in P. Clark (ed.), *The Transformation of English Provincial Towns* (1984), pp. 190–227; M. Prior, *Fisher Row. Fishermen, Bargemen, and Canal Boatmen in Oxford, 1500–1900* (1982); Clark and Slack, *English towns*, p. 142.

34 See J. Boulton, 'The limits of Formal Religion: the administration of Holy Communion in late Elizabethan and early Stuart London', *London Journal,* **10** (1984), pp. 135–54. The token books are described in full in Boulton, 'Early Seventeenth-Century Southwark', pp. 362–79.

35 The known positions of large buildings, such as inns and breweries, also

helped to establish the relative positions of households. For this 'standard procedure', see H. Carter, 'The map in urban history', *Urban History Year-book* (1979), pp. 19–20. For methodological problems encountered in studies of nineteenth-century cities see R. Lawton, 'Mobility in nineteenth-century British cities', *Geographical Journal,* **45** (1979), pp. 213–14.

36 Apart from some changes in names there was little topographical difference between the Boroughside of the 1620s and the 1740s. The only differences seem to have been that 3 Crown Court – a soaphouse in 1622 – was depicted as a residential area in 1746 and Castle Alley – a very small place in the early seventeenth century – was not shown at all by Roque. A new inn seems to have been constructed on the High Street between what was Goat Yard and Saints Alley in the later seventeenth century. Map 3 supplies the names of alleys as they were in the 1620s.

37 The exact location on the ground-plan of householders living in the Close and Counter Lane districts was particularly difficult to ascertain with full confidence. Boulton, 'Early Seventeenth-Century Southwark', p. 172.

38 In 1622 35 per cent of all householders in the sample contributed to the poor-rate compared to a figure of 31 per cent for the whole district. Boulton, 'Early Seventeenth Century Southwark', pp. 113, 223.

39 See, for example, the alien families listed in the 1618 token book, GLRO P92/SAV/207. For aliens resident in the Boroughside in 1618 see R. E. G. and E. F. Kirk (eds), *Returns of aliens in the city and suburbs of London from Henry VIII to James I*, Huguenot Society Publications, **10** (1907), vol. 3, pp. 218–19.

40 For this point see S. R. Smith, 'The London Apprentices as Seventeenth-Century Adolescents', *Past and Present,* **61** (1973), pp. 149–61. See also Finlay, *Population and Metropolis*, p. 77; D. V. Glass, 'Notes on the demography of London', pp. 281–2.

41 A 1618 survey of the Boroughside poor listed only householders and their families. Poor-relief accounts record payments only to householders: see GLRO P92/SAV/1465, 1400. For the role of the householder in London see V. Pearl, 'Social Policy in Early Modern London', in V. Pearl, H. Lloyd-Jones and B. Worden (eds), *History and Imagination: essays in honour of H. R. Trevor-Roper* (1981), p. 123; Pearl, 'Change and Stability', pp. 15–18; A. M. Dingle, 'The role of the Householder in Early Stuart London c. 1603–1630', (Unpublished M. Phil thesis, University of London 1974), *passim*.

42 For the patriarchal authority of the household head see, for example, S. R. Smith, 'The ideal and the reality: Apprentice-Master relationships in seventeenth-century London', *History of Education Quarterly,* **21** (Winter 1981), pp. 449–60; R. L. Greaves, *Society and Religion in Elizabethan England* (1981), pp. 291–326.

43 See the 1631 population survey included in the token book of the same year. This total excludes an unrecorded floating population of lodgers, inmates and guests not recorded in the token books (GLRO P92/SAV/219). For studies of household size in pre-industrial towns and cities see N. Goose, 'Household size and structure in early Stuart Cambridge', *Social History,* **5** (1980), pp. 363–4; P. and J. Clark, 'The Social Economy of the Canterbury Suburbs: the evidence of the census of 1563', in A. Detsicas and N. Yates (eds),

Studies in Modern Kentish History (1983), pp. 69–70; R. Wall, 'Regional and temporal variations in English household structure from 1650', in J. Hobcraft and P. Rees (eds), *Regional aspects of British Population Growth* (1979), p. 103; C. Phythian-Adams, *Desolation of a City* (1979), p. 246.

44 Elliott, 'Mobility and marriage', p. 281.

45 Elliott, 'Single women in the London Marriage Market', p. 92.

46 See note 10 above. For evidence of a shortening in the length of apprenticeship in London in the seventeenth century see Snell, *Annals of the Labouring Poor*, p. 239.

47 Following the precedent set by studies of nineteenth-century mobility persist- ence was measured over a ten-year period. See C. Pooley, 'Residential mobility in the Victorian City', *Transactions of the Institute of British Geogra- phers*, new series, **4**, (1979), pp. 259–61; Lawton, 'Mobility in British Cities', p. 221.

48 The following Boroughside token books were used: GLRO P92/SAV/ 198(1608), 199(1609), 200(1610), 201(1612), 203(1614), 205(1616), 207(1618), 208(1619), 211(1622), 213(1624), 215(1626), 217(1628), 219(1631), 221(1632), 223(1633), 224(1634), 227(1635), 229(1637), 233(1640), 234(1641).

49 Pooley, 'Residential mobility', p. 265. If widows remaining in the same dwelling are also counted as persistent, then after ten years 28 per cent of the 1608 sample of householders would still have been occupying the same dwelling.

50 This 1617 tax resembled a subsidy assessment, GLRO P92/SAV/1310.

51 For the burial register of St Saviour's, Southwark, see GLRO P92/SAV/3002, 3003.

52 The persistence of householders by wealth between 1618 and 1608 was as follows: after ten years forty-one out of 228 (18 per cent) of those not taxed in 1617 were still resident in the same dwelling compared to thirty-four out of eighty-five (40 per cent) of those who contributed.

53 See, for example, R. Dennis and S. Daniels, ' "Community" and the social geography of Victorian cities', *Urban History Yearbook* (1981), p. 10; Lawton, 'Mobility in British Cities', p. 220; Pooley, 'Residential mobility', p. 272.

54 GLRO P92/SAV/201.

55 GLRO P92/SAV/406. For the circumstances surrounding its composition see W. Caldin and H. Raine, 'The Plague of 1625 and the story of John Boston, Parish Clerk of St Saviour's, Southwark', *Transactions of the London and Middlesex Archaeological Society*, **23** (1971), pp. 90–9.

56 For a rehearsal of the problems of nominal linkage see E. A. Wrigley, 'Family Reconstitution', in E. A. Wrigley (ed.). *An Introduction to English Historical Demography* (1966), pp. 108–9.

57 The 1622 index was used to build up individual biographies of all householders resident in 1622: Boulton, 'Early Seventeenth-Century Southwark', pp. 4–8. The 1624 index was intended to form the basis of a study of the impact of the 1625 plague epidemic.

58 See, for example, D. Ward, 'Environs and neighbours in the "Two Nations", residential differentiation in mid nineteenth-century Leeds', *Journal of Historical Geography*, **6** (1980), p. 157; Pooley, 'Residential mobility', p. 274; Lawton, 'Mobility in British Cities', p. 220; M. Anderson, *Family Structure*

in Nineteenth-Century Lancashire (1971), pp. 41–2; Dennis and Daniels, ' "Community" and social geography', pp. 9–13.

59 See P. Laslett, 'Clayworth and Cogenhoe', in P. Laslett (ed.), *Family Life and illicit love in earlier generations* (1977), pp. 50–101; W. R. Prest, 'Stability and Change in Old and New England: Clayworth and Dedham', *Journal of Interdisciplinary History*, **6**, (1976), pp. 359–74; K. Wrightson and D. Levine, *Poverty and Piety in an English Village; Terling 1525–1700* (1979), pp. 80–1.

60 Laslett, 'Clayworth and Cogenhoe', p. 99; Finlay, *Population and Metropolis*, p. 46.

61 See Prest, 'Stability and Change', p. 361; Souden, 'Local migration fields', pp. 26, 137; R. S. Schofield, 'Age-specific mobility in an eighteenth-century rural English parish', below, pp. 253–66.

62 Boulton, 'Early Seventeenth-Century Southwark', pp. 247–9.

63 T. F. Reddaway, 'Elizabethan London – Goldsmith's Row in Cheapside, 1558–1645', *Guildhall Miscellany*, **2**, 5(1963), pp. 181–4, 192–206.

64 See, D. Keene, 'A new study of London before the Great Fire', *Urban History Yearbook* (1984), p. 17. See also D. Keene, *Cheapside before the Great Fire*, ESRC booklet (1985), pp. 17–18.

65 Boulton, 'Early Seventeenth-Century Southwark', pp. 215–17.

66 See Public Record Office (PRO), PROB 11/146, PCC Will Register, 88 Clarke; GLRO DW/PA/7/13, Archdeaconry of Surrey Will Register, 172 Harding.

67 PRO PROB 11/195, PCC Will Register, 48 Twisse.

68 See GLRO DW/PA/7/10, Archdeaconry of Surrey Will Register, 291 Peter, 134 Peter.

69 Boulton, 'Early Seventeenth-Century Southwark', pp. 192–3.

70 See, for example, A. Dyer, 'Urban housing: a documentary study of four Midland towns 1500–1700', *Post-Medieval Archaeology*, **15** (1981), p. 217; A. Dyer, *The city of Worcester in the sixteenth century* (1973), pp. 18, 164–5; M. Reed, 'Economic Structure and Change in Seventeenth-Century Ipswich', in P. Clark (ed.), *Country towns in pre-industrial England* (1981), pp. 118–19; N. Alldridge, 'House and household in Restoration Chester', *Urban History Yearbook* (1983), pp. 39–52.

71 For this interpretation of attitudes to housing see R. Garrard, 'English probate inventories and their use in studying the significance of the domestic interior 1570–1700', *A. A. G. Bijdragen* **23** (1980), p. 57. For the social role of the alehouse see P. Clark, *The English Alehouse: A social history 1200–1850* (1983); K. Wrightson, 'Alehouses, Order and Reformation in Rural England 1590–1660', in E. and S. Yeo (eds), *Popular culture and class conflict 1590–1914* (1981), pp. 1–27. For some other arenas of social activity see R. W. Malcomson, *Popular Recreations in English Society 1700–1850* (1979), pp. 5–14; Phythian-Adams, *Desolation of a city*, pp. 166–8.

72 For a tentative attempt to estimate the proportion of leaseholders to tenants-at-will see Boulton, 'Early Seventeenth-Century Southwark', pp. 215–17.

73 In 1632 of the 107 properties held by lease from the Hospital 65 per cent were held on a twenty-one year lease and 79 per cent on leases of between nineteen and twenty-six years. PRO SP/216/114.

74 GLRO P92/SAV/450, vestry minutes, 15 November 1611.

75 D. Lupton, *London and the country carbonadoed* (1632), pp. 112–13.

76 For London, see, for example, Keene, *Cheapside before the Great Fire*, p. 16; M. Power, 'The East and West in Early Modern London', in E. Ives, R. J. Knecht and J. Scarisbrick (eds), *Wealth and Power in Tudor England: essays presented to S. T. Bindoff* (1978), pp. 167–85; Finlay, *Population and Metropolis*, pp. 79–80; Pearl, 'Change and Stability', pp. 7–8. For provincial towns see J. Hindson, 'The Marriage Duty Acts and the social topography of the early modern town: Shrewsbury, 1695–8', *Local Population Studies*, **31** (1983), pp. 21–8; Dyer, *Worcester*, p. 178; D. Hibberd, 'Urban Inequalities. Social Geography and Demography in Seventeenth-Century York' (unpublished PhD thesis, University of Liverpool 1981), pp. 152–5; Phythian-Adams, *Desolation of a city*, p. 166.

77 The streets and alleys depicted in Map 3 were assigned to the sub-districts as follows: High Street (eastside and westside of main street); Close and Pepper Alley (Montague Close, Close and Pepper Alley), Counter Lane (Counter Lane, Foul Lane, Corner Brickhouse and Triangles). All the rest were classified as Alleys and Yards.

78 J. Strype, *A Survey of London* (1720), vol. 2, pp. 10–25.

79 Ibid., pp. 28–9; W. Rendle, *Old Southwark and its People* (1878), p. 227.

80 Information from survey of the poor, 1618 and 1631 token books, GLRO P92/SAV/1465, 219 respectively.

81 See, for example, Power, 'Hearths and Homes', p. 8.

82 Strype, *Survey of London*, vol. 2, p. 29. See also Power, 'East and West in Early Modern London', p. 180.

83 See above, note 76.

84 For the 1635 token book see GLRO P92/SAV/227. For the 1635 and 1637 surveys see GLRO P92/SAV/1336, 1331 respectively.

85 GLRO HI/ST/E105. High Street inns had similarly narrow frontages. For this feature of early modern urban housing see Chartres, 'The Capital's Provincial Eyes', pp. 25–9; Rendle and Norman, *Inns of Old Southwark*, pp. 124–30; M. Power, 'East London housing in the seventeenth century', in P. Clark and P. Slack (eds), *Crisis and Order in English Towns 1500–1700* (1972), pp. 247–9; M. Laithwaite, 'Totnes Houses 1500–1800', in Clark (ed.), *The Transformation of English Provincial Towns* p. 67; M. Laithwaite, 'The buildings of Burford', in A. Everitt (ed.), *Perspectives in English Urban History* (1973), p. 65.

86 Boulton, 'Early Seventeenth-Century Southwark', pp. 74–5.

87 Clark, *English Alehouse*, p. 133.

88 GLRO HI/ST/E105.

89 Information about rent taken from the views of High Street housing in GLRO HI/ST/E105.

90 For a detailed analysis of the residential distribution of occupations see Boulton, 'Early Seventeenth-Century Southwark', pp. 180–6. For London see, for example, W. M. Stern, 'The trade, art or mistery of silk throwers of the City of London in the seventeenth century', *Guildhall Miscellany*, **1**, 6 (1956), p. 27; Reddaway 'Goldsmith's Row', pp. 181–206.

91 Strype, *Survey of London*, vol. 2, p. 29.

92 A 1605 survey listed two wharves in the Close, one of which was leased by Henry Williams, a wealthy woodmonger, still resident in 1622. Strype mentioned that Montague Close had 'a wharf for the loading of corn and

other goods' and the survey of 1635 listed a woodyard. Strype, *Survey of London*, vol. 2, p. 28; GLRO P92/SAV/664 and 1336 respectively.

93 See Pooley, 'Residential mobility', p. 272; Reddaway, 'Goldsmith's Row', p. 186. Francis Place often recorded the motives for his frequent changes of address within a circumscribed area of late eighteenth-century London, see M. Thale (ed.), *The autobiography of Francis Place 1771–1854* (1972), pp. 107–215 *passim*. For a case study of the restricted mobility of one working-class Liverpudlian, see R. Lawton and C. G. Pooley, 'David Brindley's Liverpool: an aspect of urban society in the 1880s', *Transactions of the Historical Society of Lancashire and Cheshire*, **126** (1975), pp. 149–68.

94 Alldridge, 'House and household in Restoration Chester', pp. 39–52, especially pp. 49–51.

95 Keene, 'A new study of London', p. 17.

96 Boulton, 'Early Seventeenth-Century Southwark', pp. 246–7.

97 For the badging of Edith Cotten see Charity Accounts, GLRO P92/SAV/1762. For the Cottens' fortunes see also their petitions to the vestry, GLRO P92/SAV/768, 769. For the 1621–2 and 1631 poor-rate assessments see P92/SAV/1400, 219. For the 1622 subsidy roll see PRO E179/186/407. Information for this and following biographies has also been taken from parish register entries and the sacramental token books. Specific references can be found in Boulton, 'Early Seventeenth-Century Southwark', pp. 257–61.

98 GLRO P92/SAV/768.

99 See the vestry minute book, GLRO P92/SAV/450, 31 December 1627, 3 March 1628.

100 For William Mee's will see PRO PROB 11/117, PCC Will Register, 5 Wood. For the Charity Account see GLRO P92/SAV/1780.

101 See GLRO P92/SAV/1336. Soane's 1622 move can be confirmed from the parish clerk's notebook: see the baptism entries 26 November 1620 and 6 February 1623, GLRO P92/SAV/406.

102 R. B. Walker, 'Advertising in London Newspapers, 1650–1750', *Business History*, **15** (1973), pp. 112–30.

103 See, D. Cressy, *Literacy and the Social Order: Reading and Writing in Tudor and Stuart England* (1980), pp. 72–5, 132–5; I. Darlington and J. Howgego, *Printed Maps of London c. 1553–1850* (1964), pp. 1–25.

104 D. Maclean, 'London in 1689–90 by the Revd R. Kirk', *Transactions of the London and Middlesex Archaeological Society*, new series, **6** (1929–33), p. 333.

105 Dennis and Daniels, ' "Community" and social geography', p. 10.

106 PRO STAC8/125/7. See also Boulton, 'Early Seventeenth-Century Southwark', pp. 276–7.

107 Ibid., pp. 303–8.

108 Ibid., pp. 282–332.

109 Ibid., p. 325.

110 It can be shown that eighty-nine manorial and parish offices were held by 823 male householders in 1622. Female householders were ineligible. See the householders listed in the 1622 token book, GLRO P92/SAV/211 and Boulton, 'Early Seventeenth-Century Southwark', p. 147.

111 For vestry membership qualifications see GLRO P92/SAV/790.

112 See the Overseers' Accounts, GLRO P92/SAV/1400.

113 See the petitions sent into the vestry, GLRO P92/SAV/749–786.

114 Boulton, 'Early Seventeenth-Century Southwark', pp. 333–51; Boulton, 'Limits of formal religion', pp. 135–54.

115 For this sociological concept see M. Stacy, 'The myth of community studies', *British Journal of Sociology,* **20** (1969), pp. 134–47; Dennis and Daniels, ' "Community" and social geography', p. 8; J. Connell, 'Social Networks in Urban Society', in B. D. Clark and M. B. Gleave (eds), *Social Patterns in Cities* (1973), pp. 41–52.

116 For similar sentiments see K. Wrightson, *English Society 1580–1680* (1981), pp. 40–4; R. Houlbrooke, *The English Family 1450–1700* (1984), pp. 39–58. For nineteenth-century cities see A. Sutcliffe, 'In search of the Urban Variable: Britain in the later nineteenth century', in D. Fraser and A. Sutcliffe (eds), *The Pursuit of Urban History* (1983), p. 246.

117 See a description of modern-day Cairo, described as, 'not one community but rather many separate social communities . . . a member of one community may pass daily through the physical site of communities other than his own. But within his own community, there is little, if any anonymity'. In C. Bell and H. Newby, 'The sociology of the inner city: introduction', in C. Bell and H. Newby (eds) *The sociology of community* (1974), p. 147.

118 See, for example, Patten, 'Patterns of migration and movement', pp. 81–2; Ramsay, 'Recruitment and fortunes', pp. 526–9.

119 Thus the fact that parishes in the western counties of England were larger than those of eastern England may partly explain their greater apparent immobility. For a description of these sources and the undercounting of very short moves see Clark, 'Migration in England', pp. 218–19; Souden, 'Local migration fields', pp. 72–3, 96–138; Clark, 'Migration in Kentish towns', pp. 118–21.

120 See Schofield, 'Age-specific mobility', p. 255.

121 See the Binfield listings held at the Cambridge Group for the History of Population and Social Structure. I would like to thank Kevin Schürer for this reference.

122 See, for example, Hibberd, 'Urban inequalities', pp. 398–442; D. Palliser, *Tudor York* (1979), p. 114; Phythian-Adams, *Desolation of a City*, pp. 191–2; M. Reed, 'Economic structure and change in seventeenth-century Ipswich', p. 94; Clark, 'Migrant in Kentish towns', pp. 125–6; Clark, 'Migration in England', p. 220–1. The latter two studies refer to inter-parish movement only.

123 For studies of housing in London see, for example, Power, 'East London housing', pp. 237–62; Power, 'East and West', pp. 167–85; M. Power, 'Shadwell: the development of a London suburban community in the seventeenth century', *London Journal,* **4** (1978), pp. 29–46; Keene, *Cheapside before the Great Fire*; A. F. Kelsall, 'The London House Plan in the later seventeenth century', *Post-Medieval Archaeology,* **8** (1974), pp. 80–91; M. Power, 'The social topography of Restoration London', in A. L. Beier and R. Finlay (eds), *The making of the metropolis* (1986), pp. 199–223; F. E. Brown, 'Continuity and change in the urban house: developments in domestic space organisation in seventeenth-century London', *Comparative Studies in Society and History,* **28**, 3 (1986), pp. 558–90. I would like to thank Tony Wrigley for this latter reference. For provincial housing see P. Corfield and

U. Priestly, 'Rooms and room use', *Post-Medieval Archaeology*, **16** (1982), pp. 93–124; Dyer, 'Urban housing', pp. 207–18; Garrard, 'English Probate Inventories', pp. 55–77; R. Taylor, 'Town houses in Taunton 1500–1700', *Post-Medieval Archaeology,* **8** (1974), pp. 63–79; Laithwaite, 'Buildings of Burford', pp. 60–90; Laithwaite, 'Totnes Houses', pp. 62–98.

5

'Rogues, whores and vagabonds'? Indentured servant emigration to North America and the case of mid seventeenth-century Bristol

David Souden

David Souden examines here the Bristol registers of indentured servants emigrating in the years 1654 to 1662 in order to investigate the origins of those leaving the country. The author indicates the broad social mix of the emigrants from Bristol, although most were in low-status occupations. He also reveals the essentially regional (south-western) topography of movement but with important streams of long-distance movers. The main conclusion is that emigration at this time was an extension of internal migration patterns. It should be noted that the sample is restricted to a short period in a relatively exceptional phase of English emigration, while more might have been said in the piece about the organization of the trade and colonial demand.

'Virginia and Barbados were first peopled', wrote Sir Josiah Child in 1694,

by a sort of loose vagrant people, vicious and destitute of means to live at home (being either unfit for labour, or such as could find none to employ themselves about, or had so misbehaved themselves by whoreing, thieving or other debauchery, that none would set them to work) which merchants and masters of ships by their agents (or spirits as they were called) gathered up about the streets of London and other places, clothed and transported them to be employed upon plantations. . . .[1]

Young men and women left the British Isles in their hundreds of thousands for the colonies of mainland North America and the West Indies during the seventeenth century. A majority of these emigrants were bound under indenture to work in the colonies

150

for a term of years, in return for their passage, keep, and a payment upon gaining their freedom. Providing labour principally for the plantation colonies, especially before the widespread introduction of negro chattel slavery, these 'indentured servants' were obviously crucial to the development of the nascent colonies of the New World.[2] Demand for labour was kept high by the expansion of production in the cash-crop staples – sugar in the West Indies, and tobacco in the Chesapeake – and by the prevailing high levels of mortality.[3] Contemporary writers, and particularly those engaged in arguments against colonial development and the consequent drain upon domestic resources of capital and labour, had little favourable to say about those who emigrated as indentured servants.[4]

In the absence of much other documentation, these commentators have provided us with the conventional view of these seventeenth-century emigrants. According to the received stereotype, indentured servants were commonly unemployed labourers, coming particularly from the criminal and vagrant classes, and many were so young as to have been easy victims of the unscrupulous recruiting agents who operated the trade. 'There were rogues, whores, vagabonds, cheats, and rabble of all descriptions, raked from the gutter and kicked out of the country. . . . People of every age and kind were decoyed, seduced, inveigled, or forcibly kidnapped and carried as servants to the plantations.'[5]

Despite increasing interest in recent years in the levels of physical mobility within early modern England, and massive interest in the history of negro slavery in the New World, little attention has been paid to these emigrants. It is the aim of this paper to re-examine indentured servants. Physical mobility, and the institution of labour service for men and women before full maturity and marriage, were embedded in the lifestyle of pre-industrial England.[6] In this light, indentured servants may not have been as atypical as has long been thought, and certain characteristics may well be representative of a wider population.

There are, however, few surviving sources for the direct study of indentured servant emigration in the seventeenth century. Various sets of indentures for London over the period 1682 to 1692, lists of servants leaving Liverpool, and a collection of miscellaneous lists concentrated in the 1630s, do remain.[7] The most important extant record, and that which is employed in this study, is the two-volume register of 'Servants to foreign plantations' for the port of Bristol, covering the years 1654–79.[8] This records the names of over 10,000 men and women who emigrated under indenture; the register contains very full information on individuals in the early years of the registration procedure, where this study is concentrated.

Registration in Bristol was instituted at Michaelmas 1654, by an ordinance of the city's Common Council, in an attempt to prevent the 'Inveigling, purloining, carrying and Stealing away Boys Maides and other persons and transporting them Beyond Seas', a measure which followed a similar Parliamentary ordinance for London of May 1645.[9] The establishment of the procedure was part of the general return to civic normality that took place in Bristol during 1654, following the disruption of the Civil War years.[10] Until 1658, detail on servants entered in the register is particularly full: the most complete entries record the date, the servant's name, place of origin, and occupation, his or her·destination, term of years to serve, and the freedom due to be paid, along with the name, place of residence and occupation of the person to whom the servant was indentured. After 1658 there is a rapid deterioration in the amount of detail recorded; from mid 1661 only basic information of date, name, term and master tends to be given, with the name of the ship upon which the servant was to sail.

The monthly totals emigrating over the period covered by this paper are set out graphically in Figure 15, with an eleven-month moving mean to show the underlying trend. A total of 5138 indentures are recorded for the years 1654–62, the larger period studied here; analysis will largely be confined to the period ending in 1660, comprising 3568 indentures, since details entered may then be more intensively utilized.[11] Despite a considerable amount of detail and personal information being entered in the register, the data should not be taken simply at their face value, although they seem to exhibit no obvious systematic bias for the most part, particularly since Bristol and London were the main points of departure for the colonies. Servants may not have given truthful answers about their occupation, home parish, or even their name; however, the enormous variety of information, and occasionally very specific detail, which is given, would appear to deny this possibility on a significant scale. Since the registration procedure was instituted to prevent 'spiriting', those who were kidnapped would doubtless not have been recorded. Some servants do appear

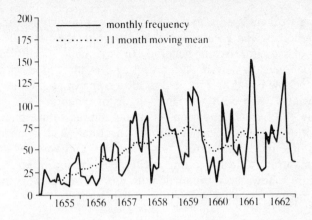

Figure 15 Numbers of indentured servants emigrating
via Bristol, 1654–62

to have been smuggled out under the noses of the civic authorities, although a vigilant eye was kept at times, as witnessed by the occasional counter-signature of the water-bailiff against entries in the register. Those found spiriting servants out were brought to trial, and the penalties involved were relatively severe.[12] The likelihood of kidnapping taking place, and thus the removal of emigrants from observation, is reduced by one finding of this study, that the major brokers in servants – those who were supposed to have been the kidnappers – were considerably less important in the emigration process than we have long imagined. More servants may have been taken on board after ships left Bristol, especially in Ireland, but that possibility is outside the scope of this article.[13]

The information which we lack on all servants is age: no indication is given, except where a servant is recorded as being a son or daughter. It is possible, however, to infer the approximate ages of the servants from the registration of the length of indenture. Most colonies enacted legislation during the seventeenth century, which generally embodied custom, tying the length of service for those arriving without indenture to their age.[14] The bulk of these Bristol indentures were for four years, suggesting that most servants were in the age group 18–22. Younger children would have had longer indentures, while those with skills appropriate to colonial agriculture and industry – coopers, metal-workers, building workers – were more likely to have got a shorter indenture, reflecting the greater value placed upon their labour. The length of indenture seems generally to have been socially rather than economically determined, reflecting prevailing ideas of when young people could be expected to have come of age. Other lists of servants, when both ages and lengths of indenture are given, do show this basic relationship.[15] Females amongst the emigrants, accounting for some 25 per cent of the total, had a narrower spread of length of indenture, suggesting that they were relatively more mature: Table 16, setting out the distribution of lengths of indenture, shows how proportionally more women were indentured for four or five years than for other terms.

Table 16 Distribution of servants' indenture terms

Length of indenture (years)	Emigrants for indenture term		Sex ratio*
	Number	Per cent	
2	1	0·0	—
3	419	11·8	1,008·3
4	2,165	60·9	234·1
5	405	11·5	216·4
6	202	5·7	417·9
7	269	7·6	767·7
8	40	1·1	900·0
9	29	0·8	1,350·0
▷10	23	0·6	226·6
Total	3,554	100·0	288·4

* The sex ratio is defined as the number of males per 100 females.

Of the total registrations to 1660, 64.5 per cent included occupational information. Not surprisingly, a large proportion were engaged in agriculture (as yeomen and husbandmen) or were described as labourers. Those registered as yeomen account for a massive 35.1 per cent of all indentures over the period 1654–60 where an occupation is registered, whilst those registred as labourers account for 10.4 per cent. These figures are in direct contradiction to the received view of the composition of the indentured servant groups, as Professor Campbell also set out in her seminal article of 1959. From this stemmed her contention that the 'middling sort' amongst indentured servants were of paramount important in the stream of emigrants to, and in the building of, early America.[16] This conclusion, however, ignores the fact of increasingly deficient registration of occupational details over the first eight years of the registration system. Until 1657, when almost all emigrants had their occupation entered, labourers consistently outnumbered yeomen 2.5:1. After that date, when registration of occupational detail was increasingly incomplete, registration of 'labourer' dwindled to an insignificant level, while specific entries for yeomen remained high. On this basis, we are unable to attach too much significance to the numbers of yeomen *vis à vis* labourers, and are thus unable to concur with Mildred Campbell's revisionist view that 'the majority of "the others" [indentured servants] who found shipping in the trading vessels that regularly plied the western waters were England's middling people – the most valuable cargo that any captain carried on his west-bound voyage'.[17]

Table 17 provides an analysis of the occupational structure of the emigrant population, within broad categories. For the men in the group, ninety-six occupations are recorded. Most were in low-status occupations, such as artisans, labourers, clothworkers or tailors, whilst few were in professional occupations. Given their age, even those emigrants in higher-status groups would undoubtedly not have attained full status.[18] Relatively little information is recorded for the women: most are entered as 'spinster', some as 'singlewoman', and a few as 'wife' or 'widow'.

Table 17 Occupational structure of indentured servants, 1654–60

Occupational group	Number	Per cent	Occupational group	Number	Per cent
Yeoman	803	35·1	Clothing industry	110	4·8
Husbandman	44	1·9	Leather industry	75	3·3
Gardener, etc.	5	0·2	Milling	5	0·2
Labouring	238	10·4	Woodworking	24	1·0
Stoneworking	3	0·1	Metalworking	57	2·5
Building trades	78	3·4	Professional	12	0·5
Dealing and service	38	1·7	Gentlemen and planters	33	1·4
Transportation	29	1·3	Miscellaneous	18	0·7
Textile industry	104	4·5	Women	611	26·7
			Total	2,287	99·7*

*Due to rounding

It is possible to hypothesize that, rather than all eventual emigrants coming to Bristol with the express intention of leaving for the colonies, a significant proportion of those emigrants who were not natives of Bristol were a subset of the general influx of people into the city. Bristol's population more than doubled during the sixteenth and seventeenth centuries, probably from just under 10,000 in the 1520s to some 20,000 in 1700.[19] With prevailing levels of urban mortality, that increase may be almost wholly ascribed to net immigration.

While emphasizing the essentially local nature of most geographical movement within early modern England, general studies of internal migration have also stressed the overlaid pattern of longer range movement into and between towns, particularly to the great magnet of London.[20] John Patten has recently suggested the size of urban migration fields to be a function of urban size, the large towns and cities drawing significant numbers from considerable distances.[21] The source which has been most intensively used to study immigration to early modern towns has been registrations of apprentices. In order to provide some comparison with the mobility patterns of indentured servants presented here, information on the origins and migration patterns of Bristol apprentices is included in this analysis.[22]

Large numbers did indeed come to Bristol from outside, both to stay and to sail for North America, at the middle of the seventeenth century. For those servants emigrating during 1654–60, the county (or country) of origin is given in 70.0 per cent of cases, and the actual place of origin in 68.9 per cent. These places have been positively identified for 60.9 per cent of all cases. The distance from Bristol of all identified places of origin has been measured within broad concentric zones centred upon the city. Studies to date of early modern urban migration fields have found that immigrants came almost exclusively from within a radius of 20 miles, and certainly from within 40 miles.[23] Although Bristol apprentices of the 1650s generally fit this pattern, indentured servants often came from greater distances. Of those servants coming from within England and Wales, 38.5 per cent came from outside a 40 mile radius of Bristol, compared with only 14.6 per cent of apprentices. Tables 18 and 19 present the data on places of origin, in terms of distances from Bristol, and of geographical areas. Map 4 plots the places from which indentured servants had come.

The areas around Bristol, as may be expected, provided large numbers of emigrants, as did South Wales and the border counties along the Severn valley. For apprentices, movement into Bristol

Table 18   Distances travelled to Bristol by indentured servants and by apprentices

Distance (miles)	Indentured servants within distance			Apprentices within distance		
	Number	Per cent	Cumulative per cent	Number	Per cent	Cumulative per cent
<10 miles	412	19·0	19·0	494	54·5	54·5
10–20 miles	354	16·3	35·3	148	16·3	70·8
20–40 miles	570	26·2	61·5	132	14·6	85·4
40–60 miles	354	16·3	77·8	67	7·4	92·8
60–80 miles	132	6·1	83·9	23	2·5	95·3
80–100 miles	142	6·5	90·4	18	2·0	97·3
100–150 miles	171	7·9	98·3	22	2·4	99·7
150–200 miles	30	1·4	99·7	2	0·2	99·9
>200 miles	8	0·3	100·0	0	0·0	99·9*
Total	2,173	100·0	—	906	99·9*	—

* Due to rounding

was of a much shorter range, and even in counties adjacent to Bristol, most apprentices came from places near the city. Relatively large numbers of those who emigrated moved to Bristol from London, some considerable distance; few in either group, however, came from the south-western peninsula and from the southern coastal counties, possibly reflecting a degree of commercial isolation from Bristol. The linear clustering of many of the mapped places of origin is accounted for by the fact that most places from which emigrants stemmed lay along or near the main roads. Information was most easily disseminated along the roads, particularly as a result of commercial traffic and movement to market. The clustering of many places in coastal counties further from Bristol suggests that many may have reached the city by sea.[24] The decision to move cannot have been random: greater information and traffic along major routes helped form the streams and counter-streams in which most migratory movements took place.[25] Comparison of both sets of seventeenth-century data with apprentice registrations for the city of a century earlier shows the general constancy of the Bristol migration field, and the degree to which migration streams and paths tended to perpetutate themselves over time.[26]

Table 19 Geographical origins of indentured servants and of apprentices

Area	Indentured servants		Apprentices	
	Number	Percentage of total	Number	Percentage of total
Bristol	272	10·9	330	33·6
Somerset	395	15·9	158	16·1
Gloucestershire	287	11·5	201	20·5
Wiltshire	225	9·0	57	5·8
Monmouthshire	241	9·7	56	5·7
South Wales[a]	225	9·0	52	5·3
Border counties[b]	283	11·4	54	5·5
Southern England[c]	74	3·0	18	1·8
South-west England[d]	87	3·5	9	0·9
London and Home Counties[e]	135	5·4	15	1·5
East Anglia[f]	18	0·7	0	0·0
Southern Midlands[g]	32	1·3	2	0·2
Northern Midlands[h]	26	1·0	4	0·4
Northern England[i]	45	1·8	5	0·5
Mid and north Wales[j]	106	4·3	12	1·2
Ireland	36	1·4	7	0·7
Elsewhere[k]	5	0·2	1	0·1
Total	2,492	100·0	981	99·7*

[a] Glamorgan, Carmarthenshire, Pembrokeshire.
[b] Herefordshire, Shropshire, Worcestershire.
[c] Dorset, Hampshire, Sussex.
[d] Cornwall, Devon.
[e] London, Middlesex, Buckinghamshire, Berkshire, Essex, Hertfordshire, Kent, Surrey.
[f] Cambridgeshire, Huntingdonshire, Norfolk, Suffolk.
[g] Bedfordshire, Leicestershire, Northamptonshire, Nottinghamshire, Oxfordshire.
[h] Derbyshire, Staffordshire, Warwickshire.
[i] Cheshire, Cumberland, Lancashire, Lincolnshire, Northumberland, Yorkshire.
[j] Breconshire, Cardiganshire, Caernarvonshire, Denbighshire, Flintshire, Montgomeryshire.
[k] Scotland, France, Jersey.
* Due to rounding.

Behind such an analysis of the spatial distribution of the places from which emigrants had come, and the illustrations of 'distance-decay' familiar from many studies, lies the character of the communities from which indentured servants stemmed.[27] Scholars in recent years have drawn attention to the pastoral farming communities of the extensive woodland areas, concentrated in the north and west of England, which were generally less rigidly

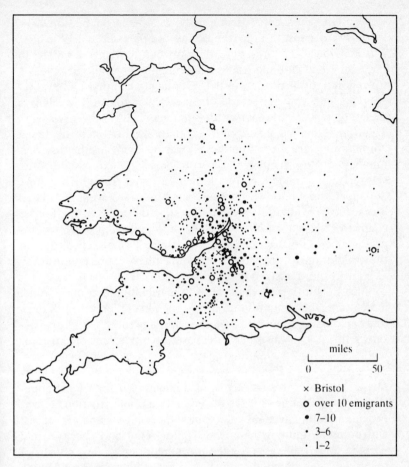

Map 4   Places of origin of indentured servants, 1654–60

controlled and more diverse than settlements in arable 'champion country'. The pastoral regions contained large, and growing, numbers of people, often engaged in rural by-employments – forestry, textile production, dairying.[28] Many emigrants came from woodland areas within western England – from such forests as Dean, Wentwood, and particularly Selwood. The forest–pasture areas were noted for the mobility of their populations: not only were large numbers attracted into these marginal areas, but large numbers also moved out.[29] Settlements within the pastoral regions were often poor, and susceptible to economic depression. The cloth-working towns along the border of Somerset and Wiltshire, and in Gloucestershire, were the previous residence of many in the textile and clothing trades who emigrated; Frome Selwood, a town noted for its poverty in the seventeenth century, had twenty-six men and women recorded in the Bristol register. Wells was the only place in Somerset to send more, with twenty-seven; Taunton provided twenty-three; Bath twenty-one; all being considerably larger communities. It was by no means the case that numbers from particular places were purely an expression of the size of their population, or of their distance from Bristol: mid Somerset, mid and west Gloucestershire were well populated areas, but provided fewer emigrants than did areas in the border counties of Herefordshire and Shropshire, or the pasture regions of Somerset, Gloucestershire and Wiltshire.[30] In direct contrast to the emigration records, these areas are rarely represented in the apprenticeship registrations for the city.

Since indentured servants were primarily intended for colonial agriculture, the assumption that has been made hitherto has been that servants' origins were almost exclusively rural.[31] This analysis shows this not to have been the case: 56.6 per cent of those for whom we have an identified place of origin came from towns.[32] For early modern England, towns were key elements in the long-range migration process, acting as a magnet for their local populations and as centres for the dissemination of information. Towns provided readily available accommodation in inns and alehouses, and potential employment, whilst poor relief and charity could provide in certain cases for the incoming poor.[33] The suburbs of towns and their neighbouring villages proved havens for incoming men and women: Salisbury, for example, provided forty-one emigrant indentured servants, its satellite parishes of Fisherton, Fisherton Anger and Harnham provided eleven. Of those coming from towns, a higher proportion were from crafts and trades, although there were also numbers of indentured servants registered as yeomen, husbandmen and labourers, emphasizing the fact that 'town' and 'country' were by no means mutually exclusive categories.[34]

A higher proportion of women came from towns, the sex ratio for the towns of 248.9 comparing with one of 291.7 for all indentured servants with an identified place of origin.[35] Indeed, the migratory pattern of women differed from that of the men, since women who emigrated came mostly from the counties nearest Bristol and along the Severn valley, whilst few came from distances greater than these. The sex ratio for Bristol was 123.3, for Somerset 277.4, for Herefordshire 217.8, Shropshire 261.1, and for Worcestershire, 266.7; curiously, the Gloucestershire sex ratio was above the mean, at 322.1, and more in line with Welsh experience than with its neighbouring English counties. High sex ratios for southern and south-western counties probably reflect the fact that many would have reached Bristol by sea from those counties, which would have led to fewer women coming from these areas. Ravenstein, in his classic work on the 'laws of migration', claimed that women would predominate amongst short-journey migrants.[36] This was not the case for indentured servants, although we have to recognize that the workings of the system of recruitment may well conceal the proportion of women entering Bristol in the general flow of migrants.[37]

A particular spatial pattern has therefore been arrived at for the immigration to Bristol of those who were then indentured as servants for the colonies. Significant numbers came from marginal forest areas and from towns. The number of servants on the whole decreased with distance, but the pattern is not smooth: peaks within the 20–40 mile band may be accounted for by the concentration of forest areas within that area, whilst the peak in the 100–150 mile range is readily explicable by the presence of London. Figure 16 graphs the comparative numbers of those who emigrated as indentured servants and those who came to Bristol

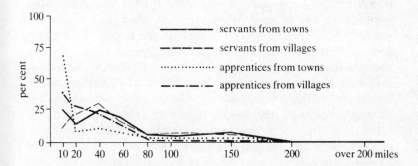

Figure 16 Distance migration 'profiles' of indentured servants and apprentices, 1654–60

as apprentices, in terms of the numbers coming from towns and from villages within each distance band.

Particular areas, especially those with extensive commercial contacts with Bristol, despatched migrants to the city. The pattern of servant migration to Bristol is not wholly reflected in the figures derived from apprenticeship registrations, which have been used in a number of studies as an indicator of immigration to early modern towns. The apprenticeship data show a smaller catchment area, and that few came from the marginal forest–pasture areas. Large numbers of apprentices came from towns, and from craft and trade backgrounds. Although the evidence is limited, and is problematic in that it stems from a procedure recording trans-Atlantic migration, comparison of the indentured servants data with other studies suggests that the pattern of movement of these emigrants may well be indicative of the general patterns of lower-status mobility within southern England and Wales. The occupational and migratory profiles of servants fall between those generally found for apprentices and for vagrants.[38] Apprentice migration may be unrepresentative of general patterns because of age-, sex-, and status-bias: indentured servants indeed appear to have been substantially a subset of the general influx into Bristol.

The trend in the further movement, out of Bristol (as in Figure 15), is characterized by an annual cycle with an autumn–winter peak, overlaid by a rising secular trend peaking in 1659 and in 1661–2. The annual movement reflects particularly sailings to the colonies, and the seasonal rhythm of the tobacco trade: ships bound for the Chesapeake would leave Bristol during the latter part of the year to reach North America when the tobacco was ready to be shipped out. The dangers to the health of the newly arrived were also lessened by arriving during those months, avoiding the malarial 'seasoning' diseases.[39] The longer-term trend may well, at least in part, reflect the incidence of harvest failure and dearth in these years, and the effect that would have had in driving many onto the roads, especially those from marginal areas.[40] The numbers are an artefact of the actual emigration process, in which the key elements were the level of colonial demand for labour, and the instruments through which that demand operated, namely those persons to whom servants were indentured, and who rapidly responded to shifts in colonial prices and labour demand. Masters would not have recruited servants if there were no sales likely in the colonies, particularly when prices were low and planters were threatened by the spectre of over-production.[41] Trading arrangements helped determine the trade in servants, since in numerous cases planters seem to have had arrangements for procuring indentured servants, along with other goods, shipped to them by Bristol merchants.[42]

Table 20 Number of servants per master, 1654–60

No. of servants per master	No. of masters	Per cent of masters	No. of servants	Per cent of servants
≥ 20	13	1·3	503	14·2
10–19	55	5·4	731	20·6
9	18	1·8	162	4·6
8	11	1.1	88	2.5
7	25	2·4	175	4·9
6	31	3.0	186	5.2
5	52	5·1	260	7·3
4	70	6·8	280	7·9
3	112	11·0	336	9·5
2	187	18·3	374	10·6
1	448	43·8	448	12·6
Total	1,022	100·0	3,543	99·9*

* Due to rounding.

For the period 1654–60, 945 men and seventy-seven women had servants indentured in their name, a mean 3.49 servants per person. The traditional bogeymen of the servant trade have always been considered to have been the large-scale operators, those who took across large numbers of servants, either under indenture or by kidnapping the unsuspecting and smuggling them out of the ports.[43] However, the majority of masters had only one or two servants indentured to them in the years studied, and the bulk of servants went to those masters who had no more than seven or eight under indenture. Even though a third of the servants went across the Atlantic under the aegis of those who were larger-scale operators in the trade, the majority were emphatically not the victims of the grasping few who appear in the mythology surrounding the subject. The whole Bristol trading community appears to have been involved in the trade of sending servants to the colonies.[44] Only a handful – Henry Banks, a merchant who sent across 108 servants, John Morgan, an upholsterer with seventy-six and Gabriel Blike, another merchant, with fifty-three – approach the traditional stereotype. Blike himself is a particularly

interesting case: a gentleman's son from Hereford, he was apprenticed in May 1653 to Walter Tocknell, a Bristol merchant (who
was himself to indenture two servants); Blike was taking servants
across by late 1654. We would anticipate that Tocknell financed
the transportation of the servants, whilst Blike went with the
ship to guard his master's interests – a practice common amongst
mercantile apprentices. Although adhering to the registration
system, Blike was not above illicit dealings, since depositions were
made before the Mayor in 1656 alleging that he was trading
illegally in indigo.[45] Many of those to whom servants were indentured may have been relatively young, on the basis of information
on ages in depositions, and of dates of admission to the freedom
of the city and of the Company of Merchant Venturers.[46]

The larger-scale operators were the least discriminating in hiring
those they were to send to the colonies. Personal or business
arrangements often appear to have determined the indenturing of
servants. Wood and metal craftsmen were at a premium, and this
is reflected in the often more advantageous terms they received.[47]
Mariners, particularly on Virginia voyages, would often take one
or two servants, in order to make a quick profit on the side on
their own account. Merchants were more often connected with
Barbados, since trade with the West Indies had to be more organized, given the more capital-intensive nature of sugar production
and trade. Some Bristol merchants appear to have sent across
their own apprentices under indenture; Richard Crabb, a weaver
and clothier from Bristol, apprenticed one of his sons to himself
in 1656, having indentured another son to himself the previous
year, to serve in Barbados.[48] An example of the means of recruitment is to be found in the case of a Barbados merchant, Peter
Coker, who promised Bridget Robinson, a Bristol widow, that he
would take her son John back with him and 'did promise to prefer
him to be clerk in his storehouse there which he then would be
worth £50', adding that if John did not like it there, he would be
brought back.[49] There is, however, no record of Robinson going,
or Coker indenturing anyone else in his own name. Trade links
with particular colonies appear to have determined much of the
pattern of the despatch of servants: soap-boilers, for example,
were exclusively involved with Virginia, and it is most likely that
they sent servants over in return for the supplies of potash they
received from the colony.

Despite emphasis upon the level of kidnapping, a general

assumption that has often been made about indentured servants is that they chose the colony to which they were to go.[50] This is questionable in the light of this analysis. Figure 17 shows the pattern of emigration to the three main colonies, Barbados, Virginia and Nevis: the despatch of servants to Barbados on a significant scale ended after 1660, and had been declining before that date. Servants after 1660 went to other islands, and many more went to the mainland colonies. This change has generally been attributed to servants' reluctance to go to the harsh disease and work environment of Barbados, where the prospects of social advancement were almost nil. The change was so swift that it may only reasonably be interpreted in terms of a switch of Barbadian preferences for labour, to negro chattel slavery. Henry Banks, for example, had until 1660 sent servants almost exclusively to Barbados; thereafter, his hirings went to Nevis. Servants who wished to leave Bristol out of the main autumn-winter 'season' for sailings would have had little option other than to go to Barbados. Those who were indentured for business reasons would have had to go where they were sent.

It has often been contended that labourers, and the dregs of the servant group, were sent to Barbados, since that island had a greater expendability of labour, whilst good servants and the

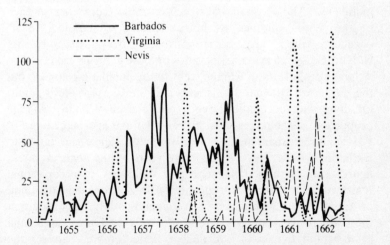

Figure 17 Numbers of indentured servants emigrating
via Bristol to the major colonies, 1654–62

Table 21 Numbers of indentured servants bound for each colony, 1654–62

Destination	Number of males	Numer of females	Number of persons for each colony	Per cent	Sex ratio
West Indies					
Barbados	1,917	603	2,520	49·1	317·9
Nevis	473	123	596	11·6	384·6
St Christophers	33	15	48	0·9	220·0
Other islands*	23	7	30	0·6	328·6
Subtotal	2,446	948	3,194	62·2	327·0
Mainland					
Virginia	1,391	507	1,898	37·0	274·4
Maryland	8	3	11	0·2	266·7
New England	24	6	30	0·6	400·0
Subtotal	1,423	516	1,939	37·8	275·8
Total	3,869	1,264	5,133	100·0	306·1

* Jamaica, Antigua, Montserrat.

majority of women were sent to the healthier environment of the mainland.[51] The occupational structure of those destined for each of the major colonies is, however, most remarkable in its constancy, with no great deviation from the overall structure, and with little difference in the sex ratios of those going to each colony. A larger proportion of women went to the mainland colonies, but the difference between the islands and the Chesapeake is slight. Of those with occupations registered, a slightly below average proportion of labourers, and higher than average percentage of yeomen and husbandmen went to Barbados. (Since emigration to Barbados was greatest in the early years of the register, these figures may be biased by increasing deficiency of occupational registrations.) A greater proportion of those from industries and professions were indentured for Virginia, possibly suggesting that the Chesapeake was considered more as a settlement area than as an exploitative one. Nevertheless, the differences between the colonies were not as great as we have been often led to believe.[52]

Despite the opprobrium of commentators of the period, and of later historians, indentured servants appear from the evidence studied here to have presented a more mundane face to the world. Rather than being a solid body of the rascally indigent, certain distinct groups are visible within the servant population: those who went to the colonies on behalf of the Bristol mercantile community, to safeguard commercial interests in the colonies and to claim land under the headright system, whereby land was given on the mainland to those bringing in servants;[53] those who were offered advantageous terms in the colonial plantations in return for their superior skills; and the many who moved to Bristol within the general migrant streams, possibly without the intention of crossing the Atlantic, but who were persuaded by the lack of opportunity in the city to move to the New World. Patterns of mobility obtained from the register of indentures, appearing as they do to represent general lower-status movement to Bristol, would seem to indicate the degree to which indentured servants were indeed part of the general system of migration.

The myth of the static, rural past has long been discounted, and considerable attention is now paid within the context of social and demographic history to migrants and mobility. Seventeenth-century men often seem to have regarded the migrant as deviant, fearing as they did the effects of dislocation, regarding the mobile as a threat to stability and movement as an explicit indication of roguery.[54] These prejudices have left us with a stereotype that still prevails. Data from Bristol for the 1650s and 1660s cannot of course be wholly representative of an institution which lasted well into the eighteenth century, and which may be expected to have undergone many changes consequent upon changes in migration and employment prospects within Britain, and with the growth of negro slavery in the plantations. Nevertheless, the Bristol emigration registers provide us with one of the few detailed insights into the operation of indentured servitude. The young emigrants represented here were fundamentally part of the general degree of extra-local mobility within pre-industrial England: they were not the rogues, the whores and the vagabonds that the prevailing mythology might still lead us to believe.

Acknowledgements

For their advice and criticism, I would like to thank particularly Lois Green Carr, Jim and Sheila Cooper, James Horn, Brian Outhwaite, Betty Wood, and the editors of *Social History*.

Notes and references

1 J. Child, *A New Discourse of Trade* (1694), 183.

2 The classic work on indentured servitude is A. E. Smith, *Colonists in Bondage: white servitude and convict labor in early America, 1607–1776* (Chapel Hill, N. Ca., 1946). For guides to an expanding literature, see R. R. Menard, 'Immigration to the Chesapeake colonies in the seventeenth century: a review essay', *Maryland Historical Magazine,* **LXVIII**, 3 (Fall, 1973), 323–32; J. P. P. Horn, 'Emigration to the Chesapeake in the seventeenth century', in T. W. Tate and D. W. Ammerman (eds), *The Chesapeake in the Seventeenth Century* (Chapel Hill, N. Ca.).

3 R. S. Dunn, *Sugar and Slaves: the rise of the planter class in the English West Indies, 1624–1713* (1973); D. B. and A. H. Rutman, 'Of agues and fevers: malaria in the early Chesapeake', *William and Mary Quarterly*, 3rd series, **XXXIII**, 1 (January 1976), pp. 31–60; L. S. Walsh and R. R. Menard, 'Death in the Chesapeake: two life tables for men in early colonial Maryland', *Maryland Historical Magazine,* **LXIX**, 2 (Summer 1974), pp. 211–27.

4 M. Campbell, ' "Of people either too few or too many": the conflict of opinion on population and its relation to emigration', in W. A. Aitken and B. D. Hening (eds), *Conflict in Stuart England* (1960), pp. 171–201; Smith, *Colonists in Bondage*, for example pp. 56–60, 69–77. Both cite extensively the large contemporary literature.

5 Smith, *Colonists in Bondage*, p. 5 and *passim*; W. F. Craven, *White, Red and Black: the seventeenth-century Virginian* (Charlottesville, Va. 1971), p. 5.

6 See P. Laslett, *The World We Have Lost* (2nd edn. 1972), for example, pp. 1–19, 66–70; A. Macfarlane, *The Family Life of Ralph Josselin* (Cambridge, 1970), esp. pp. 205–10.

7 C. D. P. Nicholson (ed.), 'Some early emigrants to America', *Genealogists' Magazine,* **XII** (1955–8) and **XIII** (1959–62), *passim*; J. Wareing (ed.), 'Some early emigrants to America, 1683–1684. A supplementary list', ibid., **XVIII**, 5 (March 1976), pp. 239–46; M. Ghirelli (ed.), *A List of Emigrants from England to America, 1682–1692* (Baltimore, Md., 1968): E. French (ed.), 'List of emigrants to America, 1697–1707', *New England Historical and Genealogical Register,* **LXIV** (1910) and **LXV** (1911), *passim*; J. C. Hotten (ed.), *Original Lists of . . . Emigrants . . . Who Went from Great Britain to the American Plantations AD 1600–1700* (1874).

8 Bristol Archives Office (subsequently BAO), 04220 (1) and (2); some 600 more indentures were recorded in BAO 04355 (6) and 04356 (1), *Actions and Apprentices*, covering the years 1683–6. These and the first set of London indentures were used by Mildred Campbell in her seminal article, 'Social origins of some early Americans', in J. M. Smith (ed.), *Seventeenth Century America* (Chapel Hill, N. Ca., 1959), 63–89.

9 Both ordinances are bound into BAO 04220 (1).

10 J. Latimer, *The Annals of Bristol in the Seventeenth Century* (Bristol, 1900), pp. 248–50.

11 BAO 04220 (1), fos. 1–400, 29 September 1654 to 31 December 1660, and fos. 1–533, 29 September 1654 to 31 December 1662. All dates are in Old Style, except that the year begins at 1 January. Subsequent tables, unless

stated otherwise, relate to the period 1654–60, and not all tables sum to the appropriate total, because of missing data.

12 Ordinance of Common Council, 29 September 1654, in BAO 04220 (1). The prescribed fine was £20; Latimer, *The Annals of Bristol*, p. 235, has examples of men being pilloried and committed to trial for kidnapping.

13 For similar discussion of French data, see J.-P. Poussou, 'Les mouvements migratoires en France et à partir de la France de la fin du XVe siècle au début du XIXe: approche pour une synthèse', *Annales de démographie historique 1970* (Paris, 1971), pp. 11–78, esp. pp. 28–30.

14 R. R. Menard, 'From servant to freeholder: status mobility and property accumulation in seventeenth century Maryland', *William and Mary Quarterly*, 3rd series, **XXX**, 1 (January 1973), pp. 37–64, esp. pp. 49

15 See note 7, above; Horn 'Emigration to the Chesapeake', Table 2.

16 Campbell, 'Social origins', pp. 71, 89: she explicitly defines yeomen as 'middling sort'.

17 Ibid, p. 89.

18 Horn, 'Emigration to the Chesapeake'. The suspiciously low numbers of 'husbandmen' may also indicate that the clerks in the Bristol Tolzey used 'yeoman' as a generic term for agricultural occupations.

19 P. Corfield, 'Urban development in England and Wales in the sixteenth and seventeenth centuries', in D. Coleman and A. H. John (eds), *Trade, Government and Economy in Pre-Industrial England. Essays presented to F. J. Fisher* (1976), pp. 214–47, esp. pp. 222–3.

20 E. J. Buckatzsch, 'The constancy of local populations and migration in England before 1800', *Population Studies,* **V** 1 (January 1951), pp. 62–9; J. Patten, *Rural-Urban Migration in Pre-Industrial England*, University of Oxford School of Geography, research paper 6 (Oxford, 1973); P. Spufford, 'Population mobilty in pre-industrial England', *Genealogists' Magazine*, **XVIII**, 8 (December 1973), pp. 420–29, 9 (March 1974), pp. 475–81, 10 (June 1974), pp. 537–43.

21 Patten, *Rural-urban Migration*, p. 47.

22 For example, J. Patten, 'Patterns of migration and movement of labour to three pre-industrial East Anglian towns', above, pp. 77–106; S. R. Smith, 'The social and geographic origins of the London apprentices, 1630–60', *Guildhall Miscellany,* **IV**, 3 (1973), pp. 195–206; A. J. Willis and A. L. Merson, *A Calendar of Southampton Apprenticeship Registers, 1609–1740*, Southampton Records Series **XII** (Southampton, 1968). Apprentice data are from BAO 04352 (6), *Apprentices 1640–1658*, fos. 325–421, 437–8; the subsequent registrations to 1664 are lost.

23 See note 20, above.

24 For similar results, see P. A. Slack, 'Vagrants and vagrancy in England, 1598–1664', above, pp. 49–76 esp. p. 62; P. Clark, 'The migrant in Kentish towns, 1580–1640' in P. Clark and P. Slack (eds), *Crisis and Order in English Towns, 1500–1700* (1972), pp. 117–63, esp. pp. 138.

25 E. Lee, 'A theory of migration', in J. A. Jackson (ed.), *Migration* (Cambridge, 1969), pp. 282–97.

26 D. Hollis (ed.), *Calendar of the Bristol Apprentice Book, 1532–1565, 1532–1542*, Bristol Record Society, **XIV** (Bristol, 1948).

27 For the general inadequacy of simple distance formulations, see R. P. Shaw, *Migration Theory and Fact* (Philadelphia, Pa., 1975), p. 49.
28 J. Thirsk, 'Farming regions of England', in J. Thirsk (ed.), *Agrarian History of England and Wales, iv: 1500–1640* (Cambridge, 1967), pp. 1–112, esp. pp. 2–25, 67–71, 79–80, 110–112; A. Everitt, 'Farm labourers' in ibid., pp. 396–465, esp. pp. 409–12; J. Thirsk, 'Seventeenth century agriculture and social change', *Agricultural History Review*, **XVIII**, Supplement (1970), pp. 148–77, esp. pp. 167–76.
29 Thirsk, 'Farming regions', p. 80; Slack 'Vagrants and vagrancy', pp. 66–7.
30 Thirsk, 'Farming regions', pp. 64–72, 76–80; G. D. Ramsay, *The Wiltshire Woollen Industry in the Sixteenth and Seventeenth Centuries*, 2nd edn (1965), p. 72.
31 Dunn, *Sugar and Slaves*, pp. 53–7; C. Bridenbaugh, *Vexed and Troubled Englishmen, 1590–1642* (New York, 1968, revised 1976), pp. 412–13.
32 Towns as identified in J. Adams, *Index Villaris* (1688).
33 Clark, 'The migrant in Kentish towns', pp. 139–42; A. Everitt, *Change in the Provinces: the seventeenth century*, University of Leicester, Department of English Local History, occasional papers, 2nd series, **1** (Leicester, 1969), pp. 25; H. J. Wilkins (ed.), *The 'Poor Book' of the Tithings of Westbury-on-Trym, Stoke Bishop, and Shirehampton from AD 1656–1698* (Bristol, 1910), *passim*.
34 J. Patten, 'Village and town: an occupational study', *Agricultural History Review*, **XX**, 1 (January, 1972), pp. 1–16.
35 The sex ratio is defined as the number of men per 100 women.
36 E. G. Ravenstein, 'The laws of migration', *Journal of the Royal Statistical Society*, **XLVIII** (1885), pp. 167–235, and **LII** (1889), pp. 241–305, esp. pp. 288.
37 Slack's finding that vagrant women often travelled considerable distances is not mirrored here: 'Vagrants and vagrancy', pp. 65.
38 Patten, 'Patterns of migration', Patten, *Rural-urban Migration*, pp. 15–17, 34–6; Clark, 'The migrant in Kentish towns'; Slack, 'Vagrants and vagrancy'; A. L. Beier, 'Vagrants and the social order in Elizabethan England', *Past and Present*, **64** (August, 1974), pp. 3–29.
39 W. S. Morgan, *American Slavery, American Freedom, the ordeal of colonial Virginia* (New York, 1975), p. 184; Rutman and Rutman, 'Of agues and fevers'; Menard, 'Immigration', pp. 328–31.
40 W. G. Hoskins, 'Harvest fluctuations and English economic history, 1620–1759', *Agricultural History Review*, **XVI**, 1 (January 1968), pp. 15–31; J. Walter and K. Wrightson, 'Dearth and the social order in early modern England', *Past and Present*, **71** (May 1976), pp. 22–42; the level of poor relief in Wilkins (ed.), *The 'Poor Book'* follows the general trend of dearth, peaking c. 1659–61.
41 Menard, 'Immigration', pp. 330. For A. E. Smith, the mainspring of the servant trade was the pecuniary advantage of the merchants and mariners: *Colonists in Bondage*, pp. 5, 18–19, 39–42, 52.
42 For example, BAO 04439 (2), *Depositions 1654–1657*, fo. 12.
43 For the classic picture, see Smith, 'The social and geographic origins', pp. 43–86; Bridenbaugh, *Vexed and Troubled Englishmen*, pp. 413–17.
44 P. McGrath, 'Merchant shipping in the seventeenth century: the evidence of

the Bristol deposition books', *Mariner's Mirror*, **XL**, 2 (May 1954), pp. 282–93, and **XLI**, 1 (January 1955), pp. 23–37. Relatively fewer were involved in the London trade: Horn, 'Emigration to the Chesapeake'.

45 BAO 04352 (6), fo. 283; 04439 (2), fo. 75; 04220 (1), fo. 5.

46 BAO 04439 (2) and (3), *Depositions 1657–1659*, for example (2), fos. 16, 37; P. McGrath (ed.), *Records Relating to the Society of Merchant Venturers of the City of Bristol in the Seventeenth Century*, Bristol Record Society, **XVII** (Bristol, 1952); McGrath (ed.), *Merchants and Merchandise in Seventeenth Century Bristol*, Bristol Record Society, **XIX** (Bristol, 1955), pp. 30–3.

47 The most detailed freedom due is promised in BAO 04220 (1), fo. 60.

48 BAO 04352 (6), fo. 392; 04220 (1), fo. 12.

49 BAO 04439 (2), fo. 37. Recruitment may have been by public proclamation of the need for servants, as in Norwich: Norwich and Norfolk Record Office, *Mayor's Court Book, vol. 25, 1675–1695*, Press D, case 16, fo. 57, 15 November 1679.

50 For example, Dunn, *Sugar and Slaves*, p. 123.

51 Ibid, pp. 68–75, 325–6.

52 J. P. Greene, 'Society and economy in the British Caribbean during the seventeenth and eighteenth centuries', *American Historical Review*, **LXXIX**, 5 (December 1974), pp. 1499–1517.

53 Craven, *White, Red and Black*, pp. 9–20; Menard, 'Immigration', pp. 324–6.

54 Slack 'Vagrants and vagrancy', and Clark, 'The migrant in Kentish towns', *passim*.

6
Moving on in the New World: migration and out-migration in the seventeenth-century Chesapeake

J. P. P. Horn

Analysis of population 'turnover' is the basis of this paper which uses a wide range of primary and secondary material to explain what happened to some of the English emigrants discussed in chapter 5 when they arrived in the Middle Colonies of North America. It shows how the settlers took with them their experience of English household forms and migration practices, bending them to the new demands of colonial life. The settlers remained highly mobile with many servants and poor freedmen travelling long distances because of shortages of work and land. There was also some more respectable betterment migration. At the same time, because of the absence of towns in the Chesapeake area, movement was rural dominated. Mobility patterns in this area were closely related to the development of the regional economy and there were significant differences in migration in New England.

Early in the 1630s Randall Revell made the most important decision of his life: to leave familiar surroundings, friends and kin in England and 'pass beyond the Seas' to the Chesapeake colonies of Maryland and Virginia. Whatever motives prompted his decision to emigrate it is clear that Revell's voyage across the Atlantic was not the end of his travels. Two years after arriving on the Eastern Shore of Virginia in 1634, he moved with his wife and two sons across the Chesapeake Bay to the newly-founded colony of Maryland where he settled on a modest plantation of 300 acres in St Mary's County (see Map 5). By 1645 he had returned to the Eastern Shore of Virginia, almost certainly as a consequence of the near collapse of Maryland during the political turmoil and plundering of Ingle's rebellion, and spent the next fifteen years in Accomack–Northampton County. He became a respected member of the community, serving in the colonial legislature in 1657 and joining the county bench four years later. His obviously considerable standing did not, however, persuade him to stay in Virginia and in late 1661 or early 1662 he and his family moved again to Maryland. On this occasion, he chose to remain on the Eastern Shore, moving north to Manokin, later part of Somerset County, where he died in 1687.[1]

Randall Revell's movements were by no means exceptional. Thousands of settlers who made the long journey across the Atlantic in the seventeenth century to work in the tobacco fields of Maryland and Virginia trekked from one part of the Chesapeake to another in search of improved opportunities: better land, work, or perhaps the chance to marry.[2] For many men and women, the long distances travelled to English ports and cities which eventually led to taking ship for America, prefaced a further period of movement within the colonies.[3] Tramping along the roads or travelling by river in Maryland and Virginia was thus a continuation of tramping the countryside in England; one facet of a far-flung transatlantic system which linked the parent country's economy to Ireland, the West Indies and mainland America.[4] In the Chesapeake, as in England, migration represented a principal mechanism for readjusting to changing economic realities. 'Moving on' was a means of keeping alive hopes for eventual prosperity, modest comfort, or at least subsistence.[5]

While historians are in general agreement about the significance of migration to the development of society along the tobacco coast in the seventeenth century, remarkably little is known about it. Much recent research has been devoted to describing the main demographic and economic characteristics of Chesapeake society but migration is often featured only tangentially.[6] The main reason for this is that sources for the analysis of Chesapeake migration flows are more intractable than English materials. The kinds of sources that are standard for the study of mobility in England are almost wholly missing for seventeenth-century Maryland and Virginia.[7] There are few records which provide a convenient and reliable means of reconstructing migration or estimating the strength and direction of movement.[8]

The purposes of this essay are to bring together recent research on geographical mobility in the Chesapeake; to provide new evidence about the nature of migration flows; and to place migration in the broader context of the adaptation of English emigrants to their new environment. First is a brief consideration of general social and economic factors which influenced migration in the Chesapeake in this period. Secondly, a case study of Lancaster County, Virginia, is used to examine the mechanics of settlement of new areas: the different sorts of settlers who peopled the county and the ways by which they came to enter the region. Thirdly, the movement of men and women beyond the Chesapeake to other colonies and back to England is discussed. And finally, there is an assessment of Chesapeake migration patterns compared to mobility in early modern England.

I

Little can be understood of the development of Chesapeake society in the seventeenth century without reference to tobacco. Settled in 1607, the first fifteen years of Virginia's existence witnessed a desperate struggle for survival. Financially and demographically the colony proved a disaster, despite the strenuous efforts of the Virginia Company to promote a sound economy based on the production of a range of manufactured goods in demand in England: silk, iron, salt, potash and pitch.[9] Tobacco, however, was the key to the colony's fortunes. Considered a luxury in Europe, it could be produced cheaply in Virginia and sold initially at a handsome profit in London. From the early 1620s, when extensive cultivation began, the 'Stinking Weed' governed the course of Chesapeake society and economy until the end of the colonial period.[10] 'We have [no] trade at home and abroad,' a contemporary stated, 'but that of Tobacco . . . [it] is our meat, drink, clothes, and monies.'[11]

Cycles of opportunity for settlers were strongly influenced by the boom and bust character of the tobacco economy. Production rose from about 400,000 lbs in 1630 to 15 million by the 1660s. The growth rate slowed in the 1670s and 1680s, and was followed by a quarter of a century of stagnation during which output fluctuated around 28 million pounds. Within this general trend, 'alternating periods of prosperity and depression, with peaks and troughs at remarkable regular intervals, afflicted the Chesapeake economy'.[12] During good times, such as the 1620s, mid 1630s, 1645 to 1654 and mid 1670s, planters sought to increase their output by acquiring more land and labour. When the price of leaf was high the number of ships trading to the tobacco coast rose and greater numbers of servants were imported. Settlement expanded into new areas where land was cheap and plentiful. Free immigrants and ex-servants alike took advantage of the availability of credit to set up their own plantations. Output increased not only because the same planters were producing more but also because the number of units of production rose. Increased production eventually saturated European markets and the price of leaf fell rapidly. Planters attempted to reduce costs and become more self-sufficient. Fewer servants were brought into the region and opportunites for ex-servants declined. Many were unable to afford the expense of establishing plantations of their own and were forced to become labourers and tenants of richer planters or move out of the Chesapeake altogether. Yet while the tobacco industry remained depressed low prices encouraged the expansion of the European market and demand for leaf began to increase. With a rise in demand tobacco prices increased and the whole cycle began again.[13]

The phenomenal growth of the tobacco industry created and maintained the need for a continuing supply of cheap labour. Throughout the seventeenth century Maryland and Virginia were immigrant societies populated mainly by young men and women from central and southern parts of Britain. Between 70 and 85 per cent arrived as indentured servants: bound labourers who had contracted to work for a fixed term in return for their passage across the Atlantic and certain 'freedom dues' when their servitude ended.[14] Not until the turn of the century was the majority of inhabitants along the tobacco coast native born.[15] Like London in this period, the Chesapeake depended on large-scale immigration from British provinces to maintain population growth.[16]

Population grew rapidly: from 104 settlers who arrived at Jamestown in 1607 to about 8000 inhabitants in 1640, 25,000 in 1660, 60,000 in 1680 and 100,000 by 1700.[17] Nevertheless these figures tend to obscure one of the salient features of the region's demographic history: 'a mortality of extraordinary dimensions'.[18] Recent estimates suggest that 105,400 to 111,700 persons emigrated from Britain to the Chesapeake between 1630 and 1700, and yet the total population at the end of the century was barely 100,000.[19] There had been a massive wastage of life as well as extensive outmigration.

The Chesapeake Tidewater is a vast, low-lying, riverine environment where settlers were subject to 'much sickness or death' during the seventeenth century.[20] According to George

Gardyner, writing in 1650, 'the air is exceeding unwholesome, insomuch as one of three scarcely liveth the first year at this time'.[21] Mortality rates were even higher than those found in the notoriously unhealthy fenlands and marshlands of England.[22] Up to 40 per cent of new arrivals may have died within their first few years in the Tidewater, commonly of a variety of ailments associated with malaria and intestinal diseases. Those who survived 'seasoning' led short lives by English standards and had usually succumbed to the environment by their mid to late forties.[23] Natural population growth was retarded also by the considerable sexual imbalance which characterized early Chesapeake society. Far fewer women emigrated than men. In 1625 there were approximately seven men to every woman in Virginia, while even in the last quarter of the century the ratio was two or three to one. A shortage of women restricted family formation and forced many males to remain single.[24] Consequently, as Carr and Menard point out, 'High mortality and sexual imbalance, along with a late age at first marriage for immigrant females, prevented reproductive population increase until near the end of the seventeenth century . . . and kept the society sensitive to changes in the character of the immigrant group and the opportunities offered new arrivals.'[25]

Early Chesapeake society was therefore subject to a variety of influences which encouraged migration. Immigrants, free and unfree, having severed ties with their native communities were likelier to continue moving than their more sedentary contemporaries in England. Virginia and Maryland were peopled by highly mobile elements of the parent country's population: the poor, young and unmarried. Rapid growth of the tobacco industry, cheap, plentiful land and the development of extensive trading networks along the Tidewater's rivers encouraged the expansion of settlement and movement into new areas. Rivers and creeks, as Durand of Dauphiné noted in 1686, served 'all the inhabitants as a common highway', facilitating migration from one region to another. Finally, high mortality rates may have influenced the movement of people into areas where land became available owing to the death of landowners. High population turnover naturally led to a rapid turnover of property.

Map 5 The Chesapeake in the seventeenth century

Sources: Edward B. Mathews (ed.), *The Counties of Maryland. Their Origin, Boundaries, and Election Districts* (Baltimore, 1907); Morgan P. Robinson, 'Virginia Counties: Those Resulting from Virginia Legislation', *Bulletin of the Virginia State Library*, **9** (1916).

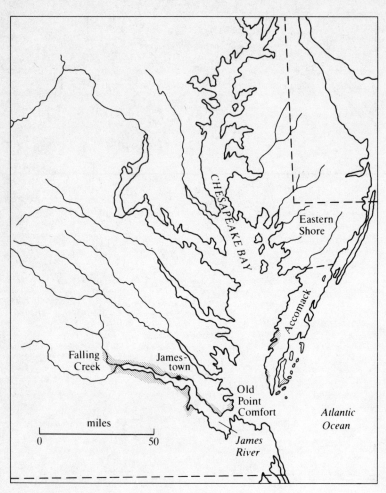

Map 6   Settlement patterns in the seventeenth-century
Chesapeake, 1622

Sources: see Map 5.

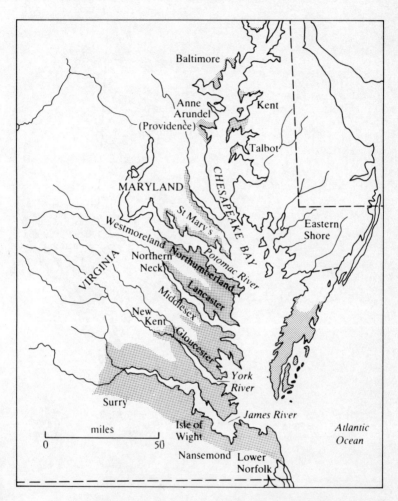

Map 7 Settlement patterns in the seventeenth-century
Chesapeake, 1652

Sources: see Map 5.

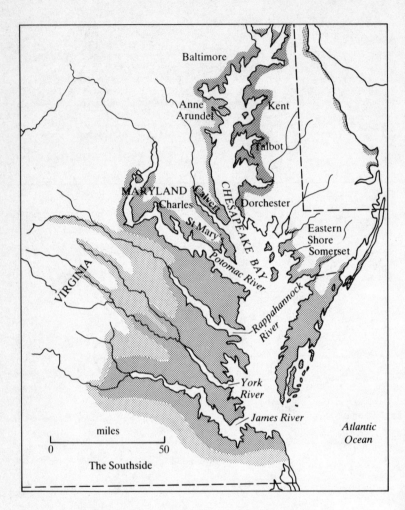

Map 8 Settlement patterns in the seventeenth-century
Chesapeake, 1671

Sources: see Map 5.

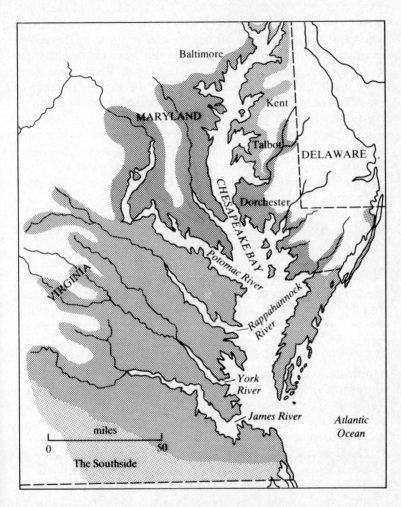

Map 9 Settlement patterns in the eighteenth-century
Chesapeake, 1702

Sources: see Map 5.

II

Maps 5 to 9 illustrate the spread of settlement across the Chesapeake between 1622 and 1702. The pattern of expansion is well known and requires only an outline here.[26] Prior to the Indian massacre of 1622 settlements reached out from the original seat at Jamestown along the banks of the James River from Point Comfort in the east to Falling Creek in the west, a distance of over 70 miles. Plantations were established also on the southern tip of the Eastern Shore of Virginia across the Bay (Map 6). During the 1620s and 1630s, as the pace of immigration quickened, there was a thickening of settlement along the banks of the James and the filling up of the James–York peninsula. The reorganization of Virginia into eight counties in 1634 testifies to this rapid expansion. Further north, Kent Island was settled in the early 1630s and Maryland in 1634.[27]

By the mid seventeenth century there had taken place a substantial expansion of settlement in Virginia northward beyond the York River to the Gloucester–Middlesex peninsula and the Northern Neck. Significant numbers of Virginia planters moved further north across the Potomac into Maryland, the 'Chesapeake frontier' of the 1650s and 1660s.[28] On the Eastern Shore settlers pushed up the Delmarva peninsula to the border of Maryland. Many of the first settlers of Somerset County, Maryland, were from Virginia's Eastern Shore counties of Accomack and Northampton.[29] Thus a northward expansion of settlement was the central feature of the four decades following the 1622 massacre (Map 7). The axis of population shifted from the older-settled region of the James River basin to the more northerly rivers of the York, Rappahannock and Potomac.

The third quarter of the century was an expansive period in the region's history. Between 1650 and 1680 approximately 60,000 immigrants arrived in the Chesapeake.[30] Eight new counties were formed in Maryland and Virginia between 1648 and 1654 and a further seven during the next decade.[31] Whereas almost all the growth in Maryland before the 1650s occurred along the lower Western Shore, after 1660 there was a major expansion of population in Maryland's Eastern Shore counties and in frontier counties such as Baltimore[32] (Map 8). In Virginia the population of the James River counties rose from 4589 tithables in 1653 to 5430 in 1682, but the region's share of the colony's total population fell from 63.8 to 35.8 per cent. During the same period the population of the York River counties quadrupled to 4848 tithables and its share of the total population increased from 17.6 to 32.0 per cent. The Rappahannock and Potomac counties exhibited an equally impressive growth rate and increased their share of the colony's population from 11.6 to 24.7 per cent (834 to 3746 tithables).[33]

By the beginning of the long tobacco depression (around 1680) settlement had virtually reached its seventeenth-century limits. In the remainder of the century less desirable land in the interiors of established counties was taken up and there was a drift of population westwards across the fall line; the latter trend foreshadowing the major impulse of the eighteenth century (Map 9). There was relatively little movement into new areas of the Chesapeake because the best tobacco lands had been patented and the depression, which would last about thirty years, did not encourage expansion.[34] Instead of seeking new land on the frontiers of Maryland and Virginia, thousands of settlers began moving to other colonies, notably Pennsylvania, the Carolinas, Delaware and the Jerseys.[35]

So much for the general picture. Settlement patterns indicate the direction of population movement and regional differentials in growth but tell us little about the magnitude or nature of migration flows in the Chesapeake. Several studies have been made of population turnover in Virginia and Maryland counties for the seventeenth century and may be compared to similar studies for England and New England (see Tables 22 and 23 pp. 194–6),[36] although there are considerable problems with using the data in this way.

Gross turnover rates measure those persons who 'disappear' from records over given time periods. A substantial proportion of those who disappeared (leaving aside the issue of the reliability of the sources) suffered, in Walsh's words, 'vertical mobility into the grave',[37] as Table 23 suggests. In Cogenhoe, for example, a slightly larger proportion of household heads remained in their home village than in Clayworth, but a much larger proportion moved also, as a result of different mortality rates.[38] Similarly, the apparent stability of New England communities compared to England and the Chesapeake is likely to be as much a function of lower levels of mortality as less mobility.[39] Secondly, the geographical units compared are very different, which raises the issue of how to assess the significance of distances moved in the three societies.[40] A person in England rarely had to travel more than a few miles to cross the parish boundary, but in the Chesapeake and New England, where settlement was far more dispersed, much longer distances are involved. Insufficient data exist to measure intra-county or -town movement and hence no attempt has been made to standardize distances travelled by migrants. Even if such data were available it is improbable that moving 5 miles in the Chesapeake had the same implications for migrants as moving 5 miles in England, given the very different population densities, economic organization and local government structures.[41] Finally, the composition of the samples vary: the Virginia and English data include only heads of households, most of whom were male; the Maryland data are confined to male landowners; and the New England sample consists of householders and some non-householders. It should be stressed that the figures do not deal with women and that persistence rates·will be higher for householders and landowners than the population as a whole since the most mobile elements in society – non-householders and non-landowners – have largely been excluded. Differential mobility rates of lower-class inhabitants are discussed in a subsequent section.

Table 22 shows that between 40 and 60 per cent of male householders (or landowners) in the Chesapeake disappeared during ten- and fifteen-year periods in the second half of the seventeenth century. Death accounted for 27 to 46 per cent of the turnover in Lancaster and Charles counties, leaving 12 to 28 per cent of the sample as migrants; close to the range for householders in Clayworth and Cogenhoe (Table 23).[42] There appears to have been considerable variation in levels of mobility: a much larger proportion of householders moved out of Lancaster County than Charles for example. The English and New England data also display significant differences. Variation can be explained in part by reference to the different types of communities used in this study and to timing. English society experienced much higher levels of mobility in the early seventeenth century compared to the 1680s.[43] It may not be surprising therefore that twice the proportion of people moved out of Cogenhoe, 1618–1628, than Clayworth sixty years later. Dedham, Massachusetts, was a far smaller and closed society in comparison to the burgeoning seaport of Boston.[44] But this is not the whole story. The Chesapeake evidence suggests that important regional differences existed with respect to mortality rates and levels of mobility; a consequence of the differential maturation of local economies throughout the Tidewater, and different demographic mixes (varying proportions of free and unfree settlers, immigrants and native-born). Local society in the Chesapeake during the second half of the seventeenth century may have been much more variegated than has been generally recognized.[45]

Traditionally New England communities have been considered the epitome of residential stability.[46] Recent research however has revised this view. Both Windsor, Connecticut, and Boston have greater turnovers of population than is usually assumed for New England (Table 22, pp. 194–5).[47] At the same time, persistence rates tend to be higher in New England than elsewhere but the differences are not as large as once thought. 'Dispersion of settlement over broad geographical areas in New England', as Douglas Lamar Jones says, 'almost from the moment of arrival was the common experience'.[48] R. J. Crandall characterizes the movement of Puritan families north and south along the Atlantic seaboard and into the interior, between 1630 and 1700, as the 'second Great Migration'.[49] Overall, the level of mobility among householders in the Chesapeake appears similar to that experienced in England and may not have been substantially greater than that of New England settlers.

Putting faces to the movers reveals some interesting parallels between Old and New World experiences. In Charles County four-fifths of free immigrants who survived for fifteen years or more, and who acquired land, stayed in the county permanently. Almost all free immigrants who did not possess land moved out. Similarly, 80 to 90 per cent of former servants stayed if they acquired land, while 57 to 61 per cent of non-landowners migrated.[50] Ex-servants were the most mobile group in Chesapeake society. Less than 10 per cent of servants freed between 1662 and 1678 in Lancaster appear as householders in the county in 1679.[51] Lorena Walsh estimates that about 60 per cent of servants left Charles as soon as their terms expired during the second half of the century: 'a combination of death and emigration must explain the fates of most of the Charles County servants who disappeared'.[52] On the Eastern Shore of Virginia only 17 and 9 per cent respectively of servants who arrived in Accomack and Northampton counties between 1663 and 1697 eventually acquired land as freemen.[53] At no time during the seventeenth century in either Maryland or Virginia was more than a small proportion of servants able to own land and settle in their home counties. The majority of those who survived servitude either chose or were forced to move elsewhere.

In seventeenth-century England, too, servants were the most mobile element of the population.[54] They composed 35 per cent of the people leaving Clayworth, 1678–88 and from 22 to 68 per cent of those leaving Cogenhoe between 1618 and 1628.[55] Typically, from a half to all the farm servants in a given parish moved out annually. Much of the parochial mobility of the seventeenth century, in Kussmaul's opinion, can be attributed to the movement of servants.[56] Comparing English farm servants to indentured servants in the Chesapeake is imprecise, the former usually served one-year contracts in contrast to the common minimum of four years along the tobacco coast. Nonetheless, freemen found themselves in an increasingly analogous position to their English labouring counterparts as the century progressed. In England and the Chesapeake it was mainly the young, un- or underemployed men and women who tramped the countryside in search of job openings or better opportunities.

General influences which encouraged people to stay or move were broadly similar in all three societies. The ability to acquire land and establish a household was probably the most important factor. Other considerations of significance were the proximity of kin, the availability of marriage partners, the number of existing ties with the 'home' community and perceived advantages of moving.[57] These factors are closely linked, of course, to an individual's sex, life cycle and status. To explore these issues further, in the context of Chesapeake migration patterns, the settlement of Lancaster County, Virginia, will be examined in detail.

Lancaster County is situated in the Northern Neck of Virginia and originally included land on both sides of the Rappahannock, from the Piankatank in the south to the border of Northumberland County in the north (see Map 6). The first settlers found a countryside of gently rolling hills, heavily wooded and dissected by numerous streams and creeks. Fertile soils and good lines of communication provided by the larger rivers guaranteed that it would become a prime tobacco-producing area. Interest in the region dates from the early 1640s. The first land patents were issued mainly for speculative purposes and were frequently extensive. Captain Samuel Mathews, for example, patented 4000 acres on the north side of the Rappahannock in 1643, one of the largest grants of the period.[58] Eight of the thirteen patents issued for the Piankatank–Rappahannock area in 1642 and 1643 were for tracts of over 1000 acres.[59] Wealthy and well-connected planters took up land in the expectation of handsome returns when the region came to be settled. Those involved in governing the colony were in an especially advantageous position to assess the possibilities of new lands for settlement and, by making use of the headright system (50 acres were granted for every person transported to the Chesapeake), could patent large areas at small expense.[60]

Large-scale movement into the region would probably have taken place in the mid 1640s had it not been for the Indian war of 1644 to 1646. The peace treaty of October 1646 prohibited English settlers from patenting land north of the York.[61] Two years later, however, all restrictions on settlement were removed and the flood gates were thrown open. The rapidity with which land was taken up is striking: by the end of 1650 alone sixty patents had been granted for land along the Rappahannock River totalling over 53,000 acres.[62] During the next two years a further 123,000 acres were patented along the north side of the Pianka-tank, both banks of the Rappahannock and inland along the major creeks and tributaries. Well over half the total area of Lancaster, as created in 1651, had been patented by the time of the first division of the county in 1656. In the late 1650s and 1660s, as the land boom continued, virtually all the remainder was taken up.[63]

Population increase in the area was equally rapid: from 380 tithables in 1653, to 663 in 1656 and 945 by 1663.[64] In the same period, the total number of tithables in Virginia rose from just over 7000 to 12,500.[65] The bulk of the increase in Lancaster was generated by the immigration from England of free settlers and servants. At least fifty (and probably nearer eighty) of the 141 householders who appear on the 1655 tithing list entered Lan-caster directly from the parent country.[66] They were a diverse group. A number of the free immigrants were politically influential men of high status. Sir Henry Chicheley, Sir Thomas Lunsford and Grey Skipwith were royalist sympathizers who had left England after the execution of Charles I.[67] Lunsford had been appointed Lieutenant of the Tower of London in 1641 and fought for the king in both civil wars. He may have met Sir Henry Chicheley, a fellow officer, while imprisoned in the Tower in 1648.[68] Another cavalier emigré, Colonel Henry Norwood, describes meeting both of them at Ralph Wormeley's plantation on the York River in early 1650, where they passed an evening 'feasting and carousing' with other ex-royalist officers 'lately come from England'.[69]

Other immigrants, like Raleigh Travers, William Ball and Thomas Powell, were merchants and 'Gentleman-Tradesmen' from London and the outports.[70] Ball arrived in Lancaster County from London in 1650 and quickly developed an extensive trade provisioning deep-water ships at anchor in the Corotoman River, one of the principal tributaries of the Rappahannock. Despite his evident success it does not appear that he was initially committed to staying in the Chesapeake since his wife and children remained in England until the mid 1660s. During part of this period his eldest son, William, was responsible for running the English end of the family business.[71] Similarly, Henry Corbin, an influential and well-connected planter of Lancaster and Middlesex counties, emigrated to Virginia in the mid 1650s while his two brothers, merchants of London, remained in England.[72] Strong ties of commerce and kinship were characteristic of Anglo-Chesapeake trade after the Restoration.[73]

The majority of new arrivals in Lancaster, as elsewhere in the Chesapeake in the second half of the seventeenth century, were servants. Between 1653 and 1656 the number of labourers rose from approximately 350 to 550, or about half the total population of the county in these years.[74] Planters lived in 'a sea of servants'.[75] At the time of the formation of Middlesex County, in 1668, 45 per cent of the population were bound labourers (16 per cent of whom were slaves).[76] Little is known about them. Most were probably recruited in London since the majority of merchants trading to the Rappahannock were from the metropolis. A large proportion were aged in their mid teens: only thirty-two of 296 servants who arrived in Lancaster without indentures between 1662 and 1680 were 19 years or more.[77] The typical length of service was seven years. A few ex-servants became householders in Lancaster. Sam Sloper, who appears on the listing of 1655, was transported by Major Andrew Gilson of Lancaster in or before 1650, while Charles King, who patented 40 acres at the mouth of the Corotoman River in 1657, had been brought into the colony by Modecai Cooke of Mobjack Bay, Gloucester County seven years earlier.[78] Such men were very much in a minority however; 90 per cent disappeared. 'Lancaster in the seventeenth century was a rich man's county . . . it was not a land of opportunity for its newly freed servants'.[79]

About a third of the householders who had arrived in Lancaster by 1655 were from other parts of Virginia.[80] Their importance to the political and economic development of the county far outweighs their relatively small numbers. Free Virginia settlers brought their experience of tobacco husbandry and marketing to the new area. Through former contacts they may well have encouraged English merchants to re-route their shipping to the Rappahannock, and their political connections must have been vital in the establishment of orderly rule on the frontier. Richard Lee, John Carter, James Bagnoll and a number of other planter-merchants had extensive experience of local government as justices of the peace, burgesses or members of the colony's Council of State.[81] Such men provided the backbone of govern-ment in their new county and represented Lancaster in the colonial legislature. They played a crucial role in helping newcomers (of their own rank) acclimatize to conditions in the Chesapeake.

Two regions contributed most of the free Virginia householders who moved into the region prior to 1656. Of thirty-six families for whom reliable evidence exists, seventeen came from the counties immediately to the south (eleven from York and six from Gloucester) and thirteen were from the three easternmost counties south of the James River (eight from Isle of Wight, four from Nansemond and one from Lower Norfolk). Of the remaining six families, two were from Charles City County, one from Elizabeth City and three from the Eastern Shore of Virginia.

The proximity of York and Gloucester counties, together with the general south-north axis of migration, explains the prominence of families from this area.[82] Settlements along the York River, which had increased rapidly in the 1630s and 1640s, provided an excellent springboard for the exploration of lands on the Rappa-hannock. In the late 1650s Rowland Haddaway related how he and four other men from York explored the Rappahannock several years earlier to survey new land: 'Going into a Creek . . . we gave it the name of Haddaways Creek and I . . . did take up the land that Hugh Brent lives upon.' On sighting a tract that looked promising, one of the members of the expedition 'took a book out of his pocket and did set down the bounds'.[83] This process must have been repeated thousands of times as settlers moved into new regions.

Movement from the counties south of the James is less easy to explain. Considerable distances were involved. A family migrating from Isle of Wight County faced a journey of about 20 miles downriver to Old Point Comfort, 40 miles up the Bay to Windmill Point at the mouth of the Rappahannock and possibly another 20 to 30 miles up the river before reaching their final destination; a total of 80 to 90 miles. The most likely reason for movement out of the Southside (the counties of Surry, Isle of Wight, Nansemond and Lower Norfolk) is that it was a low-grade tobacco area. John White, a merchant of London, explained to Robert Shepard of Surry in 1646 that although his crop was 'sound good Leafe' it was 'of the common sort' and would not fetch as high a price as the more fashionable sweet-scented tobacco.[84] The Southside developed in the second half of the seventeenth century as 'a small planter society',[85] an area which attracted large numbers of ex-servants, many of whom subsisted near the poverty line.[86] Planters with sufficient resources may have decided to take advantage of the northern land boom to move to an area of prime tobacco soils.

What of the negative evidence: why was migration weak or non-existent from other regions in Virginia? There is little concrete information but it is possible to speculate about general influences. Counties to the north, along the Potomac, were linked to the same migratory flow as Lancaster and were receptors rather than producers of migrants. Settlers in this area had only recently arrived by the early 1650s, and it was probably too soon to move again.[87] If they did decide to push on it was more likely they would cross the Potomac into Maryland than return south. The Eastern Shore may have experienced a migratory system of its own since there appears to have been little large-scale movement westward across the Bay. Most movement in this period was northerrlly, taking migrants eventually to Maryland and the Delaware region.[88] Lastly, the historic counties along the north bank of the James River sent few migrants to Lancaster. These counties produced high-quality leaf and exported more tobacco than any other single region throughout the century.[89] Proximity to the seat of the colony's government at Jamestown may have also encouraged landowners in the region to stay put. Wealthy men like Samuel Abbott, of James City County, were prepared to speculate in northern lands but not to move.[90]

A range of clues exists about the influences which lay beneath the decision of individuals and families to migrate. First, as has been suggested, political connections were important in alerting planters to opportunities elsewhere in the Chesapeake. Toby Smith, Captain Moore Fauntleroy and John Carter arrived in Virginia at about the same time, in the early 1640s, and settled in Nansemond. All three served regularly in the House of Burgesses as representatives of their county.[91] Carter may have discussed with Smith and Fauntleroy his speculative venture of 1642 (he had patented 1300 acres on the Rappahannock)[92] and the possibility of moving north. Smith and Fauntleroy probably knew Rowland Burnham and Richard Lee, both of York County, who sat in the same assemblies of the 1640s.[93] At meetings of the colonial legislature in Jamestown and on court days in the counties at large there would have been plenty of opportunity to gather information and discuss the potential of the newly-settled area of the Rappahannock.[94]

Kinship and neighbourliness played an important role in encouraging migration, or at least in determining the choice of destination. Smith was married to Fauntleroy's sister,[95] while influential early settlers Ralph Wormeley, William Brocas and Rowland Burnham were brothers-in-law by virtue of their marriage to three of the four Eltonhead sisters.[96] Epaphroditus Lawson, who settled in Nansemond prior to 1635, was the brother of Rowland and Richard Lawson who also moved to Lancaster in the early 1650s.[97] As one of the wealthiest men in the area and a member of the bench, Epaphroditus Lawson was well known to other important planters in Nansemond. Moore Fauntleroy was a close neighbour and Carter had assigned land to him in the early 1640s.[98] Of twenty-four families who settled on the south side of the Rappahannock by 1653 over half had lived in a cluster of households along the York River, and just under half had known each other previously as relatives or acquaintances.[99]

Again and again, one is struck by the small world that early Chesapeake planters of this rank inhabited. Linked by a 'tangled web of cousinry', friendship, political and business connections, planters were brought into frequent face-to-face contact with one another. Such links helped to shape the pattern of migration and would profoundly influence the development of society in the new county. Settlers chose to move to Lancaster not only because of the abundance of fertile land but also because they had kin and friends in the region. Similar factors probably influenced the immigration of numerous free settlers from England.

The movement of well-connected families such as the Carters, Lees and Lawsons constitutes an important aspect of Chesapeake migration but was not the most common form. Thousands of poor people – ex-servants, labourers, and small planters – who did not enjoy the political and social advantages of their wealthier contemporaries, composed the majority of migrants in the seventeenth century.[100] There is little evidence about their movements. E. S. Morgan argues that they tended to move away from the rich counties of the lower York, Rappahannock and Potomac to more marginal regions such as the Southside. Here were the largest concentrations of single-tithable householders, an indication of the persistence of poverty among small planters.[101]

Opportunities for the poor undoubtedly declined after the Restoration. By the 1660s levels of poverty along the tobacco coast were approaching Old World proportions.[102] In Maryland 40 per cent of the population died worth less than £35 between 1656 and 1696, and about half died worth less than £50.[103] A petition of 1664 from Virginia to the king stated that planters had at most £5 per year for all necessities, and described the colony as 'this dying Country'. The king was warned that poor planters had such a struggle to survive that they would soon become desperate.[104] Sixteen years and one rebellion later, Governor Culpepper remarked that 'the low price of tobacco staggers . . . the continuance of it will be the fatal and speedy ruin of this noble Colony . . . a whole year's crop will not give the planters enough meanly to clothe themselves'.[105] Virginia in 1684 was reduced to 'a Barbarous and Melancholy part of the world'.[106]

The response of the poor was to use their feet. Complaints were made to Charles City court in 1688 that people were wandering up and down the country who were not residents and hence did not pay the annual levy.[107] Taxpayers of Accomack petitioned the court in the 1690s about 'loose and vagrant persons that have not any settled Residence' who 'remove from place to place on purpose to defraud the County of their Levies. . . . '[108] According to Carr and Menard, the experiences of servants who immigrated to Maryland between 1680 and 1710 followed a uniform pattern, 'When they completed their terms they found themselves free men with no capital and little chance of advancement. After a few years as hired hands or sharecroppers, or perhaps a brief attempt at tenant farming, they left the tobacco coast for more promising regions.'[109] The proportion of freedmen in Maryland dropped from nearly 11 per cent of all male decedents in 1658–1670 to 2.4 per cent by 1721–1730. 'Immigrants without capital were moving on.'[110] The last quarter of the century witnessed extensive out-migration from both Virginia and Maryland.

III

During the last twenty to thirty years of the seventeenth century out-migration from the Chesapeake was primarily a consequence of the deepening tobacco depression as well as developing opportunities in other colonies. But out-migration was not unique to this period and should be interpreted in the broad context of migration systems which embraced other parts of the English Atlantic world. The scale and direction of out-migration had altered by the late seventeenth century, but not the impulse. People had been moving out of the Chesapeake almost as long as people had been moving in.

Out-migration took a variety of forms. First, throughout the century there was a steady, if relatively small, flow of people back to England.[111] As early as 1612 the Virginia Company complained of 'divers lewd ill-disposed persons, both sailors and soldiers, artificers, husbandmen, labourers, and others' who after receiving wages, clothing and food from the Company had returned 'most treacherously by stealth' to England.[112] Sufficient people were leaving the colony in the 1620s to force the Assembly to address the issue in 1626. It was decided 'there should be noe generall restraint of people from goeing for England, but that such as desire theire passes shall repaire to the Court held weekly at James Cittye'.[113] Two years later fourteen passengers leaving Virginia were released from an agreement to sail in the *Sun* because she was exceedingly leaky.[114] Fifty men and boys who left 'Kiekoutan' in December 1629 in the *Gift* were not so fortunate and were lost in a storm off Cape Hatteras on their way to England.[115]

Some passengers merely visited England for business or personal reasons: to market tobacco, obtain servants, or see kin and friends.[116] Planter-merchants such as Thomas Burbage appear to have led a quasi-amphibious existence, travelling to England

frequently.[117] Others, however, had no intention of going back to
the Chesapeake. William Tucker emigrated to Virginia in 1610
and became one of the most powerful planters of the 1620s and
1630s. He returned to England for good on the eve of the Civil
War.[118] His brother-in-law, Maurice Thompson, lived in Virginia
for several years before becoming an influential London
merchant.[119] Major Robert Bristow and Otho Thorpe left Virginia
after Bacon's rebellion in the late 1670s.[120] Colonel Philip Ludwell,
a prominent member of Virginia's elite, returned to England in
the late seventeenth century and died in London.[121] Even the
darling of Virginia biographers, Richard Lee, went back to his
estate at Stratford-Langton, Essex, before deciding that he
preferred Virginia where he died in 1664.[122]

There is no indication of the scale or pace of migration back to
England in the seventeenth century. Nonetheless, the evidence
suggests that not all settlers were committed to staying in the
colonies permanently. Whether they did or did not depended on
their connections and prospects in their native country as well as
prospects in the Chesapeake. As John Goode explained in 1676,
'here are many people in Virginia that receive considerable
benefitts and advantages, by Parents, . . . Friends and Correspon-
dents in England, and many expect Patrimonys and Inheritances'.[123] People returned home to take up bequests or to marry.
Goode was speaking of the wealthier members of society, but the
attitude of at least a section of the poor may have been similar,
if for different reasons. They had little hope of receiving an
inheritance in England but neither did they necessarily envisage
staying in the Chesapeake the rest of their lives. For some indentured servants emigrating to the tobacco coast approximated
signing up for a tour of service in the armed forces: in return for
the immediate benefits of board and lodging they sold their labour
for a fixed period (and risked their lives).[124] After their terms
expired they may have thought of returning to England or would
wait and see what turned up in the Chesapeake and surrounding
region.

They can be compared to lower-class migrants in England who
were characterized not so much by 'purposeful linear migration'
as 'untidy, irregular and often circular wandering'.[125] Not every
servant left England with the preconceived idea of becoming a
tobacco planter. Some had little notion of their eventual

Table 22 Gross turnover of householders in the Chesapeake, England, and New England, 1618–1710

Region/country		Per cent of householders remaining in county, parish, or town
Chesapeake:	Charles County, Maryland[a]	
	1660–1675	47
	1675–1690	42
	1690–1705	51
	Surry County, Virginia[b]	
	1668–1678	46
	Lancaster County, Virginia[c]	
	1669–1679	39
	1678–1688	43
	1688–1698	45
	1700–1710	47
	Accomack-Northampton, Virginia[d]	
	1646–1655	53–57
England:	Clayworth, Nottinghamshire[e]	
	1676–1688	50
	Cogenhoe, Northamptonshire[e]	
	1618–1628	52
New England:	Rowley, Massachusetts[f]	
	1643–1653	59
	Dedham, Massachusetts[f]	
	1648–1660	52
	1660–1670	78
	1680–1690	73
	1690–1700	83
	Boston, Massachusetts[f]	
	1687–1695	53
	Windsor, Connecticut[f]	
	1676–1686	57

Sources:

a Lorena S. Walsh, 'Mobility, Persistence, and Opportunity in Charles County, Maryland, 1650–1720', *William and Mary Quarterly*, (forthcoming), Table 3.

b Kevin P. Kelly, 'Economic and Social Development of Seventeenth-Century Surry County, Virginia', (PhD diss., University of Washington, 1972), Table 5, p. 23.

c Robert A. Wheeler, 'Lancaster County, Virginia, 1650–1750: The Evolution of a Southern Tidewater Community', (PhD diss., Brown University, 1972), pp. 66, 82.

d James R. Perry, 'The Formation of a Society on Virginia's Eastern Shore, 1615–1655', (PhD diss., The Johns Hopkins University, 1980), p. 64.

e Peter Laslett, *Family Life and Illicit Love in Earlier Generations: Essays in Historical Sociology*, (1977), Table 2.22, p. 98.

f Douglas Lamar Jones, 'The Strolling Poor: Transiency in Eighteenth-Century Massachusetts', *Journal of Social History*, **8** (1975), Table 1, p. 30.

Table 23 Rates of turnover of householders in the Chesapeake and England, 1618–1710

Region	Per cent of householders who died	Per cent who left	Per cent who stayed
Charles County, Maryland			
1660–1675	39	15	47
1675–1690	46	12	42
1690–1705	38	12	51
Lancaster County, Virginia			
1669–1679	35	26	39
1678–1688	31	26	43
1688–1698	27	28	45
1700–1710	28	25	47
Clayworth, Notts., England			
1676–1688	38	12	50
Cogenhoe, Northants., England			
1618–1628	24	24	52

Sources: See Table 22

destination or occupation; much depended on the ebb and flow of available opportunities.

The first signs of a significant volume of out-migration from Virginia occur in the middle decades of the century as a consequence of the migration of settlers to Maryland. Evidence from land patent records suggests that at least 500 people moved to the sister province between 1633 and 1680, about four-fifths of whom arrived in the 1660s and 1670s.[126] Roughly half entered Maryland in family units and approximately a third were single males. It is difficult to distinguish between free emigrants and servants in all cases, but the latter appear to have composed about 15 per cent of arrivals. Most of the movement took place along the Eastern Shore. Sixty per cent of Virginia's migrants were from Accomack and Northampton, while Somerset County, Maryland, just over the border, received half of all immigrants. Western Shore counties received under 30 per cent of new arrivals, the majority of whom went to St Mary's (Tables 24 and 25, p. 202).

There are two general reasons for the exodus of settlers from Virginia to Maryland. The settlement of Annemessex, part of the border country between Virginia and Maryland, was a refuge for nonconformists who left the older colony as legislation passed against them became stricter.[127] The persecution of Quakers was especially severe. An Act passed by the Virginia Assembly in March 1660 described them as 'An unreasonable and turbulent sort of people . . . teaching and publishing lies, miracles, false visions, prophecies and doctrines . . . attempting thereby to destroy religion, lawes, communities and all bond of civil societie'. Two years later a fine of 2000 pounds of tobacco was placed on persons refusing to have their children baptized, and in 1663 measures were taken to prevent Quakers from holding meetings.[128] Quaker families therefore took advantage of Calvert's offer in 1661 to open up Maryland's lower Eastern Shore for settlement and within six months fifty tithables had moved to the future Somerset County.[129] Earlier, in the late 1640s, a couple of hundred nonconformists migrated from the Southside and Eastern Shore of Virginia encouraged by promises of toleration from Governor William Stone of Maryland, himself formerly of Northampton County. Many settled at Providence, later Anne Arundel, on the Western Shore of the province.[130]

The second general reason for the influx of people into Maryland was the availability of land. On the Eastern Shore, as the lower part of the peninsula filled up, it became increasingly desirable to move further north where well-located, cheap land was abundant. The region was a 'good poor man's country' in the mid seventeenth century. For smaller planters there was a better chance of establishing themselves on the Eastern Shore of Maryland than in older-settled areas of the Tidewater. As population grew settlers moved to the Delaware Bay and the back country of Talbot and Queen Anne's counties in the 1680s and 1690s.[131]

In October 1695 the Council of Maryland proposed 'that some sort of Remonstrance or Declaration' be drawn up to warn inhabitants of the hazards of moving to Carolina or Pennsylvania. People had been 'deceived and led into such ffancy through a Common Empty rumour and report of the great plenty those two places live in which Reports are Raised by persons travelling from those parts . . . others have been Ignorantly persuaded and terrified out of the province through a Vain and giddy headed notion and noise of Great and heavy taxes'.[132] Earlier in the year, Governor Francis

Nicholson complained that 'the trade of this Province of Maryland is much impared and damnifyed by several Sloopes Shallops and Boats belonging to Pensilvania. . . . And that they make it their dayly practice to intice tradesmen, Seamen and other persons out of this province Under Specious pretences and fair promises'.[133] He commented later to the Board of Trade that 'the reasons as I conceive which induce the Inhabitants of the Province to leave it, are the incouragement which they have from the Carolinas and the Jerseys, but particularly from Pensilvania, which being so very nigh they easily remove thither, and their Handicraft Tradesmen have incouragement for illegal Traders   for privateers, or rather pyrats. . . . ' [134]

Similar anxieties were being voiced in Virginia. As early as 1677 the General Assembly stated that inhabitants were 'frequently deserting this Colony under pretence of gaineing Lands in Maryland, Soe that lands already taken up here (That might else be leased out) continue uncultivated for want of Tennants. . . .' Servants, slaves and debtors often 'Runn away' to Maryland and Carolina.[135] The latter colony was described in 1681 as a resort for the 'scumme and refuse of America . . . the refuge of our Renagadoes'.[136] Governments in Maryland and Virginia voiced their indignation about the poaching of their inhabitants (taxpayers and potential tenants) by other colonies.

British imperial authorities were agreed that the major reason for high levels of out-migration in the late seventeenth century was the engrossment of huge tracts of land by a tiny minority of wealthy speculators.[137] 'Some persons', it was said in 1697, 'have taken up great quantities of land both in Virginia and Maryland, of whom few or none are able to improve it all, and this is one great reason why young English Colonists and freed servants leave these Colonies and go either Southward or Northward; for they are naturally ambitious to be landlords not tenants.'[138] Engrossment, according to Edward Randolph, 'drives away the Inhabitants and servants, brought up only to planting, to seek their fortunes in Carolina and other places, which depopulates the Country. . . . ' [139] This assessment was correct but was merely part of the problem. The most important contributor to out-migration, as to internal migration, was the malaise affecting the economy. Until the price of tobacco rose there was little incentive for freedmen and small planters to remain in the Chesapeake when they could get better livings elsewhere.[140]

The ruling classes had good cause for concern. People were leaving in droves. At least a thousand male settlers left Maryland between 1704 and 1712, and thousands more left Virginia in the fifty years after Bacon's Rebellion.[141] As T. J. Wertenbaker says, 'For a full half century a large proportion of the white immigrants to Virginia seem to have remained there for a comparatively short time only, then to pass on to other settlements.'[142] Southward, Carolina developed as a vast pasture farming region supplying the population centres of the West Indies with foodstuffs and naval stores.[143] Pennsylvania's early trade was dominated by the export of grain, meat and lumber to the Caribbean, 'supplemented by occasional shipments of wheat and flour to southern Europe'.[144] The growth of Philadelphia during the last two decades of the seventeenth century must have created a powerful new magnet for migrants. Though little more than a small country town by English standards, its population of 2200 in 1700 was by far the largest concentration of people in the region.[145] Philadelphia's development, therefore, may have instigated the first examples of rural-urban migration from the Chesapeake, leaving aside movement back to England.

The direction of out-migration seems clear. Pennsylvania, where the population rose from about 700 people in 1680 to 18,000 by 1700, received most migrants.[146] North Carolina can be regarded virtually as an extension of the lower Chesapeake in the seventeenth century in demographic terms.[147] The first settlers of the Albemarle region migrated from Virginia's Southside in the 1650s and took up land along the Roanoke River.[148] The population grew from approximately 1000 people in 1660 to 10,000 by the turn of the century.[149] Mechanisms by which people heard of opportunities elsewhere in America are suggested in the views of Nicholson and others quoted above. It was perhaps inevitable that with the development of neighbouring colonies people would perceive better opportunities for themselves in newly-established areas. The same impulse led thousands of migrants to leave New England and West Indies for the southern colonies in the second half of the seventeenth century.[150] As trade between the regions of English settlement in America increased, so did the flow of information between them. The rising volume of shipping engaged in inter-colonial trade facilitated movement from one region to another. In sum, out-migration from the Chesapeake was at one and the same time an extension of intra-regional flows and an aspect of inter-regional migration between English colonies and the parent country.

IV

Obvious differences between migration in England and the Chesapeake stand out. Distances travelled within Virginia and Maryland were usually far greater than in the parent country. In the late seventeenth and early eighteenth centuries relatively few migrants in England moved more than 10 to 20 miles from their native communities, and most remained within the county boundary.[151] While long-distance migration became less common as the seventeenth century drew to a close, [152] the reverse was true in the Chesapeake. Emigration to the tobacco coast declined as migration fields contracted in England, but for people already in Virginia and Maryland long-distance movement became increasingly common. By virtue of being in the Chesapeake most settlers had travelled spectacular distances by Old World standards. Once there they continued moving. Settlers who migrated from the Southside to the Northern Neck, or beyond to Maryland, made journeys of up to 80 and 150 miles as the crow flies. Albemarle, to the south, lay 80 miles away. Pennsylvania, the Jerseys and New York were several hundred miles to the north. Movement was on a different scale in the New World.

Long-distance migration in the Chesapeake was the result of a number of factors. The Tidewater covers an enormous territorial expanse: at its maximum limits, 200 miles long by 100 miles wide. Superimposed onto a map of England it stretches from the south coast to the Humber and west-east from the Midland Plain to the Wash. Moving from one part of the region to another, therefore, often involved long journeys. Population density was much lower in the Chesapeake than in England. At the end of the seventeenth century entire counties had populations no larger than those of small English market towns and yet covered hundreds of square miles.[153] An 'abundance of land' and 'absence of people' encouraged extensive landholdings and husbandry, characteristics of Chesapeake plantation society.[154] Tracts of 400 or 500 acres enabled planters to shift tobacco fields from one area to another as soils were worn out and have plenty of land in reserve for raising cattle and swine.[155] Much larger tracts were acquired by the elite for speculative purposes or to provide for their children.

Consequently, planters were forced to move further and further in search of good, cheap land or stay put and rent.

Low population density, a simple agrarian economy and extensive landholdings were three important facets of Maryland and Virginia society in the seventeenth century, another was the lack of urban communities.[156] The Chesapeake did not develop towns prior to the end of the century, partly because rural hinterlands could not support urban populations and partly because the major marketing centres for the two colonies were in England. In a sense the cities and towns of the Chesapeake were London, Bristol, Liverpool and other outports. Migrants were denied the greater opportunities for casual employment that the more complex economies of towns provided. Whereas 'subsistence migration' in England was characterized by the movement of poor people from rural to urban communities this was not the case in Maryland and Virginia, where almost all migration took place in a rural to rural context.[157]

In view of the radically different environment encountered by colonists in the Chesapeake it may seem implausible that there were any significant similarities in migration patterns between the Old World and the New. However, it should be re-emphasized first that Chesapeake migration flows were, in part, an overseas continuation of mobility in Britain; they were not entirely autonomous sytems. Imperatives which had encouraged people to migrate within England, and later emigrate to America, frequently influenced movement in Virginia and Maryland. Clark argues that emigration to the colonies was largely an 'extension of the long-distance subsistence-type internal migration' of the first half of the seventeenth century.[158] Servants and poor freedmen were the Chesapeake equivalents of itinerant labourers and the unemployed in England. Much of the movement out of the region in the 1680s and 1690s conforms to subsistence migration on the part of the disadvantaged denied opportunities in their own communities.

The majority of Chesapeake migrants were young, poor and had developed few links with the communities into which they had been transported. Some possibly had no desire to establish themselves as planters immediately if at all. Others did not have the resources to do so and, like their English counterparts, were driven to seek work 'sometime in one place and sometime in another'.[159] Householders of the type who moved into Lancaster

Table 24   Counties of previous residence of Virginia settlers
who migrated to Maryland, 1633–1680

Region	County	N		Per cent	
Eastern Shore of Virginia	Accomack	22	} 28	47·8	} 60·8
	Northampton	6		13·0	
Northern Neck	Northumberland	6	} 7	13·0	} 15·2
	Westmoreland	1		2·2	
Middle Peninsula	York	5	} 9	10·9	} 19·6
	Gloucester	4		8·7	
Southside	Nansemond	2		4·3	
	Total	46		99·9	

Source: Tabulated from Gust Skordas, ed., *The Early Settlers of
Maryland . . . 1633–1680*, (Baltimore, 1968).

Table 25   Counties of residence in Maryland of Virginia settlers
who migrated, 1633–1680

Region	County	N		Per cent	
Eastern Shore	Somerset	95		53·4	
	Dorchester	14		7·9	
	Talbot	10		5·6	
	Kent	4	} 128	2·2	} 71·9
	(Choptank River)	3		1·7	
	Worcester	1		0·6	
	Eastern Shore	1		0·6	
Western Shore	St. Mary's	33		18·5	
	Anne Arundel	8	} 50	4·5	} 28·1
	Baltimore	6		3·4	
	Charles	3		1·7	
Total		178		100·1	

Source: See Table 24

County in the mid seventeenth century, or who migrated from
Virginia to Maryland, conform in many respects to the English
model of 'betterment migrants': those who were 'not compelled

by necessity but encouraged by the hope of social and economic improvement'.[160] Within the context of the higher rates of lower-class mobility, they composed an influential group of movers who brought capital, labour and connections with the wider community into newly-settled regions.

English settlers who immigrated to the tobacco coast in the seventeenth century left a society characterized by high levels of population turnover. The assumption that they uniformly settled down once they arrived in the Chesapeake is clearly wrong. Maryland and Virginia society were profoundly influenced not only by the flow of people into America but also by the movement of settlers within and beyond the region. Currents and cross-currents of migration were just as important to the social and economic development of the Chesapeake as they were to English society in the early modern period. Moving on quickly became as integral to life in the New World as it had been for centuries in the Old.

Acknowledgements

I would like to thank Peter Clark, Lorena Walsh, Warren Billings, James Perry, Kevin Kelly, Peter Bergstrom, Roger Ekirch, David Cressy, John Hemphill and Allan Kulikoff for allowing me to read or use unpublished research, and for their advice and support. Thad Tate, Michael McGiffert and David Souden provided valuable criticism of an earlier version of this article.

Notes and references

1 Clayton Torrence, *Old Somerset on the Eastern Shore of Maryland: A Study in Foundations and Founders* (Richmond, Va., 1935), pp. 306–10, 455–7; Susie M. Ames, ed., *County Court Records of Accomack-Northampton, Virginia, 1640–1645* (Charlottesville, Va., 1973), pp. 445, 446–7, 448; Northampton County Orders: Deeds, Wills, etc., No. 3, 1645–1651, ff. 3, 17, 61. I am indebted to James Ferry for these last two references. For Ingle's Rebellion see Russell R. Menard, 'Maryland's "Time of Troubles": Sources of Disorder in Early St Mary's', *Maryland Historical Magazine*, (hereafter *MHM*), **76** (1981), pp. 136–8.

2 A similar case could be made for New England and the West Indies. See Ralph J. Crandall, 'New England's Second Great Migration: The First Three Generations of Settlement, 1630–1700', *The New England Historical and Genealogical Register*, **129** (1975), pp. 347–60; T. H. Breen and Stephen Foster, 'Moving to the New World: The Character of Early Massachusetts Immigration', *William and Mary Quarterly*, (hereafter *WMQ*), 3rd series, **30** (1973), pp. 208–13; Richard Waterhouse, 'England, the Caribbean, and the Settlement of Carolina', *Journal of American Studies*, **9** (1975), pp. 259–81; Richard S. Dunn, *Sugar and Slaves: The Rise of the Planter Class in the*

English West Indies, 1624–1713 (New York, 1973), pp. 110–16. See also N. Canny, 'Migration and Opportunity: Britain, Ireland and the New World', *Irish Economic and Social History,* **12** (1985), pp. 7–32.

3 On the movement of emigrants in England before leaving for America, see David Souden, ' "Rogues, Whores and Vagabonds"? Emigrants to North America, and the Case of Mid Seventeenth-Century Bristol', above, pp. 150–71; Anthony Salerno, 'The Social Background of Seventeenth-Century Emigration to America', *Journal of British Studies,* **10** (1979–80), pp. 31–52; James Horn, 'Servant Emigration to the Chesapeake in the Seventeenth Century', in Thad W. Tate and David L. Ammerman (eds), *The Chesapeake in the Seventeenth Century: Essays on Anglo-American Society,* (Chapel Hill, 1979), pp. 51–95; John Wareing, 'Migration to London and transatlantic emigration of indentured servants, 1683–1775', *Journal of Historical Geography,* **7** (1981), pp. 356–378.

4 David W. Galenson, *White Servitude in Colonial America. An Economic Analysis,* (Cambridge, 1981); David Souden, 'English Indentured Servants and the trans-Atlantic Colonial Economy', in S. Marks and P. Richardson (eds), *International Labour Migration: Historical Perspectives* (London, 1984), pp. 19–33; Abbot Emerson Smith, *Colonists in Bondage: White Servitude and Convict Labor in America, 1607–1776* (Gloucester, Mass., 1965. First pub. 1947).

5 E. G. Ravenstein, 'The Laws of Migration', *Journal of the Royal Statistical Society,* **48** (1885); Peter Clark, 'The Migrant in Kentish Towns, 1580–1640', in Peter Clark and Paul Slack, (eds), *Crisis and Order in English Towns, 1500–1700, Essays in Urban History* (London, 1972), pp. 117–63; idem, 'Migration in England during the late Seventeenth and early Eighteenth Centuries', below, pp. 213–52; Paul Slack, 'Vagrants and Vagrancy in England, 1598–1664', above, pp. 49–76.

6 Excellent summaries of recent research on the seventeenth-century Chesapeake can be found in John J. McCusker and Russell K. Menard, *The Economy of British America, 1607–1789* (Chapel Hill, 1985), *passim*: Allan Kulikoff, *Tobacco and Slaves: The Development of Southern Cultures in the Chesapeake, 1680–1800* (Chapel Hill, 1986), ch. 1; Gloria L. Main, *Tobacco Colony: Life in Early Maryland, 1650–1720* (Princeton, 1982), chs. 1–3; Darrett B. Rutman and Anita E. Rutman, *A Place in Time, Middlesex County, Virginia, 1650–1750* (New York, 1984).

7 English sources for the study of migration are discussed by Peter Clark, 'Migration in England', pp. 216–19. See also David Souden, 'Migrants and the Population Structure of later seventeenth-century Provincial Cities and Market Towns', in Peter Clark, ed., *The Transformation of English Provincial Towns, 1600–1800* (London, 1984), pp. 137–42; idem., 'Movers and Stayers in Family Reconstitution Populations', *Local Population Studies,* **17** (1984), pp. 11–27; and John Wareing, 'Changes in the Geographical Distribution of the Recruitment of Apprentices to London Companies, 1486–1750', *Journal of Historical Geography,* **6** (1980), pp. 241–9.

8 Chesapeake historians have relied upon a variety of sources to describe migration: colony-wide and county lists of tithables (essentially a tax on labourers), land patents, deeds, county records in general and literary evidence. The best published guide to population changes in Virginia is E. S.

Morgan, *American Slavery, American Fredom. The Ordeal of Colonial Virginia* (New York, 1975), Appendix, pp. 395–432. See also Rutman and Rutman, *A Place in Time*, vol. 1, pp. 48–9, 236–40. For Maryland see Lorena S. Walsh, 'Mobility, Persistence, and Opportunity in Charles County, Maryland, 1650–1720', (Paper presented to the Social Science History Association, October 1982); Russell R. Menard, 'Immigrants and their Increase: The Process of Population Growth in Early Colonial Maryland', in Aubrey C. Land, Lois Green Carr, and Edward C. Papenfuse (eds), *Law, Society, and Politics in Early Colonial Maryland* (Baltimore, 1977), pp. 88–110; P. M. G. Harris, 'Integrating Interpretations of Local and Region-Wide Change in the Study of Economic Development and Demographic Growth in the Colonial Chesapeake, 1630–1775', *Working Papers from the Regional Economic History Research Center*, 1, No. 3 (1978), pp. 35–72. For literary evidence see *Calendar of State Papers, Colonial Series*, ed. W. Noel Sainsbury *et al*, (London, 1860–); H. R. McIlwaine, ed., *Journals of the House of Burgesses of Virginia, 1659/60–1693* (Richmond, Va., 1914); William Hand Brown *et al* (eds). *Archives of Maryland . . .* (Baltimore, 1883–), hereafter cited as *Md Arch*. For eighteenth-century migration see Kulikoff, *Tobacco and Slaves*, pp. 76–7, 145–57.

9 Morgan, *American Slavery*, chs 3–6; Wesley Frank Craven, *The Southern Colonies in the Seventeenth Century, 1607–1689* (Baton Rouge, La., 1949), chs 3–5.

10 T. J. Wertenbaker, *The Planters of Colonial Virginia* (New York, 1958. First pub. 1922),. pp. 23–4.

11 'Part of a Letter from the Rev. Mr. Hugh Jones to the Rev. Dr. Benjamin Woodruff, F.R.S., concerning Several Observables in Maryland', 23 January 1698 [1699], Royal Society Archives, LBC **II** (2), p. 247, f. 247.

12 Russell R. Menard, 'Economy and Society in Early Colonial Maryland' (Phd diss., Universy of Iowa, 1975), pp. 285.

13 Idem, 'The Tobacco Industry in the Chesapeake Colonies, 1617–1730: An Interpretation', *Research in Economic History*, 5 (1980), pp. 109–77.

14 Horn, 'Servant Emigration': Galenson, *White Servitude*. Freedom dues varied considerably from one colony to another throughout the seventeenth century but typically comprised clothing, corn and tools. The rights to 50 acres of land or a cash payment were sometimes granted. Main, *Tobacco Colony*, pp. 98, 116–17; Smith, *Colonists in Bondage*, pp. 238–41.

15 Menard, 'Immigrants and their Increase', pp. 88–110.

16 E. A. Wrigley and R. S. Schofield, *The Population History of England, 1541–1871. An Interpretation* (Cambridge, Mass., 1981), pp. 166–70; E. A. Wrigley, 'A Simple Model of London's Importance in Changing English Society and Economy, 1650–1750', *Past and Present*, **37** (1967), pp. 44–9; J. Patten, 'Rural-Urban Migration in Pre-Industrial England', *Research Paper No. 6* (School of Geography, Oxford University, 1973), p. 27; C. G. A. Clay, *Economic Expansion and Social Change: England, 1500–1700.* (Cambridge, 1984), vol. 1, p. 27.

17 Menard, 'Immigrants and their Increase', p. 88.

18 Ibid., p. 93.

19 Henry A. Gemery, 'Emigration from the British Isles to the New World, 1630–1700: Inferences from Colonial Populations', *Research in Economic*

History, **5** (1980), pp. 179–231; Main, *Tobacco Colony*, pp. 10–16; McCusker and Menard, *Economy of British America*, pp. 222–4.

20 Arthur P. Middleton, *Tobacco Coast, A Maritime History of the Chesapeake Bay: the Colonial Era* (Newport News, Va., 1953), ch. 2.

21 George Gardyner, *A Description of the New World* (London, 1650), p. 99.

22 Mary Dobson, ' "Marsh Fever" – the Geography of Malaria in England', *Journal of Historical Geography,* **6** (1980), pp. 357–89.

23 Lorena S. Walsh, 'Servitude and Opportunity in Charles County, Maryland, 1658–1705', in Land, Carr, and Papenfuse (eds), *Law, Society and Politics*, p. 130; Lorena S. Walsh and Russell R. Menard, 'Death in the Chesapeake: Two Life Tables for Men in Early Colonial Maryland', *MEM,* **69** (1974), pp. 211–27; Daniel Blake Smith, 'Mortality and Family in the Colonial Chesapeake', *Journal of Interdisciplinary History,* **8** (1978), pp. 403–27; Darrett B. and Anita H. Rutman, ' "Now-Wives and Sons-in-Law": Parental Death in a Seventeenth-Century Virginia County', in Tate and Ammerman (eds), *The Chesapeake in the Seventeenth Century*, pp. 153–82; idem. ' "Of Agues and Fevers": Malaria in the Early Chesapeake', *WMQ*, 3rd series, **33** (1976), pp. 31–60.

24 Menard, 'Immigrants and their increase', p. 96.

25 Lois Green Carr and Russell R. Menard, 'Immigration and Opportunity: the Freedman in Early Colonial Maryland', in Tate and Ammerman (eds), *The Chesapeake in the Seventeenth Century*, p. 209.

26 Edward B. Mathews, (ed.), *The Counties of Maryland. Their Origin, Boundaries, and Election Districts* (Baltimore, 1907); Morgan P. Robinson, 'Virginia Counties: Those Resulting from Virginia Legislation', *Bulletin of the Virginia State Library,* **9** (1916); Richard L. Morton, *Colonial Virginia, vol. 1, The Tidewater Period, 1607–1710* (Chapel Hill, 1960), pp. 52, 58, 62–5, 122–30, 155–8, 163, 242; Robert D. Mitchell, 'American Origins and Regional Institutions: The Seventeenth-Century Chesapeake', *Annals of the Association of American Geographers,* **73** (1983), pp. 404–20.

27 Robinson, 'Virginia Counties'; Mathews, *The Counties of Maryland*; Warren M. Billings (ed), *The Old Dominion in the Seventeenth Century: A Documentary History of Virginia, 1606–1689* (Chapel Hill, 1975), pp. 8, 68, 71; Morton, *Colonial Virginia*, pp. 58, 125; Menard, 'Maryland's "Time of Troubles" ', pp. 129–33.

28 Menard, 'Economy and Society', pp. 223.

29 Torrence, *Old Somerset*, pp. 257–81, 297–334, 435–60; J. C. Wise, *Ye Kingdome of Accawmacke, or the Eastern Shore of Virginia in the Seventeenth Century* (Baltimore, 1967. First pub. 1911), pp. 93, 105–9. 'Delmarva' refers to the entire peninsula between the Chesapeake and the Delaware bays, which includes parts of Delaware, Maryland and Virginia.

30 Main, *Tobacco Colony*, p. 10.

31 Menard, 'Tobacco Industry', pp. 133, 134.

32 Idem., 'Economy and Society', p. 216.

33 Morgan, *American Slavery*, Table 4, p. 414.

34 Ibid., chs 11–14; Menard, 'Tobacco Industry', pp. 137–42, 153–6.

35 Wertenbaker, *The Planters of Colonial Virginia*, pp. 139–47.

36 Walsh, 'Mobility, Persistence, and Opportunity', Table 2; Kevin P. Kelly, 'Economic and Social Development of Seventeenth-Century Surry County,

Virginia', (PhD diss., University of Washington, 1972), Table 5, p. 23; Robert A. Wheeler, 'Lancaster County, Virginia, 1650–1750: The Evolution of a Southern Tidewater Community' (PhD diss., Brown Univeristy, 1972), pp. 66, 82; James R. Perry, 'The Formation of a Society on Virginia's Eastern Shore, 1615–1655) (PhD diss., The Johns Hopkins University, 1980), 64; Peter Laslett, *Family Life and Illicit Love in Earlier Generations: Essays in Historical Sociology*, (1977), Table 2.22, 98; Douglas Lamar Jones, 'The Strolling Poor: Transiency in Eighteenth-Century Massachusetts', *Journal of Social History*, **8** (1975), Table 1, pp. 30; Thomas R. Cole, 'Family, Settlement, and Migration in Southeastern Massachusetts, 1650–1805: The Case for Regional Analysis', *The New England Historical and Genealogical Register*, **132** (1978), p. 174; Crandall, 'New England's Second Great Migration'; Breen and Foster, 'Moving to the New World'; Douglas Lamar Jones, *Village and Seaport: Migration and Society in Eighteenth-Century Massachusetts* (Hanover and London, 1981), p. 107; W. R. Prest: 'Stability and Change in Old and New England: Clayworth and Dedham', *Journal of Interdisciplinary History*, **6** (1976), pp. 359–74.

37 Walsh, 'Mobility, Persistence, and Opportunity', p. 3.

38 Laslett, *Family Life and Illicit Love*, pp. 68, 98.

39 Crandall, 'New England's Second Great Migration'; Cole, 'Family, Settlement and Migration'; Prest, 'Stability and change'; Jones, *Village and Seaport*.

40 Prest, 'Stability and Change'.

41 Ibid.

42 Laslett, *Family Life and Illicit Love*, p. 98.

43 P. Clark, 'Migration in England'.

44 Jones, 'The Strolling Poor'; Kenneth A. Lockridge, *A New England Town, the First Hundred Years* (New York, 1970); Darrett B. Rutman, *Winthrop's Boston: Portrait of a Puritan Town, 1630–1649* (Chapel Hill, 1965).

45 Harris, 'Integrating Interpretations of Local and Region-Wide Change'.

46 Lockridge, *A New England Town*; Philip J. Greven, *Four Generations: Population, Land, and Family in Colonial Andover, Massachusetts* (Ithaca, New York, 1970); Sumner Chilton Powell, *Puritan Village: The Formation of a New England Town* (Middletown, Conn., 1963).

47 Jones, 'The Strolling Poor', Table 1, p. 30.

48 Idem, *Village and Seaport*, p. 104.

49 Crandall, 'New England's Second Great Migration', p. 347.

50 Walsh, 'Mobility, Persistence, and Opportunity', Table 3.

51 Morgan, *American Slavery*, p. 226.

52 Walsh, 'Servitude and Opportunity', p. 116.

53 Joseph D. Deal, 'Race and Class in Colonial Virginia: Indians, Englishmen, and Africans on the Eastern Shore during the Seventeenth Century' (PhD diss., University of Rochester, 1981), p. 114.

54 Laslett, *Family Life and Illicit Love*, pp. 35–43, 72–3; A. S. Kussmaul, 'The Ambiguous Mobility of Farm Servants', *EcHR*, 2nd series, **34** (1981), pp. 222–35.

55 Laslett, *Family Life and Illicit Love*, p. 98.

56 Kussmaul, 'The Ambiguous Mobility of Farm Servants', pp. 224–5.

57 Walsh, 'Mobility, Persistence, and Opportunity', pp. 5–9; Breen and Foster, 'Moving to the New World', pp. 208–13; Cole, 'Family, Settlement and

Migration', pp. 171–85; Crandall, 'New England's Second Great Migration', pp. 351–6; Jones, 'The Strolling Poor', pp. 39–41; Laslett, *Family Life and Illicit Love*, pp. 68–75; Clark, 'Migration in England', pp. 227–31 idem., 'The Migrant in Kentish Towns', pp. 134–49.

58 Nell Marion Nugent, *Cavaliers and Pioneers, Abstracts of Virginia Land Patents and Grants, 1623–1800*, vol. 1 (Richmond, Va., 1934), p. 144.

59 Ibid., pp. 132–48.

60 See Rutman and Rutman, *A Place in Time*, vol. 1, p. 74, for land speculation; Morgan, *American Slavery*, pp. 218–20. For the headright system see Smith, 'Mortality and Family', pp.14–15.

61 Morton, *Colonial Virginia*, vol. 1, pp. 153–6.

62 Nugent, *Cavaliers and Pioneers*, vol. 1, pp. 177–209.

63 Wheeler, 'Lancaster County, Virginia', pp. 16–17, 27, 36–42, 62, 87.

64 Lancaster County Deeds etc., No. 1, 1652–1657, pp. 90–4, 302–7; Orders etc., 1655–1666, pp. 236–8. Menard, 'Economy and Society', Appendix 4, 460–4. Tithables were the taxable population of the Chesapeake colonies in the seventeenth and eighteenth centuries; essentially a tithable was a field hand or labourer (see Morgan, *American Slavery*, pp. 400–1).

65 Menard, 'Tobacco Industry', Appendix, pp. 158–9.

66 Lancaster County Deeds etc., No. 1, 1652–1657, pp. 234–9; *Virginia Colonial Abstracts, vol. 22, Lancaster County, 1652–1655*, Beverley Fleet, abs. (Baltimore, 1961), pp. 105–9; J. P. P. Horn, 'Lancaster County, Virginia, Biographical Files'. Nugent, *Cavaliers and Pioneers*, vol. 1, *passim*.

67 Morton, *Colonial Virginia*, vol. 1, p. 167; Steven D. Crow, ' "Your Majesty's Good Subjects": A Reconsideration of Royalism in Virginia, 1642–1652', *Virginia Magazine of History and Biography* (hereafter *VMHB*), **87** (1979), pp. 158–73.

68 Lunsford had shocked Sussex society in 1632 by his attempt on the life of his influential neighbour, Sir Thomas Pelham. He spent a year in Newgate before fleeing to France. On his appointment to the Lieutenantship of the Tower of London, he was described by a group of City petitioners as 'a man of decayed and desperate fortune, most notorious for outrages'. The House of Commons voted for his immediate removal. See Anthony Fletcher, *A County Community at Peace and War: Sussex, 1600–1660* (London, 1975), pp. 54–5; Brian Manning, *The English People and the English Revolution* (London, 1976), pp. 74–6; C. V. Wedgwood, *The King's War, 1641–1647* (New York, 1959), 49–53, 59; 'Note – Sir Thomas Lunsford', *Virginia Historical Magazine*, **17** (1909), pp. 26–33.

69 Colonel Norwood, 'A Voyage to Virginia, [1649]', in Peter Force, comp., *Tracts and Other Papers relating principally to the Origin, Settlement, and Progress of the Colonies in North America from the discovery of the country to the year 1776* (Gloucester, Mass., 1963), vol. 3, no. 10, pp. 49.

70 Horn, 'Lancaster County Files'. The phrase 'Gentleman-Tradesman' is from Daniel Defoe, *Moll Flanders*, ed. Edward Kelly (New York, 1973), p. 48.

71 N. T. Mann, 'William Ball, Merchant', *Northern Neck Historical Magazine*, **23** (1973), pp. 2523–9.

72 Rutman and Rutman, *A Place in Time*, vol. 1, p. 50.

73 J. M. Sosin, *English America and the Restoration Monarchy of Charles II; Transatlantic Politics, Commerce, and Kinship* (Lincoln, Na., 1980), ch. 1.

74 Wheeler, 'Lancaster County, Virginia', p. 22.

75 Rutman and Rutman, *A Place in Time*, vol. 1, p. 71.

76 Ibid., pp. 71–2.

77 Morgan, *American Slavery*, p. 216.

78 Nugent, *Cavaliers and Pioneers*, vol. 1, pp. 197, 200, 290; Fleet, *Virginia Colonial Abstracts*, pp. 105–9.

79 Morgan, *American Slavery*, pp. 226–7.

80 Horn, 'Lancaster County Files'.

81 H. R. McIlwaine (ed.), *Journals of the House of Burgesses of Virginia, 1619–1658/9* (Richmond, Va., 1915), xvi–xxiii; Rutman and Rutman, *A Place in Time*, vol. 1, p. 48.

82 Rutman and Rutman, *A Place in Time*, vol. 1, pp. 44–9, provides an excellent account of the settlement of the south side of the Rappahannock River (the future Middlesex County).

83 Ibid., p. 46.

84 *Surry County Records, Surry County, Virginia, 1652–1684*, abs., Elizabeth T. Davis (n.p.), pp. 15–16.

85 Kelly, 'Economic and Social Development, p. 139.

86 Morgan, *American Slavery*, pp. 227–30.

87 Northumberland was founded in 1648 and Westmoreland in 1653.

88 Torrence, *Old Somerset*, pp. 257–81, 297–334, 435–60.

89 Morgan, *American Slavery*, p. 415.

90 Nugent, *Cavaliers and Pioneers*, vol. 1, p. 141.

91 McIlwaine (ed.), *Journals of the House of Burgesses, 1619–1658/9*, pp. xvi–xx; Horn, 'Lancaster County Files'.

92 Nugent, *Cavaliers and Pioneers*, vol. 1, p. 132.

93 In 1643/4, 1644, 1647/8, 1649, McIlwaine (ed), *Journals of the House of Burgesses, 1619–1658/9*, pp. xvi–xx.

94 Rutman and Rutman, *A Place in Time*, vol. 1, pp. 47–8.

95 Fleet, *Virginia Colonial Abstracts*, pp. 36–8.

96 Rutman and Rutman, *A Place in Time*, vol. 1, p. 49.

97 Horn, 'Lancaster County Files'.

98 Nugent, *Cavaliers and Pioneers*, vol. 1, pp. 135, 151; Horn, 'Lancaster County Files'.

99 Rutman and Rutman, *A Place in Time*, vol. 1, pp. 48–9.

100 Much of the internal movement is very difficult to trace; more evidence exists of out-migration at the end of the century. See Morgan, *American Slavery*, p. 237.

101 Ibid., pp. 225–30.

102 J. P. P. Horn, 'Adapting to a New World: A Comparative Study of Local Society in England and Maryland', in Lois Green Carr, J. P. Greene, and Philip Morgan, eds, *Essays on the Colonial Chesapeake* (Chapel Hill, forthcoming).

103 Main, *Tobacco Colony*, Table 11.5, p. 60. See also Russell R. Menard, P. M. G. Harris, and Lois Green Carr, 'Opportunity and Inequality: The Distribution of Wealth on the Lower Western Shore of Maryland, 1638–1705', *MHM*, **69** (1974), pp. 169–84; Virginia Bernhard, 'Poverty and Social Order in Seventeenth-Century Virginia', *VMHB*, **85** (1977), pp. 141–55.

104 CO1/18, ff. 311–13.

105 *Cal. State Papers, Col. Series, 1677–1680*, ed., Sainsbury, *et al*, pp. 568–9.

106 McIlwaine (ed.), *Journals of the House of Burgesses, 1659/60–1693*, pp. 228.

107 *Charles City County, Virginia, Court Orders, 1687–1695*, Benjamin B. Weisiger, comp. (Richmond, Va., 1980), p. 24.

108 Morgan, *American Slavery*, p. 238.

109 Carr and Menard, 'Immigration and Opportunity', pp. 233–4.

110 Ibid., pp. 235, 240.

111 It is unlikely that we will ever know the full extent of return migration to England in this period: the subject remains tantalizing but elusive. For New England see William L. Sachse, 'The Migration of New Englanders to England, 1640–1660', *American Historical Review*, **53** (1948), pp. 251–78.

112 Richard B. Morris, *Government and Labor in Early America* (Boston, 1981. First pub. 1946), p. 170.

113 H. R. McIlwaine (ed.), *Minutes of the Council and General Court of Colonial Virginia* (Richmond, Va., 1979), p. 116.

114 P. W. Coldham, *English adventurers and emigrants 1609–1660* (Baltimore, 1984), p. 22.

115 Ibid., p. 23.

116 Luke Petley arrived in London from Virginia in 1656 and stated that 'his business is to see his friends'. Similarly, Baker Brooke, 'planter in Virginia', returned to England in the same year 'at the request of his Brother who sent for him'. British Library, Add. Mss 34015, vol.2, pp. 6, 33. John Jones wrote from Virginia to Sir Lionel Jenkins in the summer of 1682 requesting money in order to visit Wales to see his parents, CO1/49, ff. 71, 72. Christopher Boyse (Boyce) and Richard Rutherford, both of Virginia, were in England in the mid 1630s to obtain servants; Coldham, *English adventurers*, pp. 58–9. These examples could be multiplied.

117 Coldham, *English adventurers*, pp. 22, 23, 25, 43, 76, 76, 89–90, 144, 153, 156.

118 Wesley Frank Craven, *White, Red, and Black: the Seventeenth-Century Virginian* (Charlottesville, Va., 1971), pp. 23; L. Withington, 'Virginia Gleanings in England', *VMHB*, **22** (1914), pp. 267–8.

119 Craven, *White, Red, and Black*, p. 23; W. G. Stanard, 'Abstracts of Virginia Land Patents', *VMHB*, **1** (1893–1894), pp. 188–9.

120 C. M. Andrews (ed.), *Narratives of the Insurrections, 1675–1690* (New York, 1943. First pub. 1915), pp. 24, 121.

121 Ibid., pp. 128; 'Philip Ludwell's Account of Bacon's Rebellion', *VMHB*, **1** (1893–1894), pp. 174–8.

122 Burton J. Hendrick, *The Lees of Virginia, Biography of a Family* (New York, 1935), pp. 25–6.

123 Cited in Stephen Saunders Webb, *1676: The End of American Independence* (New York, 1984), p. 82.

124 It was said in the mid eighteenth century that poor people recently arrived in London who were unable to find work 'will not go home to be laughed at . . . but enlist for soldiers, go to the plantations etc., if they are well-inclined; otherwise they probably commence thieves or pick-pockets'; see Horn, 'Servant Emigration', p. 84.

125 Slack, 'Vagrants and Vagrancy', p. 64; For a similar view, see Smith, 'Mortality and Family', pp. 297–300.

126 Gust Skordas, ed., *The Early Settlers of Maryland . . . 1633–1680* (Baltimore, 1968), *passim*.

127 Torrence, *Old Somerset*, p. 25; Wise, *Ye Kingdome of Accawmacke*, pp. 105–9.

128 Kenneth L. Caroll, 'Quakerism on the Eastern Shore of Virginia', *VMHB*, **74** (1966), pp. 172, 174–5.

129 Torrence, *Old Somerset*, pp. 25, 275–81.

130 Babette M. Levy, 'Early Puritanism in the Southern and Island Colonies', *Proceedings of the American Antiquarian Society*, **70** (1960), pp. 122–3, 130–3, 140; J. Reaney Kelly, *Quakers in the Founding of Anne Arundel County, Maryland* (Baltimore, 1963); Clayton C. Hall (ed.), *Narratives of Early Maryland, 1633–1684* (New York, 1925), pp. 218–19, 235.

131 Paul G. E. Clemens, 'Economy and Society on Maryland's Eastern Shore, 1689–1733', in Land, Carr, and Papenfuse (eds), *Law, Society and Politics* pp. 153–70.

132 *Md Arch.*, pp. 19, 225.

133 Ibid., pp. 20, 279.

134 Ibid., pp. 33, 84.

135 McIlwaine (ed.), *Journals of the House of Burgesses, 1659/60–1693*, p. 74.

136 CO1/47, ff. 193–194; Morgan, *American Slavery*, p. 239.

137 Wertenbaker, *The Planters of Colonial Virginia*, pp. 141–4.

138 *Cal. State Papers, Col. Series, 1696–1697*, ed., Sainsbury *et al*, p. 422.

139 CO5/1359, f. 22.

140 Menard, 'Tobacco Industry', pp. 138–42, 153–54; Carr and Menard, 'Immigration and Opportunity', p. 236.

141 Carr and Menard, 'Immigration and Opportunity', p. 236; Wertenbaker, *The Planters of Colonial Virginia*, pp. 139–46.

142 Wertenbaker, *The Planters of Colonial Virginia*, p. 146.

143 *Cal. State Papers, Col. Series, 1693–1696*, ed. Sainsbury *et al*, p. 511; McCusker and Menard, *The Economy of British America*, pp. 170–73; Waterhouse, 'England, the Caribbean, and the Settlement of Carolina', p. 278.

144 Jacob M. Price, 'Economic Function and the Growth of American Port Towns in the Eighteenth Century', *Perspectives in American History*, **8** (1974), p. 152; McCusker and Menard, *The Economy of British America*, p. 194.

145 Gary B. Nash, *The Urban Crucible: Social Change, Political Consciousness, and the Origins of the American Revolution* (Cambridge, Mass., 1979), p. 3.

146 Price, 'Economic Function', p. 175; McCusker and Menard, *The Economy of British America*, p. 203.

147 McCusker and Menard, *The Economy of British America*, pp. 169–70, 172.

148 W. P. Cumming, 'The Earliest Permanent Settlement to Carolina', *American Historical Review*, **45** (1939), pp. 82–9.

149 McCusker and Menard, *The Economy of British America*, p. 172.

150 J. K. Hosmer, ed., *Winthrop's Journal, 'History of New England', 1630–1649* (New York, 1908), vol.1, p. 333; Waterhouse, 'England, the Caribbean, and the Settlement of Carolina', Dunn, *Sugar and Slaves*, pp. 110–16.

151 Clark, 'Migration to England', p. 59.

152 Ibid., pp. 72–6; Wareing, 'Changes in the Geographical Distribution', pp. 241–9; Souden, 'Movers and Stayers', Table 3, pp. 20–2.

153 Morgan, *American Slavery*, Table 3, pp. 412–13; Menard, 'Economy and Society', Appendix 3. pp. 457–9.
154 Morgan, *American Slavery*, p. 158.
155 Carville V. Earle, *Evolution of a Tidewater Settlement System: All Hallows Parish, Maryland, 1650–1783* (University of Chicago, 1975), 29, 141.
156 John C. Rainbolt, 'The Absence of Towns in Seventeenth-Century Virginia', *Journal of Southern History,* **35** (1969), pp. 343–60; Peter V. Bergstrom and Kevin P. Kelly, 'The Country Around the Towns: Society, Demography, and the Rural Economy of York County, Virginia, 1695–1705' (Paper presented to a conference on 'Maryland, A Product of Two Worlds', St Mary's City, Maryland, May 1984).
157 Clark, 'The Migrant in Kentish Towns', p. 149.
158 Idem, 'Migration in England', p. 89.
159 Idem, 'The Migrant in Kentish Towns', p. 138.
160 Ibid., p. 137.

7
Migration in England during the late seventeenth and early eighteenth centuries

Peter Clark

The author exploits church court witness statements for the late seventeenth and early eighteenth centuries to delineate the overall pattern of migration, principally in southern England. Though indicating regional variations, Peter Clark argues for continuing high levels of physical mobility, but with most migration short distance and the apparent disappearance of long-distance subsistence movement. The analysis stresses the importance of rising living standards, urbanization, agrarian differentiation, the Old Poor Law and settlement controls in influencing the new patterns of migration after the Restoration. The source does not provide a good measure of gross migrant flows. The data are also less reliable after 1700 and it is problematical whether the pattern observed here obtains far into the eighteenth century.

Physical mobility had a profound and pervasive effect on early modern society. Its central role in the demographic matrix is increasingly clear. In many towns population growth depended heavily on the recruitment of outsiders: perhaps as many as one in six of English adults had visited the capital in the period 1650 to 1750.[1] Immigration also helped shape the demographic structure of communities. Detailed work indicates how the influx of migrants, particularly female domestics, was of major importance in determining the large households, regressive age pyramids, and surplus of women found in the wealthy inner parishes of cities.[2] Again the level of physical mobility may have affected the elasticity of the labour supply,[3] while it certainly had wide-ranging social repercussions. In the decades before the Civil War the multitudes of poor migrants on the tramp across England precipitated an avalanche of problems for public order, housing and food supply.[4] Physical mobility also probably contributed to the

213

communication of new ideas and attitudes, particularly those generated in the forcing-ground of the metropolis, as well as encouraging changes in the status and importance of women.[5] On the other hand, migration continued to serve as a powerful adhesive force in provincial society, integrating towns with the villages of their hinterlands, linking together the communities of a sub-regional 'country' or *pays*.[6] Nor is the importance of internal migration in this period confined to its impact on society at large. As we shall see, it was also a sensitive barometer of economic, social and political change.

This paper will look first at the current state of research on physical mobility in early modern England, then at the existing sources and their problems, before going on to present new data for the years 1660 to 1730, making use of biographical material provided by seven thousand or so witnesses appearing in the church courts. From this and other evidence we shall attempt to map the main contours of migration in the late seventeenth and early eighteenth centuries, paying particular attention to regional and social variations and the forces which affected them.

I

Most recent research on physical mobility in pre-industrial England has tended to concentrate on the century or so before 1640. Julian Cornwall has exploited a small group of biographical statements made by witnesses before Sussex church courts and found that about three-quarters of his mainly rural sample had moved at least once in their lives. Mining a similar source, the depositions of a hundred or so east Londoners before the London commissary court, David Cressy concluded that 89 per cent of his witnesses were born in different parishes or other parts of the country, notably the west midlands and the north. In an earlier essay on movement into three Kent towns between 1580 and 1640 I analysed just over a thousand deposition statements and put forward the view that these centres were affected by a substantial amount of longer-distance *subsistence* migration by poorer folk, alongside more localized movement by respectable men and women.[7]

Other sources have also been investigated. Working on the freemen rolls for New Romney in the fifteenth and early sixteenth centuries, A. F. Butcher has argued for a large influx of immigrants into that Kentish port, with as many as a quarter drawn from outside the county. From the apprenticeship records of certain London gild companies in the period 1630–60, Steven R. Smith has shown that up to 40 per cent of those indentured came from the north and the midlands. As for poorer migrants, Paul Slack has examined a mixture of town and central government records and determined that during the critical decades before 1640 many paupers travelled long distances in search of employment and relief – up to 22 per cent of his sample had moved more than a hundred miles.[8]

While more studies are still needed to provide local detail, the broad pattern of physical mobility in England before the Civil War is already visible. First, migration was an almost universal phenomenon affecting the great mass of the national population. Secondly, most of this migrational activity involved what we might term 'circular mobility', with servants, apprentices, would-be spouses, and others out to better themselves, travelling fairly limited distances, to a neighbouring town or village, usually within an area defined by traditional notions of a sub-regional 'country'. Thirdly, there was a significant level of longer distance *subsistence* migration, involving mainly poor people, pushed by hardship on to the road, often moving towards towns.

Compared with the sustained attack on the problem in the earlier period, work on migration after the Restoration has been small-scale and exploratory. Peter Laslett and John Harrison have compared parish listings for Clayworth in Nottinghamshire in 1676 and 1688 in order to calculate overall mobility rates.[9] Using the apprenticeship records of the Cutlers' Company in Hallamshire, E. J. Buckatzsch has tabulated the places of origin of certain immigrants into Sheffield, while David Glass has taken the list of apprentices admitted to the freedom of the City of London in 1690 to make crude calculations about the flow of migrants to the metropolis. R. A. Pelham and E. G. Thomas have both analysed settlement records to track the mobility of poorer men and women, the former concentrating on movement to Birmingham in the years 1686–1726, the latter comparing migrational patterns in Essex, Berkshire and Oxfordshire during the eighteenth century.[10] A variety of minor pieces have also appeared.[11] Nevertheless a number of important questions remain outstanding relating to the overall level of mobility, the origins of migrants, the distances travelled, the ages of those moving, and regional and social variations. Most of these questions will be considered in later sections of this paper.

Part of the explanation for the limited research on migration in the late seventeenth and early eighteenth centuries is to be found in the quality of the sources. They are noticeably more intractable and less reliable than for the preceding period. The limitations of the data need to be carefully spelt out before we can attempt to construct any general analytical framework.

II

Many sources offer shards of information on physical mobility after the Restoration,[12] but only five or six provide quantifiable data to any extent: nominal listings of inhabitants; marriage records; settlement papers; apprenticeship and freemen registers; and church court deposition books.

Nominal listings such as those used by Laslett and Harrison for their Clayworth study are quite rare and generally only tell us who moved, not where the migrants went. An exception (though somewhat outside our period) is the Cardington listing of 1782, which sheds light on the ages, occupations and birthplaces of parishioners, as well as giving similar details for all surviving children including the location of those no longer resident.[13] Data on a wider range of communities are provided by marriage records, since some registers note the residence of incoming spouses. There are problems however: marriage records suffer from under-registration as a result of clandestine or dissenting weddings and common-law unions; the data are biased towards younger members of society; and even after the Hardwicke Marriage Act of 1753, registers note only the place of residence at the time of marriage.[14]

Apprenticeship registers (mostly kept by boroughs) have frequently been used for the study of migration, particularly rural/ urban movement. Though age–selective like the previous source, records specify the apprentice's place of origin, the type of trade entered and (quite often) the name and occupation of the father. On the other hand, apprenticeship was never a neutral process by which boys were recruited to learn a craft or trade prior to induction as full members of the community. Rather, apprenticeship served to regulate entrance into the principal occupations of a town and, in conjunction with the grant of freedom, operated as a check on the number of townsmen enjoying civic rights. Apprenticeship data have to be seen then as age- and sex-selective, relating almost wholly to teenage boys, and as discriminatory, affecting only some of the large numbers of young males flocking to town. For instance, at Norwich we find repeated references to masters employing country youths and servants who had not been apprenticed.[15] Under-registration is another major drawback with apprenticeship records. To cite one from many examples, in 1604 the Southampton leet complained of the 'many inconveniences [that] arise by means of the not enrolment of apprentices of all trades in this town'. The widespread failure to have agreements registered stemmed partly from the negligence of town officials and partly from the reluctance of masters to pay the necessary fees. Masters often delayed enrolment for several years, doubtless because of the high drop-out rate among apprentices, particularly in the poorer trades. At Norwich, for example, many poor apprentices never had their agreements registered. In consequence the data are heavily biased towards more respectable occupations.[16]

The problems with apprenticeship records escalate from the late seventeenth century as gild organizations and controls disintegrated in many towns, and it became increasingly easy to work or set up in business without having been apprenticed. At the same time, we discover people entering fictitious apprenticeships in order to acquire the freedom for party political ends. To compound the difficulty, most borough records were kept more erratically after the Restoration.[17]

Freemen registers are less informative than apprenticeship papers (at best they only tell us occupations and birthplaces). They are also socially-selective, strongly biased towards the upper echelons of urban society, while the data are progressively undermined during the later Stuart period by the partisan practice of making armies of paper freemen for electoral purposes.[18] More valuable for studies of migration are settlement papers, the two main series – removal orders and certificates – appearing after the 1662 Settlement Act. As well as covering both town and countryside, they detail the movement of all members of the family grouping and also yield information about the ages and occupations of migrants. Settlement papers do not deal with the destitute alone. Because the law affected most persons without residential property of £10 or more per annum, many marginal and respectable poor were also caught in the settlement net. On the debit side, only a few parishes kept registers of orders or certificates, so we rarely have any idea of the total number of cases handled or the typicality of surviving papers, while the urban coverage is generally incomplete owing to the multiplicity of parishes in most larger towns. But despite these reservations settlement records tell us a great deal about physical mobility and we shall need to refer to them again in the later analysis.[19]

Finally, there are the church court deposition papers. When witnesses in civil and criminal actions appeared before the diocesan courts they generally prefaced their testimony with a brief autobiographical statement. From the late sixteenth century the statement normally listed name, age, occupation or status, place and length of residence, and sometimes details of previous residence. This practice was more or less the rule in most parts of the province of Canterbury, though not in the northern province.

As John Patten has remarked, deposition records are 'invaluable for the study of mobility and migration.'[20] But the source is by no means unimpeachable. Clerks in diocesan courts were not always conscientious in keeping accurate records, and witnesses might prove forgetful or unintelligible. Comparison of statements by the same witness on different occasions, however, suggests that the information recorded is reasonably accurate. More serious and unavoidable is the tendency for the witnesses to be respectable people able to impress the court with their standing, though before the Civil War a fair number of poorer men and women also testified.[21] In the late seventeenth century the difficulties multiply. In some dioceses the church courts never regained their momentum after the English Revolution. In many areas the number of cases heard was falling markedly by 1700, though most courts managed to carry on until about 1730. Exceptionally, the Norwich diocesan courts remained functioning into the second half of the eighteenth century. Again the problem of the social selectivity of the data becomes more acute after the Restoration: poorer witnesses are less common. A final difficulty for the historian stems from the growing fluidity of occupational styles.[22]

Nonetheless, deposition records are still our most extensive and illuminating source for the study of physical mobility in the late seventeenth and early eighteenth centuries. They supply detailed evidence of the migrational experience of men and women, town and countryside, different regions and varying social and economic groups. From deposition records we can sketch an outline picture of physical mobility in England after the Restoration which can then be checked and substantiated by reference to some of the other sources examined earlier – settlement records, nominal listings and the like.

III

For the purposes of this paper I have collected and analysed the biographical data relating to over seven thousand witnesses appearing in the diocesan courts of Canterbury, Norwich, Oxford, Salisbury, Gloucester, and Coventry and Lichfield, between 1660 and 1730. Because of the large size of the Norwich sample, I have distinguished between Norfolk and Suffolk witnesses. In the case of Canterbury diocese the sample is drawn from east and mid Kent. The Salisbury evidence covers Wiltshire and parts of Dorset; the Oxford and Gloucester data relate to Oxfordshire and Gloucestershire respectively. Coventry and Lichfield diocese embraced parts of Warwickshire, Worcestershire, Staffordshire and Derbyshire. As the sample here is small the data have been aggregated to form a single west midlands category.[23] The overall sample provides a fairly representative cross-section of southern and midland England. (See Table 26.).

To complete this discussion of the sample, three further points need to be made. First, all the data are derived from orthodox deposition statements such as those described earlier, with the exception of the material from Coventry and Lichfield diocese. There the courts failed to ask witnesses to supply biographical details before they testified. Fortunately the interrogatories which deponents answered in the course of their testimony usually included a standard question concerning their personal status and background. As a result, one can unearth the relevant biographical data in a substantial number of cases. While this data may be less reliable than that for other areas, detailed analysis suggests no glaring discrepancies. Secondly, on period coverage, the depositions for Gloucester, Salisbury, and Coventry and Lichfield dioceses relate to the first three decades after the Restoration only; for the other dioceses there are data for the whole of the period up to 1730, though it is less abundant after about 1700. A final point. Witnesses usually made their statements in one of several courts appearing within a diocese. But since there is nothing to indicate that courts differed in the types of cases they

Table 26   Sample: number of deponents 1660–1730*

	Male			Female			Total Male and Female
	Rural	Urban	All	Rural	Urban	All	
Gloucestershire	473	212	685	142	57	199	884
Kent	458	355	813	142	112	254	1,067
Norfolk	1,356	828	2,184	282	417	699	2,883
Oxfordshire	291	191	482	76	86	162	644
Suffolk	308	196	504	70	68	138	642
West Midlands	221	117	338	64	39	103	441
Wiltshire and Dorset	230	147	377	60	49	109	486
							7,047

Notes and sources: Data have been derived from church court deposition books and papers as follows: Gloucestershire, from Gloucestershire Record Office, GDR 205, 211, 219, 221, 232; Kent, from Canterbury Cathedral Library, PRC 38/1-3, and PRC 39/51-5 (previously at the Kent Archives Office); Norfolk and Suffolk, from Norfolk Record Office, DEP 46-8 (books), 49-64 (files); Oxfordshire, from Bodleian Library, MSS. Oxford dioc. c. 28–31, 96–7, and Oxford archd. c. 119-20; west midlands, from Lichfield Joint Record Office, Cause Papers, B/C/5, 1660-85; Wiltshire and Dorset, from Salisbury Diocesan Record Office, Bishop's Court, Deposition Books, 58-64, together with Archdeacon's Court, Deposition Papers, and Dean's Court, Deposition Books, 15-19. Salisbury diocese had extensive peculiars in Dorset. The data for Gloucestershire, the west midlands, and Wiltshire and Dorset only survive for the period *c.* 1660–*c.* 1685.

heard or witnesses they called, curial distinctions have been ignored in the analysis of the data.

Let us turn to the light the deposition material sheds on the pattern of physical mobility between 1660 and 1730. The salient features of male migration can be discerned from Table 27. Among town deponents[24] the overall proportion of those who had moved at least once in their lives – whether within or from outside their county, to an unspecified destination, or from parish to parish within their home town – was just over six in every ten. The incidence of mobility was somewhat less in the west (as low as 49 per cent in Gloucestershire) and greater in eastern England (roughly about 70 per cent in Suffolk, Norfolk and Kent). As for countrymen, the overall rate of movement was rather higher – with nearly seven in every ten mobile – though this masked wider regional variations, with the incidence of migration in Suffolk almost twice that in Gloucestershire.

Geographical contrasts are less striking when we look at the female evidence. (See Table 28). Of the townswomen deposing,

Table 27 Incidence of migration among male deponents*

Gloucestershire:	rural	54·1	4·2	—	30·1	11·6
	urban	50·9	2·8	1·4	27·9	17·0
Kent:	rural	19·7	7·4	—	62·4	10·5
	urban	29·0	6·2	7·3	42·3	15·2
Norfolk:	rural	21·5	8·6	—	58·9	11·0
	urban	30·9	4·1	10·7	38·1	16·2
Oxfordshire:	rural	41·6	6·9	—	32·6	18·9
	urban	38·7	4·2	9·9	23·6	23·6
Suffolk:	rural	16·6	5·2	—	50·0	28·2
	urban	29·1	7·7	0·5	32·6	30·1
West Midlands:	rural	40·3	5·0	—	38·5	16·2
	urban	46·2	4·3	0·0	29·0	20·5
Wiltshire and Dorset:	rural	35·6	17·0	—	35·5	13·9
	urban	46·9	14·3	0·0	21·1	17·1
Mean of county percentages:	rural	32·8	7·8	—	43·7	15·8
	urban	38·8	6·2	4·3	30·7	20·0
	overall	35·8	7·0	4·3	37·2	17·9
Weighted mean of county percentages:	rural	31·3	8·1	—	45·7	15·2
	urban	38·4	6·4	4·3	31·5	19·5
	overall	34·9	7·2	4·3	38·6	17·4

Notes and sources: Data and sources are as given in Table 26. All figures are percentages. Local figures represent percentages of group sample. The weighted mean adjusts for the relative population sizes of counties calculated from P. Deane and W. A. Cole, *British Economic Growth, 1688–1959* (Cambridge, 1962), p. 103.

only about one in three had never moved, with the highest levels of mobility recorded in Kent and the west midlands. In all areas the incidence of mobility was even more common among country-women: on average about three-quarters had migrated at some time, with the proportion again particularly high in Kent.

What about changes in mobility rates over time? How far, for instance, did amendments to the settlement law in the 1690s permit or encourage any acceleration in migrational activity?[25] Our data here are confined to Kent, Suffolk, Norfolk and Oxford-shire. Nonetheless, a crude comparison of deposition statements

Table 28   Incidence of migration among female deponents*

Gloucestershire:	rural	33·8	4·9	—	47·9	13·4
	urban	40·4	1·7	0·0	45·6	12·3
Kent:	rural	17·6	4·9	—	74·0	3·5
	urban	31·3	2·7	11·6	44·6	9·8
Norfolk:	rural	20·6	5·3	—	62·4	11·7
	urban	41·0	2·4	9·6	33·3	13·7
Oxfordshire:	rural	32·9	5·3	—	40·8	21·0
	urban	43·0	1·2	13·9	27·9	14·0
Suffolk:	rural	18·6	4·3	—	48·5	28·6
	urban	33·8	2·9	4·4	26·5	32·4
West Midlands:	rural	23·4	1·6	—	57·8	17·2
	urban	28·2	0·0	0·0	43·6	28·2
Wiltshire and Dorset:	rural	25·0	8·3	—	46·7	20·0
	urban	40·8	6·1	0·0	38·8	14·3
Mean of county percentages:	rural	24·6	4·9	—	54·0	16·5
	urban	36·9	2·4	5·6	37·2	17·8
	overall	30·8	3·7	5·6	45·6	17·2
Weighted mean of county percentages:	rural	23·7	5·0	—	55·3	16·0
	urban	36·9	2·6	5·3	37·5	17·8
	overall	30·3	3·8	5·3	46·4	16·9

Notes and sources: Data and sources are as given in Table 26. All figures are percentages. Local figures represent percentages of group sample. For the weighted mean, see Table 27.

made before and after 1697 yields few signs of any rise in the level of mobility; among townswomen, the incidence of migration actually fell in the second half of our period.

Having established the general extent of mobility we need to examine how far our migrants had travelled. To begin with, a rough and ready distinction can be made between migration within the home county and migration from outside. Looking first at the men (see Table 27) and taking urban and rural deponents together, it is evident that extra-county migration was running at less than half the rate of movement inside the county. At the same time, migration from outside the home county was more common among townsmen than countrymen. In the case of

women (see Table 28) movement within the home county was still
more frequent, though again a rather greater proportion of urban
(as against rural) deponents had migrated from another county.
Even when migrants had travelled from outside the home county
the great majority, both men and women, had come from neighbouring shires.

At the same time, it would be wrong to give too much credence
to figures dependent on the vagaries of county boundaries, where
(as in the west midlands) walking only a few miles might entail
traversing several shires. Rather more reliable is evidence derived
from the measurement of migrational distances as the crow flies.

Table 29 demonstrates that roughly half of all the migrants had
travelled no more than 10 miles, while only about one in ten had
moved over 40 miles, and less than one in twenty over 100 miles.
Localized migration was particularly notable among country-
women, with countrymen a close second. Townsmen were most
liable to move long distances. Predictably, there were some
regional variations in the mileages moved, a point we shall return
to later in the paper. However, there is no evidence in any of our
areas of the fairly large-scale, longer-distance movement, north-
south and to some extent west-east, which has been observed for
the years before 1640.[26]

Table 29 Mileage travelled by migrants between birthplaces
and places of residence*

| | Male | | Female | |
	Rural	Urban	Rural	Urban
10 miles or less	59·4	45·0	64·6	47·9
Over 40 miles	9·3	19·2	6·7	11·4
Over 100 miles	3·2	8·2	0·8	1·7

*Notes and sources: Data and sources are as given in Table 26. All figures are
percentages and represent an arithmetical means of county percentages; the
weighted mean shows no significant statistical variations.

This leads us on to the question, how far there were marked
variations in the migrational experience of different social and
economic groups, as there had been in the sixteenth and early
seventeenth centuries. Any attempt to answer this question is
obviously complicated by the growing imprecision of occupational
styles after the Restoration and the need to employ somewhat
arbitrary occupational groupings. Yet while admitting that our

findings must be treated with caution, they do shed some limited light on the problem.[27]

In the case of urban migrants (see Table 30) it was professional men – lawyers, clergy, physicians – who had travelled furthest (on average over 60 miles). Next came those claiming gentle status, among them perhaps numerous pseudo-gentry and small land-owners who had moved into town; these had migrated an average of 39 miles. Another group of townsmen with a relatively high average mileage were the food and drink traders, closely connected with inland trade. At the opposite end of the mileage spectrum were yeomen and those engaged in the building and clothing trades, all of whom had travelled quite short distances. Yet, despite these differences, what is also striking about the findings presented in Table 30 is the general bunching of distances travelled, with the great majority of the occupational groups

Table 30 Average mileage moved since birth by male immigrants (urban deponents) according to occupational grouping*

Gentry	18·2	30·2	56·4	77·6	36·3	—	14·3	38·8
Professional	33·4	112·6	54·7	30·7	84·5	82·4	—	66·4
Clothing trades	16·7	8·0	39·7	—	17·5	—	—	20·5
Leather trades	—	26·6	35·8	6·4	—	21·2	28·9	23·8
Food and drink	14·9	52·4	44·3	19·2	50·1	97·6	17·1	42·2
Textile	21·0	37·7	32·1	16·4	25·5	—	19·2	25·3
Household goods	—	—	33·3	12·7	—	—	—	23·0
Distributive	—	31·9	61·0	—	18·9	25·1	—	34·2
Building trades	—	13·8	33·9	12·4	22·8	—	—	20·7
Yeomen	18·8	38·1	17·2	14·3	9·6	18·9	15·3	18·9
Husbandmen	—	39·8	15·1	—	76·9	17·8	—	37·4
Labourers	—	—	—	—	—	—	—	—
Rural miscellaneous	—	24·6	40·3	—	—	—	—	32·5
Service industries	—	78·1	20·7	11·7	15·0	—	—	31·4
Servants	—	31·7	17·1	—	—	—	—	24·4
Miscellaneous	—	8·9	34·3	—	49·9	—	—	31·0
Unspecified	9·5	—	27·8	—	62·2	—	—	33·2

Notes and sources: Data and sources are as given in Table 26. All mileages are calculated as the crow flies. Small occupational samples have been excised from the analysis.

having moved on average between 20 and 35 miles. There were of course some regional variations in the pattern but they do not detract from the surprisingly uniform bias towards shorter-distance migration right across the occupational board. Neither the overall mean figures already cited nor the sample findings for post-Restoration Kent tabulated in Table 30 show any sign of the high mileages recorded for poorer groups of migrants travelling into Kentish towns before 1640.

In the case of rural migrants (see Table 31) the pattern of movement was a telescoped version of the urban picture. The distances moved were shorter and the variations between occupational groups even less marked. Once again, professional people and gentlemen figure prominently among those moving furthest: servants, yeomen and husbandmen had travelled least far. But there was an obvious concentration of movement in the 10 to 25

Table 31   Average mileage moved since birth by male immigrants (rural deponents) according to occupational grouping*

Gentry	21·2	44·9	26·3	18·2	20·6	43·9	18·5	27·7
Professional	36·5	80·6	37·2	65·4	36·9	13·8	55·2	46·5
Clothing trades	—	48·7	20·0	5·5	22·3	—	—	24·1
Leather trades	—	9·1	23·7	—	17·6	—	—	16·8
Food and drink	—	20·9	24·0	9·1	43·7	10·6	—	21·7
Textile	6·3	11·7	16·7	—	35·1	—	8·1	15·6
Household goods	—	—	—	—	—	—	—	—
Distributive	—	—	7·4	—	—	—	—	7·4
Building trades	12·2	12·9	11·7	10·4	13·8	34·7	9·8	15·1
Yeomen	15·2	15·4	12·7	8·8	7·8	11·5	10·7	11·7
Husbandmen	13·2	13·7	10·6	12·2	17·8	9·6	8·9	12·3
Labourers	—	—	55·0	11·5	—	10·7	—	25·7
Rural miscellaneous	—	9·8	12·9	8·9	23·6	19·2	—	14·9
Service industries	—	40·9	13·4	9·5	14·3	—	9·3	17·5
Servants	—	—	14·5	—	—	—	—	14·5
Miscellaneous	—	—	9·8	—	—	—	—	9·8
Unspecified	8·5	—	29·1	11·1	10·4	7·2	—	13·3

Notes and sources: Data and sources are as given in Table 26. All mileages are calculated as the crow flies. Small occupational samples have been excised from the analysis.

mile range, with two-thirds of the occupational groupings recording mileages of that order.

Deposition evidence for the period after the Restoration is not sufficiently detailed to afford any precise idea of the frequency of moves, but we know more about the age at which migrants arrived at their place of residence. The majority had moved between the ages of 11 and 30. This undoubtedly reflected the personal life cycle of the migrant, the rigours of travel, and the combined pressures of employment, marital and (possibly) educational opportunities.[28] Of course there were some contrasts between town and countryside. As Table 32 indicates, migrants to towns were most likely to move between the ages of 11 and 20. Migration among rural deponents was more heavily weighted towards the 21 to 30 age category. The high level of teenage migration to towns was consistent with the continuing role of the apprenticeship system in urban labour recruitment in the later Stuart period. From the 1690s, however, there are signs of a possible contraction of teenage migration to towns – coinciding, arguably, with the decline of apprenticeship. The rural evidence would suggest that, while entering service often entailed leaving home, many teenagers quite often worked initially in the same community; afterwards they would move further afield to be hired as farm servants living in their masters' houses. Eventually they would marry and work as labourers or set up in farming or a trade on their own.[29] As for migrants coming from outside the home county, these included a high proportion of men from the older age categories – higher than among county-born migrants.[30] Finally, what do we know about the age of migration for women? Though the evidence

Table 32 Ages of male migrants on arrival at places of residence*

		Under 11	11–20	21–30	31–40	Over 40
Rural:	county-born	7·9	19·0	40·0	20·2	12·9
	extra-county	6·7	17·5	38·2	22·2	15·4
Urban:	county-born	9·0	32·3	34·1	15·8	8·8
	extra-county	4·4	29·0	37·9	19·3	9·4

Notes and sources: Data and sources are as given in Table 26 but with the west midlands material excluded because it omits ages. All figures are percentages and represent an arithmetical mean of county percentages; the weighted mean shows no significant statistical variations.

here is more sparse, there are indications that migration into towns by teenage girls was less common than among their male counterparts and that the most popular age of movement by women, whether in town or countryside, was between 21 and 30.

To complete this discussion of the deposition data we need to look at the previous contacts of our migrants, whether with town or village. Here I have included places of birth and (where known) places of intermediate residence. From Table 33 it can be seen that there was a significant level of movement between towns. For town deponents born in their home counties, approximately a quarter of their contacts had been urban; for those coming from outside the county the proportion was nearer a half. By contrast, the experience of the country deponents was predominantly rural, though again extra-county migrants had had more contacts with towns. The female pattern of rural/urban contacts seems to have been roughly similar.

IV

So much then for the information on physical mobility in post-Restoration England presented by the deposition statements. The sample is relatively small (just over 1 per cent of the total adult population of our areas) and not all the material is equally convincing. But the data do provide a rough sketch of the anatomy of internal migration in the period. Such a picture can

Table 33 Rural/urban contacts of male migrants before current residence*

	Rural contacts	*Urban contacts*
Rural deponents		
county-born	84·0	16·0
extra-county	73·4	26·6
Urban deponents		
county-born	74·6	25·4
extra-county	55·3	44·7

Notes and sources: Data and sources are as given in Table 26. All figures are percentages and represent an arithmetical mean of county percentages; the weighted mean shows no significant statistical variations.

be tested by reference to some of the other sources and published work mentioned earlier in this paper.

The most striking and fundamental finding of the deposition evidence is that the great mass of English people, men and women, country-dwellers as well as townspeople, migrated at some time in their lives in the late seventeenth and early eighteenth centuries. This is in close accord with Laslett and Harrison's view that nearly 40 per cent of the Clayworth villagers had changed parishes between 1676 and 1688, and the evidence for late eighteenth-century Cardington that about 70 per cent of the inhabitants had been born elsewhere.[31] Combining the post-Restoration evidence with what is known of physical mobility before the English Revolution, we must conclude that migration was not the exception but the social and demographic norm, indeed the usual way of life, in early modern England.[32]

Another conclusion of the deposition material – that the great majority of moves took place within the home county, usually involving travel of little more than 10 or so miles – is also borne out by other sources. Thus Buckatzsch calculated that 73 per cent of his Sheffield apprentices in the years 1650–1724 had come from within a radius of 15 miles and only just over 4 per cent from over 40 miles. Even among poorer, settlement migrants we discover the same preponderance of short-distance mobility. Of those arriving in the prosperous county town of Maidstone with settlement certificates during the period 1691–1740, well over half had travelled no more than 10 miles, while only about 15 per cent had walked or ridden over 40 miles. (See Table 34.) Further north, in Derbyshire, removal orders for the years 1720–4 reveal a similar bias

Table 34 Mileages travelled by immigrants with settlement certificates at Maidstone 1691–1740*

	Male	Female
10 miles or less	56·5	53·0
Over 40 miles	15·1	14·2
Over 100 miles	7·5	6·5
Size of sample	345	247

Notes and sources: Figures are taken from Kent Archives Office, P 241/ 13/1, a well-kept register of settlement certificates covering the whole town. Apart from the sample size all figures are percentages.

towards localized mobility – 67 per cent of the migrants there had gone less than 11 miles.[33]

All this would seem to argue for a shift in the late seventeenth century away from the fairly high incidence of longer-distance mobility observed for the period before the Civil War. Such a shift can be traced to some extent through the deposition data. In Gloucester diocese between 1595 and 1640 nearly a quarter (23.1 per cent) of townsmen appearing in the church courts had been born outside the county, often coming from far afield; among countrymen the proportion was 14.7 per cent. In the decades following the Restoration the corresponding figures, as we saw above (Table 27), were 17 per cent and 11.6 per cent respectively. Among Kentish townsmen there was an equally significant decline in longer-distance mobility, from about 22 per cent in the period 1580–1640 to about 15 per cent in the late seventeenth and early eighteenth centuries.[34] It is possible that comparisons of this sort are distorted by the increasing social selectivity of the deposition data during the seventeenth century, with fewer poor men appearing in court. At the same time, if we are to believe the settlement records, most poorer folk in later Stuart England moved only short distances. Certainly the apprenticeship evidence we have indicates a growing localization of migration. According to Lawrence Stone, and based on his tabulation of the records of the London Carpenters' and Fishmongers' Companies, by 1700 only 20 per cent or less of apprentices were recruited from the highland zone, compared with 40 per cent in the pre-revolutionary era. A contraction in the catchment area for Norwich apprentices also occurred during the same period.[35] Some of the factors behind this development will be considered shortly.

Overall then, internal migration in England in the period 1660–1730 was broadly characterized by high rates of turnover but limited geographical movement. When looked at more closely, however, a number of variations can be observed within this general pattern relating to a range of differential factors – sex, location, region and so on.

As we saw earlier, the deposition evidence indicates that women in our period tended to be more mobile than men, though they moved shorter distances (many of these women doubtless shifted to neighbouring villages to get married). Comparable data are in short supply, but the Cardington survey of 1782 supports both these findings while work on migration into Kentish towns before

1640 confirms the last.[36] At the same time, such generalizations need careful qualification, as we can see when we look at the differences between urban and rural migration. In the countryside, mobility was markedly higher among women than men, but in towns the divergence was small, partly affected by the important role of apprenticeship in bringing boys to town.

Differences between town and countryside are also emphasized in other ways. The deposition data suggest that while overall mobility may have been more pronounced among countrypeople than townspeople (in the ratio 7:6) urban migration was more geographically extensive. (See Table 29 above.) On the latter point Thomas's research comes to similar conclusions: whereas most rural labourers had travelled only 5 or 6 miles, urban migrants had frequently travelled further, often on an inter-town basis.[37] The more extensive catchment area of the urban community was sustained by a complex of factors, including the greater number and variety of employment opportunities there, the town's marketing links with the villages of its hinterland, and the operation of the apprenticeship system which served as a surrogate kinship network, encouraging parents to send their children further and earlier from home.[38]

In principle one can say that the larger the town, the wider its catchment area. In Kent before the English Revolution Canterbury's attractive pull was strongest in an arc of about 15 miles, compared with 11 miles each for Maidstone and Faversham, whose respective populations were less than half that of Canterbury. According to Wrigley and others the great metropolis of London recruited throughout the kingdom in the seventeenth century.[39] Yet it would be simplistic to construct a hierarchy of urban recruitment zones based on demographic criteria alone. Thus deposition evidence for post-Restoration Norwich, the second largest city in the kingdom (population of about 30,000 in *circa* 1700), indicates that the proportion of immigrants from outside the county was roughly similar to that for the port of Yarmouth whose inhabitants probably numbered only about 10,000. Here it seems likely that Norwich's attractive power was muted by indifferent cross-country communications, while Yarmouth's maritime connections along the east coast amplified its recruiting pull.[40]

The pattern of mobility was certainly not unilinear. Women, though probably more mobile than men, tended to move shorter distances; townspeople, if less prone to migrate than those who had stayed in the country, moved further when they actually took to the road. Even so, these variations do not seriously impugn our main findings: that most people moved in their lives, but that their travels usually spanned only short distances. Two problems remain to be considered however. How far were there significant variations in the migrational experience of different areas of the country and different social and economic groups? And particularly important, what lay behind such variations?

V

The deposition data analysed earlier suggested that there were a number of differences in the level and type of physical mobility between the regions of southern and midland England. Indeed it seems likely that the ground plan of migration in our period was highly variegated, almost to the point where it defies overall interpretation. Nonetheless, certain landmarks are visible. In the first place it can be seen from Tables 27 and 28 that the overall rate of mobility, for both sexes, was lowest in the west – in Oxfordshire, Gloucestershire, Wiltshire and Dorset – and highest in the east, particularly in Kent and Suffolk. In line with this finding, localized migration (involving distances of 10 miles or less) seems to have been more important in the west, most obviously in Gloucestershire. So far as longer-distance movement is concerned, the picture is more complicated. True, Suffolk in the east had a high percentage of people moving over 40 miles, and indeed over 100 miles, but so it would seem did Oxfordshire. Surprisingly perhaps, Kent and Norfolk were notable for the low incidence of longer-distance mobility in both town and village.

Local variations in migrational activity have also been described by Slack in his work on vagrancy before the Civil War and by Thomas in his study of eighteenth-century settlement papers.[41] Far less is known, however, about the actual variables shaping regional or sub-regional patterns. No exhaustive checklist can be offered here, but six or seven factors clearly deserve attention. One is communications. It was noted earlier how the flow of migrants into Norwich between 1660 and 1730 was apparently distorted by poor cross-country communications. At the general level, there may be a positive correlation between the high mobility rates found in Kent and Suffolk in our period with their relatively good communications – Roman roads, turnpikes (from the 1690s), and river and coastal transportation. By contrast the more immobile western counties suffered fairly primitive communications, at least before the 1730s.[42] At the local level, we know that many Suffolk men travelled into south Essex in the eighteenth century by coastal shipping, while marital migrants in the east midlands tended to make their way along important drove roads.[43]

Another variable affecting the regional kaleidoscope of physical mobility is the local level of urbanization. One might reasonably expect substantial urban growth to generate an above-average incidence of migration in the area, including some longer-distance mobility. Thus the high number of immigrants found in certain Kent towns before 1640 may well have been affected by the advanced level of urbanization in the county.[44] The evidence for the later period is hardly as positive as one would like. The west midlands, despite its numerous industrializing centres, was not in fact one of the more mobile regions nor was it apparently prone to longer-distance movement, though it must also be said that the deposition sample for the area is small and drawn from an early period (1660–85). The picture is more convincing when we look at the possible links between urban decay and low levels of migrational activity. For example, Gloucestershire, which ranked on almost all counts as one of the least mobile areas after 1660, experienced fairly widespread urban dislocation and decline. Gloucester itself was only slowly recovering from the severe economic depression which had affected the city in the 1620s and 1630s and which had been prolonged by the devastation of the Civil War, while the number of market towns in the county fell by nearly a half between the Restoration and 1720 as a result of economic decay.[45]

Needless to say, London was by far and away the most powerful urban influence on regional patterns of mobility. The capital functioned as an enormous pair of revolving doors, pulling migrants in one side and pushing those that survived its disease-stricken world out on the other. While men and women travelled there from most parts of the kingdom, many of those who departed from the metropolis tended to take up residence in neighbouring counties.[46] Thus the deposition evidence records a sizeable efflux of Londoners to East Anglia and Kent; migration to the western counties was negligible.

Local variations in the pattern of physical mobility also have to be seen in the context of developments in the agrarian economy of the area. Here, fortunately, the deposition material is ample enough for Norfolk to plot the divergent trends in migrational activity of the principal farming 'countries' of that shire: the sheep-corn 'country', mainly to the north and west, and the wood-pasture 'country', mostly to the south and east. A recent detailed survey allows us to identify the farming bias of the majority of parishes in the county and to correlate this with our data on mobility. (See Table 35.)

Table 35 Migration patterns of male deponents born in Norfolk*

	Born in wood-pasture parish	Born in sheep-corn parish
Stationary	24·0	22·0
Move unspecified	8·7	11·0
Move to Norwich	10·2	13·1
Move to Yarmouth	2·2	2·8
Move to other towns	5·5	8·0
Move to wood-pasture parish	41·0	23·5
Move to sheep-corn parish	8·4	19·6
Size of sample	641	327

Notes and sources: Deposition data are derived from Norfolk Record Office, DEP 46–64. Wood-pasture and sheep-corn parishes are as identified in A. Hassell Smith and D. N. J. MacCulloch, 'The Authorship of the Chorographies of Norfolk and Suffolk', *Norfolk Archaeology*, **xxxvi** (1977), fig. 1 (facing p. 334). I am indebted to Dr Smith for sending me a draft version of this map. Movements from parishes with an unidentified farming bias have been excised from the analysis. Apart from the sample size all figures are percentages.

Allowing for the limitations of the evidence, and uncertainty concerning the relative population densities of the two farming 'countries', we can draw a number of conclusions from Table 35. First, male villagers migrating from wood-pasture parishes showed a clear preference for residence in other wood-pasture settlements. Secondly, migrants from sheep-corn areas more often went to urban or wood-pasture communities than to sheep-corn parishes. This predilection for wood-pasture areas among our county-born migrants is underlined by a similar trend among extra-county newcomers to Norfolk villages: eight out of ten opted for a wood-pasture centre.

These migrational trends are compatible with what is known about the divergent economic experience of the two farming areas during the seventeenth century. In the sheep-corn country, a land of poorish soils, unenclosed fields and heathlands, worked in uneasy tandem by large sheep-masters and small corn-growing tenant farmers, the period witnessed the erosion of customary farming arrangements. *Rentier* landowners greatly enlarged their flocks and extended the fold courses, thereby precipitating local conflict, piecemeal depopulation and, after 1700, the collapse of open-field farming. The deteriorating position of the small tenantry may also have been aggravated by the fall in corn prices in the late seventeenth century. In comparison, conditions were far more favourable for villagers in the wood-pasture 'country'. By 1700 much of this fertile, boulder-clay land had been enclosed by agreement. Barely affected by manorial controls, the numerous small farmers concentrated on rearing cattle and dairying, largely for the London market. Even more important, many inhabitants had an industrial by-employment. They dressed and combed wool, and prepared yarn, principally for the buoyant worsted industry centred at Norwich. As Defoe enthused:

this side of Norfolk is very populous and thronged with great and spacious market-towns . . . but that which is most remarkable is [that] the whole country round them is so interspersed with villages and those villages so large and so full of people that they are equal to market-towns in other counties. . . .

Many of the people crowding these settlements we can be sure were migrants, often from the sheep-corn areas.[47]

Thus developments in the agarian economy of an area almost certainly played an influential role in fashioning the local physiognomy of internal migration. Yet one must view these regional variations in perspective. In Norfolk, despite the differences between the two farming 'countries', particularly in the incidence of immigration, their migrational experience was very similar in certain important respects – and also close to the national norm. Mobility rates were uniformly high: in both areas only about one in five of the sample had not moved at some time. In addition, localized migration predominated, with average mileages only marginally higher among migrants from the sheep-corn areas.

Other potential influences on local mobility patterns also need consideration here: inheritance customs, the institution of service, and the operation of the settlement laws. In the first two instances we know all too little about their precise relationship to migration. The national topography of inheritance customs is still largely incomplete, particularly at the level of the smallholder and ordinary villager. It is conceivable that adherence to partible inheritance or (in some places) borough-English in the wood-pasture 'country' of Norfolk contributed to the high rate of localized mobility found there, but without detailed communal studies this must remain speculation. For the century after the Restoration one might conjecture that inheritance customs were a less powerful determinant of mobility than in the preceding period, primarily because of the general decline of the push factors in the migrational equation, a point we must return to shortly. The impact of service, particularly on farms, is clearer. Farm service, with unmarried servants-in-husbandry living in their masters' houses, encouraged spasms of large-scale mobility at the end of every hiring year as servants went in search of a new master – usually no more than a few miles away. At the same time the incidence of this type of service varied from area to area, with the highest levels in regions of pastoral agriculture and small farms. In the lowland areas during the eighteenth century, servants-in-husbandry were increasingly replaced by farm labourers, usually married and living out, men more closely tied to the parish by the need to maintain their settlement rights. In some parishes vestries ordered that no labourer was to be employed unless he was a parishioner, with a fine for offending employers.[48] In fact the settlement laws and the administrative diversity in enforcing them at the local level, were almost certainly a major determinant in this period of regional variations in migrational activity. With little central direction, counties went their own way in the interpretation and implementation of the law. At the communal level, the different attitudes of overseers and vestries consecrated the distinction, notorious by the late eighteenth century, between open and closed parishes: the former with their numerous freeholders and large, ineffective vestries had lax controls on settlement and a rising population density; in the latter a small knot of major landowners dominated the vestry and kept migrants at bay through the rigorous execution of the law.[49] In the next section we shall see how the working of the settlement laws may also have contributed to changes in the level and direction of migration among the lower orders in post-Restoration England.

VI

Earlier in this chapter it was noted that before the English Revolution the main social and economic groupings in the country had quite distinct characteristics so far as migration was concerned. Whereas substantial men – gentlemen, or members of respectable trades – tended to move relatively short distances, for marriage, apprenticeship, or general betterment, those people engaged in poorer occupations – labourers, husbandmen and the like – were frequently forced to travel long distances, often through dire necessity. The deposition evidence for the years 1660–1730 reveals a somewhat different picture. Migrational variations between groupings are less marked, while long-distance migration is not only less common generally, in town and countryside, but it is no longer closely identified with the lower orders. Instead, upper social groups – gentlemen and merchants, as well as professional men – registered the greatest average distances travelled. This last point is confirmed by work on settlement records which demonstrates the low level of longer-distance migration even into industrializing towns like Birmingham or Halifax.[50]

The advent of more extensive movement by the better-off members of society is fairly straightforward, and the reasons for it well-established. Increasingly prosperous, the upper classes travelled in pursuit of leisure and the fashionable 'high life', often residing part time or permanently in London, a provincial capital, or one of the major county towns. Their travels were aided by improvements in transport, including the coach and the turnpike.[51] Rather less is known about the apparent decline of long-distance *subsistence* migration and the general prevalence of localized mobility among the poor. Here a wide range of factors was involved, reflecting important changes in the economic and social order of post-Restoration England.

One vital influence was the apparent slow-down in population growth, discernible for many areas of the country in the late seventeenth century. Taken in conjunction with the continuing expansion in agricultural production, this may well have alleviated some of the pressure to migrate.[52] In the highland zone, for instance, there is little evidence for the period after 1660 of the kind of large-scale subsistence crises which had overwhelmed parts of the north during the 1590s and 1620s, and which had helped propel many uplanders into the towns and villages of southern England in the decades before the revolution. In mid Wharfedale in the West Riding, baptismal and burial rates were fairly stable in the late seventeenth century; in Cumberland and Westmorland the marriage rate was relatively low, with couples marrying later from the 1670s onwards and producing smaller families. Poverty remained a problem here as elsewhere in the north, but it never got out of control. Poor migrants were not found close to the north-south roads, and those who did drift southwards were probably attracted by the intervening opportunities provided by the new textile and metal-working towns of Yorkshire and the north-west.[53] In many pastoral villages poverty was now relieved by a growing array of industrial by-employments, particularly in the new consumer industries, while increased specialization in live-stock husbandry 'successfully absorbed much additional labour into farming'.[54]

Yet *subsistence* migration had never been determined solely by push factors – overpopulation and economic opportunities (or the lack of them) at home. It had also been stimulated by the high turnover of population in towns (the most important reception centres) as a result of the recurrent excess of deaths over births. The imbalance was largest and most spectacular in the case of London, but most county towns before 1640 suffered a similar problem, relying on heavy recruitment of outsiders to maintain or increase their numbers. The influx into towns was particularly great after critical decades like the 1590s and 1620s when urban populations were decimated by epidemic disease and food shortage.[55] After the Restoration the situation eased. Though larger towns retained running deficits of births over deaths, there were few full-scale mortality crises (even during decades of poor harvests like the 1690s) which required the massive replacement of inhabitants over a short time. Sudden influxes of newcomers into towns were now more often in response to cyclical trade booms. After peace with Spain in 1713, Defoe tells us, demand for manufactured goods was so great and workshops so busy that dairymaids and ploughmen 'all ran away to Bocking, to Sudbury, to Braintree and to Colchester and other manufacturing towns of Essex and Suffolk', where wages were higher. But as Defoe implies, most of these immigrants probably came from neighbouring villages, and returned to them when commercial activity declined.[56]

Nor were changing demographic and economic pressures the only factors behind the reduction of *subsistence* migration into towns. From the beginning of the seventeenth century many towns had erected increasingly elaborate barriers to pauper immigration. In the later Stuart period these municipal controls were buttressed by legislation and the growing efficiency of civil administration. Again, the old attraction of towns as fairly generous dispensers of charitable relief may also have waned. Though expenditure on the poor continued to grow, civic relief may have become less indiscriminate than in the past – for instance, town grain stocks seem to have disappeared. The Corporations of the Poor, established in a blaze of publicity from the 1690s onwards, emphasized the harsher aspect of urban relief (outdoor doles were curtailed and most of the new workhouses were little more than glorified houses of correction).[57]

Moreover it is essential to remember that these urban developments occurred against a backcloth of major changes in settlement controls and poor relief right across the country. In villages, as in towns, settlement measures had appeared, mainly on local initiative, before the Restoration, but their operation in rural areas was mostly ineffectual and haphazard, with communities only taking concerted action in years of economic crisis. The Settlement Act of 1662 and subsequent legislation created a permanent national framework for dealing with the mobile poor, a framework which embraced both town magistracies and the increasingly powerful county governments. The settlement law and its enforcement is too large an issue to be considered here in any detail, but certain aspects need comment because of their implications for mobility in the late seventeenth and early eighteenth centuries. In the first place, as the Webbs argued long ago and as our own deposition data have amply confirmed, the settlement statutes did not stop migration: this remained almost universal. But they did inhibit longer-distance movement. Even the amending laws of 1691 and 1697, the last of which permitted movement on a certificate basis by unmarried as well as married poor, seem to have done little to make long-distance movement easier. Unlike someone moving locally, a poor person wishing to travel long distance probably faced considerable difficulty in securing a certificate from his home parish and getting it accepted by the overseers at his destination. Local officials were increasingly conscious of the high cost of removing long-distance travellers if they became a charge, particularly when cases were contested and involved protracted litigation. In such cases it was not just the parish chest which lost out: the paupers themselves were sometimes shunted back and forth from one county to another for months on end. These miserable refugees served as a powerful warning of the dangers of poorer folk travelling far afield on the tramp.[58]

Those members of the lower classes who did take to the road in our period ran the risk of running foul not just of the settlement laws but of the vagrancy statutes as well. Following the Restoration, legislation against vagrants was steadily strengthened with major codifying measures in 1714, 1740 and 1744. There was also a great deal of home-grown harassment of vagrants. In the North Riding, we are told, 'the justices consistently pursued a policy of repression largely unmitigated by recourse to statutory provisions'. In 1670 the Norfolk justices sitting at Norwich agreed unanimously on the need for tough action against vagrants and others, ordered petty sessions to take all necessary steps, and offered a reward of two shillings for each offender captured.[59] A decade or so later the Leicestershire bench drew up detailed regulations codifying the law as it affected vagrants and directed that these orders should be read publicly in churches and entered in parish books. Sporadic efforts were made in various counties to ensure that vagrants were whipped before they were passed – the Northamptonshire justices who made such an order in 1726 wrote to their colleagues in Hertfordshire, Bedfordshire and Buckinghamshire urging them to follow suit.[60] Some vagrants were still branded; a growing number suffered transportation. In principle at least, the passing of vagrants back to their home parishes was also reformed: in 1699 this became a county rather than a parochial charge and soon afterwards a number of counties, led by Buckinghamshire and Warwickshire, appointed salaried contractors to cart these folk through their shires.[61]

Many ordinary poor people thus found it increasingly difficult, if not dangerous, to move extended distances. Even that vital stopover place and succouring refuge of the tramping poor, the

alehouse, was now stringently regulated, with minor establishments suppressed.[62] By 1700 long-distance movement was
progressively confined to a rump of three or four groups of itinerant poor. Some were Scots or Irish (a growing number); some
were gypsies, more or less authentic, like Richard Stanley of
Kerton in Devon who in 1700 admitted travelling selling 'taps
[possibly stoppers] in Somerset, Gloucestershire and Wiltshire . . .
[where] the country people . . . use to call him, his brother and
others of his company Egyptians'; other migrants, an overlapping
category, were petty chapmen, pedlars and travelling entertainers.[63] The later Stuart authorities apparently mounted a
campaign to tie such folk to particular areas – with partial
success.[64] The last and probably most important group of
continuing long-distance travellers were servicemen and their
families. Of the migrants who passed through Lichfield in 1692
nearly 30 per cent comprised soldiers and seamen. These service
migrants were subject not just to the settlement and vagrancy
statutes but were also liable to martial law: after 1688 desertion
was punishable by death.[65]

On the other hand, one should not exaggerate the negative role
of the settlement and poor laws in curbing long-distance movement by the lower orders. This type of migration may also have
declined owing to the increased sophistication and generosity of
parish relief in country areas. Following the example of urban
centres, most rural parishes had by the late seventeenth century
adopted much of the paraphernalia of statutory relief. So far as
one can judge, expenditure on relief continued to grow, though
there was an apparent stabilization in the actual numbers of the
poor – suggesting a rise in *per capita* payments.[66] When overseers
proved stingy, quarter sessions intervened to order adequate
maintenance. In Derbyshire during the 1680s, sessions regularly
heard between twenty and thirty petitions a meeting asking for
relief orders; most were granted. In the West Riding some overseers were fined £1 a month as long as they neglected to provide
satisfactory relief; others were referred to the local JPs or sent to
gaol.[67] To pay for the higher level of parish expenditure there was
a shift towards a more uniform system of poor-rate assessment
with the pound rate replacing customary levies.[68]

After the Restoration, quarter sessions sometimes linked the
removal of a poor person to his native parish with an order that
he or she have work there.[69] Removal orders were also frequently

accompanied by directives to parish officials to supply accommodation for the incoming poor. The proliferation of what one might
term habitation orders – authorizing the erection of cottages for
the poor, the provision of rented housing, and so on – was one
of the most striking developments in poor relief during the second
half of the seventeenth century. Such orders had been issued from
time to time in the late sixteenth century and were permitted by
the 1598 poor legislation. But in most areas before 1640 magistrates were hostile to the raising of cottages for the poor, and
prosecuted offenders under the 1589 Depopulation Act (31 Eliz.,
cap. 7) which required that every cottage should have 4 acres of
adjacent land.[70] In some counties, like Northamptonshire,
presentments continued to be made for offences under this Act
until about 1670 or later, but by that time magisterial attitudes
were changing. From the 1650s many JPs showed themselves more
and more sympathetic to the building of new cottages for the poor
or the continuance of existing homes.[71] In 1676, for example,
when John Rivett and his family of Sisland in Norfolk were turned
out of their home and forced to live in the church porch, the
overseer's refusal to offer them a house was angrily reversed by
county sessions. Justices insisted that overseers build or help build
cottages and repair them when they decayed. Occupants paid little
or no rent and had security of tenure, possibly for three or seven
years, usually for life – provided that they stayed in the same
place. Poor folk in private accommodation had their rents paid.[72]
Parochial opposition was cowed by the tactic of making the parish
pay double or treble relief until the housing was ready; a recalcitrant official might even have to lodge the pauper himself. The
justices moreover attempted to make sure that the housing for
the poor was of a reasonable standard. The Derbyshire bench was
especially fussy. About 1683 Elvaston parish had to construct 'a
convenient habitation with a chimney' for one pauper; ten years
later a poor family of eight had to be housed in a cottage 'twelve
foot high on the side wall, so as to make two convenient chambers'.[73] Nearly a quarter of all the orders made by Derbyshire
quarter sessions in 1683, a fairly typical year, related to the habitation of the poor. Other county sessions making large numbers
of similar orders included Gloucestershire, Kent, Lancashire,
Leicestershire, Northamptonshire, Nottinghamshire, Shropshire,
Somerset, Warwickshire, and the North and West Ridings.[74]

In these varied ways, through the mobilization of the settlement and poor laws, the ruling classes of provincial England launched a pincer attack on the whole problem of long-distance *subsistence* migration, offering incentives – housing, generous relief, work – to those who stayed at home or in a particular area, and ensuring that life was difficult and unpleasant for those who still dared to go tramping the highways of the kingdom.

Having said all this, it is important not to view *subsistence* migration, and its apparent decline, in isolation from the wider context of physical mobility and the migrational options – or 'ploys' – open to the lower orders. It can hardly be a coincidence that the same post-Restoration period which witnessed the declining importance of long-distance movement among the poor also saw the growth of two alternative types of mobility: seasonal migration and emigration. For France J. P. Poussou has claimed that seasonal migration, widespread and large-scale during the sixteenth and seventeenth centuries, was the vital complement to a highly sedentary population where, if we are to believe some reports, the great majority of the people lived in the same place as they were born.[75] In England seasonal migration, except on a very local basis, seems to have been relatively unimportant before the Civil War. However, it was specifically allowed by the 1662 Settlement Act and had become increasingly widespread by the end of the century. Inhabitants of the highland zone travelled south into East Anglia and the south midlands for harvesting, and Londoners migrated every summer into the Home Counties for hop-picking and general harvest work. By the late eighteenth century seasonal migration, including long-distance movement, was a major force in rural society. No doubt this was partly a result of the labour-intensifying changes affecting English agriculture at this time, changes which aggravated the seasonal peaks in demand for workers. But it was also possibly a natural demographic and economic counterpart to the mainly localized pattern of internal migration in Hanoverian England.[76]

Another option open to the lower classes after the Restoration was emigration. Though evidence is patchy on the precise scale of the exodus to the Caribbean, Virginia and New England, it is possible that the total English population across the Atlantic rose from about 70,000 in 1660 to over 200,000 by 1700. Assuming fairly high mortality rates, particularly in the West Indies, probably somewhere between 100,000 and 150,000 people emigrated over that period, despite limited demographic growth in England.

Most went as indentured servants and were young, able-bodied males. However, recent research would suggest that the outflow was at its height in the 1660s and thereafter declined considerably. It is arguable, in fact, that emigration was an extension of the long-distance *subsistence*-type internal migration observed for the earlier period. Movement to the colonies probably had only a minor role to play in the new context of localized migration which evolved in post-Restoration England.[77]

In this study then we have sought to examine not just one isolated flow of migrants, but rather the broad structure of physical mobility and the changes and pressures which affected it during the late seventeenth and early eighteenth centuries. Clearly no single model can be devised to comprehend the complex pattern of internal migration at that time. There were important variations between town and countryside, between towns at different levels of the urban hierarchy, between one region, one sub-regional 'country', and the next – variations which helped to define and distinguish the highly disparate network of local communities which structured early modern England. There were also significant variations in the migrational experience of different social groupings. At the same time, we can now be sure that physical mobility was widespread, indeed part of the usual way of life of most English people. No less important, it seems fairly certain that there was little of the long-distance, push-dominated migration found in the period before 1640. Instead most (though not all) movement was localized and basically circular, whether it involved settlement or marital migrants, apprentices, itinerant traders, or rural labourers exchanging one employer for another through the mediation of the hiring fair: here, 'pull forces' held sway.[78] This kind of local migration remained the most striking feature of the English demographic and social order into the early Victorian era, though with an increasing emphasis on more effective, ripple-type movement as against circular mobility, particularly once the pace of urbanization accelerated from the mid eighteenth century onwards.[79]

The general implications of this picture are far-reaching. The localization of migration may help to explain the slow rate of urban growth after the Restoration despite the improvement in the economic fortunes of many of the middling and larger towns. At the same time, as the rate of longer-distance *subsistence* migration declined, town rulers managed at last to bring under control many of their acute social problems.[80] In the countryside the new-found stability of post-Restoration society was underpinned by the predominance of localized migration. Old traditions of community, neighbourliness and gentle patriarchalism might flourish anew in a world where most people once again recognized their local 'countrymen'.[81] On the other hand, the generally high incidence of mobility during the period ensured a steady but flexible labour response to economic change. Thus the pattern of internal migration in late seventeenth- and early eighteenth-century England played an important role in the orderly progress towards early industrialization.

Acknowledgements

Part of the field-work for this paper was supported by a grant from the British Academy; the Gloucestershire material is derived from my study of Gloucester and its region 1550–1800 which has been generously funded by the Social Science Research Council. I am very grateful to Jenny Clark for her help in analysing the data. An early version of this paper was read at graduate seminars in London, Aberdeen and Cambridge and I am indebted to those present for their comments and suggestions. I am also indebted to Dr P. Corfield, Dr D. W. Jones and Mr D. Souden for detailed criticism, and to Dr H, Fox and Dr P. Cottrell for advice on specific points.

Notes and references

1 P. Clark and P. Slack, *English Towns in Transition, 1500–1700* (London, 1976), pp. 86–7; see also J. de Vries, *The Dutch Rural Economy in the Golden Age* (London, 1974), pp. 108–9; E. A. Wrigley, 'A Simple Model of London's Importance in Changing English Society and Economy, 1650–1750', *Past and Present*, **37** (July 1967), pp. 44–70, at p. 49. For a somewhat different view of the role of urban immigration, see A. Sharlin, 'Natural Decrease in Early Modern Cities: A Reconsideration', *Past and Present*, **79** (May 1978), pp. 126–38.

2 See E. Helin, *La démographie de Liège aux XVIIe et XVIIIe siècles* (Brussels, 1963), ch. 2.

3 D. C. Coleman, 'Labour in the English Economy of the Seventeenth Century', reprinted in E. M. Carus-Wilson (ed.), *Essays in Economic History*, 3 vols (London, 1954–62), ii, p. 304.

4 P. Clark, 'The Migrant in Kentish Towns, 1580–1640', in P. Clark and P. Slack (eds), *Crisis and Order in English Towns, 1500–1700* (London, 1972), pp. 150–2; A. Fletcher, *A County Community in Peace and War: Sussex, 1600–1660* (London, 1975), pp. 165–6.

5 Wrigley, 'A Simple Model of London's Importance' pp. 50–1; R. Thompson,

Women in Stuart England and America (London, 1974), pp. 32–5, 240–3; Clark, 'Migrant in Kentish Towns', p. 153.

6 Clark, 'Migrant in Kentish Towns', pp. 156–7; P. Styles, 'A Census of a Warwickshire Village in 1698', *University of Birmingham Historical Journal,* **iii** (1951–2), p. 49.

7 J. Cornwall, 'Evidence of Population Mobility in the Seventeenth Century', *Bulletin of the Institute of Historical Research,* **xl** (1967), p. 146; see also H. Hanley, 'Population Mobility in Buckinghamshire, 1578–1583', *Local Population Studies,* **15** (1975), pp. 33–9, which found that 18 per cent of the rural sample had moved over 40 miles (ibid., p. 35); D. Cressy, 'Occupations, Migration and Literacy in East London, 1580–1640', *Local Population Studies,* **5** (1970), pp. 57–8; Clark, 'Migrant in Kentish Towns', pp. 117–50.

8 A. F. Butcher, 'The Origins of Romney Freemen, 1433–1523', *Economic History Review,* 2nd series, **xxvii** (1974), pp. 16–27; for more use of freedom records, see G. D. Ramsay, 'The Recruitment and Fortunes of Some London Freemen in the Mid Sixteenth Century', *Economic History Review,* 2nd series, **xxxi** (1978), pp. 528–40, S. R. Smith, 'The Social and Geographical Origins of the London Apprentices, 1630–60', *Guildhall Miscellany,* **iv** (1971–3), pp. 195–206; P. Slack, 'Vagrants and Vagrancy in England, 1598–1664', above, pp. 49–76.

9 P. Laslett and J. Harrison, 'Clayworth and Cogenhoe', in H. E. Bell and R. L. Ollard (eds), *Historical Essays, 1600–1750, Presented to David Ogg* (London, 1963), pp. 177–80; certain of the figures presented in this article have been modified slightly by Laslett in his *Family Life and Illicit Love in Earlier Generations* (Cambridge, 1977), pp. 65–75.

10 E. J. Buckatzsch, 'Places of Origin of a Group of Immigrants into Sheffield, 1624–1799', *Economic History Review,* 2nd series, **ii** (1949–50), pp. 303–6; D. V. Glass, 'Socio-Economic Status and Occupations in the City of London at the End of the Seventeenth Century', in P. Clark (ed.), *The Early Modern Town* (London, 1976), pp. 228–30; R. A. Pelham, 'The Immigrant Population of Birmingham, 1686–1726', *Trans. Birmingham Archaeol. Soc.,* **lxi** (1940), pp. 45–80; E. G. Thomas, 'The Treatment of Poverty in Berkshire, Essex and Oxfordshire, 1723–1834' (London University PhD thesis, 1971), esp. pp. 217–59.

11 For example, L. Bradley, 'Derbyshire Quarter Sessions Rolls: Poor Law Removal Orders', *Derbyshire Miscellany,* **vi** (1971–3), pp. 98–114; B. Maltby, 'Parish Registers and the Problem of Mobility', *Local Population Studies,* **6** (1971), pp. 39–42; J. M. Martin, 'The Rich, the Poor and the Migrant in Eighteenth-Century Stratford-on-Avon', *Local Population Studies,* **20** (1978), pp. 40–5.

12 For the use of wills and surnames, see P. Spufford, 'Population Movement in Seventeenth-Century England', *Local Population Studies,* **4** (1970), pp. 42–3, 46.

13 Laslett and Harrison 'Clayworth and Cogenhoe'; D. Souden and G. Lasker, 'Biological Inter-relationships between Parishes in East Kent: An Analysis of Marriage Duty Act Returns for 1705', *Local Populations Studies,* **21** (1978), pp. 30–9, examines the surnames of inhabitants of certain Kentish parishes listed in 1705 to provide 'a useful, if gross, measure of "contact", and by extension of past migratory experience'; R. S. Schofield, 'Age-Specific Mobility

in an Eighteenth Century Rural English Parish', *Annales de démographie* below, pp. 253–66; see also D. Baker (ed.), *The Inhabitants of Cardington in 1782* (Beds Hist. Rec. Soc., **lii**, Bedford, 1973).

14 See R. F. Peel, 'Local Intermarriage and the Stability of Rural Population in the English Midlands', *Geography*, **xxvii** (1942), pp. 25–9; Maltby 'Parish Registers'; J. D. Chambers, *Population, Economy and Society in Pre-Industrial England* (London, 1972), p. 47; E. A. Wrigley, 'Clandestine Marriage in Tetbury in the Late Seventeenth Century', *Local Population Studies*, **10** (1973), pp. 15–21. Laslett has noted the relative unimportance of marital migration in the overall context of mobility at Clayworth; Laslet, *Family Life and Illicit Love in Earlier Generations*, p. 70.

15 Clark and Slack, *English Towns in Transition*, p. 94; *Minutes of the Norwich Court of Mayoralty, 1630–1*, ed. W. L. Sachse (Norfolk Rec. Soc., **xv**, Norwich, 1942), pp. 142, 147–8, and *passim*. According to D. Souden, 'apprentice migration may be unrepresentative of general patterns (of mobility) because of age-, sex-, and status-bias': D. Souden, 'Rogues, Whores and Vagabonds? Indentured Servant Emigrants to North America, and the Case of Mid Seventeenth-Century Bristol', above, pp. 150–71.

16 *A Calendar of Southampton Apprenticeship Registers, 1609–1740*, ed. A. J. Willis and A. L. Merson (Southampton Rec. Soc., **xii**, Southampton, 1968), p. xii; see also *The Records of the Borough of Northampton*, ed. J. C. Cox, 2 vols (Northampton, 1898), ii, pp. 324–5; *The Chamber Order Book of Worcester, 1602–1650*, ed. S. Bond (Worcs. Hist. Soc., new series, **viii**, Worcester, 1974), pp. 427–8. For delayed enrolments, see Gloucestershire Record Office (hereafter Gloucs. RO), GBR 1458; see also Norfolk Record Office (hereafter Norfolk RO), Norwich Apprentice Enrolments, II, fo. 206, and *passim*; Norwich Assembly Book, V, fos. 307, 351; Norwich Sessions Book, VII (1591–1602), fo. 2.

17 J. R. Kellett, 'The Breakdown of Gild and Corporation Control over the Handicraft and Retail Trade in London', *Economic History Review*, 2nd series, **x** (1957–8), pp. 382–9; Clark and Slack, *English Towns in Transition*, p. 109; Warwickshire Record Office (hereafter Warwicks. RO), Coventry Sessions Book, QS/64/1/1, pp. 9–10, 13–14, 28–30; Bedford Town Hall, Bedford Town Minute Book, 1664–88, pp. 172, 252–3, and 1688–1718, fo. 40 *v*; Kent Archives Office (hereafter Kent AO) Maidstone Borough Records, Burghmote Book D, fos. 218*v*ff.

18 J. Patten, 'Urban Occupations in Pre-Industrial England', *Trans. Institute of British Geographers*, new series, **ii** (1977), pp. 298–9; D. M. Woodward, 'Sources for Urban History: 1, Freemen's Rolls', *Local Historian, ix*, (1970–1), p. 91; Kent AO, Maidstone Burghmote Book D, fos. 225 *r-v*; Gloucs. RO, GBR 1466B.

19 D. Marshall, *The English Poor in the Eighteenth Century* (London, 1926), pp. 161–2; Pelham, 'Immigrant Population of Birmingham'; Thomas, 'Treatment of Poverty in Berkshire, Essex and Oxfordshire'.

20 J. Patten, *Rural-Urban Migration in Pre-Industrial England* (University of Oxford, School of Geography, Research Papers, vi, Oxford, 1973), p. 20.

21 For a discussion of some of the general problems, see Clark, 'Migrant in Kentish Towns', p. 119.

22 Misson noted 'the abuse of every man's calling himself gentleman in England':

H. Misson, *Memoirs and Observations in his Travels over England* (London, 1719 edn), p. 200; see also L. Stone, 'Social Mobility in England, 1500–1700', *Past and Present,* **33** (April 1966), pp. 16–55, at pp. 53–4.

23 For references, see Table 26, Notes and sources.

24 Towns are as identified in John Adams, *Index Villaris: or, An Alphabetical Table of all the Cities, Market-Towns, Parishes, Villages, and Private Seats, in England and Wales* (London, 1680).

25 Some liberalization of the law in the 1690s is suggested in P. Styles, 'The Evolution of the Law of Settlement', *University of Birmingham Historical Journal,* **ix** (1963–4), pp. 49–52; see also pp. 83–4 below.

26 Slack, 'Vagrants and Vagrancy in England', pp. 64–5; Clark, 'Migrant in Kentish Towns', pp. 126–8.

27 Clark, 'Migrant in Kentish Towns', pp. 129–31. For the difficulties of occupational classification, see Patten, 'Urban Occupations in Pre-Industrial England', pp. 301–11.

28 T. H. Hollingsworth, 'Historical Studies of Migration', *Annales de démographie historique 1970* (1971), p. 88.

29 Schofield, 'Age-Specific Mobility in an Eighteenth Century Rural English Parish', p. 261; for migration as a *rite de passage* for boys in developing countries, see J. Connell *et al., Migration from Rural Areas* (Delhi, 1976), pp. 40–1.

30 The general connection between longer-distance movement and older population groups is noted in Connell *et al., Migration from Rural Areas,* p. 41.

31 Laslett, *Family Life and Illicit Love in Earlier Generations,* p. 68; Schofield, 'Age-Specific Mobility', p. 256.

32 For a possibly similar situation in New England, see W. R. Prest, 'Stability and Change in Old and New England: Clayworth and Dedham', *Journal of Interdisciplinary History,* **vi** (1976), esp. pp. 372–3.

33 Buckatzsch, 'Places of Origin of a Group of Immigrants into Sheffield', pp. 304–5; Kent AO, P 241/13/1; Bradley, 'Derbyshire Quarter Sessions Rolls', p. 111.

34 The early Gloucestershire data (rural sample of 1679; urban sample of 440) were derived from diocesan deposition books: Gloucs. RO, GDR 79, and *passim*; I am grateful to Dr P. Morgan for help with this source. See pp. 221ff. above; Clark, 'Migrant in Kentish Towns', p. 122 (the mean figure for Canterbury, Faversham and Maidstone).

35 Stone, 'Social Mobility in England' p. 31. The trend was already evident by the mid seventeenth century: Smith, 'Social and Geographical Origins of the London Apprentices', pp. 202–4. Patten, *Rural-Urban Migration in Pre-Industrial England,* p. 33.

36 Schofield, 'Age-Specific Mobility', pp. 256, 262 (combining adults and children); Clark, 'Migrant in Kentish Towns', p. 123. This accords with one of Ravenstein's so-called 'laws': D. B. Grigg, ' E. G. Ravenstein and the "Laws of Migration" ', *Journal of Historical Geography,* **iii** (1977), p. 49.

37 See p. 68 above; Thomas, 'Treatment of Poverty in Berkshire, Essex and Oxfordshire', pp. 220–1, 233.

38 From detailed analysis of the catchment areas of several eastern towns (albeit relying solely on apprenticeship data), see J. Patten, 'Patterns of Migration

and Movement of Labour to Three Pre-Industrial East Anglian Towns', above, pp. 77–106.

39 Clark, 'Migrant in Kentish Towns', p. 126; Wrigley, 'A Simple Model of London's Importance', pp. 48–9; Smith 'Social and Geographical Origins', pp. 204–6.

40 The same point is made in Patten, 'Patterns of Migration and Movement of Labour to Three Pre-Industrial East Anglian Towns', p. 97.

41 Slack, 'Vagrants and Vagrancy in England', pp. 66–7; Thomas, 'Treatment of Poverty', pp. 220 ff.; see also D. Souden, 'Movers and Stayers in Family Reconstitution Populations, 1600–1780', *Local Population Studies*, **33** (1984), pp. 11–28.

42 The localized pattern of pauper migration in Norfolk is noted in Slack, 'Vagrants and Vagrancy in England', p. 371. For the old road network, see B. P. Hindle, 'The Road Network of Medieval England and Wales', *Journal of Historical Geography,* **ii** (1976), p. 220; E. Pawson, *Transport and Economy: The Turnpike Roads of Eighteenth Century Britain* (London, 1977), pp. 27, 137.

43 Thomas, 'Treatment of Poverty', pp. 225, 227; A. Constant, 'The Geographical Background of Inter-Village Population Movements in Northamptonshire and Huntingdonshire, 1754–1943', *Geography,* **xxxiii** (1948), p. 83.

44 Clark, 'Migrant in Kentish Towns', pp. 122–3; P. Clark, *English Provincial Society from the Reformation to the Revolution: Religion, Politics and Society in Kent, 1500–1640* (Hassocks, 1977), p. 9; C. W. Chalklin, *Seventeenth-Century Kent* (London, 1965), pp. 30–2; see also generally S. Akerman, 'Internal Migration, Industrialisation and Urbanisation, 1895–1930: A Summary of the Västmanland Study', *Scandinavian Economic History Review,* **xxiii** (1975), p. 151.

45 P. Clark, ' "The Ramoth-Gilead of the Good": Urban Change and Political Radicalism at Gloucester, 1540–1640', in P. Clark, A. G. R. Smith and N. Tyacke (eds), *The English Commonwealth, 1547–1640: Essays in Politics and Society Presented to Joel Hurstfield* (Leicester, 1979), pp. 169–73, 185; J. A. Chartres, 'The Marketing of Agricultural Produce in Metropolitan Western England in the Late Seventeenth and Eighteenth Centuries', *Exeter Papers in Economic Hisstory,* **viii** (1973), p. 64.

46 Wrigley, 'A Simple Model of London's Importance', pp. 46–9; Glass, 'Socio-Economic Status and Occupations in the City of London', pp. 228–30.

47 M. R. Postgate, 'Field Systems of East Anglia', in A. R. H. Baker and R. Butlin (eds), *Studies of Field Systems in the British Isles* (Cambridge, 1973), p. 282, and *passim*; K. J. Allison, 'The Sheep-Corn Husbandry of Norfolk in the Sixteenth and Seventeenth Centuries', *Agricultural Historical Review,* **v** (1957), pp. 12, 22–5, 28; J. Patten, 'Population Distribution in Norfolk and Suffolk during the Sixteenth and Seventeenth Centuries', *Trans. Institute of British Geographers,* **65** (1975), p. 55 and *passim*, indicates the growing population density in woodland areas; for immigration into such districts generally in the seventeenth century, see J. Thirsk, 'Seventeenth-Century Agriculture and Social Change', in J. Thirsk (ed.), *Land, Church and People: Essays Presented to Professor H. P. R. Finberg* (Supplement to *Agricultural Historical Review,* **xviii** (1970)), pp. 172–3; also Souden, 'Movers and Stayers

in Family Reconstitution Populations'. Daniel Defoe, *A Tour through the Whole Island of Great Britain*, ed. G. D. H. Cole and D. C. Browning, 2 vols (London, 1962), i, p. 61.

48 For inheritance customs, see H. P. R. Finberg (ed.), *The Agrarian History of England and Wales, iv, 1500–1640*, ed. J. Thirsk (Cambridge, 1967), p. 48; for a comment on the connection with migration, see C. Howell, 'Peasant Inheritance Customs in the Midlands, 1280–1700', in J. Goody, J. Thirsk and E. P. Thompson (eds), *Family and Inheritance: Rural Society in Western Europe, 1200–1800* (Past and Present Publications, Cambridge, 1976), p. 154. For farm service, see the excellent study by A. S. Kussmaul, 'Servants in Husbandry in Early Modern England' (Toronto University, PhD thesis, 1978), esp. p. 194, and *passim*. Berkshire Record Office, Coleshill Vestry Minutes, D/P40/8/1 (December 1741).

49 E. M. Hampson, *The Treatment of Poverty in Cambridgeshire, 1597–1834* (Cambridge, 1934), pp. 127 ff.; D. R. Mills, 'The Poor Laws and the Distribution of Population, c. 1600–1860, with Special Reference to Lincolnshire', *Trans. Institute of British Geographers,* **26** (1959), pp. 186, 191, 193; see also J. S. Taylor, 'The Impact of Pauper Settlement, 1691–1834', *Past and Present,* **73** (November 1976), pp. 42–74, at p. 66. For the situation at the open parish of Wigston, Leicestershire, see W. G. Hoskins, *The Midland Peasant* (London, 1957), pp. 208–12.

50 Pelham, 'Immigrant Population of Birmingham', pp. 50–1 (though Pelham notes more longer-distance movement after 1700); R. Bretton, 'Settlement Certificates and Removal Orders', *Trans. Halifax Antiq. Soc.* (1959), pp. 9–26; for a general comment on changes in mobility patterns over time, see Akerman, 'Internal Migration, Industrialisation and Urbanisation', p. 151.

51 Clark (ed.), *Early Modern Town*, pp. 205–6, 210, 306–7; P. Borsay, 'The English Urban Renaissance: The Development of Provincial Urban Culture, c. 1680–1760', *Social History,* **ii** (1977), pp. 582 ff.

52 D. C. Coleman, *The Economy of England, 1450–1750* (London, 1977), chs 6–7; see also J. D. Chambers, *The Vale of Trent, 1670–1800* (*Economic History Review* Supplement, **3**, London, 1957), pp. 34–5, 38–42.

53 A. B. Appleby, *Famine in Tudor and Stuart England* (Liverpool, 1978), pp. 113–18, 121–34, 146, 155–81; W. G. Howson, 'Plague, Poverty and Population in Parts of North-West England, 1580–1720', *Trans. Hist. Soc. Lancs. and Cheshire,* **cxii** (1961), pp. 53–4; M. F. Pickles, 'Mid Wharfedale, 1721–1812', *Local Population Studies,* **16** (1976), p. 33; for movement to Kendal, a growing textile and hosiery centre in the early eighteenth century, see J. D. Marshall, 'Kendal in the Late Seventeenth and Eighteenth Centuries', *Trans. Cumberland and Westmorland Antiq. and Archaeol. Soc.,* new series, **lxxv** (1975), pp. 189, 208 ff.

54 J. Thirsk, *Economic Policy and Projects* (Oxford, 1978), pp. 164–9; see also Appleby, *Famine in Tudor and Stuart England*, pp. 161 ff.

55 Clark and Slack, *English Towns in Transition*, pp. 86–9; see also P. Slack, 'Social Problems and Social Policies' in *The Traditional Community under Stress* (Open University course A322, Milton Keynes, 1977), pp. 79–81.

56 A. B. Appleby, 'Nutrition and Disease: The Case of London, 1550–1750', *Journal of Interdisciplinary History,* **vi** (1975–6), pp. 13–18; Chambers, *Vale*

of Trent, pp. 22, 26, 28; Daniel Defoe, *A Plan of the English Commerce* (London, 1728), pp. 267–8. I owe this last reference to Dr P. Corfield.

57 Styles, 'Evolution of the Law of Settlement', pp. 36–40; S. and B. Webb, *English Poor Law History*, Pt. 1, *The Old Poor Law* (London, 1927), pp. 120–1; Marshall, *English Poor in the Eighteenth Century,* pp. 47–8, 127–8; see also *Bristol Corporation of the Poor, 1696–1834*, ed. E. E. Butcher (Bristol Rec. Soc., **iii**, Bristol, 1932).

58 F. G. Emmison, *Early Essex Town Meetings* (London, 1970), pp. viii, xiii: Styles, 'Evolution of the Law of Settlement', pp. 43–52; Webb, *English Poor Law History*, pp. 334–6; the 1697 Act only confirmed local practice: Hampson, *Treatment of Poverty in Cambridgeshire*, p. 144; A. Redford, *Labour Migration in England, 1800–1850* (Manchester, 1926), p. 76; for parish refusals to grant certificates to long-distance migrants, see M. F. Lloyd Prichard, 'The Treatment of Poverty in Norfolk from 1700 to 1850' (Cambridge University PhD thesis, 1949), p. 198.

59 Webb, *English Poor Law History*, pp. 351–5; J. S. Cockburn, 'The North Riding Justices, 1690–1750: A Study in Local Administration', *Yorkshire Archaeological Journal*, **xli** (1966), p. 509; Norfolk RO, County Quarter Sessions, C 3/S2/3 (unfol., January 1669/70); rewards had been offered in some counties since the 1650s and had been sanctioned by the 1662 Act: Nottinghamshire Record Office (hereafter Notts. RO), QSM 13 (unfol., April 1656); *The Statutes of the Realm*, ed. A. Luders *et. al.*, 11 vols in 12 (Rec. Comm., London, 1810–28), v, p. 404.

60 Leicestershire Record Office (hereafter Leics. RO), Quarter Sessions, QS 6/1/2/1, fos.58v–62; see also Warwicks. RO, QS 40/1/7, fos. 43v–v; *Buckingham Sessions Records: i, 1678–94*, ed. W. Le Hardy (Aylesbury, 1933), p. 258; Northamptonshire Record Office (hereafter Northants. RO), Quarter Sessions Minute Book, 1708–27 (unfol., Michaelmas 1726); see also Warwicks. RO, QS 1/40/9 (unfol., June 1723); Leics. RO, QS 6/1/2/1, fo. 120.

61 West Yorkshire Record Office (hereafter W. Yorks. RO), Sessions Order Book, III, fo. 293; Warwicks. RO, QS 40/1/7, fo. 143; Leics. RO, QS 6/1/2/1, fo. 126; Webb, *English Poor Law History*, pp. 379–80; Warwicks. RO, QS 40/1/7, fo. 70 and QS 40/1/8, pp. 19, 101–2, and *passim*; see also Cockburn, 'The North Riding Justices', p. 511; for further action to regulate the passing of vagrants: Buckinghamshire Record Office, Quarter Sessions Transcripts, IV, pp. 48–9.

62 P. Clark, 'The Alehouse and the Alternative Society', in D. Pennington and K. Thomas (eds), *Puritans and Revolutionaries: Essays in Seventeenth-Century History Presented to Christopher Hill* (Oxford, 1978), pp. 70–1.

63 *Buckinghamshire Sessions Records, i,* ed. Le Hardy, p. 156; Hampshire Record Office, Basingstoke Town MSS, 2/6/4; see also J. C. Cox, *Churchwardens' Accounts* (London, 1913), p. 339. For entertainers, see Bedfordshire Record Office (hereafter Beds. RO), QSR 1742/57; Warwicks. RO, CR 103, fo. 99: one Price 'wandered about the county showing tricks of dexterity or sleight of hand . . . known by the name of the Fire-Eater'. Gregory King's estimates of the vagrant population vary widely and are clearly speculative. In his MS book he noted that the number of 'soldiers, seamen, crate-carriers, hawkers, peddlers, thieves and beggars cannot be esteemed much less than

80,000': *The Earliest Classics,* ed. P. Laslett (Farnborough, 1973), p. 160; but without the servicemen the number of vagrants is elsewhere put at 30,000, a strikingly low figure: Gregory King, *Natural and Political Observations and Conclusions upon the State and Condition of England* (London, 1696), reprinted in *Earliest Classics,* ed. Laslett, p. 36.

64 Notts RO, QSM 13, January 1656/7; Derbyshire Record Office (hereafter Derbys. RO) Sessions Order, I, fo. 90*v*. I am also grateful for information on this point to Dr D. Hey.

65 Lichfield Joint Record Office, Lichfield Town Accounts, 1657–1707 (unfol.); see also Kent AO, Q/SB 31, fo. 231; *Statutes of the Realm,* vi, pp. 146–7.

66 For example, F. G. Emmison, 'The Relief of the Poor at Eaton Socon, 1706–1834' (Beds. Hist. Rec. Soc., **xv**, Apsley Guise, 1933), pp. 12–20; S. A. Cutlack, *The Gnossall Records 1679 to 1837: Poor Law Administration* (Collections for a History of Staffordshire, Stafford, 1936), pp. 19–43. At Cowden in Kent, for example, average annual expenditure on relief nearly trebled between 1636–40 and 1696–1701, though the number of pensioners and others receiving relief rose only marginally: Kent AO, P 99/12/1; for a parallel rise in *per capita* relief in towns, see Slack, 'Social Problems and Social Policies', pp. 94–5. The increased sophistication of poor relief is also discussed in A. L. Beier, 'Studies in Poverty and Poor Relief in Warwickshire, 1540–1680' (Princeton University PhD thesis, 1969), p. 197, and *passim*; J. Hill, 'A Study of Poverty and Poor Relief in Shropshire, 1550–1685' (Liverpool University MA thesis, 1973), pp. 121–31. For criticism of the rising level of relief in this period, see Charles Davenant, *The Political and Commercial Works,* ed. Sir Charles Whitworth, 5 vols (London, 1771; reprinted Farnborough, 1967), i, pp. 72–3, 100.

67 Derbys. RO, Sessions Orders, I, fos. 6–7*v*, 9*v*; W. Yorks. RO, Sessions Order Book, III, pp. 125, 388.

68 For example, Northants. RO, QSR 1/45/59; Leics. RO, QS 6/1/2/1, fos. 107, 126, 135*v*; Gloucs. RO, Q/SO 1, fo. 95*v*.

69 For example, Northants RO, QSR 1/39/129. Parish stocks to set the rural poor on work were not successful however: Emmison, 'Relief of the Poor at Eaton Socon', pp. 9–10; Hampson, *Treatment of Poverty in Cambridgeshire,* pp. 66–7, 69–70.

70 For example, *Wiltshire County Records: Minutes of Proceedings in Sessions, 1563, and 1574 to 1592,* ed. H. C. Johnson (Wilts. Arch. and Nat. Hist. Soc., Records Branch, **iv**, Devizes, 1949), pp. 138, 142, 147; *Statutes of the Realm,* iv, pt 2, pp. 804–5; Emmison, *Early Essex Town Meetings,* p. xiii.

71 For example, Northants. RO, QSR 1/56/53; for Northamptonshire JPs overruling presentments of poor cottagers, see ibid., QSR 1/52/119; for the mass licensing of cottages, see ibid., QSR 1/10/70.

72 Norfolk RO, C/S2/3 (unfol., October 1676); Derbys. RO, Sessions Orders, I, fos.68*v*, 98; Northants. RO, QSR 1/55/60; QSR 1/57/164–5; QSR 1/60/73; Leics. RO, QS 6/1/2/1, fo. 121; Derbys. RO, Sessions Orders, I, fo. 41*v*.

73 Northants. RO, QSR 1/60/84; Derbys. RO, Sessions Orders, I, fos. 9*v*, 42; Leics. RO, QS 6/1/3, p. 141; Northants. RO, QSR 1/58/94; Derbys. RO, Sessions Orders, I, fos. 30, 230*v*; see also Notts. RO, QSM 20, fo. 35*v*.

74 Derbys. RO, Sessions Orders, I, fos. 30ff.; Gloucs. RO, Q/SO 1, fo. 22*v*, and *passim*; Kent AO, Q/SOW 2, *passim*; Marshall, *English Poor in the*

Eighteenth Century, p. 108; Leics. RO, QS 6/1/2/1, fos. 24*v*, 25, 27*v*, and *passim;* Shropshire *County Records: Orders of the Shropshire Quarter Sessions*, ed. R. L. Kenyon, 2 vols (Shrewsbury, 1908), ii, pp. 13, 29, 31, 37, and *passim; Quarter Sessions Records for the County of Somerset, 1607–77*, ed. E. H. Bates-Harbin and M. C. B. Dawes (Somerset Rec. Soc., **xxiii, xxiv, xxviii, xxxiv**, London, 1907–19), iv, pp. 2, 4, 15, 16, and *passim*; Northants. RO, QSR 1/34, and *passim*; Notts. RO, QSM 12, *passim*; Warwicks. RO, QS 40/1/7–8, *passim*; Cockburn, 'North Riding Justices', p. 505; W. Yorks. RO, Sessions Order Books, II-III, *passim*.

75 For emphasis on the variety of migrational 'ploys' open to peasants in developing societies, see R. F. Spencer (ed.), *Migration and Anthropology* (London, 1970), pp. 27 ff.; J. P. Poussou, 'Les mouvements migratoires en France et à partir de la France de la fin du XVe siècle au début du XIXe siècle', *Annales de démographie historique 1970* (1971), pp. 42–8, 62–3; P. Goubert, *The Ancien Régime*, trans. S. Cox (London, 1973), p. 43; for more on seasonal migration in France, see M. A. Carron, 'Prélude à l'exode rural en France: les migrations anciennes des travailleurs creusois', *Revue d'histoire économique et sociale*, **xliii** (1965), esp. pp. 293–4. The growth of *subsistence* migration in the eighteenth century is described by O. Hufton, 'Begging, Vagrancy, Vagabondage and the Law: An Aspect of the Problem of Poverty in Eighteenth-Century France', *European Studies Review,* **ii** (1972), pp. 98ff., 105 ff.

76 Clark, 'Migrant in Kentish Towns', p. 137; *Statutes of the Realm,* v, p. 401; Styles, 'Evolution of the Law of Settlement', pp. 48–9; Thirsk, *Economic Policy and Projects,* p. 162; Beds. RO, QSR 1714/14; Warwicks. RO, CR 103, fo. 58; Kent. AO, Q/SB 2, fo. 48, and Q/SB 32, fos. 25, 210; Redford, *Labour Migration in England*, p. 122; E. J. T. Collins, 'Migrant Labour in British Agriculture in the Nineteenth Century', *Economic History Review*, 2nd series, **xxix** (1976), pp. 38–59; see also D. H. Morgan, 'The Place of Harvesters in Nineteenth-Century Village Life', in R. Samuel (ed.), *Village Life and Labour* (London, 1975), pp. 27–38.

77 R. C. Simmons, *The American Colonies: From Settlement to Independence* (London, 1976), pp. 74, 87, 100; for the West Indies, see R. S. Dunn, *Sugar and Slaves: The Rise of the Planter Class in the English West Indies* (London, 1973), p. 313; Souden, 'Rogues, Whores and Vagabonds?', pp. 27, 29; D. Souden, 'Seventeenth-Century Indentured Servants Seen within a General English Migration System' (Paper read to a session of the Organization of American Historians, St Louis, April 1979).

78 For the role of the hiring fair and its influence on rural migration, see Kussmaul, 'Servants in Husbandry in Early Modern England', pp. 118–48.

79 Redford, *Labour Migration*, pp. 56, 160–1; see also Akerman, 'Internal Migration, Industrialisation and Urbanisation', p. 156.

80 C. W. Chalklin, *The Provincial Towns of Georgian England* (London, 1974), p. 17; Clark and Slack, *English Towns in Transition*, pp. 124–5.

81 For the revival of patriarchalism, see R. W. Malcolmson, *Popular Recreations in English Society, 1700–1850* (Cambridge, 1973), pp. 13–14.

8
Age-specific mobility in an eighteenth-century rural English parish

R. S. Schofield

This is a classic analysis of a unique source, the highly detailed enumeration for the farming and lace-making village of Cardington, Bedfordshire, in 1782. The author reveals a high level of mobility with almost universal migration among married adults and young people, with valuable data on age at leaving home. Most of the movement was rural-rural and very localized, though with a significant degree of migration to London. The chapter demonstrates the beauties and perils of exploiting a single source. Recent work has suggested a greater variety of age migration patterns, and it is clear that these may be affected by local economic and social circumstances. Almost certainly relevant to the Cardington experience were changes in the rural economy of Bedfordshire in the late eighteenth century with the spread of enclosure and the problems of craft industries.

Recent work on the turnover of population has suggested that a high degree of mobility obtained in the villages of pre-industrial England.[1] In Clayworth, Notts., for example, at the end of the seventeenth century 61 per cent of the population was no longer resident in the village after a period of twelve years. About a third of those no longer resident had died, but the rest had left the village and others had entered to take their place.[2] In another village, Cogenhoe in Northants., in the early seventeenth century the most mobile element in the population was the group of unmarried children no longer residing in the parental home, known as servants. After a period of two years, over three-quarters of the servants in Cogenhoe were no longer living in the village.[3] It is known from listings of inhabitants that children were frequently sent out into service from about the age of 15 until marriage. Listings of six communities which give the ages of inhabitants, ranging in date from 1599 to 1796, show that on average the proportion of children of ages 15–24 in service was about 33 per cent. In these same communities the servants comprised on average 12 per cent of the population, a figure very close to that of 13 per cent obtained for a larger group of listings for one hundred communities for the period from the late sixteenth to the early nineteenth century.[4]

The custom of sending children away from home into service is therefore likely to be of major importance in determining the nature and extent of mobility in the past. But further questions arise: How far from home did children travel when they went into service? Did they merely go to work in neighbours' households, or did they journey long distances? Was the experience of boys and girls similar, or did they go into service at different ages and travel different distances in their search for work? When the children married, did they return to their home parish, or did they found a family elsewhere, and at what distance from their parents' home? In order to answer questions of this kind fully, we should need to know the residence patterns of the inhabitants of past communities at each age, or life-cycle stage, from birth to death. Needless to say the evidence for so ambitious an undertaking does not exist. The listings of inhabitants, for example, even when available for a series of years, state neither the place of origin of servants and other newcomers nor the destination of those who left the community. Indeed one cannot even tell from these documents whether those who left did so to go into service or to get married.

One listing of inhabitants, however, has been discovered which provides a quite exceptional amount of information on the migration patterns of the families resident in the parish and their children. The listing states for the heads of families and their wives not only their names, ages, occupations, and religious affiliations, but also the places where they were born. In addition the listing gives the names, ages, occupational and marital statuses, of all their surviving children, whether they are resident with them or not. If a child is living elsewhere, the listing specifies the location.[5]

The listing refers to the parish of Cardington, in Bedfordshire in the east midlands, in the year 1782. According to the listing the parish comprised 180 households (199 families) living in four distinct settlements. The three subsidiary settlements lie on what was even then a main road from Bedford to London, while the main settlement of Cardington itself lies about 0.75 miles to the east of the main road.[6] Cardington is only 2½ miles from Bedford, the county town, which lies to the north-west and shares with Cardington a common parish boundary. London is 45 miles to the south-east. The parish is situated at an altitude of about 100 feet above sea level in the fertile shallow valley of the river Ouse, which passes through Bedford and then forms the northern boundary of the parish. Two-thirds of the heads of households in the parish in 1782 were engaged in agriculture: 16 per cent were farmers and 51 per cent were labourers. Fourteen per cent of the households were headed by craftsmen, employed in the usual agricultural service occupations (for example, carpenter, blacksmith, bricklayer) while 3 per cent were headed by gentry and clergy, and the rest (16 per cent) by widows and others of unspecified occupation. Unfortunately the listing gives only summary information for the gentry and clergy households and for all except one of the farmer households. The information on mobility contained in the listing therefore relates to the families of labourers, craftsmen and widows, who together comprise about 80 per cent of the families in the parish. Amongst this group of families, the labourers are heavily predominant. Initially separate tables were drawn up for labourer, craftsman and widow families, as well as for the two religious divisions given in the listing (Anglican and Baptist), but the numbers for all groups other than Anglican labourers, was too small for meaningful comparisons to be made. Accordingly all families have been combined in arriving at the figures given below.

The first aspect of mobility which the listing permits us to investigate is the movement of families during the year the listing was being compiled. In the course of 1782, seven families changed their domicile, but remained within the parish; four families entered the parish from other parishes, 2½, 7, 9 and 12 miles away; and five families left the parish, four to go to other parishes within 10 miles and one to go to London. For three of the five families leaving the parish kinship ties seem to have influenced their destination: two families moved to the parish stated in the listing to be the wife's birthplace, and a woman who was widowed during 1782 went to the parish where her only child (a married daughter) was residing. The proportion of families entering and leaving the parish during the course of the year is about 3 per cent, which is high by comparison with other published figures.[7]

The second aspect of mobility on which the Cardington listing throws some light is the place of birth of the heads of families and their wives. Table 36 summarizes the distribution of birthplaces for men and women separately.

Table 36   Place of birth of heads of families and their wives

Place of birth	Males		Females	
	Number	*Per cent*	*Number*	*Per cent*
Cardington	41	33	33	27
Under 5 mls	45	36	42	34
5–10 mls	26	21	25	21
Over 10 mls	14	11	22	18
	126	101*	122	100

*In this and subsequent tables percentages are rounded to the nearest whole percent; consequently they may not always add up exactly to 100.

The impression given by Table 36 is that there was considerable mobility amongst the married adults in the parish: only 33 per cent of the men and 27 per cent of the women had been born in the parish. This mobility, however, was predominantly local, for slightly over two-thirds of the men and slightly under two-thirds of the women had been born in Cardington or neighbouring parishes not more than 5 miles away. Relatively few men (11 per cent), but rather more women (18 per cent) had come from parishes more than 10 miles away. The married adults in Cardington in 1782 were therefore by no means predominantly the children of the previous generation who had replaced their parents. Unless special demographic conditions obtained[8], the listing suggests that two out of three of the children of the previous generations had left the parish to found families elsewhere, their places being taken by the children of other parishes.

But was this widespread mobility at marriage an isolated phenomenon, or was it part of a larger pattern of mobility? A study of the current generation of children in the Cardington listing enables us to examine the pattern of mobility at different ages, before and after marriage. Table 37 summarizes, for each

Table 37 Children at home, in service, or married, by age and sex

	0–4 No.	0–4 Per cent	5–9 No.	5–9 Per cent	10–14 No.	10–14 Per cent	15–19 No.	15–19 Per cent	20–24 No.	20–24 Per cent	25–29 No.	25–29 Per cent	30– No.	30– Per cent
							Males							
At home														
No occupation	51		19		34		1		2		0		0	
At school	1		23		7		0		0		0		0	
Occupation	0		0		1		4		1		1		0	
Married	0		0		0		0		0		1		0	
	52	100	42	100	42	84	5	22	3	14	2	12	0	0
*In service**	0	0	0	0	8	16	18	78	15	68	5	29	1	6
Married	0	0	0	0	0	0	0	0	4	18	10	59	17	94
	52	100	42	100	50	100	23	100	22	100	17	100	18	100
							Females							
At home														
No occupation	47		19		9		4		2		0		0	
At school	0		13		4		0		0		0		0	
Occupation	0		10		27		19		12		4		4	
Married	0		0		0		1		1		0		2	
	47	100	42	100	40	91	24	71	15	48	4	22	6	30
*In service***	0	0	0	0	4	9	10	29	10	32	2	11	3	15
Married	0	0	0	0	0	0	0	0	6	19	12	67	11	55
	47	100	42	100	44	100	34	100	31	99	18	100	20	100

*Including 2 at sea, 5 soldiers, 3 apprentices, and 1 craftsman not stated to be in service.
**Including 4 unmarried girls resident elsewhere, but not stated to be in service.

standard five-year age group the numbers of children residing at home in different circumstances, or living elsewhere, in service or married.

The first point that is clear from the table is that all children under the age of 10 were living at home with their parents. Most were listed as being without occupation, although in the 5–9 age group about one-quarter of the girls were assigned an occupation. The girls' occupations given in the listing reveal a widespread domestic industry of pillow-lace making and to a lesser extent of linen and jersey spinning, which provided a considerable amount of employment for the women of the parish at this date, but which was almost extinct a century later.[9] As a result, at all ages a far higher proportion of the girls are assigned a specific occupation than are the boys, although it is possible that the boys were also employed, but more generally in assisting their fathers. Schooling was available in the parish thanks to two benefactors, but with one exception only children between the ages of 5 and 11 are stated in the listing to be at school. School attendance was more common amongst the boys than amongst the girls: in the 5–9 age group, just over one-half of the boys and just under one-third of the girls were at school.

In the next age group, 10–14, the overwhelming majority of children were still at home, 84 per cent of the boys and 91 per cent of the girls; those who were not at home were out in service. A higher proportion of boys than girls was out in service at this age, a pattern which persists until the mid 20s, when it is overlaid by marriage, and which probably reflects the availability of alternative employment at home for the girls in lace making. In the next age group, 15–19, however, there is a massive change in the residence pattern of the boys: now only 22 per cent remained at home, and 78 per cent were out in service. In the age groups 20–24 and 25–9 even fewer boys were living at home (between 10 per cent and 15 per cent); the great majority were living elsewhere, either in service (20–24: 68 per cent, 25–29: 29 per cent), or, increasingly with age, married and heading families of their own (20–24: 18 per cent, 25–29: 59 per cent). Over the age of 30 none of the boys was still living with his parents: indeed all were married, except one who remained in service.

If we were to characterize the age-specific residence expectations of a Cardington boy in 1782, we should say that he would be certain to live at home with his parents during the first nine years of his life, and that between the ages of 5 and 11 he would have a 50:50 chance of attending a school. From 10 to 14 there would only be a 1 in 4 chance that he would be living away from home in service, but the odds in favour of his being away in service would increase dramatically to 4 to 1 between the ages of 15 and 19. In his twenties he would very probably (6 or 7 to 1) be living away from home, either in service or married. He would not marry before he was 20, and he would probably marry in his late 20s. He would be unlikely to remain celibate. The pattern is therefore one of a general expectation for a boy to leave the parental home after the age of 15, first as an unmarried servant, and then married, as head of his own family. Relatively few boys over the age of 15 remained at home, and only one, the third of a carpenter's four sons, and himself a carpenter, continued to live with his parents after he was married.

The residence pattern for the girls of Cardington differs some-what from that of the boys after the age of 15. In general a higher proportion of girls remained living at home, mostly occupied in lace making and textile spinning. In the age group 15–19 when only 22 per cent of the boys remained at home, no less than 71 per cent of the girls were still living with their parents. This percentage fell to 48 per cent of the age group 20–24, reflecting the fact at this age girls were beginning to leave home to get married, for the percentage of girls in service remained more or less the same. Above the age of 25 the percentage of girls still living at home fell further to between 20 per cent and 30 per cent, and the percentage in service also fell from around 30 per cent to between 10 per cent and 15 per cent. The percentage of girls of this age who were married accordingly rose, for like the boys, most girls seem to have married in the mid or late 20s. Unlike the boys, however, a fairly high percentage of the girls over the age of 30 (35 per cent) remained unmarried; about half of these were still living at home, and about half were in service. Four married girls were living with their parents.

The age-specific residence expectations of a Cardington girl would therefore begin, as for her brother, with the certainty of living at home during the first nine years of her life, but she would have a chance of only 1 in 3 of attending a school between the ages of 5 and 9. From 10 to 14 she would almost certainly still be at home, probably employed in lace making or textile spinning. From 15 to 19 she would still most probably (3.5 to 1) be similarly employed; otherwise she would be out in service. From 20–24 she would be almost equally likely either to remain at home, or to leave home either as a servant or to be married. If she were to leave home, she would be 1.5 times more likely to be a servant than to be married. In her late 20s, however, she would be unlikely to be at home (5 to 1 against), or a servant (10 to 1 against); most probably she would be married. Over the age of 30 she would still most probably be married and living away from home, but there is some chance that she would remain unmarried (1 in 3), and in this case she would be equally likely to live at home, or out in service. If she were married, she would not be likely at any age, to be living with her parents, although she would be more likely than her brother to do so.[10]

These age-specific mobility profiles, which the listing enables us to draw for the children of Cardington, emphasize the paramount importance of the custom of sending children into service in determining the migratory experience of children for the ten years from the age of 15 until the mid 20s when marriage finally sundered

Table 38 Residence of children absent from parent's home, by age and sex

	0–4/5–9 No.	Per cent	10–14 No.	Per cent	15–19 No.	Per cent	20–24 No.	Per cent	25–29 No.	Per cent	30– No.	Per cent	Total No.	Per cent
In service*							*Males*							
Cardington	0	0	5	62	8	44	3	20	1	20	1	10	18	38
Under 5 mls	0	0	1	12	5	28	7	47	0	0	0	0	13	28
5–10 mls	0	0	0	0	2	11	2	13	0	0	0	0	4	9
Over 10 mls	0	0	0	25	3	17	3	20	4	80	0	0	12	26
(incl. London)	(0)	(0)	(0)	(0)	(1)	(6)	(1)	(7)	(0)	(0)	(0)	(0)	(2)	(4)
	0	0	8	99	18	100	15	100	5	100	1	100	47	101
							Females							
Cardington	0	0	1	25	3	30	1	10	0	0	0	0	5	17
Under 5 mls	0	0	2	50	5	50	6	60	2	100	1	33	16	55
5–10 mls	0	0	0	0	0	0	1	10	0	0	0	0	1	3
Over 10 mls	0	0	1	25	2	20	2	20	0	0	2	66	7	24
(incl. London)	(0)	(0)	(1)	(25)	(1)	(10)	(1)	(10)	(0)	(0)	(1)	(33)	(4)	(14)
	0	0	4	100	10	100	10	100	2	100	3	99	29	99
Married							*Males*							
At home	0	0	0	0	0	0	0	0	1	9	0	0	1	3
Cardington	0	0	0	0	0	0	1	25	3	27	3	18	7	22
Under 5 mls	0	0	0	0	0	0	1	25	2	18	5	29	8	25
5–10 mls	0	0	0	0	0	0	1	25	2	18	2	12	5	16
Over 10 mls	0	0	0	0	0	0	1	25	3	27	7	41	11	34
(incl. London)	(0)	0	(0)	0	(0)	0	(1)	(25)	(3)	(27)	(6)	(35)	(10)	(31)
	0	0	0	0	0	0	4	100	11	99	17	100	32	100
							Females							
At home	0	0	0	0	1	100	1	14	0	0	2	15	4	12
Cardington	0	0	0	0	0	0	0	0	2	17	2	15	4	12
Under 5 mls	0	0	0	0	0	0	4	57	6	50	3	23	13	39
5–10 mls	0	0	0	0	0	0	2	29	2	17	2	15	6	18
Over 10 mls	0	0	0	0	0	0	0	0	2	17	4	31	6	18
(incl. London)	(0)	(0)	(0)	(0)	(0)	(0)	(0)	(0)	(2)	(17)	(3)	(23)	(5)	(15)
	0	0	0	0	1	100	7	100	12	101	13	99	33	99

*Including some not explicitly stated to be servants; see note to Table 37.

most children from their parental home. But the listing also enables us to observe the distance from their parents' home at which children of different ages resided, when they were married or in service. Table 38 above summarizes the information given in the listing on residential distances from home for male and female children in each age group who are in service or married.

Although the numbers in some parts of Table 38 are too small for any firm conclusions to be drawn, the overall patterns in the residential distribution of servants and married children are not in doubt. Taking all ages together, the most common location of boys living away from home in service was another household in the same parish. About two-thirds of the youngest boys in service remained in the parish, but this proportion fell sharply with age, so that over three-quarters of the boys aged 20–29 were employed outside the parish. Between the ages of 15 and 24, when the greatest proportion of boys was out in service, a substantial percentage was employed in neighbouring parishes not more than 5 miles from home. Most of these parishes lay alongside the river Ouse, which formed the northern boundary of Cardington, and there was a tendency for servants to prefer the parishes on the Cardington side of the river. The nearby country town of Bedford seems to have been no more attractive to male servants than other neighbouring parishes. Relatively few boys were in service in parishes between 5 and 10 miles away; but a quarter of the servants of all ages were in service more than 10 miles away from home. Two points should be made about this last figure. Firstly only two boys had reached London, and secondly two-thirds of this group who were living so far from home were not actually servants.[11] Thus although this figure of one-quarter usefully indicates the extent of long-distance migration among the unmarried male children of the parish, it exaggerates the proportion of those who were employed *as servants* so far from home.

The residence pattern of the girls who went into service is somewhat different. At all ages most servant girls were working in another parish, but predominantly in one which was less than 5 miles away. By far the most popular place for female servants from Cardington was the county town, Bedford, where about one-third of them found employment. Service in other households in Cardington was by comparison less frequent. Like the boys, few girls went to be servants in parishes between 5 and 10 miles away; but a sizeable proportion (24 per cent) went to parishes more than

10 miles away. London was the most favoured of the distant locations: about one girl servant in seven was to be found there.

In general, however, most servants (about two-thirds of the boys, and almost three-quarters of the girls) were employed either within the parish, or in neighbouring parishes within 5 miles of home. Since servants rarely stayed in one place for more than a year or two, it was this wider area within a radius of 5 miles of their parents' home, rather than their home parish itself, which constituted the normal geographical horizon of the 60 per cent of the boys and 26 per cent of the girls, who were out in service between the ages of 15 and 24.

After the age of 25 most children had left their parents to get married rather than to go into service. Only one-quarter of the male children continued to live in the parish after marriage. Another quarter were residing in neighbouring parishes, so that about a half of the married male children were living within a radius of 5 miles from their parents' home. On the other hand about a third of the married male children were living in London. This is a far higher proportion than went to London as unmarried servants or apprentices and suggests that the capital city offered economic opportunities to a man burdened with family responsibilities which the local economy was unable to provide.

About the same proportion, one-quarter, of the girls remained in the parish after marriage, but one-half of those that remained continued to live with their parents. Nearly 40 per cent of the married girls lived in neighbouring parishes so that about two-thirds of them, compared with only one-half of the married boys, resided within 5 miles of their parents' home. On the other hand a far lower proportion of married girls lived in London: 15 per cent, compared with 31 per cent of the boys. Taking girls and boys together, about a quarter (23 per cent) of the married children of the parish were living in London. It has recently been suggested that the massive increase in the population of London between the mid seventeenth and the mid eighteenth century could only have been achieved, in the face of its persistently large surpluses of deaths over births, by substantial migration to the capital, involving the adult survivors of about one-sixth (17 per cent) of all children aged 25–29, and 30 and above, who were resident in the national cohort of births.[12] In Cardington in 1782 the proportions in London were 14 per cent and 26 per cent respectively. Cardington has the advantage of being situated on a

main road only 45 miles from the capital, yet given the high degree
of local rural mobility which the listing reveals, it is possible that
other Bedfordshire parishes were sending similarly high
proportions of their adult married children to London at the
end of the eighteenth century. The importance of London in
Cardington's migration pattern is underlined by the fact that three
times more married children were resident there than in Bedford,
only 2½ miles away.

Table 39 summarizes the age-specific migration patterns of the
children of Cardington in 1782. The table shows for each age
group the proportion of children resident in different locations,
and also, in the 'cumulative' column, the proportion of children
living less than a given distance from their parents' home.

From the table it is clear that the children of Cardington spent
the first nine years of their lives at home with their parents. A
few boys, and fewer girls, left home between the ages of 10 and
14 to go into service, the boys tending to go into households
within the parish, and the girls into households in neighbouring
parishes.[13] From the age of 15 the percentage of boys at home is
drastically reduced, the older the boys are the further away from
home they reside. The percentage of boys still resident *in the
parish* falls from 57 per cent in the age group 15–19 to around 35
per cent between the ages of 20 and 29, and falls again to about
20 per cent in the age group of 30 and above. The percentage of
boys resident *within 5 miles* also falls with age from about 80 per
cent at 15–19 to around 50 per cent at age 25 and upwards.
Conversely the percentage of boys living *more than 5 miles* from
their parent's home rises steeply with age, from around 20 per
cent at 15–19 to about 50 per cent from the age of 25.

Many more girls than boys remain at home after the age of 15,
and far fewer girls are to be found living in other households
within the parish. Possibly a number of girls who would otherwise
have gone out into service in the parish were kept at home
employed in making lace. In addition no less than half of the
married daughters resident in the parish were living with their
parents rather than in separate households of their own. Otherwise the girls' migration profile was not unlike that of the boys;
the older they were, the further from the parish they resided. The
proportion of girls living more than 5 miles away from home was
less than half that of the boys at all ages under 30. This reflects
three special aspects of the girls' migration which have already

Table 39 Percentage distribution of children's residence, by age and sex

	0–4		5–9		10–14		15–19		20–24		25–29		30–	
	Per cent	cum per cent	Per cent	cum per cent	Per cent	cum per cent	Per cent	cum per cent	Per cent	cum per cent	Per cent	cum per cent	Per cent	cum per cent
Males														
Within parish														
At home	100	100	100	100	84	84	22	22	14	14	12	12	0	0
Other households	0	100	0	100	10	94	35	57	18	32	24	36	22	22
Outside parish														
Under 5 mls	0	100	0	100	2	96	22	79	36	68	12	48	28	50
Over 5 mls	0	100	0	100	4	100	22	101	32	100	53	101	50	100
(incl. London)	(0)		(0)		(0)		(4)		(9)		(18)		(33)	
Females														
Within parish														
At home	100	100	100	100	91	91	71	71	48	48	22	22	30	30
Other households	0	100	0	100	2	93	9	80	3	51	11	33	10	40
Outside parish														
Under 5 mls	0	100	0	100	5	98	13	93	32	83	44	77	20	60
Over 5 mls	0	100	0	100	2	100	6	99	16	99	22	99	40	100
(incl. London)	(0)		(0)		(2)		(3)		(3)		(11)		(20)	

been mentioned: their tendency to stay at home in domestic industry, their preference as servants for employment in neighbouring Bedford, and the lower proportion residing after marriage in London.

In general, however, the listing reveals a remarkable degree of migration amongst the sons and daughters of the labourers and craftsmen of Cardington. From the age of 15 a large proportion of the population was in service, mobile, and living increasingly distant from the parental home. Marriage continued, and possibly accelerated, this pattern. If we take the children aged 30 and above as representing the adult second generation of the Cardington families with families of their own, over three-quarters of the men and nearly two-thirds of the women are found to have left the parish. Furthermore about half of this second generation have settled more than 5 miles from their parents' home.

The Cardington listing is exceptional, and we shall be fortunate indeed to discover another which provides a comparable wealth of information on migration. There can therefore be no guarantee that the picture it yields of the patterns of migration is typical of other parishes. Rural communities in the past were by no means alike, and certain features of Cardington, for example its location and the prevalence of a domestic industry, may have given the pattern of mobility of its inhabitants a particular cast. But until it can be shown that Cardington was in some fundamental way different from other rural parishes, we may perhaps accept the age-specific profiles given here as a provisional paradigm of English rural migration on the eve of the industrial revolution.

Notes and references

1 Peter Laslett, 'Le brassage de la population en France et en Angleterre au XVIIe et XVIIIe siècles', *Annales de démographie historique* (1968), pp. 99–109: 'Clayworth and Cogenhoe', *Historical essays, 1680–1750, presented to David Ogg*, eds H. E. Bell and R. L. Ollard (1963), pp. 157–184.

2 Laslett, 'Le brassage', p. 106.

3 Laslett, 'Clayworth and Cogenhoe', p. 179.

4 Laslett, 'Size and structure of the household in England over three centuries; part I', *Population Studies* (1969), p. 219; unpublished analyses at Cambridge Group for the History of Population and Social Structure.

5 A preliminary demographic and social structural analysis of this listing has been published by N. Tranter in 'Population and social structure in a Bedfordshire parish: the Cardington listing of inhabitants, 1782', *Population Studies*, **xxi** (1967), pp. 261–82. Tranter also carried out a family reconstitution study of some of the families, which substantially confirmed the accuracy of the

listing. Mr D. Baker of the Portsmouth College of Technology is also engaged on a full study of this remarkable document.

6 Thomas Jeffreys, *Map of the county of Bedford* (c. 1780).

7 Laslett, 'Le brassage', p. 107, gives figures for the percentages entering and leaving Clayworth, Hallines and Longuenesse over a period of twelve years, ranging between 6 per cent and 15 per cent, and 11 per cent and 19 per cent, respectively.

8 A large increase in the number of families in the parish, for example, or a high mortality rate or a low mortality rate amongst the previous generation of Cardington children, would upset the reciprocity inferred in the text.

9 *Kelly's Directory of Bedfordshire, Huntingdonshire and Northamptonshire* (1898), p. 59.

10 There seems to be little evidence of the residence pattern normally associated with a stem-family structure, among the labourers and craftsmen of Cardington in 1782. The families with married sons or daughters living at home comprise 5 per cent and 15 per cent respectively of all families with married sons or daughters.

11 See note to Table 37, above.

12 E. A. Wrigley, 'A simple model of London's importance in changing English society and economy, 1650–1750', *Past and Present*, **37** (1967), pp. 44–70.

13 The high percentage of boys and girls (94 per cent and 93 per cent respectively) residing in the parish until the age of 14 is encouraging for the accuracy of child mortality rates calculated on the basis of family reconstitution. The Cambridge Group for the History of Population and Social Structure calculates child mortality rates only up to the age of 9, at whch age all the Cardington children were still resident at home.

9
Migrants in the city: the process of social adaptation in English towns 1500–1800

Peter Clark

The chapter deploys mainly literary evidence to survey the complex mechanisms by which migrants became integrated and socialized in English towns in the early modern period. The main argument is that whereas in the sixteenth and seventeenth centuries the urban access paths for many migrants were often restricted, with conventional channels for integration unable to absorb the high levels.of outsiders, by the eighteenth century a greater range of channels had emerged, including commercial and voluntary bodies which made it somewhat easier for outsiders to secure a position in urban society. The discussion provides little quantitative evidence and is in parts, of necessity, rather speculative. It is also unclear from work so far whether the developments in the larger urban centres discussed here, particularly in London, were mirrored in smaller urban communities.

Cities in the pre-industrial era were like railway termini.[1] Large numbers of people arrived every day, many moving on quickly to different places in town, others after a short stay departing for new destinations, urban or rural. Though considerable research has been done on the heavy volume of movement to English towns during the early modern period, the equally important questions of mobility within towns and outward migration have only recently attracted attention.[2] Evidence would indicate that the pattern of turnover and out-movement varied, as for immigration, according to a range of social and economic circumstances. Newcomers would stay in one place, move street or parish, or leave town, depending on the availability of jobs and housing. Other factors influencing their movement would be their personal backgrounds and attitude (some country people found urban life too fast and hectic); their position in the life cycle; the strength of ties with home; and alternative employment opportunities. Equally vital in deciding whether newcomers were successful in adjusting to their adopted community and settling down as townspeople was the quality of the channels of urban integration and assimilation. It was a two-way process. The effectiveness of social integration determined how far towns could cope with the problems created by the large-scale migrant inflows in early modern England.

For the industrial period Michael Anderson's study of Victorian Preston has shown how a complex web of social mechanisms, principally family ties, but also lodging houses, shops and other bodies, helped smooth the migrant's entry to town. In French cities during the nineteenth century it seems that kinship, regional ties, occupational specialization and voluntary associations played a significant part in assisting outsiders to find their feet. Similarly in the expanding cities of the modern developing world we can see the importance for immigrants of family connections, tribal and regional affinities, and drinking houses and clubs which served to mediate between countryside and town.[3]

Less is known, however, about these integrative channels in pre-industrial England. There are serious problems with the sources. We have only a few listings of native immigrants by the civic authorities which record places of origin, occupations, and so on.[4] Settlement records which supply information on the place of birth or origin of poorer movers do not usually tell where they resided in town. Thus one gets only a sketchy idea of the spatial distribution and employment patterns of newcomers within the community: quantitative analysis is virtually impossible. Nonetheless, despite these and other difficulties, it is possible to describe some of the varied kinds of support to which urban migrants had access in the early modern period. As we shall see, the pattern of integrative support changed over time. In this paper we consider firstly some of the traditional mechanisms of assimilation; then growing official intervention from the sixteenth century; and finally the proliferation of new informal and commercial channels of integration, particularly during the eighteenth century. The main concern is with the reception of lower-class migrants – the great mass of urban newcomers.

I

From the late Middle Ages apprenticeship was one of the principal gateways to urban society for many young migrants. By the terms of his indenture the teenage apprentice served his freeman master for a certain number of years, living in his household, learning a craft or trade; after completing his period of service he had the prospect of becoming a freeman himself, a master of his craft gild, and maybe one day a member of the town corporation. Just how widespread and organized the institution of apprenticeship was in medieval towns is unclear; it probably varied in importance from town to town according to local usage. Service outside apprenticeship was doubtless common, particularly in suburban areas.[5] But this is not to underestimate the general significance of apprenticeship for urban recruitment. By the early seventeenth century London may have had 25,000 apprentices, about 12 per cent of the overall population. At Cambridge in the 1620s 6 per cent or more of the inhabitants were apprentices. A high proportion of town apprentices were outsiders.[6]

During the Tudor and Stuart period, however, apprenticeship experienced important changes. Fundamental was the statute of 1563 which codified the procedure and made it both more comprehensive and less flexible. A seven-year term steadily became the norm; female apprentices largely disappeared (until the late seventeenth century).[7] Another factor affecting the role of apprenticeship was the rapid growth of large-scale subsistence migration to towns in the century before the Civil War. Many of these newcomers were poor people who had travelled long distances and lacked the necessary money and contacts to be apprenticed.[8] Even for those who were indentured there are signs of a two-tier system evolving. Apprenticeship in the principal urban trades, ones which generally ensured some degree of social advancement, were increasingly dominated by children from wealthier families; boys from lesser backgrounds had to make do with inferior trades and poorer masters. At this level masters often did not trouble to draw up formal agreements or failed to pay the fees to have them registered, treating them as cheap labour and sending them away when they became recalcitrant or too expensive to keep. The drop-out rate was high. At Norwich in the sixteenth and seventeenth centuries roughly three-quarters of the apprentices never became freemen. At Salisbury only 21 per cent of the boys enrolled in the 1610s took out the freedom.[9]

As the seventeenth century progressed the recruitment of apprentices was more and more localized, with a growing dependence on the immediate hinterland. At London in the years 1570 to 1640 only 19.0 per cent of the apprentices in fifteen London companies came from the home counties, while 32.5 per cent originated in the northern and western counties. But by the period 1674 to 1690 31.7 per cent of the apprentices in nine companies came from the home counties, and only 14.5 per cent came from the north and west. In Southampton after 1670 less than half the new apprentices were outsiders.[10] To some extent this contraction mirrored general migration trends, with the increase of short-distance movement and possibly immobility after the Restoration. But the narrowed range of apprentice movement was also linked with the slow but steady decline of apprenticeship as an urban institution, particularly evident after 1700. Though it remained a useful step-ladder into superior urban trades, for poorer crafts and the new consumer industries apprenticeship assumed a minor importance. From the close of the seventeenth century it was increasingly detached from the political *cursus honorum* in many towns, through the mass creation of freemen, many of whom had not been apprenticed. In the eighteenth century even those boys still apprenticed often lived outside their masters' houses in lodgings.[11]

Whereas apprenticeship declined in general effectiveness as an integrating channel for migrants, marriage may well have advanced in importance during the early modern period. For towns a substantial proportion of all marriages were exogamous. Marriage licence data for four London parishes between 1572 and 1650 indicate that in approximately half the weddings one partner was an outsider, though mostly from another city parish. Even in the minority of cases where marriages were apparently endogamous, it may well be that at least one partner was a recent immigrant. Marriage could provide newcomers with access to urban trading and social contacts. By wedding the daughter or widow of a freeman the outsider might acquire the privileges of the freedom. In London 30 per cent of craftsmen marrying for the first time took a widow as partner. If she was respectable the new husband stood a good chance of gaining a house, a business and a circle of friends and acquaintances in one swoop. An alliance with the kinswoman of a civic patrician family could open the door to commercial and political success. Marriage was an important key to civic advancement in Elizabethan Exeter and elsewhere.[12] However, one must not exaggerate the opportunities for social mobility for newcomers. Those marrying into patrician families were often from respectable or rising rural families. Most sons of village labourers or artisans, if they married in town, ended up allied to an equally poor girl with few assets – money, possessions or contacts. At this social level there was in fact precious little incentive to marry and many poorer folk lived in casual or common-law relationships. Thus Robert Gant, a Kentishman arrested at Southampton in the 1650s, claimed to have met and married his wife in Canterbury but 'afterwards confessed that he was not married by any lawful minister but that he took her to be his wife . . . and will live and die with her'. Often, however, partners separated in order to find work.[13] In the later part of the period it is possible that marriage became more important as a social and integrative institution for the artisan and labouring classes. Although unofficial or clandestine marriages were common until the reform of the marriage law in 1753, rising living standards (before the last years of the eighteenth century) and improvements in urban housing may have made it easier for people to set up home together. The operation of the poor and settlement laws may also have been biased towards married couples (at least those without children).[14]

Apprenticeship and marriage were sometimes interlinked with another traditional medium of urban contact: kinship. Country parents might seek to indenture their child to a relative in town, though this was less common than one might expect. At Salisbury in the late sixteenth and early seventeenth centuries no more than 5 per cent of servants dwelt with kin; at Bristol in the sixteenth century up to 7 per cent of rural apprentices were related to their masters. Other kin support may have come from sibling contact. Among Gloucestershire apprentices to Bristol nearly one in ten had a brother who was also indentured in the city. In the same fashion, relations in town might help the newcomer with the choice of a marriage partner. As well as this, there is evidence for close and distant kinsfolk providing temporary accommodation, food, assistance with finding a job, loans, and other help. In 1609 Katherine Lye, a widow from Yeovil in Somerset, who had travelled to Southampton in the company of a friendly cheese-trader, stopped and took up lodging with her relative Robert Gilletts, a tailor in East Street. The same year a New Romney girl, Alice Cutberde, went to the town of Cranbrook, also in Kent, saying she hoped her sister 'would help her to a service'. In the 1670s John Pinney, who had been born in a Dorset village and worked for a time at Exeter, came and stayed with his kinswoman Sabina Pinney at the small town of Chudleigh in Devon; after a few months he took his own house and set up as a cordwainer.[15] Of a sample of single female migrants living in London in the years 1565–1644 37 per cent had kin dwelling in the capital and over a fifth were living with relatives. Godparents, usually distant kin, were often supportive. They might help with accommodation and finding a job. In the late eighteenth century Thomas Bewick described how he was apprenticed to a Newcastle engraver through the intervention of his godmother Miss Simons, who also paid the apprenticeship premium; he subsequently lodged with an aunt who was the widow of one of his godfathers.[16] Kinsfolk at home might also be mobilized to help the urban migrant. If things turned difficult he could send a message to his parents for money or some other aid. Literate migrants clearly maintained ties with home through letters, particularly if they had gone long distances. In the later Stuart period the Coggeshall woolcomber Joseph Bufton corresponded monthly for several years with his brother John, who had gone to Dublin. Channels of communication between urban and rural kin were also maintained through visits, and after the late seventeenth century in particular by seasonal migration, with townspeople returning to their native areas at harvest time.[17] In these ways continuing kinship ties helped to consolidate the outsider's position in town and to establish a road which future generations of migrants would tread.

One must be wary of overstating the importance of kin ties in the context of assimilating immigrants, especially during the sixteenth and seventeenth centuries. Extended family networks were probably most effective for more respectable movers travelling relatively short distances. It is questionable whether they afforded much succour to the poor subsistence migrants coming long distances who flocked into English towns in ever growing numbers in the decades before the Civil War. Even those indigent newcomers who found a relative to lodge with in town, probably stayed, as at Salisbury, for only a brief time. Since the relation was also likely to be poor a major constraint was space and food for the incomer. Significantly, at Salisbury wealthier, better settled households tended to lodge more kin for longer periods.[18] By the eighteenth century, however, the increased localization of migration and improved living standards among townspeople (allowing lower-class families greater resources in terms of housing, food and the like) may have led to a new situation in which kin ties contributed more widely to the reception of urban newcomers. Mary Prior, in her valuable study of an Oxford riverside community, has stressed the importance of a web of kinship ties in the river trade down the Thames, which provided a conduit for movement between Oxford, Abingdon, and the towns beyond.[19]

Regional and local affinities also helped the migrant find his feet in town. When William Lilly, the future astrologer, went to London in 1620 he became the servant of Gilbert Wright and his wife, both of whom had originally come from Lilly's home district of western Leicestershire; they remained in contact with the area, sometimes going on visits there. Some years before Richard Sanger had migrated from Wiltshire to Sandwich in Kent; he had journeyed there in the company of his 'countryman' Clarke of Sandwich who helped Sanger when he got to town, and traded with him. In the 1740s when William Hutton arrived at Hinckley in Leicestershire he was asked. 'Where do you come from?' When he said 'Derby', he was told 'There is a countryman of yours in such a street.' This 'countryman' gave him temporary work and lodging. The *New London Spy* (1780) tells a similar story of a man robbed in the street in the capital being helped by a passerby who 'came from the same town as he did, acknowledged his acquaintance, lent him a great coat' and took him to his lodging.[20] The diary of John Byrom, a Manchester man who came to London for extended stays during George II's reign, reveals that he was regularly attended by poor people from the north wanting (and receiving) relief. It is also clear that he was a member of a lively network of Lancashire people meeting to talk, drink and consult together in the capital. From the seventeenth century, if not before, inns and other drinking establishments in towns commonly had regional connections. Henry Newcome noted in 1662 going to Chester and meeting an 'abundance of our Manchester folk' at the Sun tavern. In eighteenth-century Liverpool one public house was known to cater for people from Bristol. In London Thomas Bewick met his Newcastle friends every Monday at the Hole in the Wall, Fleet Street, where Newcastle newspapers were available.[21] In the seventeenth and eighteenth centuries these provincial gatherings were increasingly formalized with the establishment of county clubs and societies in London and other major cities, a development which is discussed below. To what extent regional connections in town were reinforced by occupational specialization or residential propinquity is not very clear. It has been suggested that apprentices to Newcastle from certain areas tended to cluster in particular trades – thus barber-surgeons from in and around Morpeth and glaziers from the Glasshouses; but we lack similar evidence for other towns. Again there is nothing to show that distinct geographical concentrations of Kentishmen or Yorkshiremen existed in the capital. In general provincial loyalties were probably more diluted and fragmented than was the case in continental cities.[22]

On the other hand, there may have been a contrast here in the experience of ethnic migrants. Poor Welsh immigrants were apparently clustering together at Shrewsbury in the seventeenth century near the river Severn by the Welsh Bridge. By the mid eighteenth century one hears a report from Worcester that 'one part of the town is inhabited by Welsh people who speak their own language'. In London the Welsh seem to have been widely dispersed during the seventeenth century, but the rapid expansion of the capital may have encouraged greater, if still limited, concentration during the next century in the vicinity of the Welsh school in Clerkenwell.[23] Scots people in London may also have gravitated together somewhat by the reign of George I. The records of the Scottish Presbyterian Church, first in St Martin's Lane and then in Crown Court, Covent Garden, indicate a high density of immigrants living in the western suburbs close to the old city walls – in St Martin's, the Strand, Bedfordbury, and Holborn. Favoured trades were tailoring and the hair trade (particularly in Bedfordbury).[24]

Probably the heaviest clustering, however, involved Irish immigrants. In the 1780s there were over 23,000 in London, and by the early nineteenth century distinct neighbourhood communities in the riverside parishes of east London and in St Giles. Underpinning this development was the emergence of an array of ethnic social institutions – lodging houses, public houses, cookshops, masonic clubs, and chapels with their circles of charities, societies and schools.[25] In July 1736 when anger erupted over cheap-rate

Irish labour in the capital, the mob went on a tour of alehouses and cookshops in Shoreditch and Spitalfields, attacking Irish landlords and customers. Geographical concentration may well have been fostered by popular antipathy to the Irish. It was not just competition in the workplace which upset Londoners. They disliked the squalid poverty of many Irish immigrants, their lack of skills, and their cultural distinctiveness (language as well as religion). In the mid 1730s there was a newspaper report of an Irish woman in custody in London setting up 'the Irish howl' which quickly attracted a crowd of compatriots to rescue her. The popular cry at this time among Londoners was 'down with the wild Irish'.[26]

As for the continental immigrants, evidence for London would indicate that French and Dutch 'strangers' tended to be dispersed across the capital in the early period (although one sees more clustering in provincial centres like Canterbury). By the end of the seventeenth century, however, there was greater residential concentration. The thousands of French Huguenots who fled from persecution under Louis XIV, especially after the Revocation of the Edict of Nantes, gathered in London in two main districts: Spitalfields and Bethnal Green to the east and Leicester Fields and Soho in the west. The latter community tended to be better off, conforming to the Anglican liturgy, while the other was poorer and nonconformist. Nonetheless ethnic cohesion was encouraged by a profusion of institutions serving the community: the General Assembly of French Churches (from the 1690s), the French Protestant Hospital (1718), a school, friendly societies and drinking houses. The large government grant to the Huguenots for relief purposes (about £12,000 a year after 1696) may also have boosted closer ties within the community. However it is also evident that in the course of the eighteenth century membership of the Huguenot churches declined sharply as a result of rapid assimilation into the native population.[27]

Another important ethnic community in Hanoverian London (and also some provincial towns) were the Jews. While there were divisions between the wealthier, long-established Sephardim (Portuguese) Jews and more recent poorer refugees mainly from central Europe (the Ashkenazim), the latter were increasingly united by religious and charitable organizations, by commercial specialization and by residential propinquity. In London the main Jewish grouping was around Petticoat Lane.[28] In the East End in fact one can identify neighbourhoods which provided a harbour for successive waves of ethnic immigrants – French, Irish and Jews. Overall the formation of distinct immigrant neighbourhoods or communities seems to have been most marked among those people who displayed the greatest social and cultural differentiation from the native population, and for that reason were unable to utilize conventional channels of entry into urban society.

Finally hospitality. It was not only kinsfolk and 'countrymen' who traditionally offered relief and aid to urban newcomers. In the Middle Ages new arrivals might expect neighbourly hospitality, including food, drink and shelter from wealthier and ordinary townsmen. Certain gilds had lodging chambers for migrants. But hospitality of this kind probably diminished during the sixteenth and seventeenth centuries, partly perhaps because of the Reformation and Protestant criticism of indiscriminate charity, but also because of the growing volume of immigration, threatening to overwhelm urban dispensers of hospitality. Though contemporary complaints about the decay of hospitality were not new and were rather conventional, A. L. Beier has shown that there was a real decline in the neighbourly relief of poorer migrants before the Civil War. By 1600 immigrants commonly paid for their lodging in private houses. For many needy townspeople, particularly widows, the lodging of outsiders became a valued source of income.[29] Town magistrates issued increasingly vehement orders against the practice, fining the offenders, but such efforts had only partial success.[30] At the same time, old-style hospitality did not entirely disappear. A poor migrant to Birmingham in the 1740s was approached by two townspeople. Noting that the newcomer looked 'a forlorn traveller, without money and without friends', they gave him bread, cheese and beer and found lodging for him in the neighbourhood.[31]

In sum, it is evident that English towns had a range of traditional arrangements for assimilating outsiders into the community. Nevertheless, one has a strong sense that during the sixteenth and early seventeenth centuries these mechanisms were under intense pressure, unable to absorb the high levels of immigration, particularly the inflows of impoverished subsistence movers. The situation was aggravated by the economic difficulties of numerous towns at this time. Heavy immigration contributed to mounting urban poverty and unemployment and to other serious social problems.

II

From Henry VIII's reign civic magistrates were increasingly concerned at the threat posed to the urban community by the influx of outsiders, and they introduced numerous measures to regulate it; by 1600 these controls often had statutory backing. For lower-class migrants the official strategy was largely negative and punitive. In 1536 the Southampton magistrates complained of the 'great number of beggars' who 'daily do resort' there and appointed a 'controller over all beggars'; only twenty local people were licensed to beg. At Bury St Edmunds in the 1570s a monthly search was made for vagabonds and newcomers; artificers and labourers 'suspected of loitering' had to declare to the constables where they had worked the previous week. At Lincoln in the same decade the town hired 'a master of the poor folks' to keep watch at the town gates and to drive away and punish vagabonds or strange beggars.[32] From the 1550s London had the Bridewell, a large institution where vagrants and other poor migrants could be incarcerated and punished before being sent back to their birthplaces. The number of vagrants brought before the Bridewell court rose more than tenfold between 1560 and 1624–25. In difficult months like January 1600, over 200 vagrants appeared in the court. By the close of the sixteenth century most larger provincial towns also had their houses of correction, where immigrant poor were punished.[33]

There were mass expulsions of outsiders. At Shrewsbury in 1597 the magistrates prolonged their court sessions for several days because they 'had much ado with inmates and idle persons pestering the town, in examining of them and so driven out of the town'. After the mid sixteenth century a growing number of towns insisted that newcomers should obtain magisterial consent and give sureties before they were allowed to settle. At Coventry in 1598 it was decreed that any stranger marrying a local woman should take her home for a year before coming to live in the city. Repeated orders were issued against the renting of cottages, rooms and cellars to poor migrants.[34]

Not only the poor but small craftsmen and traders experienced restrictions on movement to town during the sixteenth and early seventeenth centuries. Unenfranchised newcomers who set up in business in town were denounced by established citizens. Magistrates in alliance with the gilds often prosecuted offenders and tried to compel new arrivals to purchase the freedom or shut up shop. Access to the freedom was made more difficult in a number of provincial towns by sharp increases in the entry fines. At Lincoln the cost of the freedom by redemption rose from £1 to £5 during Elizabeth's reign; at Rochester it advanced more than fifteenfold during the course of the sixteenth century. Some other towns, including London, may have been less restrictive, but overall the urban strategy was discriminatory, endeavouring to admit into the community only those with capital or special skills and to exclude or deter most other immigrants.[35]

These restrictive policies were only partially successful, however – as the rising population figures for towns at this time indicate. Large contingents of lower-class people continued to arrive, but they were increasingly deflected into the suburbs. Here official controls were lax or ineffectual. People could work without being apprenticed or enfranchised. Accommodation was easier to obtain, with many poor inhabitants, as we have noted, taking in lodgers, and other newcomers building or renting cramped hovels. These suburban or peripheral areas of town also had high numbers of alehouses which provided numerous services for the newcomer. Spreading out from most major towns in the late sixteenth and early seventeenth centuries the suburbs played an important role in the reception of lower-class migrants. However, for many newcomers suburban habitation offered only a precarious foothold in the community. They were excluded from the mainstream of civic economic and political life. Their households were small and fragile entities with few children or servants – liable to break up under pressure. Many of these immigrants soon moved on elsewhere. Only a small minority of respectable householders tended to stay for any length of time.[36]

Another reason for the high mobility of the poor was the quality of urban poor relief. While urban relief expanded markedly in the Tudor period, it provided only marginal aid for immigrants. In periods of crisis, times of harvest failure or trade collapse, relief schemes might succour some newcomers as well as settled poor, mainly to prevent a breakdown of law and order. By 1600 most large and some smaller towns had corn-stocks which sold subsidized grain to the indigent. At Coventry, for example, the city stock served 400–600 customers a week in the spring of 1597 but the great majority were probably resident townsmen. Again town workschemes may have furnished temporary employment for migrant labourers. At Canterbury in the early 1590s large gangs worked on trying to make the river navigable for shipping; in London vagrants helped dig and repair the city ditches. Outsiders may also have benefited from the distribution by town worthies of money or food in years of famine. But generally speaking the great bulk of urban relief went to the local needy – notably the traditional 'impotent' poor, widows, orphans and the sick. Although new hospitals and almshouses were founded during the Tudor and early Stuart period, the relief they provided was usually monopolized by town residents. Parish poor-relief, introduced by law in the 1530s and reorganized by statutes in 1598 and 1601, was primarily concerned with giving weekly doles to local people. The money spent on the migrant usually took the form of small sums to encourage them to stay on the road.[37]

In sum, civic action before the English Revolution tended to be restrictive and biased against lower-class immigrants. While it failed to stop movement to town, it did contribute to high rates of turnover. As the problem of large-scale pauper migration waned in the late seventeenth and early eighteenth centuries official measures against newcomers became stricter but more selective. Local settlement controls were put on a comprehensive national footing by the Settlement Act of 1662. One effect of this statute may have been to discourage longer-distance movement to town. Poor movers travelling from afar without the necessary certificate from their home parish ran the risk of being removed back to their place of birth or settlement. But the operation of the law was selective in other ways too. Single males, married couples without children, and better-off migrants were usually permitted to stay in town without difficulty. Single women and widows, and families with children were much more likely to face removal. To some degree towns could control the mix of immigrants according to their own economic needs.[38] In the later Stuart period there was also an increased institutionalization of parish relief including the establishment of corporations of the poor at Bristol, Gloucester and other towns. The main aim of the corporations was to curtail expenditure by centralizing relief in town workhouses. But if there was any plan to make it more difficult for outsiders to obtain relief, the outcome was quite different. Many local poor refused to accept relief in the work-houses and by the late eighteenth century these institutions were mainly concerned wth aiding destitute migrants, especially the sick and homeless.[39]

Respectable migrants found fewer restrictions and controls than before the English Revolution. Not only were the settlement laws permissive, but the decline of many town gilds by the early eighteenth century and the progressive devaluation of the freedom made it increasingly easy for outsiders to set up in business. With the resurgence of urban prosperity after the Restoration towns and their rulers could afford to be less protectionist.[40]

By the Hanoverian period immigration was no longer one of the most pressing and intractable problems which faced town governments. In part this reflected the changing pattern of migration, with the eclipse of large-scale subsistence movement. When it resurfaced in the late eighteenth century it was mainly associated with the Irish. In this new climate some of the old-style channels for integrating outsiders into the community, such as kinship, may have become more important, while the increased selectivity of official controls, concentrated against the economically marginal and tramping poor, had greater effect. No less vital in the amelioration of the problem was the advent of a great variety of new-style, often commercial agencies which helped newcomers to adjust to urban society.

III

During the sixteenth and seventeenth centuries the most important of the new informal agencies was the urban alehouse. Though alehouses had existed in towns since at least the thirteenth century, their number and importance increased markedly in the hundred years or so before 1640. At Shrewsbury the ratio of alesellers to inhabitants advanced from 1:70 in 1570 to 1:29 in 1630. At Cambridge, where the population increased by a half between the 1580s and 1620s the number of alehouses doubled during the early seventeenth century. Their density was usually highest in the poorer, often peripheral areas of town: thus at Southampton the parish of St Michael had both the highest proportion of sub-tenants (mostly immigrants) and the greatest number of alehousekeepers in the town. This was no coincidence. As I have argued elsewhere, alehouses – usually small, rudimentary premises in a back room or cellar run by a poor labourer, petty craftsmen or widow – played a growing role in servicing the needs of those subsistence migrants who flooded into towns before the Civil War. They provided customers with refreshment, accommodation, contacts, credit, news of jobs, and sometimes work on the premises as pot-boys or maids. In various ways the small urban alehouse assisted those many indigent, often longer-distance migrants who could not make use of the traditional channels for settlement like apprenticeship or the extended kin network. On occasion the world of the alehouse overlapped with older-style adaptive arrangements. But in general the emerging importance of the alehouses as an integrative medium can be seen as a response to the new social circumstances created by urban growth and widespread lower-class immigration.[41]

In the decades after the Restoration the alehouse (increasingly renamed the public house) matured as an urban institution. Premises became larger, better equipped and more comfortable; the number of houses tended to stabilize before 1750 and at the end of the eighteenth century began to decline. In part this development was the result of growing official regulation of the drink trade. But it also reflected a major shift in the alehouse's social and commercial role in towns. As economic conditions began to improve from the later Stuart period, victuallers paid less attention to servicing the needs of the tramping poor, preferring instead to cater for the growing numbers of better-off migrants and travellers – carriers, chapmen and artisans.

As one indication of this trend, by the close of the seventeenth century alehouses began to function as houses of call for certain trades. At trade clubs in the alehouse itinerant artisans might ask for work and if none was available obtain relief, including lodging and refreshment, from the craft fund. Trade clubs-cum-houses of call operated in the textile towns of the west country from the start of the eighteenth century. In 1707, for instance, the Taunton clothiers spoke of weavers belonging to various clubs who were given certificates and money from the common stock 'to travel from their families' in search of work. Bristol masters at this time complained that their workers insisted they employ only members of their clubs or those 'confederated at some other place'. Influential in the spread of trade clubs was the decline or fragmentation of many craft gilds in the early eighteenth century.[42] In London many trades had networks of clubs and houses of call by 1750, and they also developed across the provinces. In the textile trade at this time it was said a man with a certificate from his craft club would be 'subsisted for one night in every town where there is a club-house'. At the end of our period tramping between trade clubs based at public houses had become widespread in many skilled crafts as a way of overcoming local unemployment and maintaining wage rates.[43]

Trade clubs were only part of a major expansion of voluntary associations in late seventeenth and eighteenth century English towns. By George III's reign there was a great repertoire of popular clubs and societies including benefit or friendly societies (London alone may have had a thousand at the close of the eighteenth century with over 50,000 members), political clubs, leisure clubs, county or regional bodies, and so on. With their regular meetings, social functions and encouragement of mutual support, many of these bodies may well have played an important informal role in the incorporation of newcomers into the complex world of urban society, rather as voluntary associations are known to operate in cities in present-day developing countries. County and regional clubs in particular gave a new, more institutional focus to those local solidarities which had traditionally helped immigrants in town. When these regional associations began is uncertain, but writing of the decade before the Civil War the northerner John Shaw claimed that it was then 'a custom for the merchants and other tradesmen that lived in London, so many of them as were all born in the same county, to meet at a solemn feast . . . [and] to consult what good they might do to their native county'.[44] By the 1650s we know of the activities of at least half a dozen county societies in the capital. After the Restoration numbers proliferated with the meeting of up to twenty different clubs or societies linked with particular shires. Though the majority may have been short-lived a number, including those for Cumberland, Westmorland, Herefordshire and Gloucestershire, developed a permanent existence in Hanoverian London.[45]

In 1727 the preacher to the Herefordshire society declared that while they were removed far from their places of birth they formed 'a colony transplanted', concerned with the aim of mutual help. As well as providing a forum for respectable immigrants from a particular area to meet and do business together, such bodies displayed a keen interest in assisting poorer folk to settle in the metropolis. Large sums were collected to apprentice poor boys to city masters and to relieve other poor immigrants.[46] There were also London societies of Scots, Welsh and Irish. In the 1680s

Robert Kirk, on a visit to London, noted a 'club of Scottish Presbyterian schoolmasters' who gathered every Saturday and lent money and found jobs for educated newcomers from Scotland. From 1665 a charitable society called the Scottish Corporation provided relief for poor Scotsmen in the capital, and when necessary repatriated them; by the end of our period over a thousand people a year were receiving aid. Other Scottish societies existed in eighteenth-century London including friendly societies and the Highland Society set up in 1778.[47] The Honorable Society of Ancient Britons, founded in the capital in 1715, was an elitist body with strong Hanoverian sympathies, but it also supported the apprenticing of poor Welsh boys to city traders; after 1718 it had its own school where the children of poor immigrants might be taught. Members of this society were involved in the formation of the London Cymmrodorion Society in 1751 which sought to promote Welsh cultural activity and which in turn fathered the similar Gwynnedigion Society (1770).[48] The Irish Charitable Society (1704) and the later Benevolent Society of St Patrick (1784) had mainly philanthropic functions and contributed along with other charitable bodies, often linked with Catholic chapels, to the growth of that fairly distinct Irish community in late Georgian London which we noted above.[49] Leading provincial cities also had their regional and ethnic societies. Thus at Bristol, we find societies of Wiltshire, Gloucestershire and Somerset men. The Gloucestershire Society was particularly well organized, meeting continuously from the late 1650s. It collected substantial sums of money to relieve poor migrants, to apprentice boys from the shire (and sometimes to educate them), and also to support immigrant women before and after childbirth. Bristol also had a Society of Ancient Britons, as did Birmingham. At Norwich a Scots Society set up in 1775 to assist destitute migrants from over the border extended its activities after a few years to relieving other ethnic movers.[50]

At the end of the eighteenth century with accelerating urbanization there was a spate of new philanthropic societies concerned in large measure with the plight of the urban immigrant poor. The Philanthropic Society, established in London in September 1788, sought to provide education for the children of the vagrant poor. Rather later came the Institution for the Protection of Young Country Girls (1801), and the Society for the Suppression of Juvenile Vagrancy (1808). In the provinces Stranger's Friend societies were founded at Leeds, Liverpool and other rapidly growing towns. The Leeds society, for example, sought to help the 'multitudes . . . utterly destitute of friends . . . frequently strangers in the place and because of some affliction incapable of applying for relief to their respective parishes'.[51]

The original impetus behind the Stranger's Friend societies came from the Methodists, and there is evidence of growing church involvement in the process of helping immigrants find their feet in urban society. By the late seventeenth century the Quakers had a system of tickets or testimonials which members took with them when they moved town and which served as a form of accreditation with their new meeting, entitling them to support and relief. The Methodists in the late eighteenth century assisted migrants in other ways. They organized a great array of social and religious events – prayer meetings, tea parties, love feasts, and concerts – which introduced newcomers to like-minded people and gave them a sense of belonging to a community.[52]

As well as voluntary associations and the churches, commercial bodies played a part in the absorption of urban immigrants during the eighteenth century. As the alehouse became more respectable and its social function narrowed, new social institutions sprang up. By George I's reign London had a large number of lodging houses providing places for labourers and other poor outsiders to stay. In the 1720s the Middlesex justices described lodging-houses in the suburbs which crowded twenty or more inmates, regardless of sex, into the same room and charged a penny a night. For the 1740s we have the account books of Betty Wright who ran two lodging-houses for sailors, probably in the East End near the Thames. The establishments were large – one had well over fifty lodgers in a month. Men (and sometimes their wives) were supplied not only with beds, but victuals and clothes – usually on credit. Of the two houses one catered mainly for Kentish men, the other for west country men, providing them with regional food and drink. Lodging-houses also began to appear in provincial towns in the Hanoverian period. By the early decades of the nineteenth century big cities such as Birmingham had nearly 400, and even small towns like Daventry or Towcester had a number. In the major centres some premises specialized in Irish lodgers, others took a wide range of tramping poor, tinkers, petty criminals, the homeless and prostitutes.[53] Among other commercial organizations offering shelter or a social home for newcomers were brothels, gin-shops, music houses and eating houses.[54]

For obtaining jobs migrants could make use of the growing numbers of registry offices in the larger towns. These acted as employment agencies helping to place servants and other workers. Various schemes for registry offices were proposed after the Restoration and by the 1680s several offices were operating in the Strand and elsewhere in the capital. About 1698 the Office for Servants in Fleet Street published its own weekly *Servants' Guide*, a kind of situations vacant column. Registry offices became an established institution in Georgian London. The Equitable Office for Servants near Ely Place advised the upper classes that 'they may be supplied with creditable servants of every denomination'; servants paid one shilling for their name to be listed; the children of the deserving poor were promised places free of charge.[55] The institution spread to the provinces. Birmingham had at least two registry offices in the mid eighteenth century, one run by Thomas Juxon who kept a register of employers wishing to take on apprentices and journeymen and of mistresses wishing to engage maidservants. Contemporary comment was usually jaundiced, Richard King complained that such offices imposed 'upon the ignorant country man and maid by pretending to help them to places of every kind of which the existence is only in idea'. The American Morgan Rhees noted that 'in these offices a certain sum of money must be paid on [servants] registering their names – and after all in 15 cases out of 20 they get nothing but disappointment for their money'. Despite these criticisms, however, it is likely that registry offices played a part in helping some groups of immigrants, particularly female servants, to find work in an urban household.[56]

Registry offices frequently advertised their services in newspapers, which multiplied first in London and then in the provinces from the late seventeenth century. Newspapers also carried other notices and advertisements directed at the mobile sector of the urban population. For servants and apprentices who had gone away from masters, probably in search of better wages and conditions, there were large numbers of notices (with descriptions) urging them to return. Lost persons, especially children and deserting soldiers, were the subject of other advertisements, again with detailed descriptions and in some cases offers of reward for information. It was less easy to drift around in town unattached and unnoticed by the eighteenth century. No less important, newspapers carried notices about urban employment. Some people advertised their services, particularly in specialist trades, but more often the notices were placed by employers. To take an early example, in 1709 Sir Ambrose Crowley advertised in a London paper for skilled men from London and elsewhere to go to his ironworks near Newcastle, offering passage by ship from Greenwich.[57] Later in the eighteenth century John Trusler recommended the *Daily Advertiser* as the best means by which an employer could make his needs known to prospective workers. In the Leeds and York newspapers job advertisements rose from about 2 per cent of all notices in 1741 to 7 per cent in 1784 and 10 per cent in 1807. Needless to say, newspaper advertisements probably comprised only a limited portion of total urban advertising; many jobs were probably publicized through handbills and posters.[58]

As we have seen elsewhere in this book, English towns experienced heavy volumes of immigration in the early modern period. During the sixteenth and early seventeenth centuries, with civic economies quite often in difficulty, the traditional mechanisms for assimilation appear to have been breaking down under the pressure of the influx of many poor migrants: draconian punitive controls on immigration were introduced. By the Hanoverian period, however, urban communities seem to have been managing the problem of social integration rather better – even when demographic growth accelerated in the late eighteenth century. Part of the explanation for this success stems from the more buoyant economic conditions in many towns at this time, with improvements in incomes, job opportunities and housing supply. But it is also arguable that another vital factor helping towns and cities to absorb the thousands of newcomers was the emergence of a variety of new-style, frequently commercial, agencies of integration, complementing or consolidating traditional arrangements. In this way urbanization and modernization went hand in hand.

Notes and references

1 An early version of this paper was published in E. François (ed.), *Immigration et Société Urbaine en Europe Occidentale XVIe-XXe Siècles* . . . (Paris, 1985), pp. 53–63.
2 For intra-urban migration see above, pp. 114 *et seq*.
3 M. Anderson, *Family Structure in Nineteenth Century Lancashire* (Cambridge, 1971), ch. 5 *et seq*; L. P. Moch and L. A. Tilly, 'Joining the urban world: Occupation, family and migration in three French cities', *Comparative Studies in Society and History*, **27** (1985), pp. 33–56; L. P. Moch, *Paths to the City*

(London, 1983), p. 89 *et passim*; M. Banton, *West African City: A Study of Tribal Life in Freetown* (London, 1957); C. Meillassoux, *Urbanization of an African Community: Voluntary Associations in Bamako* (London, 1968).

4 For some stray listings of this type see Westminster Public Library (Victoria), F4001 (returns from St Martin's 1694–5, 1707–8).

5 D. Hollis (ed.), *Calendar of the Bristol Apprentice Book 1532–1565; Part I* (Bristol Record Soc., **14**, 1948), pp. 3–12; O. J. Dunlop, *English Apprenticeship and Child Labour* (London, 1912), ch. 1.

6 R. Finlay, *Population and Metropolis* (Cambridge, 1981), p. 67 (figures adjusted for a higher depletion rate than Finlay's): N. Goose, 'Household size and structure in early-Stuart Cambridge', *Social History*, **5** (1980), 374.

7 Cf. M. G. Davies, *The Enforcement of English Apprenticeship 1563–1642* (Cambridge, Mass., 1956), p. 1 *et seq.*: A. J. Willis and A. L. Merson (eds), *A Calendar of Southampton Apprenticeship Registers, 1609–1740* (Southampton Record Society, 1968), pp. xix, li–lii (girls appear more often as pauper apprentices); M. J. Walker, 'The extent of the guild control of trade in England c. 1660–1820' (unpublished PhD thesis, Cambridge University, 1986), p. 224 *et seq.*

8 See above, pp. 30; also P. Clark, 'The migrant in Kentish towns 1580–1640' in P. Clark and P. Slack (eds.), *Crisis and Order in English Towns 1500–1700* (London, 1972) p. 126 *et seq.*

9 J. F. Pound, 'Government and society in Tudor and Stuart Norwich 1525–1675' (unpublished PhD thesis, Leicester University, 1974), p. 67 *et seq.*; S. J. Wright, 'Family life and society in 16th and early 17th century Salisbury' (unpublished PhD thesis, Leicester Univesity, 1982), p. 188.

10 Finlay, *Population and Metropolis*, p. 64, Willis and Merson (eds.), *Southampton Apprenticeship Registers*, p. xxx.

11 See above, pp. 223 *et seq.*; J. Rule, *The Experience of Labour in Eighteenth Century Industry* (London, 1981), pp. 100–1, 108 *et seq.*

12 Finlay, *Population and Metropolis*, pp. 137–8; W. G. Hoskins, 'The Elizabethan merchants of Exeter' in S. T. Bindoff *et al* (eds.), *Elizabeth Government and Society* (London, 1961), pp. 166–7; P. Clark, 'The civic leaders of Gloucester 1580–1800' in Clark (ed.), *The Transformation of English Provincial Towns* (London, 1984), pp. 316–17.

13 For a discussion of marriage and social mobility see V. B. Elliott, 'Mobility and marriage in pre-industrial England' (unpublished PhD thesis, Cambridge University, 1978), esp. p. 274 *et seq.*; Southampton City Record Office, SC 9/3/12, fol. 94v; P. Slack (ed.), *Poverty in Early-Stuart Salisbury* (Wiltshire Record Soc., **31**, 1975), p. 24 *et passim*: Clark and Slack (eds.), *Crisis and Order*, p. 143.

14 E. A. Wrigley, 'Clandestine marriage in Tetbury in the late 17th century', *Local Population Studies*, **10** (1973), pp. 15–21; see also M. D. George, *London Life in the Eighteenth Century* (London, 1965), pp. 305–6; S. W. Taylor, 'Family Formation and the Old Poor Law in 18th century Berkshire' (paper read at the Economic History Conference, York University, 1984); C. C. Pond, 'Internal population migration and mobility in eastern England in the 18th century' (unpublished PhD thesis, Cambridge University, 1980), pp. 28–9.

15 Wright, 'Family Life', p. 195; A. Yarborough, 'Geographical and social origins of Bristol apprentices 1542–1565', *Transactions of the Bristol and Gloucester-*

shire Archaeological Society, **98** (1980), 116; J. W. Horrocks (ed.), *The Assembly Books of Southampton: II* (Southampton Record Soc., 1920), p. 18; Kent Archives Office, NR/JQ f1/2 (exam. M. Watson); Devon Record Office, Charter 875, 1 March 1675 (deps. Eliz. Putt and J. Pinney). (I owe this reference to David Souden.)

16 Elliott, 'Mobility and marriage', p. 227; Clark and Slack (eds.), *Crisis and Order*, p. 136; I. Bain (ed.), *A Memoir of Thomas Bewick Written by Himself* (Oxford, 1979), pp. 35–6, 43.

17 Brotherton Library Leeds, Special Collections, MS.8; *Memoirs of Capt. Roger Clap* (Boston, Mass., 1731), p. 2; Portsmouth City Record Office, Borough MSS., 16/344a; for other evidence of kin correspondence see David Cressy, 'Kinship and kin interaction in early modern England', *Past and Present,* **113** (1986), pp. 46 *seq.* For harvest migration see above, pp. 33–4, 242.

18 Clark and Slack (ed.), *Crisis and Order*, p. 139; Wright, 'Family life', pp. 198–204; for a London master craftsman lodging incoming kin see P. S. Seaver, *Wallington's World* (Stanford, Calif., 1985), pp. 82–3.

19 Richard Wall suggests there was a significant increase in the proportion of households with resident kin in this period: 'Regional and temporal variations in English household structure from 1650', in J. Hobcraft and P. Rees (eds), *Regional Demographic Development* (London, 1979), esp. p. 98; M. Prior, *Fisher Row* (Oxford, 1982), p. 138 *et seq.*

20 W. Lilly, *History of His Life and Times* (London, 1715), pp. 7–8, 17; Kent Archives Office, NR.JQp 1/8; C. Hutton, *The Life of William Hutton* (London, 1817), p. 117. (I am grateful for this reference to Dr P. Corfield.): R. King, *The New London Spy* (London, 1780), p. 88.

21 R. Parkinson (ed.), *The Private Journal and Literary Remains of John Byrom:* I(1) (Chetham Soc., Old Series, **32**, 1854), pp. 160, 225–6 *et passim*; I(2) (ibid., **34**, 1855), 352 *et passim*; T. Heywood (ed.), *Diary of the Rev. Henry Newcome* (ibid., 18, 1849), p. 99; C. Garstin (ed.), *Samuel Kelly: An Eighteenth century Seaman* (London, 1925), pp. 136–7; Bain, *Bewick*, pp. 75, 237n.

22 R. A. Houston, 'Aspects of society in Scotland and north-east England c. 1550–1750:' social structure, literacy and geographical mobility' (unpublished PhD thesis, Cambridge University, 1981), p. 361; for example, in Bordeaux: J. P. Poussou, *Bordeaux et le Sud-Ouest au XVIIIe Siècle* (Paris, 1983).

23 J. Hill, 'A study of poverty and poor relief in Shropshire 1550–1685' (unpublished MA thesis, Liverpool University, 1973), pp. 158 *et seq.*; Worcester and Hereford Record office (Worcester), H. W. Gwilliam, 'Old Worcester: People and Places', part 2 (typescript), p. 124; E. Jones, 'The Welsh in London in the 17th and 18th centuries', *Welsh History Review*, **10** (1980–1), 461–79.

24 Analysis based on the baptismal entries 1711–26 of the Crown Court Kirk Session, London, now at the Scottish Record Office, CH2/852/1. (I am very grateful to Dr Stephen Walker for transcribing the material.)

25 L. D. Schwarz, 'Conditions of life and work in London c. 1770–1820' (unpublished DPhil thesis, Oxford University, 1976), p. 40 *et seq.*; S. Gilley, 'English Catholic charity and the Irish poor in London', *Recusant History*, **11** (1971–2), pp. 179–89; see also L. H. Lees, *Exiles of Erin* (Manchester, 1979).

26 *Read's Weekly Journal*, 31 July 1736 *et passim*: G. Rudé, *Paris and London in the 18th Century* (London, 1970), p. 204 *et seq.*; George, *London Life*, p. 120;

et seq.; *Read's Weekly Journal*, 4 December 1736; *Daily Gazetteer,* 2 August 1736; *Daily Post*, 29 July, 2 August 1736.

27 R. D. Gwynn, *Huguenot Heritage* (London, 1985), chs 2, 6, 8, 10; see also C. M. Weekley, 'The Spitalfields Silkweavers', *Proceedings of the Huguenot Society*, **18** (1947–52), pp. 285, 287; W. M. Beaufort, *Records of the French Protestant School*, **4** (1891–3), pp. 355–6.

28 T. Mendelman, *The Jews of Georgian England* (Philadelphia, 1979); George, *London Life*, pp. 131–8; C. Roth, *The Rise of Provincial Jewry* (London, 1950). (I am grateful to Dr Aubrey Newman for his advice on eighteenth-century Jewry.)

29 P. Clark, *The English Alehouse: A Social History 1200–1830* (London, 1983), pp. 25–7; F. Heal, 'The idea of hospitality in early modern England', *Past and Present*, **102** (1984), pp. 66–93; A. L. Beier, *Masterless Men* (London, 1985), pp. 79–80; Wright, 'Family Life', p. 227.

30 For example, J. P. Earwaker (ed.), *The Court Leet Records of the Manor of Manchester*: *I* (Manchester, 1884), pp. 226–7; *III* (1886), p. 122; W. H. Stevenson (ed.), *Records of the Borough of Nottingham: IV* (London, 1889), pp. 305–7 *et passim*.

31 Hutton, *Life* pp. 114–5.

32 A. L. Merson (eds.), *The Third Book of Remembrance of Southampton: I* (Southampton Record Soc., 1952), pp. 52–3; West Suffolk Record Office, Bury MSS. C2/1, fol. 1; *Historical Manuscripts Commission*, 14th Report App. 8, p. 64.

33 A. L. Beier, 'Social problems in Elizabethan London', *Journal of Interdisciplinary History,* **9** (1978–9), 204; P. Clark (ed.), *The European Crisis of the 1590s* (London, 1985), pp. 50–1, 61; Beier, *Masterless Men*, p. 164 *et seq.*

34 W. A. Leighton, 'Early chronicles of Shrewsbury', *Transactions of the Shropshire Arch, and Natural Hist. Soc.*, 1st Series, **III** (1880), p. 336; *Victoria County History*, *Warwickshire*, **8**, p. 275; Stratford Birthplace Trust, BRU/2/2, p. 37; Dorset Record Office, B3/E5 (Bridport).

35 N. Bacon, *The Annales of Ipswiche* (ed., W. H. Richardson, Ipswich, 1884), p. 365; Kent Archives Office, Fa/JV 48/7; J. W. F. Hill, *Tudor and Stuart Lincoln* (Cambridge, 1956), pp. 87–8; Rochester, City Customal, part i, fols. 55v, 74; for London see S. Rappaport, 'Social structure and mobility in sixteenth-century London: Part I', *London Journal,* **9** (1983), pp. 109–14; but assuming the large majority of freemen lived in the old city the proportion in the metropolis as a whole almost certainly fell sharply from the later sixteenth century with the rapid growth of the suburbs (cf. A. L. Beier and R. Finlay (eds), *London 1500–1700: The Making of the Metropolis* (London, 1986), p. 41 *et passim*).

36 P. and J. Clark, 'The social economy of the Canterbury suburbs' in A. Detsicas and N. Yates (eds), *Studies in Modern Kentish History* (Kent Archaeological Society, Maidstone, 1983), pp. 65–86; Goose, 'Cambridge', 357 *et seq.*; for respectable householders see above, pp. 116 *et seq.*

37 For a general discussion of urban poor relief at this time see P. Slack *et al.*, *The Traditional Community under Stress* (Milton Keynes, 1977), p. 92 *et seq.*; Coventry City Record Office, A 27; Canterbury Cathedral Library, F/A 20 *passim*; City of London Record Office, Repertories 22, fols. 258v–9, 268v–9; A. L. Beier, 'The social problems of an Elizabethan country town: Warwick

1580–90' in P. Clark (ed.), *Country Towns in Pre-Industrial England* (Leicester, 1981), p. 68 *et seq.*; P. Slack, 'Poverty and politics in Salisbury 1597–1666' in Clark and Slack (eds), *Crisis and Order*, p. 178 *et seq.*

38 Pond, 'Internal population migration', p. 24 *et passim*, pp. 73–4; see also above, pp. 238 *et seq.*

39 D. Marshall, *The English Poor in the Eighteenth Century* (London, 1926), p. 47) *et passim*; Clark (ed.), *Transformation*, p. 31; P. Anderson, 'The Leeds Workhouse under the Old Poor Law 1726–1834', *Miscellany XVII* (Thoresby Soc. **56**, 1980), p. 88 *et seq.*

40 M. J. Walker, 'Guild control': Clark (ed.), *Country Towns*, pp. 19, 236.

41 Clark, *English Alehouse*, pp. 47–50, chs 4, 6; F. J. C. Hearnshaw and D. M. Hearnshaw (eds), *Southampton Court Leet Records: I* (Southampton Record Soc., 1905–6), p. 184.

42 Clark, *English Alehouse*, ch. 8 *et seq.*; *Commons Journals*, **15**, p. 312; Walker, 'Guild control'.

43 C. R. Dobson, *Masters and Journeymen* (London, 1980), ch. 3; *The Tiverton Wool-combers Defence* (London, 1750), p. 10; R. A. Leeson, *Travelling Brothers* (London, 1980), p. 92 *et seq.*

44 Schwarz, 'London conditions', pp. 192–4. For a short survey of voluntary associations in this period see P. Clark, *Sociability and Urbanity: Clubs and Societies in the Eighteenth Century City* (H. J. Dyos Memorial Lecture, Leicester, 1986); C. Jackson (ed.), *Yorkshire Diaries & Autobiographies* (Surtees Soc., **65**, 1877), 126.

45 For the Kentish society which began about 1657 see H. R. Plomer, *The Kentish Feast* (Canterbury, 1916); S. Low, *The Charities of London* (London, 1850), pp. 169, 245, 310–1; Guildhall Library, MS. 3322/1; T. Bisse, *Society Recommended: A Sermon Preached before the Society of the Natives of Herefordshire at their Anniversary Meeting . . .* (London, 1728); Gloucester Reference Library, JX.11.3; Gloucestershire Record Office: D149, R70; SO 3(1).

46 Bisse, *Society*, pp. 13–4; for example, E. Fowler, *A Sermon Preached at the General Meeting of Gloucestershire-Men* (London, 1685), p. 33; T. White, *A Sermon Preach'd to the Natives of the County of Warwick* (London, 1695), pp. 18–19.

47 D. MacLean, 'London in 1689–90', *London and Middlesex Archaeological Soc.,* New Series, **6** (1927–31), 491; *An Account of the Institution, Progress and Present State of the Scots Corporation* (London, 1807), esp. p. 12; *The Original Design, Progress and Present State of the Scots Corporation . . .* (London, 1730), p. 26; *Highland Society of London . . .* (London, 1892).

48 *A Brief Account of the Rise, Progress and Present State of the Most Honorable and Loyal Society of Ancient Britons* (London, 1825); W. D. Leathart, *The Origin and Progress of the Gwyneddigion Society of London* (London, 1831).

49 Gilley, 'English Catholic charity', p. 184; also Low, *Charities*, p. 310.

50 H. Bush, *History of the Gloucestershire Society* (Bristol, n.d.); J. Price, *A Sermon Preach'd before the Society of Ancient Britons* (Bristol, 1754); J. Money, *Experience and Identity: Birmingham and the West Midlands 1760–1800* (Manchester, 1977), p. 118; *An Account of the Scots Society in Norwich . . .* (Norwich, 1783).

51 *First Report of the Philanthropic Society* (London, 1789); F. K. Brown, *Fathers*

of the Victorians (Cambridge, 1961), pp. 333–5; R. F. Wearmouth, *Methodism and the Common People of the Eighteenth Century* (London, 1945). pp. 212–6; *An Address to the Members of the Stranger's Friend Benevolent Society and to the Inhabitants of Leeds* (Leeds, 1797), pp. 10–11.

52 M. F. Lloyd-Prichard, 'The treatment of poverty in Norfolk from 1700 to 1850' (unpublished PhD thesis, Cambridge University, 1949), pp. 310–12; J. M. Landers, 'Some problems of the historical demography of London 1675–1825' (unpublished PhD thesis, Cambridge University, 1985), pp. 93–4; G. Malgreen, *Silk Town: Industry and Culture in Macclesfield 1750–1835* (Hull, 1985), p. 159 *et seq.*

53 Greater London Record Office, MJ/OC 1, fols. 126–8; City of London Record Office Misc. MSS.353.3; Southampton Record Office, SC 9/4/347; University College, London, Archives Dept., Chadwick MSS.3, 4.

54 Portsmouth Record Office, Borough MSS. 11A/16/278–9; *Read's Weekly Journal*, 17 April 1731; *The Flying Post*, 30 July–2 Aug. 1698; Guildhall Library, Broadside 32.11 'Proposals for opening a Scotch eating house' (n.d.).

55 M. D. George, 'The early history of registry offices', *Economic Journal*, Supplement 1 (1926–9), pp. 570–90; MacLean, 'London', p. 335; *The Flying Post*, 3–6 Sept., 25–27 Oct. 1698; R. King, *The New Cheats of London* (London n.d.), pp. 41–2; Bodleian Library, J. Johnson Collection, Employment Box 1.

56 B. Walker, 'Birmingham directories', *Transactions of the Birmingham Archaeological Soc.*, **58** (1934), pp. 2 *et seq.*; see also *The Birmingham Register*, 3 Jan. 1765; King, *New Cheats*, pp. 41–2; M. J. Rhees, *The Good Samaritan* (Philadelphia, 1796), p. 13.

57 *The Post-Man*, 1705–1707 *passim*; for jobs wanted, for example, ibid., 15–18 Feb. 1706/7 and 8–10 May 1707. Ibid. 3–5 March 1708/9.

58 J. J. Hecht, *The Domestic Servant Class in Eighteenth Century England* (London, 1956), p. 32; J. J. Looney, 'Advertising and society in England 1770–1820: a statistical analysis of Yorkshire newspaper advertisements' (unpublished PhD thesis, Princeton University, 1983), pp. 106 *et seq.*, 120.

10
'East, west – home's best'? Regional patterns in migration in early modern England

David Souden

In a new approach to a much used (and abused) source, Rickman's eighteenth-century parish register data collected at the time of the 1801 Census, David Souden examines patterns of sex ratios at death on a county and regional level. The strong regional differences found are attributed to the net effects of sex-specific migration. Evidence from the seventeenth and nineteenth centuries suggests that there were persistent regional characteristics in population movement. The approach is inferential and speculative and the patterns discerned cannot be tested in a conventional manner. The results, however, are often dramatic and point to potentially important ways of understanding regionality and demographic change in English society.

Many questions have been raised in preceding chapters, and many answered, on the range and direction of migration in early modern England. The discussion has for the most part been concerned with the sixteenth and seventeenth centuries, where documentation and work have been concentrated. There are significant problems in studying the subject of migration for the eighteenth century, for which sources are fewer and research less advanced. And for the whole period with which this collection of essays is concerned, more questions remain unasked, more unanswered.

A reader of this book concerned whether distinct patterns of migration made one region of the country behave differently from another, or interested in the potential demographic impact of migration rather than its response to other forces, might well have received few answers. This is partly because the sources available to the historian are not very illuminating, but there are also methodological problems. Ultimately we do want to know about the action of migration upon the general population, and to gauge how far smaller studies of a sub-population can represent accurately the total experience. So the form a study of migration takes is important. There is always the possibility of a mismatch between a cross-sectional analysis, conducted at a single point in time, and a longitudinal study, taking a particular feature over an extended period. The scale of the analysis is critical, since only rarely do the sources cover a broad enough section of the population, let alone the whole population over anything other than a circumscribed area or a limited time span.

For pre-industrial England there are no continuous population registers which chart the movements of people from one place to another during their lifetimes – the sort of document which has produced so much interesting material from Scandinavia.[1] There are neither censuses covering the entire population at regular intervals nor full vital registration – sources which have provided the basis for considerably wider-ranging nineteenth-century studies, not least Ravenstein's work which provides the underpinning for the detailed analysis of migration.[2] In consequence, the historian of migration in the early modern period has to display rather more ingenuity, using important survivals of data which have proved, to varying degrees, partial in their coverage of the population at large. Above all there has been the use of a case-study approach.

The case study has been one of the most significant features of the recent writing of English economic and social history. Whether for town, parish, probate jurisdiction, trade gild, or manufacturing enterprise, the impulse is the same: to provide analysis in depth which is of a manageable size for the individual researcher to undertake and for the reader to grasp, which combines typicality and peculiarity. The ultimate aim of course is to produce a fully-rounded history of the particular phenomenon with a wide range of detailed exemplars.

But in that approach a note of caution should be introduced. The question to be asked is, was the whole greater than the sum of its parts? If in the end we have the history of every limited liability company, an analysis of every set of probate inventories, a study of every town (provided that we could agree on the definition of a town), would we then have a history of entrepreneurship, of personal wealth, of urban development in England? If we were able to plot the moves of every apprentice heading for the big city, every indentured servant venturing to the colonies, every vagrant apprehended and punished, the origins of every woman residing in a town in the last decades of the seventeenth century, or of every pauper examined or removed under the auspices of the settlement laws, would we then have a history of migration?

The answer in all these cases has to be no. There are enormous problems in comparability, let alone in the survival or the original recording of documentation. But even in an ideal archival world, that level of explanation may well prove insufficient. Explanations may be internal and complex – a town or a company atrophied because of unfair competition or lack-lustre leadership – or external and unspecific – real incomes were declining, there was a general failure of will, the spirit of the age was against it, and so companies, towns, personal wealth, waves of migrants rose and fell. Such explanations continue to be cast almost exclusively in terms of the concerns and analytical form of the problem in hand. And such explanations find it difficult to reconcile analyses operating at a macro-level with those operating in a specific local situation. Micro-level approaches do have enormous and obvious value. But the success of one place or enterprise, the failure of another, can only be judged in a much wider context reached by other methods.

Arguably this is so with the study of migration. Were there deep-seated trends or peculiarities within early modern English migration patterns that cannot be identified sufficiently by taking a local study 'head on', features that were marginal on a localized basis but which were of cumulative significance over a wide enough area?[3] The purpose of this article is to contend that there were such features, of cumulative significance, producing regional distinctiveness in populations and in migration trends.

From work on the nineteenth century, we know that there were regional differences in patterns of migration.[4] These have usually been related to industrial employment, the institution of service, the loss of labour from agriculture, and a rising urban population.[5] But recently there have been some suggestions of more deep-seated, possibly cultural, specifically regional effects in determining patterns of migration.[6]

Migration studies in the centuries before the nineteenth have placed stress upon local effects, the ubiquity of local migration, change over time in the frequency of movement or in distances travelled in response to economic or demographic conditions, the rise of competing alternative centres, and the efficacy of legal intervention.[7] There is a case for trying other avenues to answer the imperative of putting together different levels of study. As was suggested in the Introduction to this volume, there is a critical need to make *probabilistic* statements.[8] This means assessing not only the probability of making a move at some time in the 1620s as opposed to the 1690s or 1720s, but also of men and women making a move within or from Dorset as opposed to Kent.

In a world where data are rarely of a type or a consistency to perform the tasks we want, backdoor methods of analysis using surrogate or intermediate measures may provide a way. Already for the early modern period English social and economic historians have used marriage seasonality to measure regional agricultural change; the proportion of the population in towns and in industrial work to measure labour productivity in agriculture; varying numbers of settlement examinations to gauge seasonal unemployment; birth spacing intervals to infer the incidence and duration of breast-feeding; and differential sex ratios in urban and rural populations to show migration effects.[9]

Such methods may be blunt, and are often incapable of sustaining a fine-detailed local investigation. But they do enable us to set the local experience into a wider context – to distinguish the particular from the general, to understand the possibilities of local random variation, to square longitudinal with cross-sectional studies, to assess whether individual anomalies which are insignificant locally may not in total be of great significance.

One of the abiding difficulties of a local demographic study is the problem of scale.[10] A local population might be 'unbalanced': with fewer men or more elderly people than the average. A few extra or a few less people here and there might not make very much difference on a local basis. Indeed, localized migration existed partly to mop up these local inconsistencies. As most studies are concerned with the majority, the marginal case might be interesting but not of particular importance. Statistically, its significance would be small, and more likely to be a random result. But if that imbalance were repeated over a much greater area, and were part of a wider regional trend, then the small, barely perceptible, discrepancies would appear of greater importance.

At an overall level and on a very small scale populations might appear in a different light from that seen on a middle scale. Given the documentary resources that are available, it is just that position between the very local and the aggregated national picture which is often lacking. The model put forward in the Introduction, with its hierarchy of places, was largely self-balancing, with flows and counter-flows operating at most levels.[11] Reality is not necessarily like that, and recent studies of early modern English population and economy have pointed to its lack of such a self-balancing mechanism, and to its 'boom-and-bust' character. In those studies, various forces are shown to be moving together, later to reverse direction – the rise and fall of fertility and mortality, celibacy and illegitimacy, real wages and incomes – as opposed to varieties of local and regional homeostasis found to have operated in France.[12]

This essay is designed to provide some of the scale and context which often seems to be missing from migration studies for our period;[13] it employs coarse but potentially effective measurements, so as to begin to provide answers to some of the questions.[14] Using data available for the whole nation and on a consistent basis to identify different balances between the sexes in the regions, it is possible to build up a picture of regional differences relating to migration and its effects. Some of those differences prove to be enduring over a very long run.

I

In the 1790s a great intellectual debate raged over the course of population change during the preceding century. There were those (and perhaps surprisingly, Malthus was among them) who were of the opinion that the population had been stagnant. Others were sure that population growth had been considerable.[15] Estimates of the numbers living in the country at that time, and through the preceding century, therefore varied wildly.

The first census in 1801, which John Rickman supervised and indeed which he had proposed, put the matter straight.[16] The population of England was something over 8¼ million. But, as Rickman himself noted, 'The second object of the Population Act was to ascertain the increase or diminution of the population of Great Britain, throughout the last century.'[17] To that end, incumbents were required to furnish information from their parish registers: counts of the numbers of baptisms and burials registered for every tenth year between 1700 and 1780 and for every year thereafter, and of marriages in each year since Hardwicke's

Marriage Act came into force in 1754. However fraught with difficulty the endeavour, the results showed the direction and extent of population growth in eighteenth-century England. And until recently the returns have been the basis for most investigations of English population behaviour in those years.[18]

These *parish register abstracts* were combined at various levels of aggregation: most basically into hundreds (the only surviving counts for individual parishes are when one parish formed the whole of a hundred), then into counties, countries, and the nation. Especially at the lowest level, that of the hundred, these are not the most useful categories; but Rickman's collection has long provided an invaluable data source.[19] The abstracts themselves have a special feature often lacking from more recent demographic investigations, in that they were differentiated by sex, with separate counts of the baptisms and burials of males and females.[20]

Differentiation by sex is often the missing ingredient in a proper historical treatment of population and migration, either because separate information is not available or because men are better covered by the sources than women. The various models described in the Introduction, for instance, were not couched in terms of there being particular differences between the sexes. If the first of those models were treated as a universe functioning largely within itself, there would almost certainly also be movers in and out from that system. If we were deprived of all information about the system other than the *net balance of the sexes* as an outcome of those flows back and forth, would that still provide us with useful insights into the propensities and patterns of migration? It is the purpose of this essay to argue that such information can and will prove useful; that flows of people and local populations were differentiated not only by occupation and status but also by sex; and that that variegation was found through space and time. The data that Rickman collected provide the basis for such an argument.[21]

It seems to be a human biological fact that more boys are born than girls, usually in the ratio 1.04 or 1.05 to 1.[22] But a higher proportion of boys die young, so a slight surplus of females develops in the population at large, and with a female tendency towards longevity that surplus becomes more marked late in life.[23] Overall, these effects should cancel each other out, and sex ratios at death will be of a broadly similar order. If sex ratios at birth and at death prove to be substantially different, we should ask why.

Table 40 shows the results of calculating sex ratios at both baptism and burial from Rickman's parish register abstracts, those events being the nearest equivalent to birth and death registration that we possess until 1837. The general level of trustworthiness in the allocation of male and female names is shown by the consistency of sex ratios at baptism from the parish register abstracts. But things were different at the other end of the lifespan.

Table 40   Sex ratios at burial and baptism, England, 1700–90

year(s)	N baptisms	N burials[a]	sex ratio at baptism	sex ratio at burial
1700	138,291	120,786	1·05	0·98
1710	125,681	128,635	1·04	1·01
1720	140,280	147,763	1·05	1·03
1730	146,058	151,482	1·04	1·02
1740	153,042	154,002	1·06	0·98
1750	162,551	142,581	1·04	0·99
1760	168,999	142,651	1·04	1·00
1770	188,077	159,830	1·03	0·97
1780	200,537	176,674	1·03	1·00
1781–90	2,142,392	1,672,014	1·05	0·98

Source: BPP, 1802, VII, 1801 Census, parish register abstracts
Sex ratio: number of males per female
[a] These totals are slightly lower than those in the appendix, since they exclude Rutland and Monmouthshire.

The lower ratios at burial suggest that there was *net emigration* from England during the eighteenth century; for everyone born must die (although not necessarily in their country of origin). The ratios also suggest that the level of net emigration was probably substantial since it shows up so readily in the data, and of course that it was sex-selective.[24] That selectivity in any event is demonstrated in many studies, in this volume and elsewhere. A burial ratio of 1.01 would imply that three people (net) out of every 204 baptized were missing, or 1.47 per cent. Using these sorts of calculations, and a not unreasonable assumption of three male emigrants to every female, Wrigley and Schofield have calculated a net emigration rate in the first half of the eighteenth century at 1.20 per 1000, a figure which corresponds well to estimates derived in other ways.[25]

These types of calculations are rarely as straightforward as they seem at first sight. Even in a closed population a baptism/birth sex ratio of 1.04 would not necesssarily translate directly into a burial/death sex ratio of 1.04 unless the age structure and mortality schedules remained more or less constant. Taking individual years to provide the pattern of sex ratios over time will likewise prove difficult, since some diseases had a sex-selective impact, and many had an age-selective impact. If the individual year covered by the abstracts happened to coincide with an outbreak of disease then the result for that year might be skewed. The question of translating from *baptisms* to *births*, and from *burials* to *deaths*, remains a vexed one; and certainly during the course of the eighteenth century the shortfall between the ecclesiastical events and the biological events they are taken as representing grew wider.[26]

Even in a large population, the results for individual years suggest the action at least in part of random variability. If that stochastic process can be seen even at a national level of aggregation, how much more it must operate with smaller numbers. There are however ways and means of testing the likely extent of random variation in these ratios and of testing the degree of difference between the data for sub-populations.[27] It is to those variations and differences that much of this paper is devoted.

The changes in fertility and mortality necessary to move sex ratios at death as far as they appear to have shifted would have to be enormous, certainly greater than those identified for the century.[28] Although the eighteenth century saw an increasing failure to register baptisms and burials under the auspices of the Anglican church, it seems hard to imagine the circumstances in which this would be sufficiently different between males and females on a national basis so as to skew sex ratios in this way.

So perhaps the basic tendencies in the data are to be trusted. At a national level, the shortfall in burials represents a net outflow of people. If a population were gaining or losing members in significant numbers, then in certain circumstances that would show up in sex ratios at death. If young people were leaving in droves, then an ageing population would probably show a more female-dominated sex ratio at death; conversely, a population gaining many families and young people might see a higher proportion of males at death through this process. But the logic suggests that most of the variance will be due to the actual gain or loss of members of whichever sex, and the resulting numerical balance between them. These will be net effects: 300 males and 300 females moving out, with 300 males and 400 females moving in, would have the same observable effect as a stationary native population being swelled by 100 females, and an eventual depression of sex ratios at death; conversely, 300 males and 200 females moving out would seem to have much the same effect. In the end we require other information (especially the running totals of, and difference between, birth and death series) to be able to decide on the directions of movement. But in studying migration we are interested in its consequences as well as in the process itself; and a study using sex ratios as part-proxies for migration patterns does not use them as an end in themselves, but as the key to a wider investigation.

If the logic of making inferences about population structure and migration from sex ratios can operate at a national level, why not at a more local level? Table 41 presents data for sex ratios at burial in English counties during the period 1700–90, on the same basis as that in Table 40. Immediately, a number of features emerge from the table. First, and most obviously, the individual values vary considerably, both around the national figure in the first table, and against our 'natural' ratio of 1.04. Although some of that variation seems random, several of the counties show a marked degree of consistency over time in their recorded burial sex ratios. What do they mean?

The first task must be to ascertain whether these values are likely to be fictitious artefacts of the data, or whether they are in some sense 'real', whether there are anomalies in the coverage, major differences between counties? Just how much stochastic variation is there within these series? Counties are not necessarily the most helpful units of study; what degree of internal variation do these figures disguise?

Only in the nineteenth century do we have both cross-sectional and longitudinal data to see a relationship between sex ratios at death and in the population at large, in the decennial census and in the civil death registers. In the five years 1848–52 sex ratios at death were 1.03, considerably closer to the birth ratio than were the eighteenth-century burial sex ratios. The sex ratio in the population at large at the 1851 census was 0.95.[29] As Table 42 suggests, there was some relationship between death and general sex ratios, but there was by no means a straightforward translation. The table shows that high sex ratios in the general population and at death tend to be associated, as do low ratios. It would be very

Table 41 Sex ratios at burial, English counties, 1700–90

year(s)	Beds	Berks	Bucks	Cambs	Ches	Cornw	Cumbs	Derbs	Devon	Dors	Durh	Essex	Glos	Hants	Heref	Herf	Hunts	Kent	Lancs	Leics
1700	1·02	0·97	0·92	1·00	0·86	0·99	0·93	0·96	0·95	0·86	1·10	1·03	1·00	1·03	1·07	0·99	0·96	1·04	1·01	1·00
1710	1·12	1·04	1·04	1·08	0·97	1·07	0·95	1·09	0·88	0·93	1·03	1·06	1·04	1·10	1·02	1·04	0·97	1·09	1·06	0·99
1720	1·03	0·98	1·10	1·06	0·95	1·01	1·01	1·05	0·99	0·90	0·98	1·10	1·10	1·13	1·17	1·09	0·94	1·12	1·02	1·05
1730	0·97	1·03	0·97	1·08	0·96	0·96	1·03	1·05	0·99	0·91	1·02	1·07	1·03	1·09	1·21	1·11	1·05	1·10	1·09	1·08
1740	1·00	1·16	0·96	0·97	0·98	0·91	0·94	0·99	0·95	0·91	0·97	1·06	1·07	1·13	1·06	1·08	1·02	1·04	1·04	0·96
1750	1·04	1·01	0·92	1·07	1·01	0·96	0·99	1·04	0·95	0·95	0·98	1·14	0·99	1·00	1·07	0·98	0·98	1·11	1·00	0·86
1760	1·00	1·09	0·93	1·06	0·97	0·99	0·97	0·95	1·08	0·86	1·25	1·23	1·01	1·09	1·06	1·05	1·01	1·13	1·00	0·96
1770	0·98	0·97	0·93	0·92	0·96	1·00	1·08	0·91	0·90	0·90	0·98	1·08	0·93	1·01	0·98	1·06	0·93	1·06	0·96	0·95
1780	1·02	1·05	0·97	0·97	0·91	0·97	0·91	1·00	0·97	0·85	0·93	1·13	1·01	0·92	1·03	1·17	0·98	1·16	1·08	0·96
1781–90	0·96	0·98	0·91	0·98	0·94	1·01	0·96	0·97	0·94	0·88	0·94	1·03	0·90	1·03	1·04	1·05	1·00	1·10	0·93	0·95

year(s)	Lincs	Middx	Norfk	Nhant	Nhumb	Notts	Oxon	Salop	Somt	Staff	Suflk	Surry	Sussx	Warws	Westm	Wilts	Worcs	E Rid	N Rid	W Rid
1700	0·96	1·03	1·00	1·06	1·03	1·06	0·96	0·94	0·92	1·03	0·96	1·04	1·02	1·00	0·90	1·01	0·91	1·11	0·87	0·99
1710	1·02	1·00	1·07	0·94	1·11	0·96	1·04	1·01	0·94	0·99	0·96	1·00	1·07	0·95	0·91	1·04	0·97	1·05	0·97	1·06
1720	1·07	0·99	1·01	0·99	0·98	0·95	1·05	1·02	1·03	1·10	1·02	0·95	1·17	1·06	0·95	1·01	1·09	1·07	0·95	1·12
1730	1·00	0·94	1·04	1·03	0·96	1·02	1·04	1·04	0·98	0·95	0·95	1·19	1·15	0·98	0·95	1·04	1·08	0·99	0·89	1·06
1740	0·99	0·98	1·06	0·96	1·13	0·96	0·99	1·04	0·99	1·07	0·95	1·06	1·02	1·06	1·06	1·02	1·05	0·98	0·92	0·99
1750	1·02	0·97	0·97	0·99	1·03	0·97	0·99	0·93	0·93	1·01	0·98	1·02	1·15	0·89	0·89	0·98	0·97	0·91	0·99	1·01
1760	1·07	0·99	1·04	0·99	1·02	1·04	0·99	0·93	0·93	1·02	0·90	1·00	0·95	1·12	1·12	0·93	0·95	1·00	0·98	0·99
1770	1·03	1·03	0·97	0·89	0·99	0·92	0·99	0·98	0·89	0·97	0·92	0·87	1·36	0·89	0·89	0·88	1·02	0·95	0·92	0·95
1780	1·00	1·00	1·04	0·91	0·93	1·00	1·00	0·97	0·96	1·01	0·94	1·06	1·07	1·00	1·00	0·85	0·95	0·97	0·95	0·99
1781–90	0·99	1·03	0·94	0·95	0·96	0·98	0·99	1·01	0·91	1·02	0·91	1·04	1·11	0·93	0·91	0·89	1·00	0·99	0·93	0·98

Sex ratio, number of males per female
Source: 1801 census, parish register abstracts

Table 42 Sex ratios at death and in the population, England, c. 1851

area	sex ratios at death 1848–52	sex ratios in 1851 population	range of county values sex ratios at death 1848–52	range of county values sex ratios in population 1851
England	1·03	0·95		
London	1·02	0·88	0·91–1·40	0·87–0·97
south east	1·04	0·98	0·96–1·11	0·97–0·99
south midlands	1·01	0·98	0·91–1·14	0·93–1·01
east	1·00	0·97	0·96–1·05	0·94–1·00
south west	0·99	0·92	0·94–1·05	0·90–0·97
west midlands	1·04	0·97	0·94–1·12	0·90–1·03
north midlands	1·00	0·98	0·80–1·05	0·96–1·02
north west	1·04	0·95	0·98–1·06	0·95
Yorkshire	1·04	0·98	0·97–1·05	0·96–0·99
north	1·04	0·99	0·95–1·09	0·97–1·01

Sources: BPP,1852–3, LXXXV, 1851 Census, Population tables, *I*.
Sex ratio, number of males per female

surprising if there were a perfect match, however, given the likelihood of different age-specific mortality schedules, age structures, and of return migration. So the sex ratios at burial for the eighteenth century should not be taken as a straightforward measurement of the ratio for the population as a whole. The nineteenth-century data suggest that overall ratios were lower than those at death. Having established that there was some general relationship between the two series, the data which form the backbone of this paper need to be examined with care.

Investigations into the eighteenth-century parish register abstracts which Rickman compiled have shown counties varying considerably in the proportion of parishes for which returns were made, and have shown arithmetical lapses in the process of aggregating the figures into hundred, county, and country. The missing returns for England probably numbered 632. The first published returns showed that nationally there was a shortfall approaching 10 per cent of parishes, 952 missing returns against 9701 collected. Last-minute attempts to rectify the situation in 1801, and further collection and manipulation of the data at the four succeeding censuses, continued to confuse the issue as much as to clarify it. Nevertheless, it would appear that the final picture in 1801 was not quite as bad as Rickman had at first feared.[30] At the time and subsequently various incidents of double counting have been identified within the abstracts. And whereas overall some 6 per cent of parish returns were missing from the original 1801 returns (probably covering some 4½ per cent of the population), a few counties were missing more than 10 per cent of their returns, namely Cheshire, Hampshire, Hertfordshire, Nottinghamshire, Wiltshire, and the East and West Ridings. But only in Wiltshire did this mean that more than 10 per cent of the county population was omitted.[31]

Overall, although there clearly are differences between counties in the fullness of coverage by the parish register abstracts, the shortfall is not sufficient to render a use of the data impossible. In the first instance, investigation has shown on the whole the astonishingly high degree of accuracy that incumbents attained in making their counts. Secondly, there are statistical means of assessing the degree of randomness or significance in the data. At a national level the likely 'natural' outcome of sex ratios at death as a result of the underlying age structure and demographic level can be estimated from the results of Wrigley and Schofield's mammoth investigations. Individual observed values which fall outside the range of expected values can be interpreted as being significant. Similarly, confidence limits can be set for observed sex ratios at the smaller scale of the county, and the degree of significant variation from the national picture will thus be identified (the significance testing here being with Z-scores).[32]

Even more than when examining the national data, caution is required when looking at the individual values. Until 1780, information is only available for single years. Therefore these are very much point estimates of an underlying structure, potentially subject to the inherent variation of small-number problems and to the influence of short-term factors.

Lincolnshire is an interesting county in which to investigate these possible difficulties – a large but not too populous county, with its three administrative (and topographically quite distinctive) Parts of Holland, Kesteven, and Lindsey. It was also a county particularly fully covered by the responses to Rickman in 1801, missing only 2 per cent of its returns (about 1 per cent of the county population).

Table 43 shows the degree to which the individual ratios can be swayed by short-term changes in the demographic series. The high sex ratios at burial in Kesteven in the mid 1780s are due

Table 43 Variation in sex ratios at burial within Lincolnshire, 1780–90

| year(s) | sex ratios at burial in | | | | N burials in | | | |
	Holland	Kesteven	Lindsey	county	Holland	Kesteven	Lindsey	county
1780	0·90	0·97	1·05	0·99	1615	1586	2888	6089
1781	0·96	0·98	0·97	0·97	1438	1514	2829	5781
1782	0·99	1·00	0·98	0·99	1367	1584	2528	5479
1783	0·98	0·96	0·99	0·98	1287	1667	2653	5607
1784	0·90	1·11	1·00	1·01	1145	1532	2918	5595
1785	1·07	1·12	0·96	1·02	1037	1259	2527	4823
1786	0·98	1·18	0·96	1·09	998	1286	1956	4140
1787	0·98	1·02	1·08	1·00	874	1114	1998	3989
1788	0·97	1·05	1·01	1·02	1063	1255	2092	4410
1789	1·07	0·94	1·00	1·00	1099	1286	2308	4693
1790	1·08	0·96	0·93	0·97	970	1154	2236	4360
1780–90	0·98	1·02	1·00	1·00	12,793	15,240	26,933	54,966
1781–90	1·00	1·03	0·99	1·00	11,178	13,654	24,045	48,877

Source: BPP, 1802, VII, 1801 Census, parish register abstracts
Sex ratio: number of males per female

principally to a temporary high number of male deaths in Grantham. On the whole individual sex ratios in the table keep relatively close together. The question the table is designed to answer is, how likely is an individual value for any single year to be representative of the period within which it falls? Out of the thirty-three values, there would in fact be a 0.75 chance of a value falling in the range 0.97–1.03, a 0.6 chance of being in the range 0.98–1.02, and a 0.3 chance of being in the range 0.99–1.01. In other words, the chances of the sex ratio for a single year being a statement of the general tendency are good, although the likelihood of it being very close to the overall mean is not especially high. As long as we realize these limitations, we can interpret what is to follow as being a set of broadly reliable tendencies.

Even with the considerably greater small-number problems likely at lower levels of aggregation, that is when calculating sex ratios at burial for the individual hundreds within the county, there are clear convergent trends. For Lincolnshire as a whole, the mean of annual values for all hundreds within the county is 1.03, with a standard deviation of 0.22; for Holland the mean figure is 0.99 (standard deviation 0.14), for Kesteven 1.07 (standard deviation 0.27), for Lindsey 1.02 (standard deviation 0.12). At this level however the degree of random variation between places (expressed by the size of the standard deviations) is high. Our prime focus is the relationship between the sexes rather than numbers of vital events. So although Table 43 shows a falling number of burials being registered in Lincolnshire during the 1780s, it would seem unlikely that the overall effect on sex ratios at burial would be catastrophic.

This single county example shows the potential pitfalls of using sex ratios at burial as an index: they exhibit considerable variation, especially where small numbers are concerned. The death in a cold snap of an extra five old ladies could tip the balance in some of the smaller cases. What is reassuring, on the other hand, is the extent to which the sex ratios present a coherent picture, with a majority of the individual values pointing in a similar direction. In Lincolnshire, then, both at county level and on a more localized basis, the period 1780–90 saw sex ratios clustering around unity, with only a third of the values with sex ratios greater than 1.0. What is more, the values for Lincolnshire at those ten-yearly intervals between 1700 and 1780 are all more or less similarly aligned. Table 41, above, is more than just a sea of numbers. Approached with proper caution, it may well be able to tell us something about the regional population structure of eighteenth-century England and the migration patterns underpinning it. Moreover, the statistical tests suggest that the individual values for counties are very often sufficiently different from the national pattern as to be valid expressions of the underlying population structure.

The first task in exploring the interpretation of the sex ratios is to look for clusterings. If they too appear meaningful then we may be on the right path. If expressed as percentage deviations from the national position, the distribution of the individual county values of burial sex ratios appears to be strikingly consistent over time, and thus there may be some underlying structure and continuity within the data.

More readily intelligible results come from a reading of the figures which follow, Figures 18–24, deriving from the data in Table 41. The data on sex ratios at burial are grouped into regions of contiguous counties, with changes in their values plotted against time.[33] In these figures the sex ratios are represented on the horizontal axis (marked with the 'expected' level of 1.04) and the time periods are measured vertically. On each figure different counties are represented by different symbols, the position of the symbol at each point being the sex ratio found at that particular time. The regions are, first, a band of counties immediately south and east of London; then counties in the west country; home and

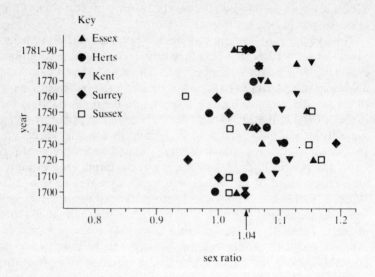

Figure 18   Sex ratios in south-eastern counties, 1700–81/90

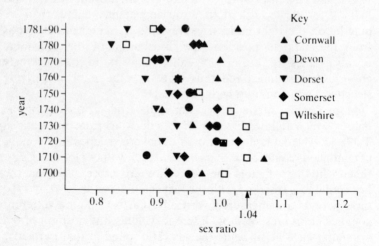

Figure 19   Sex ratios in south-western counties, 1700–81/90

midland counties north and north-west of London; a group of east midland counties; western counties along the Welsh border; counties in East Anglia; and northern counties from Lancashire and Yorkshire to the Scottish border.

There are some values well out of line, which are almost certainly the result of chance variation or some short-term factor. The Appendix at the end of this chapter shows whether or not the Z-score values from comparing the county sex-ratio data with the national evidence are significant. Those scores likewise show a degree of instability in the results, but they also highlight the number of counties with consistent results. Overall the groupings shown in the various figures cohere well, suggesting the existence of regional patterns. No less interesting, for the most part the clusters preserve their relative positions through the course of the eighteenth century. The strength and consistency of the relationships, and the generally positive result of the significance tests, argue that the varying sex ratios do indeed measure 'real' phenomena.

In Figure 18, for the counties close to London, there is almost without exception a male surplus of burials, with most values in excess of the 'expected' birth/baptism sex ratio of 1.04. Kent in particular stands out as a county with significantly high burial sex ratios (a pattern preserved at a lower level of aggregation in the various lathes).[34] The data for London and Middlesex, although not as easy to interpret, suggest by way of contrast a pattern we know to have marked the eighteenth-century metropolis, namely a high proportion of women in domestic and service occupations. In general the figures for south-eastern counties help confirm a picture which has been emerging from other work: the growth of the metropolis bit deeply into the population of its hinterland, and large numbers of women in particular were attracted to eighteenth-century London. For London itself was unable until very late to sustain a natural increase of its population, and could only maintain its numbers and grow through immigration, while every indicator suggests a contracting migration field for the capital over the course of the seventeenth century and into the eighteenth as it was affected by the growing competition of other urban centres. What we seem to be observing here is the effect on a regional population of an efflux of women, who were able to command relatively higher wages in London.[35]

The picture is quite different in those western counties which

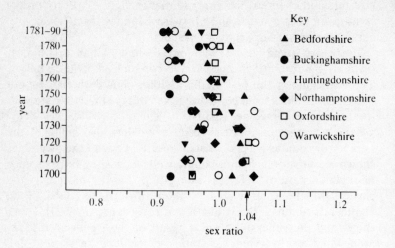

Figure 20   Sex ratios in home and south midland counties,
1700–81/90

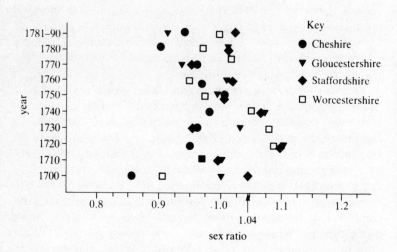

Figure 21   Sex ratios in western midland counties, 1700–81/90

are represented in Figure 19, that is to say Devon, Dorset, Somerset, and to some degree Cornwall and Wiltshire. Here population gain through the eighteenth century is unlikely to have been extraordinary. But the sex ratios at burial observable for the region are extraordinary, in the extent to which they were skewed towards females. The contrast with the south-eastern counties is very marked. Few counties in the western region saw a surplus of males at burial (a pattern also repeated at the level of the hundreds), and Dorset above all experienced very low burial sex ratios.

A reading of the pattern might therefore suggest again sex-selective outmigration, this time of males, although this is only by inference and we can say nothing about destinations. Were there, for instance, more men from western counties bound towards London? Since there was a national shortfall of male burials, some men would have died overseas, coming from seafaring counties and from a region with long traditions of emigration.[36] These were also counties with high, and growing, concentrations of pastoral agriculture by the eighteenth century, and with therefore greater opportunities for female agricultural work than was the case in arable farming regions. But they were also regions with low male wage-rates in agriculture, in contrast to the picture in many eastern counties.[37] In the western counties it is notable that the urban populations (on the occasions that they can be identified from the parish register abstracts) likewise show female burial surpluses; in contrast, not all urban parishes in the south-east had male surpluses.[38] Given that the nineteenth-century evidence showed burial sex ratios to be an underestimate of sex ratios at large, it is possible that the west country's shortfall of males was very considerable in the period covered by the parish register abstracts.

These south-western and south-eastern counties formed the most distinctive groups among the English regions. Comparison of this pair of graphs suggests that the distinction between them increased over time: the trends shown by the shifting position of the symbols suggest a shift towards greater male domination of sex ratios and so of population in the case of south-eastern counties, greater female predominance in south-western counties. Indeed, some such time trend appears in data for many regions, apart from the northern counties. The group of south midland counties in Figure 20 had in the period before 1750 as many ratios above 1 as below; but from 1750 ratios above unity were very rare. There is a similar although tighter pattern in Figure 21, for east midland counties, and in Figure 22 for the western border counties. In the latter region, most of the exceptional sex ratios above 1 (and above 1.04) are for Herefordshire, which had a very small population.

The picture is less stark for the three eastern counties (Figure 23). Cambridge (like Essex) had a fairly consistent high burial sex ratio, as did Norfolk for the most part. Suffolk, on the other hand, behaved quite differently, with sex ratios well below unity.[39] For reasons already discussed, the data at the hundred level are obviously rather less trustworthy than at the county level, but here there is a suggestion of male surpluses in northern and eastern Suffolk, and of female burial surpluses in the western part.

For northern counties (Figure 24), there is again some suggestion of a trend through the eighteenth century towards higher female proportions in the burial totals, but the trend is rather less marked than for many regions. However it was rare for the East Riding and unknown for the North Riding of Yorkshire to have a surplus of males at burial; in contrast, Northumberland frequently displayed male surpluses. Rather than being quite uniform, or differences between areas being unsystematic and random, real regional differences emerge for the English population in the eighteenth century in terms of the relative balance between the sexes (at least at burial). There are also shifts towards greater distinctiveness of these regions over the period.

It is important to fight the danger of over-interpreting these statistics, derived in such a gross manner as they are. Nevertheless, clear and suggestive patterns do seem to sing through, patterns which it is hard to avoid recognizing and hard to explain as mere random artefacts. There was a range of sex ratios at burial – and not only a range over time as the national figures show, but also a range (and a greater range) over space. Distinct regional patterns emerge, most positively in the case of groups of southern counties in the east and west. In some cases there was a trend over time, either intensifying the height or depth of the ratios, or, less often, switching from surplus to deficit. Although some counties, notably Gloucestershire and Wiltshire, moved from male to female surpluses at burial, most kept their relative local ranking within their particular region. There are strong features to suggest that deep-seated local economic and demographic mechanisms would

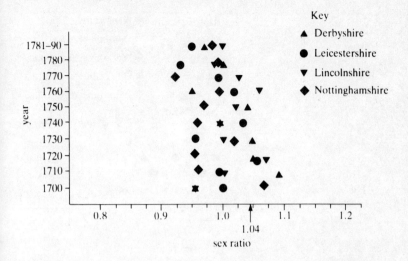

Figure 22   Sex ratios in east midland counties, 1700–81/90

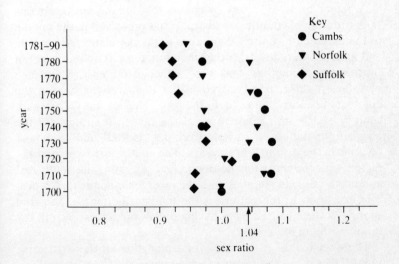

Figure 23   Sex ratios in eastern counties, 1700–81/90

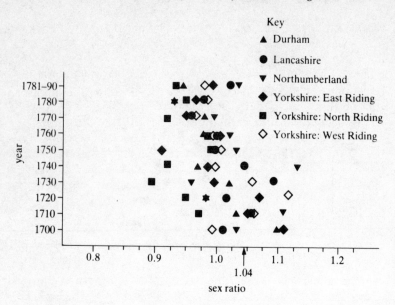

Figure 24   Sex ratios in northern counties, 1700–81/90

help produce these figures, counties tending to keep their particular burial sex ratio character, Kent always high, Dorset always low, Lincolnshire always around unity.

A glance back at Table 42 suggests that for the most part this rank ordering of counties by sex ratio was preserved in the middle of the nineteenth century. Sex ratios in the population as a whole and at death were lowest (other than in the metropolitan area) in south-western counties, and were higher in the east. The range of values in 1851, however, is smaller than was the case in the eighteenth-century data, and the first half of the nineteenth century clearly saw a narrowing of the range. Sex ratios for the English population as a whole were 0.92 in 1801 and 1811, and 0.95 in the next four census years. The south-west remained the region with the most female-dominated sex ratio, the south-east and north-midland counties with the most male-dominated ratios. The exception to the pattern is the four northernmost industrial counties, which shifted from having one of the lowest overall sex ratios to the highest.[40]

There seem to be two varieties of explanation for these patterns. Firstly, they were the result of economic change and attractions. Many of these regions underwent great change in the eighteenth century, with the rise and the consolidation of industry in some areas, and the greater intensiveness and specialization of agriculture in others. Different types of industry, and of agriculture, required different mixes of ages and sexes for their workforce. In terms of the economic changes which were in train in the eighteenth century, the variety of the sex ratios in the regional populations seem to have been appropriate, with large female populations in the metropolis and in western pastoral areas, and (in the late eighteenth century) in emerging industrial areas of the north-west. Males were more highly concentrated in eastern, and more particularly arable, regions. As urbanization continued, at a pace unmatched elsewhere in Europe, the natural increase of the rural population was in part or in whole drawn into towns. Above all, the growth and the attractiveness of London continued apace. The capital's population almost doubled in the eighteenth century; and although its relative superiority over all other urban centres diminished, its absolute size and importance remained enormous. Thus it would be surprising if the various regions did not differ one from another in their overall sex and age composition, just as smaller local populations could vary. Nevertheless the degree of such difference is quite striking.

A second type of explanation is more culturally derived. It is important to remember that the regional pictures which emerge from the sex-ratio data are net outcomes, the result of the interaction of many different elements, and single economic explanations will not suffice; but the net outcomes have great feedback possibilities. For many regions the sex-ratio effects seem to have been self-perpetuating. In demographic terms England may well have been a homogeneous nation; but that does not preclude the possibility of individual regions being distinct one from another in other ways, and that compositional effects were at work cancelling each other out to produce overall balance. The basic fertility indicators (and to a lesser extent mortality measures) may have operated on different proportions of the population at large, depending on the balance between the sexes, having different demographic results which tended to even each other out. Certainly some balance between regions appears from the consistent distribution of the data.[41] Research into migration fields suggests feedback mechanisms to be at work in maintaining, over a long period, certain flows or chains of migration. If, as seems likely, the sex-ratio data can be interpreted as net migration effects, then the continuing differences between the regions which emerge may also be culturally determined, in that certain migration mechanisms continued through time without necessarily having an identifiable economic rationale. Time and again in migration studies, certain places emerge as consistent senders of people to certain destinations (or receivers from certain origins).

The possibilities which the data provide are considerable. The suggestion that there have been very deep-seated migration patterns and propensities in early modern England may well be borne out. Returning to the concerns identified at the opening of this article, only at this level of analysis, given the insufficient range of sources otherwise available, are such forces to be seen.[42] Until more detailed work on local economies and on other sources for migration in the eighteenth century has been undertaken, these conclusions from sex ratios can only be circumstantial, inferential. The gross flows that are determined may have more to say than the overall balance. But these conclusions have in their favour the fact that they address the question of the interaction of migration with other demographic features, and that they derive from a universal and standard event, death, and a near-standard and -universal form of documentation, burial registration. Conclusions can only be drawn with the broadest of brushes, but in the absence of more direct observation in many areas of social and economic life in early modern England, such inferential 'back door' methods are important.

II

Unfortunately, until sex-specific aggregative demographic series drawn from original parish registers are available on a much larger scale than hitherto, this form of analysis cannot be extended back into the seventeenth century. However an important documentary source does exist for the study of migration in the Stuart era, namely the autobiographical preambles that witnesses provided as a heading to their depositions when appearing in church courts.[43] Surviving as they do in considerable numbers, these witnesses' depositions can provide a large-scale basis for deriving patterns of migration. A full analysis of a large set of such depositions is to be found in Peter Clark's chapter on migration in England in the later seventeenth and early eighteenth centuries.[44] Findings from another large collection of depositions covering counties in south-western England, the south midlands and East Anglia provide some indications of regionally distinctive migration patterns for the seventeenth century to match those of the eighteenth.[45]

For there were regional differences, as Peter Clark also discovered, in the extent to which witnesses had or had not moved from their native parish. Thus in seventeenth-century Devon, almost half of all male witnesses and of all female witnesses claimed still to be living in their parish of birth, in Somerset and Wiltshire villages that figure was a little more than a third of males and a quarter of females, in Oxfordshire and Leicestershire a little lower proportion still, and in Norfolk less than a fifth of men and a sixth of women. These differences are maintained even when controlling for age – since the probability of having moved increased with age – and for the varying sizes of parishes in different parts of the country. In towns, the proportions of natives were generally a little lower, reflecting the greater need for urban populations to attract newcomers from outside. A number of studies using a variety of sources, have pointed, as does the evidence from depositions, towards a slowing down of residential mobility (in the countryside at least) in the years after the Restoration compared with the decades before the Civil War. The regional distinctiveness was generally preserved in the face of this general decline.[46]

There were also regional differences in the distances that individuals had moved. In the years before 1660 (when average migration distances were higher) 75 per cent of migrant males in the countryside had moved less than 19 miles in Norfolk and Oxfordshire, less than 16 miles in Wiltshire, less than 13 miles in Somerset. The figures for women were broadly the same. After 1660 these regional distinctions were preserved, with 75 per cent of men in Norfolk moving 19 miles or less, 16 miles or less in Devon, 9½ miles or less in Wiltshire, Somerset, and Leicestershire.[47] Time and again, indices of movement show that there was a gradient of rural mobility from west to east, with lower levels of mobility (both before and after the Civil War) in the western counties, middling values in Oxfordshire and Leicestershire, and higher levels of mobility in Norfolk and Suffolk. A similar, although less clearly marked, tendency in migration patterns appears from this source for towns within the various regions.

As with any of our documentary sources, difficulties of bias, survival, and interpretation intrude. Perhaps we have not been quite cautious enough to date in using the church court deposition files. They may have tended to record those who stayed within the region; and in some instances (although by no means all) immigrants, especially those from far away, may not have been preferred as witnesses, making the population of witnesses an unrepresentative group. What is more, the depositions fail to cover adequately those who moved away entirely, and who cannot be recovered from other such archives, either because the archives do not exist, since the survival of the church courts varied from area to area, or because longer-range migrants would be less likely to appear in court. As the courts began to lose business and momentum, especially after the hiatus of the Civil War and Inter-regnum, courts in areas of higher and more directed mobility may have lost their business earlier. The source may therefore be ideally suited to investigating localized forms of migration, not always well suited to providing data on long-range movement.

On the other hand, there *is* prima facie evidence to suggest that some places, especially in Devon and Somerset, were more likely to have members of their population either immobile or long-distance movers. It is therefore possible, although not verifiable without considerably larger numbers of these depositions, that east and west differed from each other in the extent to which shorter-range movement, as opposed to leaving the area entirely, took care of local fluctuations in employment, household or population.[48]

Although this discussion is rather speculative, there can be no doubt that regional differences in basic migration indices appear in the seventeenth-century deposition data. By analogy with the previous section, those differences may well have been translated into phenomena of wider significance.

III

Thus in both the seventeenth century and the eighteenth there are signs that English regions may well have differed from each other quite considerably in their migration patterns. Although the general features of migration, that it was primarily short-distance and that movement was commonplace, hold for all regions, at the margin variations persist. And those variations seem to have held up over lengthy historical periods, suggesting that there may have been deep-seated cultural as well as economic feedback systems in maintaining migration patterns.

It has become a commonplace in recent years to suggest that England was, in demographic terms, an astonishingly homogeneous country. Although there was regional differentiation in mortality or in fertilty, it was quite muted, and changes tended to happen in the same direction more or less at the same time.[49] Homogeneity was a feature of nineteenth-century England as well as of the pre-industrial period.[50] The possibility therefore arises that regions may have been as distinguished by migration patterns as much as by any other feature – not by the general to and fro of people, but by the extent to which men or women were drawn in or drawn away, by the balance between the sexes, by the degree to which local movements predominated in the universe of moves. The simple question of how many people there are around, and of the right sex and age, is a crucial one. A superfluity of females or of males not only reflects, but has feedback consequences for, the marriage market, for fertility, for employment patterns, for wages. The extent to which certain areas were locked into longer-range migrant streams may have had an effect on the ease or otherwise of being received into their destination.[51] The patterns which emerge may be explained in terms of the diversity and increasing pace of change in economic behaviour in eighteenth-century England. What is striking is the apparent degree of diversity in one of the main constituents of the base population of a region.

Asking simple questions about the proportions of males and females in a population may have complicated repercussions. The evidence presented here suggests that in the eighteenth century, and probably before, there were distinctive regional patterns in the balance between the sexes. That was in large part the net result of sex-selective migration. The south-west and the south-east were particularly distinct. Over the course of the eighteenth century the differences between regions (and so possibly the extent and diversity of inter-regional flows) grew. In the seventeenth century, south-western counties and eastern counties also had rather distinct patterns of migration, on both a small and a larger scale. Although the two levels of analysis are not connected, the congruence between the two patterns is at the least suggestive.

No less important is the fact that this chapter has suggested new ways of advancing the study of migration in early modern

England. It has done so by finding sources which may not offer as much concrete small-scale data as do other archives, but which offer a greater chance of finding a context into which to put those data. Individual case studies and exploitation of single sources cannot always add up together. Asking different questions and inferring information from unusual and recalcitrant sources provides another perspective and provokes a new range of questions to be answered. To understand the interaction of migration and economy fully we need the particular and the general approach, the case study and the background analysis. For the whole is almost certainly greater than the sum of its parts.

Appendix

Reproduced in this Appendix are the national and county totals of burials, the sex ratios among those burials for the individual years (here expressed as *males per 100 females* and to two decimal places), and the Z-scores associated with them, comparing both the national observed sex ratios with those expected 'naturally', i.e., 105/205 or around 1.04, and the county results with the national. Values greater than +1.96 or less than −1.96 are therefore statistically significant at the 5 per cent level. Hence for Hertfordshire five out of the ten values seem to have been significantly different from the national picture (and all consistently higher, and thus male-biased, than in the nation as a whole); in Somerset six out of the ten prove significant at this confidence level, all in the opposite, female-biased direction. These results confirm the visual impression of greater divergence later in the eighteenth century than in the middle, as well as the impression of locally and regionally consistent basic patterns.

Comparing national ratios with 105/205

Date	Males	Females	Total	Rate	Z-Score	Ratio	Date
1700	60100●	61199●	121299●	0.4955	−11.65	98.20	1700
1710	64950●	64247●	129197●	0.5027	−6.81	101.09	1710
1720	75222●	73184●	148406●	0.5069	−4.11	102.78	1720
1730	81677●	80434●	162111●	0.5038	−6.73	101.55	1730
1740	77484●	79123●	156607●	0.4948	−13.79	97.93	1740
1750	71228●	71844●	143072●	0.4978	−10.85	99.14	1750
1760	71645●	71592●	143237●	0.5002	−9.09	100.07	1760
1770	78982●	81530●	160512●	0.4921	−16.13	96.87	1770
1780	88539●	88760●	177299●	0.4994	−10.79	99.75	1780
1781–90	829451●	848658●	1678109●	0.4943	−46.43	97.74	1781

Using Rickman's national ratios as expected values

Beds

Date	Males	Females	Total	Rate	Z–Score	Ratio	Date
1700	584●	572●	1156●	0.5052	0.66	102.10	1700
1710	676●	605●	1281●	0.5277	1.79	111.74	1710
1720	777●	751●	1528●	0.5085	0.13	103.46	1720
1730	866●	892●	1758●	0.4926	−0.94	97.09	1730
1740	663●	664●	1327●	0.4996	0.35	99.85	1740
1750	670●	644●	1314●	0.5099	0.87	104.04	1750
1760	630●	629●	1259●	0.5004	0.02	100.16	1760
1770	704●	715●	1419●	0.4961	0.31	98.46	1770
1780	804●	788●	1592●	0.5050	0.45	102.03	1780
1781–90	7380●	7666●	15046●	0.4905	−0.93	96.27	1781–90

Berks

Date	Males	Females	Total	Rate	Z-Score	Ratio	Date
1700	739●	764●	1503●	0.4917	−0.29	96.73	1700
1710	951●	914●	1865●	0.5099	0.62	104.05	1710
1720	978●	996●	1974●	0.4954	−1.02	98.19	1720
1730	1127●	1099●	2226●	0.5063	0.23	102.55	1730
1740	1240●	1071●	2311●	0.5366	4.02	115.78	1740
1750	1036●	1023●	2059●	0.5032	0.48	101.27	1750
1760	1068●	981●	2049●	0.5212	1.91	108.87	1760
1770	1054●	1092●	2146●	0.4911	−0.08	96.52	1770
1780	1220●	1161●	2381●	0.5124	1.27	105.08	1780
1781	11088●	11340●	22428●	0.4944	0.03	97.78	1781

Bucks

Date	Males	Females	Total	Rate	Z-Score	Ratio	Date
1700	866●	945●	1811●	0.4782	−1.47	91.64	1700
1710	1026●	991●	2017●	0.5087	0.53	103.53	1710
1720	1094●	997●	2091●	0.5232	1.49	109.78	1720
1730	1266●	1303●	2569●	0.4928	−1.12	97.16	1730
1740	1050●	1089●	2139●	0.4909	−0.36	96.42	1740
1750	1001●	1087●	2088●	0.4794	−1.69	92.09	1750
1760	975●	1043●	2018●	0.4832	−1.53	93.48	1760
1770	1155●	1242●	2397●	0.4819	−1.00	93.00	1770
1780	1237●	1270●	2507●	0.4934	−1.60	97.40	1780
1781	11035●	12198●	23233●	0.4750	−5.89	90.47	1781

Cambs

Date	Males	Females	Total	Rate	Z-Score	Ratio	Date
1700	839●	840●	1679●	0.4997	0.35	99.88	1700
1710	1141●	1058●	2199●	0.5189	1.51	107.84	1710
1720	1393●	1309●	2702●	0.5155	0.90	106.42	1720
1730	1156●	1070●	2226●	0.5193	1.46	108.04	1730
1740	945●	975●	1920●	0.4922	−0.23	96.92	1740
1750	1144●	1067●	2211●	0.5174	1.84	107.22	1750
1760	956●	903●	1859●	0.5143	1.21	105.87	1760
1770	1009●	1100●	2109●	0.4784	−1.25	91.73	1770
1780	1327●	1375●	2702●	0.4911	−0.86	96.51	1780
1781	11487●	11730●	23217●	0.4948	0.15	97.93	1781

Using Rickman's national ratios as expected values (cont.)

Ches

Date	Males	Females	Total	Rate	Z-Score	Ratio	Date
1700	1188●	1383●	2571●	0.4621	−3.39	85.90	1700
1710	1084●	1117●	2201●	0.4925	−0.96	97.05	1710
1720	1248●	1317●	2565●	0.4865	−2.06	94.76	1720
1730	1702●	1778●	3480●	0.4891	−1.74	95.73	1730
1740	1424●	1451●	2875●	0.4953	0.06	98.14	1740
1750	1258●	1248●	2506●	0.5020	0.42	100.80	1750
1760	1474●	1526●	3000●	0.4913	−0.97	96.59	1760
1770	1524●	1586●	3110●	0.4900	−0.23	96.09	1770
1780	1536●	1683●	3219●	0.4772	−2.52	91.27	1780
1781–90	16654●	17788●	34442●	0.4835	−3.99	93.62	1781–90

Cornw

Date	Males	Females	Total	Rate	Z-Score	Ratio	Date
1700	1153●	1163●	2316●	0.4978	0.23	99.14	1700
1710	1295●	1208●	2503●	0.5174	1.47	107.20	1710
1720	1347●	1336●	2683●	0.5020	−0.50	100.82	1720
1730	1977●	2056●	4033●	0.4902	−1.73	96.16	1730
1740	1688●	1847●	3535●	0.4775	−2.05	91.39	1740
1750	1326●	1379●	2705●	0.4902	−0.80	96.16	1750
1760	1383●	1397●	2780●	0.4975	−0.29	99.00	1760
1770	1444●	1448●	2892●	0.4993	0.78	99.72	1770
1780	2041●	2105●	4146●	0.4923	−0.91	96.96	1780
1781	16943●	16825●	33768●	0.5017	2.75	100.70	1781

Cumbs

Date	Males	Females	Total	Rate	Z-Score	Ratio	Date
1700	711●	767●	1478●	0.4811	−1.11	92.70	1700
1710	559●	588●	1147●	0.4874	−1.04	95.07	1710
1720	744●	740●	1484●	0.5013	−0.43	100.54	1720
1730	826●	803●	1629●	0.5071	0.26	102.86	1730
1740	660●	699●	1359●	0.4857	−0.67	94.42	1740
1750	725●	735●	1460●	0.4966	−0.10	98.64	1750
1760	711●	735●	1446●	0.4917	−0.65	96.73	1760
1770	763●	707●	1470●	0.5190	2.07	107.92	1770
1780	1053●	1154●	2207●	0.4771	−2.09	91.25	1780
1781	9763●	10201●	19964●	0.4890	−1.48	95.71	1781

Derbs

Date	Males	Females	Total	Rate	Z-Score	Ratio	Date
1700	1153●	1205●	2358●	0.4890	−0.63	95.68	1700
1710	989●	909●	1898●	0.5211	1.60	108.80	1710
1720	1042●	989●	2031●	0.5130	0.56	105.36	1720
1730	1313●	1250●	2563●	0.5123	0.86	105.04	1730
1740	990●	1003●	1993●	0.4967	0.18	98.70	1740
1750	1001●	967●	1968●	0.5086	0.96	103.52	1750
1760	1070●	1128●	2198●	0.4868	−1.25	94.86	1760
1770	1214●	1327●	2541●	0.4778	−1.44	91.48	1770
1780	1387●	1382●	2769●	0.5009	0.16	100.36	1780
1781	13527●	13942●	27469●	0.4924	−0.61	97.02	1781

Using Rickman's national ratios as expected values (cont.)

Devon

Date	Males	Females	Total	Rate	Z-Score	Ratio	Date
1700	2818●	2954●	5772●	0.4882	−1.10	95.40	1700
1710	2873●	3253●	6126●	0.4690	−5.28	88.32	1710
1720	2918●	2944●	5862●	0.4978	−1.39	99.12	1720
1730	3299●	3318●	6617●	0.4986	−0.86	99.43	1730
1740	3670●	3879●	7549●	0.4862	−1.50	94.61	1740
1750	2784●	2935●	5719●	0.4868	−1.67	94.86	1750
1760	3400●	3160●	6560●	0.5183	2.93	107.59	1760
1770	2838●	3146●	5984●	0.4743	−2.75	90.21	1770
1780	3859●	3964●	7823●	0.4933	−1.08	97.35	1780
1781–90	32017●	33992●	66009●	0.4850	−4.75	94.19	1781–90

Dorset

Date	Males	Females	Total	Rate	Z-Score	Ratio	Date
1700	882●	1030●	1912●	0.4613	−2.99	85.63	1700
1710	909●	896●	1805●	0.5036	0.07	101.45	1710
1720	912●	1016●	1928●	0.4730	−2.97	89.76	1720
1730	1188●	1311●	2499●	0.4754	−2.84	90.62	1730
1740	1004●	1108●	2112●	0.4754	−1.78	90.61	1740
1750	912●	966●	1878●	0.4856	−1.06	94.41	1750
1760	862●	999●	1861●	0.4632	−3.19	86.29	1760
1770	989●	1101●	2090●	0.4732	−1.72	89.83	1770
1780	1116●	1315●	2431●	0.4591	−3.97	84.87	1780
1781	9871●	11285●	21156●	0.4666	−8.06	87.47	1781

Durham

Date	Males	Females	Total	Rate	Z-Score	Ratio	Date
1700	1160●	1055●	2215●	0.5237	2.66	109.95	1700
1710	1252●	1219●	2471●	0.5067	0.39	102.71	1710
1720	1226●	1249●	2475●	0.4954	−1.15	98.16	1720
1730	1667●	1633●	3300●	0.5052	0.15	102.08	1730
1740	1451●	1502●	2953●	0.4914	−0.37	96.60	1740
1750	1519●	1215●	2734●	0.5556	6.04	125.02	1750
1760	1492●	1530●	3022●	0.4937	−0.71	97.52	1760
1770	1722●	1755●	3477●	0.4953	0.38	98.12	1770
1780	1702●	1829●	3531●	0.4820	−2.06	93.06	1780
1781	17625●	18820●	36445●	0.4836	−4.07	93.65	1781

Essex

Date	Males	Females	Total	Rate	Z-Score	Ratio	Date
1700	1857●	1809●	3666●	0.5065	1.34	102.65	1700
1710	2204●	2087●	4291●	0.5136	1.43	105.61	1710
1720	2909●	2644●	5553●	0.5239	2.53	110.02	1720
1730	2638●	2579●	5217●	0.5057	0.26	102.29	1730
1740	2329●	2282●	4611●	0.5051	1.40	102.06	1740
1750	2681●	2558●	5239●	0.5117	2.01	104.81	1750
1760	2353●	2276●	4629●	0.5083	1.11	103.38	1760
1770	2591●	2334●	4925●	0.5261	4.78	111.01	1770
1780	3751●	3430●	7181●	0.5224	3.89	109.36	1780
1781	26866●	25772●	52638●	0.5104	7.39	104.24	1781

Using Rickman's national ratios as expected values (cont.)

Glos

Date	Males	Females	Total	Rate	Z-Score	Ratio	Date
1700	1669●	1672●	3341●	0.4996	0.47	99.82	1700
1710	1925●	1843●	3768●	0.5109	1.00	104.45	1710
1720	2349●	2143●	4492●	0.5229	2.15	109.61	1720
1730	2308●	2234●	4542●	0.5081	0.58	103.31	1730
1740	2604●	2446●	5050●	0.5156	2.97	106.46	1740
1750	2123●	2139●	4262●	0.4981	0.04	99.25	1750
1760	2308●	2290●	4598●	0.5020	0.24	100.79	1760
1770	2562●	2744●	5306●	0.4828	−1.34	93.37	1770
1780	2370●	2354●	4724●	0.5017	0.32	100.68	1780
1781–90	23518●	26205●	49723●	0.4730	−9.50	89.75	1781–90

Hants

Date	Males	Females	Total	Rate	Z-Score	Ratio	Date
1700	1143●	1109●	2252●	0.5075	1.15	103.07	1700
1710	1402●	1275●	2677●	0.5237	2.17	109.96	1710
1720	1538●	1364●	2902●	0.5300	2.49	112.76	1720
1730	1615●	1478●	3093●	0.5221	2.04	109.27	1730
1740	2204●	1943●	4147●	0.5315	4.73	113.43	1740
1750	1425●	1418●	2843●	0.5012	0.36	100.49	1750
1760	1925●	1758●	3683●	0.5227	2.73	109.50	1760
1770	1642●	1620●	3262●	0.5034	1.29	101.36	1770
1780	2466●	2667●	5133●	0.4804	−2.72	92.46	1780
1781	20278●	19749●	40027●	0.5066	4.93	102.68	1781

Heref

Date	Males	Females	Total	Rate	Z-Score	Ratio	Date
1700	591●	552●	1143●	0.5171	1.46	107.07	1700
1710	594●	582●	1176●	0.5051	0.16	102.06	1710
1720	703●	603●	1306●	0.5383	2.27	116.58	1720
1730	849●	703●	1552●	0.5470	3.40	120.77	1730
1740	611●	578●	1189●	0.5139	1.32	105.71	1740
1750	615●	577●	1192●	0.5159	1.25	106.59	1750
1760	625●	592●	1217●	0.5136	0.93	105.57	1760
1770	633●	649●	1282●	0.4938	0.12	97.53	1770
1780	791●	767●	1558●	0.5077	0.66	103.13	1780
1781	7118●	6863●	13981●	0.5091	3.51	103.72	1781

Hertf

Date	Males	Females	Total	Rate	Z-Score	Ratio	Date
1700	820●	828●	1648●	0.4976	0.17	99.03	1700
1710	880●	847●	1727●	0.5096	0.57	103.90	1710
1720	914●	839●	1753●	0.5214	1.22	108.94	1720
1730	1233●	1112●	2345●	0.5258	2.13	110.88	1730
1740	1049●	970●	2019●	0.5196	2.23	108.14	1740
1750	1107●	1131●	2238●	0.4946	−0.30	97.88	1750
1760	1032●	987●	2019●	0.5111	0.98	104.56	1760
1770	1118●	1052●	2170●	0.5152	2.16	106.27	1770
1780	1275●	1091●	2366●	0.5389	3.84	116.87	1780
1781	10184●	9678●	19862●	0.5127	5.20	105.23	1781

Using Rickman's national ratios as expected values (cont.)

Hunts

Date	Males	Females	Total	Rate	Z-Score	Ratio	Date
1700	371●	387●	758●	0.4894	−0.33	95.87	1700
1710	430●	445●	875●	0.4914	−0.67	96.63	1710
1720	609●	650●	1259●	0.4837	−1.64	93.69	1720
1730	616●	587●	1203●	0.5121	0.57	104.94	1730
1740	475●	465●	940●	0.5053	0.65	102.15	1740
1750	437●	446●	883●	0.4949	−0.17	97.98	1750
1760	462●	456●	918●	0.5033	0.19	101.32	1760
1770	477●	513●	990●	0.4818	−0.64	92.98	1770
1780	667●	679●	1346●	0.4955	−0.28	98.23	1780
1781–90	5390●	5383●	10773●	0.5003	1.26	100.13	1781–90

Kent

Date	Males	Females	Total	Rate	Z-Score	Ratio	Date
1700	2060●	2018●	4078●	0.5051	1.24	102.08	1700
1710	2665●	2566●	5231●	0.5095	0.98	103.86	1710
1720	3219●	2809●	6028●	0.5340	4.21	114.60	1720
1730	2820●	2672●	5492●	0.5135	1.43	105.54	1730
1740	2928●	2772●	5700●	0.5137	2.86	105.63	1740
1750	2978●	2743●	5721●	0.5205	3.43	108.57	1750
1760	3223●	2698●	5921●	0.5443	6.79	119.46	1760
1770	3177●	2968●	6145●	0.5170	3.91	107.04	1770
1780	4643●	3867●	8510●	0.5456	8.53	120.07	1780
1781	35080●	31777●	66857●	0.5247	15.73	110.39	1781

Lancs

Date	Males	Females	Total	Rate	Z-Score	Ratio	Date
1700	2270●	2252●	4522●	0.5020	0.88	100.80	1700
1710	2197●	2068●	4265●	0.5151	1.62	106.24	1710
1720	2481●	2422●	4903●	0.5060	−0.12	102.44	1720
1730	3530●	3224●	6754●	0.5227	3.09	109.49	1730
1740	3528●	3382●	6910●	0.5106	2.63	104.32	1740
1750	3341●	3325●	6666●	0.5012	0.55	100.48	1750
1760	3322●	3307●	6629●	0.5011	0.15	100.45	1760
1770	4963●	5147●	10110●	0.4909	−0.23	96.43	1770
1780	4781●	4438●	9219●	0.5186	3.69	107.73	1780
1781	54716●	58676●	113392●	0.4825	−7.91	93.25	1781

Leics

Date	Males	Females	Total	Rate	Z-Score	Ratio	Date
1700	769●	768●	1537●	0.5003	0.38	100.13	1700
1710	712●	718●	1430●	0.4979	−0.36	99.16	1710
1720	982●	937●	1919●	0.5117	0.43	104.80	1720
1730	1073●	995●	2068●	0.5189	1.37	107.84	1730
1740	865●	903●	1768●	0.4893	−0.46	95.79	1740
1750	893●	1040●	1933●	0.4620	−3.15	85.87	1750
1760	951●	996●	1947●	0.4884	−1.04	95.48	1760
1770	1095●	1154●	2249●	0.4869	−0.49	94.89	1770
1780	1203●	1249●	2452●	0.4906	−0.87	96.32	1780
1781	12199●	12758●	24957●	0.4888	−1.73	95.62	1781

Using Rickman's national ratios as expected values (cont.)

Lincs

Date	Males	Females	Total	Rate	Z-Score	Ratio	Date
1700	2052●	2137●	4189●	0.4899	−0.73	96.02	1700
1710	2090●	2041●	4131●	0.5059	0.41	102.40	1710
1720	3710●	3483●	7193●	0.5158	1.51	106.52	1720
1730	2961●	2951●	5912●	0.5008	−0.46	100.34	1730
1740	1837●	1852●	3689●	0.4980	0.39	99.19	1740
1750	2075●	2044●	4119●	0.5038	0.76	101.52	1750
1760	2087●	1950●	4037●	0.5170	2.13	107.03	1760
1770	2234●	2167●	4401●	0.5076	2.06	103.09	1770
1780	3034●	3034●	6068●	0.5000	0.10	100.00	1780
1781–90	24129●	24361●	48490●	0.4976	1.47	99.05	1781–90

Middx

Date	Males	Females	Total	Rate	Z-Score	Ratio	Date
1700	4603●	4454●	9057●	0.5082	2.43	103.35	1700
1710	5276●	5276●	10552●	0.5000	−0.56	100.00	1710
1720	6007●	6066●	12073●	0.4976	−2.05	99.03	1720
1730	6199●	6580●	12779●	0.4851	−4.24	94.21	1730
1740	7494●	7683●	15177●	0.4938	−0.24	97.54	1740
1750	6439●	6665●	13104●	0.4914	−1.48	96.61	1750
1760	5811●	5852●	11663●	0.4982	−0.42	99.30	1760
1770	6704●	6531●	13235●	0.5065	3.33	102.65	1770
1780	6783●	7347●	14130●	0.4800	−4.60	92.32	1780
1781	67164●	65236●	132400●	0.5073	9.46	102.96	1781

Norfk

Date	Males	Females	Total	Rate	Z-Score	Ratio	Date
1700	2646●	2640●	5286●	0.5006	0.74	100.23	1700
1710	3445●	3211●	6656●	0.5176	2.42	107.29	1710
1720	3247●	3222●	6469●	0.5019	−0.79	100.78	1720
1730	3185●	3057●	6242●	0.5103	1.01	104.19	1730
1740	2768●	2623●	5391●	0.5134	2.74	105.53	1740
1750	2550●	2630●	5180●	0.4923	−0.80	96.96	1750
1760	2743●	2644●	5387●	0.5092	1.32	103.74	1760
1770	2996●	3077●	6073●	0.4933	0.20	97.37	1770
1780	3347●	3218●	6565●	0.5098	1.69	104.01	1780
1781	29788●	31618●	61406●	0.4851	−4.55	94.21	1781

Nhant

Date	Males	Females	Total	Rate	Z–Score	Ratio	Date
1700	1221●	1155●	2376●	0.5139	1.80	105.71	1700
1710	1080●	1153●	2233●	0.4837	−1.80	93.67	1710
1720	1437●	1451●	2888●	0.4976	−1.00	99.04	1720
1730	1588●	1548●	3136●	0.5064	0.28	102.58	1730
1740	1252●	1309●	2561●	0.4889	−0.60	95.65	1740
1750	1384●	1401●	2785●	0.4969	−0.09	98.79	1750
1760	1246●	1260●	2506●	0.4972	−0.30	98.89	1760
1770	1493●	1674●	3167●	0.4714	−2.32	89.19	1770
1780	1615●	1769●	3384●	0.4772	−2.57	91.29	1780
1781	14627●	15435●	30062●	0.4866	−2.68	94.77	1781

Using Rickman's national ratios as expected values (cont.)

Nhumb

Date	Males	Females	Total	Rate	Z–Score	Ratio	Date
1700	1039●	1011●	2050●	0.5068	1.03	102.77	1700
1710	1256●	1136●	2392●	0.5251	2.19	110.56	1710
1720	1103●	1121●	2224●	0.4960	−1.03	98.39	1720
1730	1108●	1153●	2261●	0.4900	−1.31	96.10	1730
1740	1307●	1156●	2463●	0.5307	3.56	113.06	1740
1750	1151●	1120●	2271●	0.5068	0.86	102.77	1750
1760	1192●	1166●	2358●	0.5055	0.52	102.23	1760
1770	1309●	1321●	2630●	0.4977	0.58	99.09	1770
1780	1176●	1264●	2440●	0.4820	−1.72	93.04	1780
1781–90	13899●	14504●	28403●	0.4893	−1.66	95.83	1781–90

Notts

Date	Males	Females	Total	Rate	Z–Score	Ratio	Date
1700	788●	742●	1530●	0.5150	1.53	106.20	1700
1710	702●	729●	1431●	0.4906	−0.92	96.30	1710
1720	992●	1039●	2031●	0.4884	−1.66	95.48	1720
1730	1219●	1196●	2415●	0.5048	0.09	101.92	1730
1740	796●	825●	1621●	0.4911	−0.30	96.48	1740
1750	840●	869●	1709●	0.4915	−0.52	96.66	1750
1760	967●	934●	1901●	0.5087	0.74	103.53	1760
1770	1189●	1299●	2488●	0.4779	−1.41	91.53	1770
1780	1260●	1259●	2519●	0.5002	0.08	100.08	1780
1781	13121●	13416●	26537●	0.4944	0.05	97.80	1781

Oxon

Date	Males	Females	Total	Rate	Z–Score	Ratio	Date
1700	878●	912●	1790●	0.4905	−0.42	96.27	1700
1710	1002●	964●	1966●	0.5097	0.62	103.94	1710
1720	926●	883●	1809●	0.5119	0.43	104.87	1720
1730	1164●	1117●	2281●	0.5103	0.62	104.21	1730
1740	1089●	1105●	2194●	0.4964	0.15	98.55	1740
1750	977●	982●	1959●	0.4987	0.08	99.49	1750
1760	972●	981●	1953●	0.4977	−0.22	99.08	1760
1770	1081●	1076●	2157●	0.5012	0.85	100.46	1770
1780	1188●	1240●	2428●	0.4893	−0.99	95.81	1780
1781	10572●	10653●	21225●	0.4981	1.11	99.24	1781

Salop

Date	Males	Females	Total	Rate	Z–Score	Ratio	Date
1700	1214●	1295●	2509●	0.4839	−1.16	93.75	1700
1710	1185●	1164●	2349●	0.5045	0.17	101.80	1710
1720	1282●	1260●	2542●	0.5043	−0.26	101.75	1720
1730	1785●	1724●	3509●	0.5087	0.58	103.54	1730
1740	1555●	1500●	3055●	0.5090	1.57	103.67	1740
1750	1076●	1162●	2238●	0.4808	−1.61	92.60	1750
1760	1170●	1254●	2424●	0.4827	−1.72	93.30	1760
1770	1518●	1554●	3072●	0.4941	0.23	97.68	1770
1780	1413●	1457●	2870●	0.4923	−0.75	96.98	1780
1781	15269●	15078●	30347●	0.5031	3.09	101.27	1781

Using Rickman's national ratios as expected values (cont.)

Somt

Date	Males	Females	Total	Rate	Z–Score	Ratio	Date
1700	1866●	2040●	3906●	0.4777	−2.22	91.47	1700
1710	2015●	2148●	4163●	0.4840	−2.41	93.81	1710
1720	2272●	2215●	4487●	0.5064	−0.07	102.57	1720
1730	2916●	2963●	5879●	0.4960	−1.20	98.41	1730
1740	2766●	2809●	5575●	0.4961	0.21	98.47	1740
1750	1975●	2125●	4100●	0.4817	−2.07	92.94	1750
1760	2170●	2346●	4516●	0.4805	−2.64	92.50	1760
1770	2111●	2363●	4474●	0.4718	−2.71	89.34	1770
1780	2683●	2809●	5492●	0.4885	−1.61	95.51	1780
1781–90	24118●	26416●	50534●	0.4773	−7.65	91.30	1781–90

Staff

Date	Males	Females	Total	Rate	Z–Score	Ratio	Date
1700	1335●	1302●	2637●	0.5063	1.11	102.53	1700
1710	1221●	1237●	2458●	0.4967	−0.59	98.71	1710
1720	1485●	1352●	2837●	0.5234	1.77	109.84	1720
1730	1800●	1895●	3695●	0.4871	−2.03	94.99	1730
1740	1744●	1632●	3376●	0.5166	2.54	106.86	1740
1750	1933●	1912●	3845●	0.5027	0.61	101.10	1750
1760	1901●	1855●	3756●	0.5061	0.73	102.48	1760
1770	1914●	1981●	3895●	0.4914	−0.08	96.62	1770
1780	1980●	1968●	8948●	0.5015	0.27	100.61	1780
1781	22829●	22489●	43318●	0.5038	4.03	101.51	1761

Suffk

Date	Males	Females	Total	Rate	Z–Score	Ratio	Date
1700	1587●	1653●	3240●	0.4898	−0.64	96.01	1700
1710	1863●	1935●	3798●	0.4905	−1.50	96.28	1710
1720	2429●	2384●	4813●	0.5047	−0.30	101.89	1720
1730	2229●	2339●	4568●	0.4880	−2.15	95.30	1730
1740	1802●	1889●	3691●	0.4882	−0.80	95.39	1740
1750	1808●	1847●	3655●	0.4947	−0.38	97.89	1750
1760	1761●	1967●	3728●	0.4724	−3.40	89.53	1760
1770	1997●	2161●	4158●	0.4803	−1.52	92.41	1770
1780	2440●	2609●	5049●	0.4833	−2.29	93.52	1780
1781	19707●	21561●	41268●	0.4775	−6.80	91.40	1781

Surry

Date	Males	Females	Total	Rate	Z–Score	Ratio	Date
1700	2247●	2153●	4400●	0.5107	2.02	104.37	1700
1710	2667●	2677●	5344●	0.4991	−0.53	99.63	1710
1720	2759●	2916●	5675●	0.4862	−3.12	94.62	1720
1730	3296●	2778●	6074●	0.5426	6.05	118.65	1730
1740	3383●	3179●	6562●	0.5155	3.37	106.42	1740
1750	2999●	2941●	5940●	0.5049	1.08	101.97	1750
1760	2823●	2829●	5652●	0.4995	−0.11	99.79	1760
1770	3073●	3525●	6603●	0.4662	−4.21	87.32	1770
1780	3148●	2982●	6130●	0.5135	2.22	105.57	1780
1781	30469●	29292●	59761●	0.5098	7.61	104.02	1781

Using Rickman's national ratios as expected values (cont.)

Sussx

Date	Males	Females	Total	Rate	Z–Score	Ratio	Date
1700	1008●	991●	1999●	0.5043	0.79	101.72	1700
1710	1023●	955●	1978●	0.5172	1.29	107.12	1710
1720	1520●	1299●	2819●	0.5392	3.43	117.01	1720
1730	1448●	1262●	2710●	0.5343	3.17	114.74	1730
1740	1225●	1197●	2422●	0.5058	1.08	102.34	1740
1750	1227●	1065●	2292●	0.5353	3.59	115.21	1750
1760	1221●	1291●	2512●	0.4861	−1.42	94.58	1760
1770	1867●	1376●	3243●	0.5757	9.53	135.68	1770
1780	1622●	1518●	3140●	0.5166	1.93	106.85	1780
1781–90	12628●	11424●	24052●	0.5250	9.54	110.54	1781–90

Warwicks

Date	Males	Females	Total	Rate	Z–Score	Ratio	Date
1700	1003●	1001●	2004●	0.5005	0.45	100.20	1700
1710	1247●	1319●	2566●	0.4860	−1.70	94.54	1710
1720	1220●	1152●	2372●	0.5143	0.73	105.90	1720
1730	1592●	1634●	3226●	0.4935	−1.18	97.43	1730
1740	1429●	1348●	2777●	0.5146	2.09	106.01	1740
1750	1805●	1888●	3693●	0.4888	−1.10	95.60	1750
1760	1858●	2013●	3871●	0.4800	−2.51	92.30	1760
1770	2017●	2006●	4023●	0.5014	1.18	100.55	1770
1780	2091●	2193●	4284●	0.4881	−1.48	95.35	1780
1781	21823●	22088●	43911●	0.4970	1.13	98.80	1781

Westmld

Date	Males	Females	Total	Rate	Z–Score	Ratio	Date
1700	399●	444●	843●	0.4733	−1.29	89.86	1700
1710	315●	348●	663●	0.4751	−1.42	90.52	1710
1720	303●	319●	622●	0.4871	−0.98	94.98	1720
1730	455●	477●	932●	0.4882	−0.95	95.39	1730
1740	417●	395●	812●	0.5135	1.07	105.57	1740
1750	421●	471●	892●	0.4720	−1.55	89.38	1750
1760	338●	303●	641●	0.5273	1.37	111.55	1760
1770	353●	395●	748●	0.4719	−1.10	89.37	1770
1780	416●	418●	834●	0.4988	−0.03	99.52	1780
1781	3914●	4302●	8216●	0.4764	−3.24	90.98	1781

Wilts

Date	Males	Females	Total	Rate	Z–Score	Ratio	Date
1700	1427●	1412●	2839●	0.5026	0.76	101.06	1700
1710	1332●	1284●	2616●	0.5092	0.66	103.74	1710
1720	1495●	1475●	2970●	0.5034	−0.38	101.36	1720
1730	1880●	1803●	3683●	0.5105	0.80	104.27	1730
1740	1791●	1760●	3551●	0.5044	1.14	101.76	1740
1750	1422●	1459●	2881●	0.4936	−0.46	97.46	1750
1760	1703●	1830●	3533●	0.4820	−2.16	93.06	1760
1770	1631●	1865●	3496●	0.4665	−3.02	87.45	1770
1780	1686●	1980●	3666●	0.4599	−4.78	85.15	1780
1781	15453●	17355●	32808●	0.4710	−8.43	89.04	1781

Using Rickman's national ratios as expected values (cont.)

Worcs

Date	Males	Females	Total	Rate	Z–Score	Ratio	Date
1700	1019●	1116●	2135●	0.4773	−1.68	91.31	1700
1710	1052●	1080●	2132●	0.4934	−0.86	97.41	1710
1720	1231●	1132●	2363●	0.5209	1.37	108.75	1720
1730	1413●	1307●	2720●	0.5195	1.63	108.11	1730
1740	1093●	1041●	2134●	0.5122	1.61	105.00	1740
1750	1272●	1316●	2588●	0.4915	−0.65	96.66	1750
1760	1085●	1143●	2228●	0.4870	−1.25	94.93	1760
1770	1338●	1318●	2656●	0.5038	1.21	101.52	1770
1780	1361●	1440●	2801●	0.4859	−1.43	94.51	1780
1781–90	14905●	14794●	29699●	0.5019	2.62	100.75	1781–90

Yks ER

Date	Males	Females	Total	Rate	Z–Score	Ratio	Date
1700	978●	833●	1811●	0.5400	3.79	117.41	1700
1710	926●	882●	1808●	0.5122	0.80	104.99	1710
1720	1520●	1416●	2936●	0.5177	1.18	107.34	1720
1730	1176●	1190●	2366●	0.4970	−0.66	98.32	1730
1740	1049●	1072●	2121●	0.4946	−0.02	97.85	1740
1750	973●	1073●	2046●	0.4756	−2.02	90.68	1750
1760	892●	892●	1784●	0.5000	−0.02	100.00	1760
1770	989●	1045●	2034●	0.4862	−0.53	94.64	1770
1780	1220●	1257●	2477●	0.4925	−0.68	97.06	1780
1781	12450●	12677●	25127●	0.4955	0.38	98.21	1781

Yks NR

Date	Males	Females	Total	Rate	Z–Score	Ratio	Date
1700	1028●	1184●	2212●	0.4647	−2.89	86.82	1700
1710	1014●	1042●	2056●	0.4932	−0.86	97.31	1710
1720	1195●	1256●	2451●	0.4876	−1.91	95.14	1720
1730	1213●	1359●	2572●	0.4716	−3.27	89.26	1730
1740	1000●	1083●	2083●	0.4801	−1.34	92.34	1740
1750	1036●	1048●	2084●	0.4971	−0.07	98.85	1750
1760	1175●	1201●	2376●	0.4945	−0.55	97.84	1760
1770	1179●	1285●	2464●	0.4785	−1.35	91.75	1770
1780	1249●	1312●	2561●	0.4877	−1.18	95.20	1780
1781	14194●	15288●	29482●	0.4814	−4.41	92.84	1781

Yks WR

Date	Males	Females	Total	Rate	Z–Score	Ratio	Date
1700	3156●	3186●	6342●	0.4976	0.34	99.06	1700
1710	2734●	2576●	5310●	0.5149	1.77	106.13	1710
1720	3312●	2953●	6265●	0.5287	3.45	112.16	1720
1730	3586●	3393●	6979●	0.5138	1.67	105.69	1730
1740	3293●	3337●	6630●	0.4967	0.31	98.68	1740
1750	3395●	3346●	6741●	0.5036	0.95	101.46	1750
1760	3448●	3478●	6926●	0.4978	−0.39	99.14	1760
1770	4016●	4215●	8231●	0.4879	−0.75	95.28	1770
1780	4468●	4530●	8998●	0.4966	−0.54	98.63	1780
1781	51777●	52607●	104384●	0.4960	1.13	98.42	1781

Notes and references

1 For example, I. Eriksson and J. Rogers, 'Mobility in an agrarian community: practical and methodological considerations' in K. Ågren *et al.*, *Aristocrats, farmers, and proletarians: essays in Swedish demographic history* (*Studia Historica Upsaliensia*, **xlvii**, Uppsala, 1973), pp. 60–88; T. Hägerstrand, 'Migration and area. Survey of a sample of Swedish migration fields and hypothetical considerations on their genesis', *Lund Studies in Geography*, Series B, **xiii** (1957), pp. 27–158.

2 E. G. Ravenstein, 'The laws of migration', *Journal of the [Royal] Statistical Society*, **xlviii** (1885), pp. 167–235, and **lii** (1889), pp. 241–305; A. Redford, *Labour migration in England 1800–1850* (Manchester, 1926); M. Anderson, 'Urban migration in nineteenth century Lancashire: some insights into two competing hypotheses', *Annales de démographie historique 1971* (Paris, 1972), pp. 13–26; D. Baines, *Migration in a mature economy: emigration and internal migration in England and Wales, 1861–1900* (Cambridge, 1985).

3 In another but related context, see A. S. Kussmaul, 'Time and space, hoofs and grain: the seasonality of marriage in England', *Journal of Interdisciplinary History*, **xv** (1984–5), pp. 755–79.

4 For example, R. Lawton, 'Regional population trends in England and Wales 1750–1971' in P. Hobcraft and P. Rees (eds), *Regional demographic development* (1979); J. Saville, *Rural depopulation in England and Wales 1851–1951* (1957).

5 For example, Anderson, 'Urban migration'; T. McBride, *The domestic revolution* (1976); Saville, *Rural depopulation*.

6 Baines, *Migration*, p. 282.

7 See, for example, the contributions of Boulton, Schofield, and Clark, above.

8 Above, p. 13ff.

9 A. Kussmaul, 'Agrarian change in seventeenth century England: the economic historian as paleontologist', *Journal of Economic History*, **xlv** (1985), pp. 1–30; E. A. Wrigley, 'Urban growth and agricultural change: England and the continent in the early modern period', *Journal of Interdisciplinary History*, **xv** (1984–5), pp. 683–728; K. D. M. Snell, *Annals of the labouring poor: social change and agrarian England 1660–1900* (Cambridge, 1985), pp. 15–66; C. Wilson, 'Natural fertility in pre-industrial England', *Population Studies*, **xxxviii** (1984), pp. 225–40; D. Souden, 'Migrants and the population structure of later seventeenth century provincial cities and market towns' in P. Clark (ed.), *The transformation of English provincial towns 1600–1800* (1984), pp. 133–68.

10 D. S. Smith, 'A perspective on demographic methods and effects in social history', *William and Mary Quarterly*, 3rd series, **xxxix** (1982), pp. 942–68.

11 Above, p. 13ff.

12 R. M. Smith, 'Fertility, economy, and household formation in England over three centuries', *Population and Development Review*, **vii** (1981), pp. 595–622; D. R. Weir, 'Life under pressure: France and England, 1670–1870', *Journal of Economic History*, **xliv** (1984), pp. 27–47; D. S. Smith, 'A homeostatic demographic regime: patterns in west European family reconstitution studies' in R. D. Lee (ed.), *Population patterns in the past* (New York, 1977), pp. 19–52.

13 The question of scale in these types of analysis is a vexed one. It is a common

problem in demographic and other analysis to be able to distinguish a change in a pattern or a distribution and the base population to which it relates. See the comments in Souden, 'Migrants and population structure', pp. 139–40; also D. Souden, 'Mortality crises and Europe in the 1590s' in P. Clark (ed.), *The European crisis of the 1590s* (1985), pp. 231–43.

14 See the comments on measures of migration in Eriksson and Rogers, 'Mobility in an agrarian community', pp. 63–9.

15 E. A. Wrigley and D. Souden (eds), *The works of Thomas Robert Malthus*, 8 vols (1986), i, pp. 22, 110–1.

16 See the special issue on Rickman, *Local Population Studies*, **17** (1976).

17 BPP, 1802, VI, *1801 Census, parish register abstracts*. The data used in the main part of this paper are abstracted from this volume.

18 See E. A. Wrigley and R. Schofield, *The population history of England 1541–1871. A reconstruction* (1981), pp. 563–87.

19 Wrigley and Schofield, *Population history*, appendix 8, pp. 631–7.

20 This is probably the single most important omission from the study undertaken by Wrigley and Schofield, *Population history*.

21 BPP, 1802, VI. I owe much to Tony Wrigley, whose questions concerning sex ratios and emigration coincided with my initial interest in exploring sex ratios, thereby spurring me on, and to the ESRC Cambridge Group who gave me a short research consultancy in 1985 to help me work on the topic. Some of the early results from this were reported in a paper to the conference on British and American society 1600–1820, in Williamsburg, 1985, to the organisers of and participants in which I am grateful.

22 s.v. 'Sex ratio', R. Pressat, ed. C. Wilson, *The dictionary of demography* (Oxford, 1985), p. 209.

23 s.v. 'Sex differential mortality', Pressat, ed. Wilson, *Dictionary of demography*, pp. 205–7.

24 Wrigley and Schofield, *Population history*, pp. 224–6

25 Wrigley and Schofield, *Population history*, pp. 219–28.

26 Wrigley and Schofield, *Population history*, pp. 83–154. The shortfall in the eighteenth century between Anglican registered burials and deaths may have risen from 3 per cent to 13 per cent and more: Wrigley and Schofield, *Population history*, p. 141.

27 Jim Oeppen generously produced the calculations on expected and observed death sex ratios used in this article to test the data derived from the Rickman series, and also advised me on the forms of significance testing reported below.

28 See Wrigley and Schofield, *Population history*, pp. 242–3.

29 BPP, 1852–3, LXXXV, *1851 Census;* BPP, *12th–16th annual reports of the Registrar-General, 1848–52*.

30 Wrigley and Schofield, *Population history*, pp. 597–630.

31 Wrigley and Schofield, *Population history*, p. 621.

32 E. A. Wrigley, 'Checking Rickman', *Local Population Studies*, **17** (1976), pp. 9–15; Wrigley and Schofield, *Population history*, pp. 613–9. For Z-score testing, see H. M. Blalock, *Social statistics*, 2nd edn (New York and London, 1972), pp. 401–5.

33 In each figure the highest and lowest single values have been excluded, as being the extreme product of chance.

34 High sex ratios were recorded in the 1705 Marriage Duty Act returns for East

Kent, see Souden, 'Migrants and population structure', p. 150; while the same area retained a high proportion of male servants well into the nineteenth century, against the general trend, A. Kussmaul, *Servants in husbandry in early modern England* (Cambridge, 1981), p. 131. For another inferential approach to long-run migration patterns in that area, see D. Souden and G. Lasker, 'Biological inter-relationships between parishes in East Kent: an analysis of the Marriage Duty Act returns for 1705', *Local Population Studies,* **21** (1978), pp. 30–9.

35 E. A. Wrigley, 'A simple model of London's importance in changing English society and economy 1650–1750', *Past and Present,* **37** (1967), pp. 44–70; V. Brodsky [Elliott], 'Marriage and mobility in pre-industrial England', unpublished University of Cambridge PhD thesis, 1978, pp. 197–233. There is interesting material on real wages which is particularly germane to this discussion in Snell, *Annals of the labouring poor*, pp. 37–49 and *passim*.

36 See the articles above by Horn and Souden, and for an instructive nineteenth-century continuation of these patterns, Baines, *Migration*, pp. 159–60, 210–1.

37 Kussmaul, 'Agrarian change'; Snell, *Annals of the labouring poor*, pp. 15–66, shows the regionally different patterns of male and female agricultural unemployment, and suggests that unemployment patterns were similarly distinct between south east and south west; E. H. Hunt, 'Industrialization and regional inequality: wages in Britain 1760–1914', *Journal of Economic History,* **xlvi** (1986), pp. 935–66, esp. pp. 936–41.

38 The situation in Hampshire is of male surplus at burial – and often high surpluses – throughout. The inclusion of Portsmouth (and Southampton) with their very high male burial surpluses, coupled with less than full coverage of returns to Rickman, cloud the picture.

39 For other differences in migration patterns between Norfolk and Suffolk, gauged from church court deposition data, see D. C. Souden, 'Pre-industrial English local migration fields', unpublished University of Cambridge PhD thesis, 1981, pp. 139, 143.

40 BPP, 1852–3, LXXXV, *1851 Census*, pp. 4–5.

41 Smith, 'Fertility and household formation', suggests how various such mechanisms may have been at work in early modern England, while for an instructive comparison E. A. Wrigley, 'The fall of marital fertility in nineteenth century France: exemplar or exception?', *European Journal of Population,* **i** (1985), pp. 31–60, is an elegant analysis of the 'zero sum' effects of divergent regional demographic behaviour in France during the early nineteenth century.

42 Souden, 'Migrants and population structure' attempts such a cross-sectional analysis, based upon local censuses and concentrating upon urban-rural differences. There is much more yet to be gained from investigating cross-sectional analyses of aggregative demographic data. The early stages of research undertaken by Ann Kussmaul, David Weir, and myself, investigating relationships between growth in vital series and baptism-burial ratios (from the national parish register sample kindly made available to us by the ESRC Cambridge Group), and interpreting those relationships as potentially of migration, seems to confirm the general tenor of this research.

43 See for instance, Clark, 'Migration in England during the late seventeenth and early eighteenth centuries', above; Souden, 'Migrants and population structure'; Souden, 'Pre-industrial English local migration fields', pp. 25–149; P.

Clark, 'The migrant in Kentish towns 1580–1640' in P. Clark and P. Slack (eds), *Crisis and order in English towns 1500–1700* (1972), pp. 117–63.

44 Above, pp. 213–44.

45 9837 depositions were collected in this project, using a clustered sampling framework, and the analysis upon them is reported in Souden, 'Pre-industrial English local migration fields', pp. 25–149. The area covered consisted broadly of the counties of Devon, Somerset, Wiltshire, Oxfordshire, Leicestershire, Norfolk and (to a lesser extent) Suffolk. Devon, Devon RO, Chanter 868–70, 872–8, Consistory court depositions, diocese of Exeter; Somerset, Somerset RO, D/D/Cd 32, 34, 36–7, 45–6, 51, 55, 57–9, 64–5, 67, 70–1, 76, 80, 82, 84, 91–3, 95–7, 102, 106, 108, 135, diocese of Bath & Wells; Wiltshire, Wiltshire RO, B/DB 18–21, 24–6, 28, 31–3, 38–40, 42–3, 45–7, 54–5, 57–61, diocese of Salisbury; Oxfordshire, Bodleian Library, MS Oxf Dioc paps c 26–30, MS Oxf Archd paps c 119–20, MS Oxf Archd Oxon paps b 54, c 38, diocese of Oxford; Leicestershire, Leicestershire RO, 1D 41/4 III, VII, XIV, XVII, XX, XXIX–XXXIII, XXXV–XXXVI, XXXIX, XLI, XLVI–XLVIII, archdeaconry of Leicestershire; Norfolk and Suffolk, Norfolk RO, DEP/32, 34, 37–8, 40, 43, 45–54, ANW/7/9, diocese of Norwich.

There are 2052 depositions from the diocese of Exeter (all post-1662), 2352 from Bath & Wells; 1205 from Salisbury; 871 from Oxford; 981 from the archdeaconry of Leicester; and 2376 from the diocese of Norwich.

46 See the introduction, above, p. 32; Clark, 'Migration in England', above, pp. 220ff.; Souden, 'Migrants and population structure', pp. 141–2, 161; D. Souden, 'Movers and stayers in family reconstitution populations', *Local Population Studies,* **33** (1984), pp. 11–28.

47 Souden, 'Pre-industrial English local migration fields', pp. 124–39.

48 Souden, 'Pre-industrial English local migration fields', pp. 141–7. Support for this position is also to be found in my analysis of family reconstitution data: Souden, 'Movers and stayers', pp. 26–7.

49 Wilson, 'Natural fertility'; Wrigley and Schofield, *Population history,* pp. 454–80.

50 M. S. Teitelbaum, *The British fertility decline: demographic transition in the crucible of the industrial revolution* (Princeton, 1984).

51 See Clark, 'Migrants in the city', above, pp. 267ff.

Bibliography

This bibliography is intended as a structured guide to published work on migration in early modern England, to be read principally in tandem with the Introduction to the book. The items are organized according to the variety of migration or the source with which they are concerned (with cross-references where necessary), and extend beyond the confines of sixteenth, seventeenth, and eighteenth century England where appropriate. Additional references, particularly to unpublished material, will be found in the notes to the individual chapters.

The basic categories are general studies of migration; source-based studies; particular varieties of migration, which will not readily fit these individual source categories; and studies which, in part or in whole, assess the impact of migration. These are followed by sections on continental European historical studies, on relevant nineteenth century studies, and a section on theoretical and contemporary studies as a guide for further reading.

A General surveys

Patten, J., *Rural-urban migration in pre-industrial England*, University of Oxford School of Geography research paper, 6 (1973).

Spufford, P., 'Migration in pre-industrial England', *Genealogists' Magazine*, **xvii** (1972–4), pp. 420–9, 475–80, 537–42.

B Source-based studies

i Parish registers

Buckatzsch, E. J., 'The constancy of local populations and migration in England before 1800', *Population Studies,* **v** (1951–2), pp. 62–9.

Constant, A., 'The geographical background of inter-village movements in Northamptonshire and Huntingdonshire, 1754–1943', *Geography*, **xxxiii** (1948), pp. 78–88.

Holderness, B. A., 'Personal mobility in some rural parishes of Yorkshire, 1772–1822', *Yorkshire Archaeological Journal*, **xlii** (1967–70), pp. 444–54.

Long, M., and Maltby, B., 'Personal mobility in three West Riding parishes, 1777–1812', *Local Population Studies*, **24** (1980), pp. 13–25.

Maltby, B., 'Parish registers and the problem of mobility', *Local Population Studies*, **6** (1971), pp. 32–42.

Millard, J., 'A new approach to the study of marriage horizons', *Local Population Studies*, **28** (1982), pp. 10–31.

Pain, A. J., and Smith, M. T., 'Do marriage horizons accurately measure migration? A test case from Stanhope parish, .Co. Durham', *Local Population Studies*, **33** (1984), pp. 44–8.

Sheils, W. J., 'Mobility and registration in the north in the late eighteenth century', *Local Population Studies*, **23** (1979), pp. 41–4.

Snell, K. D. M., 'Parish registration and the study of labour mobility', *Local Population Studies*, **33** (1984), pp. 29–43 [critique of next citation].

Souden, D., 'Movers and stayers in family reconstitution populations', *Local Population Studies*, **33** (1984), pp. 11–28.

Wrigley, E. A., 'A note on the lifetime mobility of married women in a parish population of the later eighteenth century', *Local Population Studies*, **18** (1977), pp. 22–9.

see also Deane and Cole, *British economic growth*, in **D**, p. 340.

ii   Settlement law and other parish documentation

Hampson, E. M., 'Settlement and removal in Cambridgeshire, 1662–1834', *Cambridge Historical Journal*, **ii** (1926–8), pp. 273–89.

Holderness, B. A., ' "Open" and "close" parishes in England in the eighteenth and nineteenth centuries', *Agricultural History Review*, **xx** (1972), pp. 126–39.

Houston, R. A., 'Geographical mobility in Scotland, 1652–1811: the evidence of testimonials', *Journal of Historical Geography,* **xi** (1985), pp. 379–94.

Kent, J. R., 'Population mobility and alms: poor migrants in the midlands during the early seventeenth century', *Local Population Studies,* **27** (1981), pp. 35–51.

Mills, D., 'Spatial implications of the settlement laws in rural England', in P. Clark *et al., Poverty and social policy 1750–1850* (Milton Keynes, 1974), pp. 18–23.

McClure, P., 'Patterns of migration in the late Middle Ages: the evidence of English place-name surnames', *Economic History Review,* 2nd series, **xxxii** (1979), pp. 167–82.

McIntosh, M. K., 'Servants and the household unit in an Elizabethan English community', *Journal of Family History,* **ix** (1984), pp. 3–23.

Pelham, R. A., 'The immigrant population of Birmingham, 1686–1726', *Birmingham Archaeological Society Transactions and Proceedings,* **lxi** (1940), pp. 45–80.

Pond, C. C., 'Eighteenth century migration and mobility in rural Essex', *Essex Journal,* **xvii** (1) (1982), pp. 15–19.

Snell, K. D. M., *Annals of the labouring poor: social change and agrarian England 1660–1900* (Cambridge, 1985).

Styles, P., 'The evolution of the law of settlement', in P. Styles, *Studies in seventeenth century west midlands history* (Kineton, 1978), pp. 175–204.

Taylor, J. S., 'The impact of pauper settlement, 1691–1834', *Past and Present,* **73** (1976), pp. 42–74.

Thomas, E. G., 'The poor law migrant to Oxford, 1700–1795', *Oxoniensia,* **xlv** (1980), pp. 300–5.

see also Kussmaul, *Servants in husbandry*, in **D**, p. 340; Marshall, *The English poor*, in **D**, p. 341.

iii Local censuses

Laslett, P., 'Clayworth and Cogenhoe' in P. Laslett, *Family life and illicit love in earlier generations* (Cambridge, 1977), pp. 50–101.

Martin, J. M., 'The rich, the poor, and the migrant in eighteenth century Stratford-on-Avon', *Local Population Studies,* **20** (1978), pp. 38–48.

Souden, D., 'Migrants and the population structure of later seventeenth century provincial cities and market towns' in P. Clark (ed.), *The transformation of English provincial towns, 1600–1800* (1984), pp. 133–68.

Souden, D., and Lasker, G., 'Biological inter-relationships between parishes in east Kent: an analysis of the Marriage Duty Act returns for 1705', *Local Population Studies,* **21** (1978), pp. 30–9.

Wall, R., 'The age at leaving home', *Journal of Family History,* **iii** (1978), pp. 181–202.

iv   Church court depositions, etc.

Brodsky Elliott, V., 'Single women in the London marriage market: age, status, and mobility, 1598–1619', in R. B. Outhwaite (ed.), *Marriage and society: studies in the social history of marriage* (1981), pp. 81–100.

Clark, P., 'The migrant in Kentish towns, 1580–1640' in P. Clark and P. Slack (eds), *Crisis and order in English towns 1500–1700* (1972), pp. 117–63.

Cornwall, J., 'Evidence of population mobility in the seventeenth century', *Bulletin of the Institute of Historical Research,* **xl** (1967), pp. 143–52.

Cressy, D., 'Occupations, migration, and literacy in East London,' 1580–1640', *Local Population Studies,* **5** (1970), pp. 53–60.

Goldberg, P. J. P., 'Marriage, migration, servanthood and life-cycle in Yorkshire towns of the later Middle Ages', *Continuity and Change,* **i** (1986), pp. 141–69.

Hanley, H., 'Population and mobility in Buckinghamshire, 1578–1583', *Local Population Studies,* **15** (1975), pp. 33–9.

Siraut, M., 'Physical mobility in Elizabethan Cambridge', *Local Population Studies,* **27** (1981), pp. 65–70.

see also McIntosh, 'Servants and the household unit', in **B** ii, above; Souden, 'Migrants and the population structure', in **B** iii, above.

v Apprentice and freeman records

Butcher, A. F., 'The origins of Romney freemen, 1433–1523', *Economic History Review*, 2nd series, **xxvii** (1974), pp. 16–27.

Hammer, C. I. jr, 'The mobility of skilled labour in late medieval England: some Oxford evidence', *Vierteljahrschrift für Sozial- und Wirtschaftsgeschichte,* **lxiii** (1976), pp. 194–210.

Holman, J. R., 'Apprenticeship as a factor in migration: Bristol, 1675–1726', *Transactions of the Bristol and Gloucestershire Archaeological Society,* **xcvii** (1979), pp. 85–92.

Kitch, M., 'Capital and kingdom: migration to later Stuart London', in A. L. Beier and R. Finlay (eds), *London 1500–1700: the making of the metropolis* (1986), pp. 224–51.

Lovett, A. A., Whyte, I. D., and Whyte, K. A., 'Poisson regression analysis and migration fields: the example of the apprenticeship records of Edinburgh in the seventeenth and eighteenth centuries', *Transactions of the Institute of British Geographers*, new series, **x** (1985), pp. 317–32.

Palliser, D. M., 'A regional capital as magnet: immigrants to York, 1477–1566', *Yorkshire Archaeological Journal,* **lvii** (1985), pp. 111–23.

Ramsay, G. D., 'The recruitment and fortunes of some London freemen in the mid-sixteenth century', *Economic History Review*, 2nd series, **xxxi** (1978), pp. 526–40.

Rappaport, S., 'Social structure and mobility in sixteenth century London. Part 1', *London Journal,* **ix** (1983), pp. 107–35.

Smith, S. R., 'The social and geographical origins of the London apprentices 1630–60', *Guildhall Miscellany,* **iv** (1971–3), pp. 195–206.

Wareing, J., 'Changes in the geographical distribution of the recruitment of apprentices to the London Companies, 1486–1750', *Journal of Historical Geography,* **vi** (1980), pp. 241–9.

Yarbrough, A., 'Geographical and social origins of Bristol apprentices 1542–1565', *Transactions of the Bristol and Gloucestershire Archaeological Society,* **xcviii** (1980), pp. 113–30.

see also Souden, ' "Rogues, whores, and vagabonds"?' in **C** ii, p. 340.

C   Types of migration

i   *Vagrancy*

Aydelotte, F., *Elizabethan rogues and vagabonds* (Oxford, 1913).

Beier, A. L., *Masterless men: the vagrancy problem in England 1560–1640* (1985).

Beier, A. L., 'Social problems in Elizabethan England', *Journal of Interdisciplinary History,* **ix** (1978–9), pp. 203–21.

Beier, A. L., 'Vagrants and the social order in Elizabethan England', *Past and Present,* **64** (1974), pp. 3–29; also 'Debate' with J. F. Pound, *Past and Present,* **71** (1976), pp. 126–34.

Davies, C. S. L., 'Slavery and Protector Somerset: the Vagrancy Act of 1547', *Economic History Review,* 2nd series, **xix** (1966), pp. 533–49.

Houston, R. A., 'Vagrants and society in early modern England', *Cambridge Anthropology,* **iv** (1980), pp. 18–32.

Pound, J. F., *Poverty and vagrancy in Tudor England* (1971).

Slack, P. (ed.), *Poverty in early Stuart Salisbury*, Wiltshire Record Society, **xxxi** (Devizes, 1975) [see Slack article, above, pp. 49–70].

see also Clark, 'The migrant in Kentish towns', in **B** v, above; Kent, 'Population mobility and alms', in **B** ii, above.

ii   *Emigration and immigration*

Bailyn, B., *Voyagers to the West* (New York, 1986).

Breen, T. H., and Foster, S., 'Moving to the New World: the character of early Massachusetts immigration', *William and Mary Quarterly*, 3rd series, **xxx** (1973), pp. 189–222.

Campbell, M., 'English emigration on the eve of the American Revolution', *American Historical Review,* **lxi** (1955), pp. 1–20.

Canny, N., 'Migration and opportunity: Britain, Ireland,and the New World', *Irish Economic and Social History*, **xii** (1985), pp. 7–32; debate with R. Gillespie, *Irish Economic and Social History*, **xiii** (1986), pp. 90–100.

Cressy, D., 'The vast and furious ocean: the passage to Puritan New England', *New England Quarterly*, **lvii** (1984), pp. 511–32.

Ekirch, R., 'Bound for America: a profile of British convicts transferred to the colonies, 1718–75', *William and Mary Quarterly*, **xlii** (1985), pp. 184–200.

Galenson, D. W., *White servitude in colonial America* (Cambridge, 1981).

Gemery, H. A., 'Emigration from the British Isles to the New World, 1630–1700: inferences from colonial populations', *Research in Economic History*, **v** (1980), pp. 179–231.

Goose, N., 'The Dutch in Colchester: the economic influence of an immigrant community in the sixteenth and seventeenth century', *Immigrants and Minorities,* **i** (1982), pp. 261–80.

Gwynn, R. D., *Huguenot heritage: the history and contribution of the Huguenots in Britain* (1985).

Gwynn, R. D., 'The number of Huguenot immigrants in England in the late seventeenth century', *Journal of Historical Geography,* **ix** (1983), pp. 384–95.

Horn, J., 'Servant emigration to the Chesapeake in the seventeenth century' in T. W. Tate and D. L. Ammerman (eds), *The Chesapeake in the seventeenth century: essays on Anglo-American society* (Chapel Hill, 1979), pp. 51–95.

Jones, E., 'The Welsh in London in the seventeenth and eighteenth centuries', *Welsh History Review,* **x** (1980–81), pp. 461–79.

Mendelman, T., *The Jews of Georgian London* (Philadelphia, 1979).

Pettegree, A., *Foreign Protestant communities in sixteenth-century London* (Oxford, 1986).

Salerno, A., 'The social background of seventeenth-century

emigration to America', *Journal of British Studies,* **xix** (1979–80), pp. 31–52.

Souden, D., 'English indentured servants and the trans-Atlantic colonial economy' in S. Marks and P. Richardson (eds), *International labour migration: historical perspectives* (1984), pp. 19–33.

Wareing, J., 'Migration to London and trans-Atlantic emigration of indentured servants, 1683–1775', *Journal of Historical Geography,* **vii** (1981), pp. 356–78.

see also Wrigley and Schofield, *Population history of England*, in **D**. p. 341.

D   Impact of migration

Clark, P., 'The reception of migrants in English towns in the early modern period' in E. François (ed.), *Immigration et société urbaine en Europe occidentale, XVIᵉ–XXᵉ siècle* (Paris, 1985), pp. 53–63.

Corfield, P., *The impact of English towns, 1700–1800* (Oxford, 1982).

Crafts, N. F. R., 'Income elasticities of demand, and the release of labour by agriculture during the British Industrial Revolution', in J. Mokyr (ed.), *The economics of the industrial revolution* (1985), pp. 151–63.

Deane, P., and Cole, W. A., *British economic growth, 1688–1959: structures and trends,* 2nd edn (Cambridge, 1967).

Finlay, R. A. P., 'Natural decrease in early modern cities', *Past and Present,* **92** (1981), pp. 169–74; see also Sharlin, below, and A. J. Sharlin, 'Rejoinder', *Past and Present,* **92** (1981), pp. 175–80.

Hey, D., *An English rural community: Myddle under the Tudors and Stuarts* (Leicester, 1974). Also, R. Gough, *The History of Myddle* (ed. D. Hey, Harmondsworth, 1981).

Kussmaul, A., *Servants in husbandry in early modern England* (Cambridge, 1981).

Kussmaul, A., 'The ambiguous mobility of farm servants', *Economic History Review,* 2nd series, **xxxiv** (1981), pp. 222–35.

Levine, D., *Family formation in an age of nascent capitalism* (1977).

Macfarlane, A., *The origins of English individualism: the family, property and social transition* (Oxford, 1978).

Marshall, D., *The English poor in the eighteenth century* (1926).

Sharlin, A. J., 'Natural decrease in early modern cities: a reconsideration', *Past and Present*, **79** (1978), pp. 126–38.

Skipp, V., *Crisis and development: an ecological case study of the Forest of Arden, 1570–1674* (Cambridge, 1978).

Tranter, N. L., 'The labour supply, 1780–1860', in R. Floud and D. McCloskey (eds), *The economic history of England since 1700, i: 1700–1860* (Cambridge, 1981), pp. 204–26.

Walton, J. R., 'The residential mobility of farmers and its relationship to the parliamentary enclosure movement in Oxfordshire' in A. D. M. Phillips and B. J. Turton (eds), *Environment, man and economic change: essays presented to S. H. Beaver* (1975), pp. 238–52.

Wrightson, K., and Levine, D., *Poverty and piety in an English village: Terling, 1525–1700* (1979).

Wrigley, E. A., and Schofield, R., *The population history of England, 1541–1871: A reconstruction* (1981).

Wrigley, E. A., 'A simple model of London's importance in changing English society and economy, 1650–1750', *Past and Present,* **37** (1967), pp. 44–70.

Yasumoto, M., 'Urbanization and population in an English town: Leeds during the Industrial Revolution', *Keio Economic Studies,* **x** (1973), pp. 61–94.

E Continental comparisons

Bouchard, G., 'Family structures and geographic mobility at Laterrière, 1851–1935', *Journal of Family History,* **ii** (1977), pp. 350–69.

Eriksson, I., and Rogers, J., 'Mobility in an agrarian community: practical and methodological considerations' in K. Ågren *et al., Aristocrats, farmers, proletarians: essays in Swedish demo-*

graphic history (*Studia Historica Upsaliensia,* **xlvii**, Uppsala, 1973), pp. 60–88.

François, E. (ed.), *Immigration et société urbaine en Europe occidentale, XVIᵉ–XXᵉ siècles* (Paris, 1985).

Garden, M., and Lequin, Y. (eds), *Habiter la ville, XVᵉ–XXᵉ siècles* (Lyon, 1984).

Gaunt, D., 'Pre-industrial economy and population structure: the elements of variance in early modern Sweden', *Scandinavian Journal of History,* **ii** (1977), pp. 183–210.

Gribaudi, M., 'Stratégies migratoires et mobilité relative entre village et ville', *Population,* **xxxvii** (1982), pp. 1159–81.

Hägerstrand, T., 'Migration and area. Survey of a sample of Swedish migration fields and hypothetical considerations on their genesis', *Lund Studies in Geography,* Series B, **xiii** (1957), pp. 27–158.

Hufton, O., *The poor of eighteenth-century France* (Oxford, 1974).

Moch, L. P., *Paths to the city: regional migration in nineteenth century France* (1983).

da Molin, G., 'Mobilità dei contadini pugliesi tra fine '600 a primo '800' in A. Bellettini (ed.), *La popolazione italiana nel settecento* (Bologna, 1980).

Poussou, J. P., *Bordeaux et le sud-ouest au XVIIIᵉ siècle: croissance économique et attraction urbaine* (Paris, 1983).

Poussou, J. P., 'Les mouvements migratoires en France et à partir de la France de la fin du XVᵉ siècle au début du XIXᵉ siècle: approches pour une synthèse', *Annales de démographie historique 1970* (Paris, 1971), pp. 11–78.

Tilly, C., 'Migration in modern European history' in J. Sundin and E. Söderlund (eds), *Time, space, and man: Essays on microdemography* (Stockholm, 1979), pp. 175–97.

Todd, E., 'Mobilité géographique et cycle de vie en Artois et en Toscane au XVIIIᵉ siècle', *Annales, E.S.C.,* **xxx** (1975), pp. 726–44.

F Nineteenth-Century studies

Anderson, M., *Family structure in nineteenth century Lancashire* (Cambridge, 1971).

Anderson, M., 'Urban migration in nineteenth century Lancashire: some insights into two competing hypotheses', *Annales de démographie historique 1971* (Paris, 1972), pp. 13–26.

Anderson, M., 'Indicators of population change and stability in nineteenth century cities: some sceptical comments' in J. H. Johnson and C. G. Pooley (eds), *The structure of nineteenth century cities* (1982), pp. 283–98.

Baines, D., *Migration in a mature economy: emigration and internal migration in England and Wales, 1861–1900* (Cambridge, 1985).

Collins, E. J. T., 'Migrant labour in British agriculture in the nineteenth century', *Economic History Review*, 2nd series, **xxix** (1976), pp. 38–59.

Huzel, J. P., 'The demographic impact of the Old Poor Law: more reflexions on Malthus', *Economic History Review*, 2nd series, **xxxiii** (1980), pp. 367–81.

Lawton, R., 'Regional population trends in England and Wales, 1750–1971' in J. Hobcraft and P. Rees (eds), *Regional demographic development* (1977), pp. 29–70.

Mills, D., *Lord and peasant in nineteenth century Britain* (1980).

Pooley, C. G., 'Residential mobility in the Victorian city', *Transactions of the Institute of British Geographers*, new ser., **iv** (1979), pp. 258–77.

Ravenstein, E. G., 'The laws of migration', *Journal of the [Royal] Statistical Society*, **xlviii** (1885), pp. 167–227, and **xlii** (1889), pp. 214–301.

Redford, A., *Labour migration in England, 1800–1850* (Manchester, 1926; 3rd ed., Manchester, 1976).

Samuel, R., 'Comers and goers' in H. J. Dyos and M. Wolff (eds), *The Victorian city*, 2 vols (1973), i, pp. 123–60.

Saville, J., *Rural depopulation in England and Wales, 1851–1951* (1957).

G   Modern and theoretical studies

Bideau, A., 'La distribution spatiale des populations et leurs migrations', *La recherche en sciences humaines, 1979–80* (Paris, 1980), pp. 92–7.

Courgeau, D., *Migrants et migrations* (Paris, 1979).

Hogan, D. P., and Kertzer, D. I., 'Longitudinal approaches to migration in social history', *Historical Methods,* **xviii** (1985), pp. 20–30.

Keyfitz, N., 'Do cities grow by natural increase or by migration?', *Geographical analysis,* **xii** (1980), pp. 142–56.

Keyfitz, N., and Philipou, D., 'Migration and natural increase in the growth of cities', *Geographical Analysis,* **xiii** (1981), pp. 287–99.

Kosinski, L. A., and Prothero, R. M., (eds), *People on the move: studies on internal migration* (1975).

Lee, E. S., 'A theory of migration' in J. A. Jackson (ed.) *Migration* (Cambridge, 1969), pp. 282–97.

Rogers, A., *The formal demography of migration and redistribution*, IIASA research memorandum 78–15 (Laxenburg, 1978).

Shaw, R. P., *Migration theory and fact*, Regional Science Institute, bibliography series, **v** (Philadelphia, 1975).

White, P., and Woods, R. (eds), *The geographical impact of migration* (1980).

Index

migration, mobility–cont.

chain 17, 313; circular 16–17, 26, 64, 215, 243, 316; circulation 16, 96; definitions 11, 13–17, 28; emigration *see* emigration, emigrants; flows 14–15, 19, 38, 297, 309, 313–14; frequency 19, 29–30, 226; group 30; harvest 17, 25, 33–4, 272; immigration *see* immigration, immigrants; immobility 22, 32, 137, 242, 270, 316; in North American colonies 37, 172–203; *see also* emigration; Maryland; Virginia; intervening opportunities 20, 32, 295; laws 19–20, 64, 161; *see also* Ravenstein; life cycle, ages 12, 13, 19, 20, 22, 24, 55–6, 80, 109, 119, 133, 138, 153–4, 185, 215–17, 226–7, 257–65; likelihood of moving 22, 29, 32, 94, 118–25, 137, 183–4, 220–1, 229–30, 234, 256–65; literacy 35, 272; local 13–15, 16–17, 19, 26, 29, 32–3, 37–8, 80–1, 183–4, 214, 223, 228–9, 230–1, 235–6, 242, 253–65, 295, 316; long-distance 17, 19, 25, 27, 29, 30–2, 34, 37–8, 58–65, 80–1, 108, 156–60, 190, 200, 214–15, 222–3, 228–9, 230–1, 236, 238–40, 243, 261–3, 272–6; measurement 17, 21, 74*n*, 81–7, 137, 156, 183, 253–4, 293–4, 316— computer mapping 82–6— models 14–17, 19–20, 243, 296–7; motivation 11–13, 15–17, 19–20, 133, 186, 267–8—cultural effects 313–14—movers/stayers *see* likelihood of moving; net 298–314; occupational differences 29, 33–4, 46*n*, 157–60, 162, 184, 215, 223–6, 230, 236, 243, 269; persistence of long-run patterns 14, 38, 157, 294, 309–10, 312–14, 316–18; probability 21, 29, 295; reactions to 21–2; relationship with demographic series 23, 32, 37–8, 292; rural-urban migration *see* towns,

migration to; seasonal 17, 33–4, 242, 272; sex differences 19, 23, 29, 33, 35, 38, 64–5, 109, 160–1, 220–1, 222–3, 229–31, 255–65, 296–328 *passim*; socialite 25, 35, 236; specialist 29, 35; step 19; subsistence 25, 27–8, 29–32, 37, 201, 214, 236–7, 242–3, 269, 272, 281—*see also* vagrants—to towns, *see* towns, migration to; *see also* towns, migration from; turnover 19, 109–38, 141*n*, 173, 176, 183–203, 237–8, 253; ubiquity of 12–13, 21, 215, 228, 294

migration patterns over time: in sixteenth century 21, 25, 28–32, 91, 95, 108, 214–15, 272, 277, 286; in early seventeenth century 21, 23, 25, 27–9, 32, 36–7, 49–69, 91–5, 97, 108, 214–15, 269, 272, 286, 315; in later seventeenth century 23–4, 32–8, 108–9, 186–203, 215–44, 270, 315; in early eighteenth century 26, 28, 32–8, 215–44, 281–2, 286, 296–314, 317; in later eighteenth century 26, 36, 231, 243, 296–314, 317; in nineteenth century 19

migration sources 11–12, 18–19; aggregative vital series 19, 38, 296–314, 318–28; apprenticeship 18, 31, 34, 78–81, 118, 137, 156, 215–17, 229, 293; censuses, local 18–19, 38, 215–16, 228–9, 245*n*, 253–65, 268, 331*n*; censuses, national 19, 293, 300, 302; church court depositions 18, 32, 80, 102, 108–9, 118, 137, 214, 218–27 *passim*, 230, 314–16; civil registers 293; Easter books 113–25; emigration and indenture registers 18, 37, 151–5, 293; family reconstitutions 32; for colonial populations 173, 184; freeman registers 31, 108, 137, 214–15, 217; hospital registers 50; marriage registers 18, 216; parish register abstracts 296–314, 318–28; population registers 18,